Stress, Coping, and Resiliency in Children and Families

Family Research Consortium:
Advances in Family Research

The Family Research Consortium was established to improve the quality of research and the breadth of collaboration in the fields of family research. It has held five summer institutes for experienced researchers. The consortium designed and ran a multisite postdoctoral training program in family process and mental health and initiated a number of collaborative research programs among its members. The consortium had 10 members: Elaine Blechman, PhD (University of Colorado), Robert Cole, PhD (Rochester), Philip Cowan, PhD (Berkeley), John Gottman, PhD (University of Washington), Mavis Hetherington, PhD (University of Virginia), Sheppard Kellam, MD (Johns Hopkins University), Ross Parke, PhD (University of California at Riverside), Gerald Patterson, PhD (Oregon Social Learning Center), David Reiss, MD (George Washington University), and Irving Sigel, PhD (Educational Testing Service).

The work of the consortium was supported by two NIMH grants: a research grant, 1R01MH40357, and a training grant, 1T32MD18262. Joy Schulterbrandt was project officer and played a major role in stimulating the current congress.

This volume is based on the fifth summer institute, *Stress, Coping, and Resiliency in Children and Families.* Other volumes in the Family Research Consortium series include:

Patterson, G. R. (Ed.) *Depression and Aggression in Family Interactions* (1990)

Cowan, P. A., & Hetherington, E. M. (Eds.) *Family Transitions* (1991)

Cole, R. E., & Reiss, D. (Eds.) *How Do Families Cope With Chronic Illness?* (1993)

Parke, R. D., & Kellam, S. G. (Eds.) *Exploring Family Relationships With Other Social Contexts* (1994)

Stress, Coping, and Resiliency in Children and Families

Edited by

E. Mavis Hetherington
University of Virginia

Elaine A. Blechman
University of Colorado

LEA LAWRENCE ERLBAUM ASSOCIATES, PUBLISHERS
1996   Mahwah, New Jersey

Lawrence Erlbaum Associates, Inc., Publishers
10 Industrial Avenue
Mahwah, New Jersey 07430

Library of Congress Cataloging-in-Publication Data

Stress, coping, and resiliency in children and families / edited by E.
    Mavis Hetherington, Elaine A. Blechman.
        p.   cm.
    Includes bibliographical references and indexes.
    ISBN 0-8058-1710-7
    1. Family—Psychological aspects.   2. Stress (Psychology).
    I. Hetherington, E. Mavis.   II. Blechman, Elaine A.
    HQ518.S75   1996
    306.85—dc20   95-41029
                                                                      CIP

Books published by Lawrence Erlbaum Associates are printed on acid-free paper,
and their bindings are chosen for strength and durability.

Printed in the United States of America
10 9 8 7 6 5 4 3 2 1

Contents

Introduction and Overview   vii
E. Mavis Hetherington and Elaine A. Blechman

1   Thinking About Risk and Resilience in Families   1
Philip A. Cowan, Carolyn Pape Cowan, and Mark S. Schulz

2   Stress, Parenting, and Adolescent Psychopathology in
Nondivorced and Stepfamilies: A Within-Family Perspective   39
Sandra H. Henderson, E. Mavis Hetherington,
Debra Mekos, and David Reiss

3   Divorce and Boys' Adjustment Problems: 67
Two Paths With a Single Model
Marion S. Forgatch, Gerald R. Patterson, and Judy A. Ray

4   Family Support, Coping, and Competence
Thomas Ashby Wills, Elaine A. Blechman, and   107
Grace McNamara

5   Risk and Resiliency in Nonclinical Young Children:
The Georgia Longitudinal Study   135
Karen S. Wampler, Charles F. Halverson, Jr., and James Deal

6   The Timing of Childbearing, Family Structure, and the
      Role Responsibilities of Aging Black Women   **155**
      Linda M. Burton

7   Family Wages, Family Processes, and Youth Competence in
      Rural Married African American Families   **173**
      Gene H. Brody, Zolinda Stoneman, and Douglas Flor

8   Attention—The Shuttle Between Emotion and Cognition:
      Risk, Resiliency, and Physiological Bases   **189**
      Beverly J. Wilson and John M. Gottman

Author Index   **229**

Subject Index   **239**

Introduction and Overview

Concern with stress and coping has a long history in biomedical, psychological and sociological research. The inadequacy of simplistic models linking stressful life events and adverse physical and psychological outcomes was pointed out in the early 1980s by Michael Rutter and Norman Garmezy in a series of seminal papers and books (Garmezy & Rutter, 1983).[1] The issues raised by Rutter and Garmezy and elaborations on their theoretical models shaped much of the subsequent research on this topic and are reflected in the chapters in this volume. The shift has been away from identifying associations between risks and outcomes to a focus on factors and processes that contribute to diversity in response to risks, with some individuals being more vulnerable and some more resilient in dealing with adversity.

Most individuals and families encounter multiple risks. In some cases, stresses occur singly and are resolved before other risks are encountered; however, in other cases, one risk, such as divorce, increases the probability of additional risks such as poverty, inept parenting, and residential moves occurring. Other cumulative risks may occur because earlier stresses are not dealt with before new ones arise. Although the challenges of moderate levels of stress accompanied by personal and social resources may actually lead to a steeling or inoculation effect reflected in enhanced competence and adaptability in dealing with future problems, when high levels of cumulative stress occur, there may be little evidence of resiliency in even the most adaptable individuals.

---

[1]Garmezy, N., & Rutter, M. (Eds.). (1983). *Stress, coping, and development in children.* New York: McGraw-Hill.

In exploring vulnerability and resiliency in response to stress, investigators have examined the contribution and interaction among individual factors such as gender, age, temperament, ethnicity, and cultural background; cognitive processes such as the perception and interpretation of events; family processes such as relationships and extrafamilial factors; and processes such as relationships in the peer group, extended family, workplace, school, and neighborhood.

In this volume, the focus is on stress and adaptability in families and family members. The chapters explore not only how a variety of stresses influence family functioning, but also how family process moderates and mediates the contribution of individual and environmental risk and protective factors to personal adjustment.

A more extensive theoretical introduction has not been included in this preface, because in chapter 1, Cowan, Cowan, and Schulz present a theoretical model and review of research issues and methodological problems in studying risk and resilience in families. They use findings from their longitudinal study of the transition to parenting to examine the relationship among mothers' and fathers' depression, marital conflict, and the buffering role of authoritative parenting in the nondepressed parent. An especially intriguing finding in this study is that girls are more at risk than boys for encountering nonauthoritative aversive parenting when parents are mentally distressed.

In chapter 2, Henderson and her colleagues explore how differential experiences and characteristics of children in the same family limit the ability of one sibling to adapt successfully to stressors but increase the ability of another sibling to overcome the same adversities. Although an increasing number of studies of the effects of nonshared environment on children's development have appeared in the last decade, the effects of stress on differential parental treatment have not been examined systematically previously. A striking finding in this study is that differential parental treatment of siblings is not greater under high stress than it is under low stress, although child temperament and "own-ness" (biological relatedness to the parent) are associated with differences in parenting.

Chapter 3 by Forgatch, Patterson, and Ray presents a mediational model of the relationship among stress, parenting, and boys' adjustment in nondivorced, divorced, and repartnered families. In all groups, the impact of stress on children's problem behavior is mediated by disruptions in parenting. The authors identify variations in the model associated with antisocial behavior, social disadvantage, and depression in mothers for the three family types, and for boys with chronic problems versus those whose problems begin after a marital transition. They also demonstrate a cyclical reciprocal process where stress leads to inept parenting, which increases child behavior problems, but over time, child behavior problems also increase maternal stress, which promotes continued or increased disruptions in parenting.

In chapter 4 by Wills, Blechman, and McNamara, epidemiological data are used to examine the way in which supportive families with effective communication skills promote the development of coping skills and competence in children and adolescents in one- and two-parent families. Supportive family relationships reduce the impact of negative life events on substance use and promote more adaptive coping. Intact families, in comparison to one-parent and stepfamilies, exhibit more family support and less substance use in children and adolescents.

Chapter 5 by Wampler, Halverson, and Deal presents the results of the Georgia Longitudinal Study on the mutual influence of the family content, child functioning over time, and minor physical anomalies in the child which are used as a proxy variable for congenital risk for child behavior problems. The results of this study support the findings by Forgatch et al. in chapter 3 and a growing body of research that reveals the importance of the effects of child characteristics and behavior on parenting and other family relationships over time. In addition, minor physical anomalies contribute to the development of both long-term externalizing and internalizing behavior, whereas family risk factors contribute only to internalizing behavior. These provocative findings appear to be inconsistent with the results of a substantial number of longitudinal studies, including the Forgatch and Patterson studies, which report bidirectional effects between parents and children that include a substantial family to child effect on the development of conduct disorders. Wampler et al. offer explanations for their findings, although none seem entirely adequate to explain the lack of family effects for externalizing and the relatively small R^2s found in predicting both internalizing and externalizing in their study in comparison to other studies that have been equally rigorous in controlling for confounding of source variance in antecedent and outcome variables. The use of minor physical anomalies as an index of biological risk free of some of the measurement problems associated with such constructs as temperament is a creative step in disentangling family and child effects. It is hoped that this chapter will stimulate more thoughtful and innovative examinations of the direction of effects between family functioning and child characteristics and behavior.

Chapter 6 by Linda Burton and chapter 7 by Brody, Stoneman, and Flor both discuss adaptation in poor African-American families. The chapter by Burton deals with multigenerational matrilineal families and the influence of normative expectations on family roles and relationships. In young adult families and in families with a teenage parent where teenaged parenting is viewed as normative, equitable distribution of parenting and caregiving is found. Where teenaged parenting is viewed as off-time or nonnormative, family caregiving responsibilities fall on the young great-grandmothers who are often overburdened and resentful.

The chapter by Brody and colleagues, in contrast to that by Burton, deals with married, rural African-American families and the impact of family wages on parental psychological functioning, the marital relationship, caregiving, and competence in youth. Although the variables and conceptual framework are similar in many ways to those in the early chapters dealing with stress, family process, and child outcome, the findings relating to optimism in caregivers, co-caregiver support, and child outcome present some additional factors that mediate responses to stress. It is a useful exercise for the reader to consider the congruence and differences in the models and findings in the various chapters dealing with stress, individual and family risk, and protective factors and child outcomes in the volume.

The final chapter by Wilson and Gottman is an unusual model and review of how attentional processes mediate between risk and the development of psychopathology in children. It is proposed that when confronting stress, attentional processes organize and regulate cognition, emotion, and the physiological responses that accompany them. Attentional processes and associated reactivity and self-regulation also influence the formation and maintenance of social relationships initially with the parents, later with sibling and extrafamilial relationships. The authors use attentional processes as the key construct in a model of risk and resiliency in the development of psychopathology and competence in children.

The chapters in this volume reveal the complexity of current theoretical models, research strategies, and analytic approaches to the study of risk, resiliency, and vulnerability in families and family members. They also reveal the central role risk, family process, and adaptability play in both normal development and childhood psychopathology.

E. Mavis Hetherington
Elaine A. Blechman

1

▼▼▼▼▼▼▼

Thinking About Risk and Resilience in Families

Philip A. Cowan
Carolyn Pape Cowan
Marc S. Schulz
University of California at Berkeley

For some children, the risks of developing serious psychological disorders are high, whereas for others the likelihood of being given a clinical diagnosis is remote. However, risks and stressors are not always followed by the consequences we expect. Some children at high risk with highly stressful environments may adapt very well, whereas others considered to be at low risk develop debilitating psychological disorders. Are researchers simply making errors in prediction, or are there lawful principles to explain both positive and negative outcomes that defy the odds? Interest in this question has been stimulated by the conceptual and empirical work on risk and resilience by Rutter and Garmezy, with important contributions from Masten, Sameroff, Seifer, Sroufe, Egeland, Rolf, Achenbach, and Cicchetti, and an increasing number of risk researchers. Together, they have given new impetus to an already active research and clinical literature on stress and coping (Garmezy & Rutter, 1983), created the new and exciting field of developmental psychopathology (Rolf, Masten, Cicchetti, Nuechterlein, & Weintraub, 1990), and provided a solid conceptual and empirical foundation for preventive intervention programs and prevention science (Coie et al., 1993).

Concepts associated with the study of risk, resilience, vulnerability, protection, and buffering now appear frequently in discussions of mental health and disorders (cf. Mrazek & Haggerty, 1994). As is usually the case when complex ideas are assimilated by a wider audience, variability and vagueness pervade the language of risk, with different theorists, researchers, clinicians, and policymakers using the same terms in very different ways. Contributing additional confusion to the discourse is the fact that risk concepts, originally developed for the study of

1

individual adaptation, have increasingly been extended to the analysis of family adaptation. The central task in this chapter, using Garmezy, and especially Rutter, as guides, is to attempt to clarify the definitions of risk, resilience, and other related concepts and to explore their implications for family research and preventive intervention. In the course of this effort at clarification, a number of issues are addressed:

1. We show how concepts of risk, vulnerability, protection, buffering, and resilience originated, and how they lead inevitably to a new theoretical and methodological paradigm—a dynamic, process-oriented view of psychopathology rather than the static, categorical picture presented by the traditional psychiatric nosology (e.g., American Psychiatric Association, 1994).

2. We emphasize the fact that distinctions among concepts from the risk and resilience literature are often blurred and we attempt to provide definitions emphasizing their differences.

3. We explore the problems that arise when risk models created to explain individual psychopathology are applied to families.

4. We argue that, from the point of view of family researchers, the elegant examples Rutter and Garmezy use to illustrate risk, buffering, and resilience effects are deceptively simple. It is necessary to develop more complex models of multiple risks and multiple vulnerabilities, buffers, or sources of resilience as they interact and unfold over time.

5. Finally, we show how risk models provide important new conceptual underpinnings to the planning and evaluation of preventive interventions designed to reduce the incidence and severity of psychological distress and to promote and enhance the development of competence.

Although risk studies are now examining psychopathology all along the individual and family lifespan, many points in this chapter are made with examples from our own research and from other investigators focused on adaptation and dysfunction during the early phases of the family developmental cycle.

RISK RESEARCH AND PSYCHOPATHOLOGY

Origins of the Concept of Risk

The concept and measurement of risk originated in the fields of commerce and insurance. Centuries ago, merchants faced with frequent disasters in shipping their goods across the seas wanted to estimate the risk of losing their cargo in order to insure themselves against potential loss. Gradually, individual bargaining and haggling about the odds of disaster and the cost of protection gave rise to an insurance industry, which relies on actuarial data concerning mortality and other natural catastrophes that affect sailors and their ships.

Risk studies also have a long history in the field of epidemiology, which focuses on documenting the health and disease patterns in human populations and the factors influencing, or at least associated with, these patterns (Kleinbaum, Kupper, & Morgenstern, 1982). What epidemiologists want to know is who gets sick, who does not, and why (Gruenberg, 1980). Answering the "why" question places us squarely in the business of understanding risk. Early epidemiological studies focused on risks associated with mortality and physical illness, with the most famous examples arising from the discovery of the fact that people living in particular locations were more likely to contract cholera, yellow fever, and typhoid.

More recently, researchers have seen rapid growth in the epidemiology of mental health and mental illness (e.g., Costello & Angold, 1993). In one example, Kellam, Brown, Rubin, and Ensminger (1983) demonstrated in a large longitudinal population study of the children of Woodlawn that those who had been described by teachers and peers as having difficulty in their academic and social adaptation to first grade were at risk for developing social and psychiatric disorders 10 years later during adolescence. Although few very large studies attempt to discover the incidence and prevalence of mental health risks and outcomes in an entire population (e.g., Rutter, 1989), most researchers choose to study individuals already identified as being at high risk for one or more specific disorders.

In one of the first applications of the "high risk" strategy, Mednick and Schulsinger (1968) sought to identify individual and family stressors that increase the likelihood of a child developing schizophrenia (see also Goldstein, 1990). Subsequent investigations focused on other subgroups at high risk for pathological outcomes including mood disorders (Radke-Yarrow & Zahn-Waxler, 1990), aggression (Patterson & Dishion, 1988; Richters & Cichetti, 1993), hyperactivity (Lambert, 1988), impaired intellectual development (Sameroff, Seifer, Baldwin, & Baldwin, 1993), and a variety of psychological and academic problems (Baldwin, Cole, & Baldwin, 1982; Sameroff, Seifer, & Zax, 1982).

It should be noted that the meaning and measurement of risk has shifted in significant ways from its beginnings in business and public health epidemiology to its current applications in the field of mental health. The field began with simple dichotomous definitions of risk: Ships returned safely to port or they did not; people developed typhoid or they did not. Risk was measured in terms of the probability of a negative, categorically defined outcome occurring in a specified population. As risk analysis was extended to the understanding of mental illness, the definition of what constitutes an "outcome" was broadened considerably. Beyond the presence or absence of a disease, investigators were also concerned with the duration of the disorder and the number or severity of symptoms regardless of the presence of a disorder. For example, studies now commonly assess the correlation between a risk factor, such as marital conflict, and the level of aggressive behavior shown by the child (e.g., Fincham, Grych, & Osborne, 1994).

A second shift in risk research has been the move from studying epidemiologically defined population samples to selecting samples of convenience with large variations in mental health status or symptom picture. Because these studies rarely provide both continuous (e.g., aggressive behavior) and categorical measures of dysfunction (e.g., Oppositional Defiant Disorder), and rarely involve epidemiologically defined samples from specified populations, it is not known whether this broadening of the concept affects the pattern of findings obtained from risk–outcome research.

From its beginnings, the study of risk has not been limited to descriptions of the chance that illness or mental disorders will occur in large populations. Epidemiologists are often motivated by the hope that their data will be used in the planning of actions to reduce both the risks and their consequences. That is, there is a close connection between the epidemiology of risk and the public health ideal of prevention. Understanding more about the risk can help researchers to make decisions and take actions that will promote good health outcomes or minimize the incidence, prevalence, and severity of disease or disorder. This point is revisited at the end of the chapter.

Causal Models and Risk Models of Psychopathology

In our view, risk analysis challenges traditional causal models of mental illness and provides a new theoretical and research paradigm for understanding psychopathology.

Causal Models. For most of this century, mental health researchers and clinicians have assumed that psychological disorders can be classified meaningfully in an array of discrete categories (e.g., schizophrenia, depression, antisocial personality disorder), and that a set of specific causes can be identified for each disorder. There are three problems associated with applying causal models to mental health. First, philosophers and scientists have a great deal of difficulty agreeing on the logical and empirical ground rules for establishing causal relationships. Furthermore, traditional definitions of causality do not always fit newer systemic conceptions of how mental health problems arise. Causal models are usually thought of as linear—from cause to effect—but family systems views, for example, assume that causality operates in a dynamic process that is circular (Steinglass, 1987) or transactional (Sameroff & Chandler, 1975). For example, in Patterson and Dishion's (1988) account of "coercive cycles" in families, a parent's ineffective responses to low levels of a child's aggression reinforce the child's negative behavior, which makes it more difficult for the parent to respond effectively, which, in turn, results in escalations in aggressive behavior. In this view, the parent's behavior is not the cause of the child's aggression, but one element in a reciprocal transactional process.

A second problem with applying traditional causal models to the etiology of mental illness as defined by mutually exclusive diagnostic categories is that many diagnoses show extensive overlap or comorbidity. For example, as Hinshaw (1992b) pointed out, children who are diagnosed as having Attention Deficit Hyperactivity Disorder also tend to exhibit features of conduct disorder and are frequently diagnosed with learning disabilities. Beyond accounting for the emergence of each of these problems, researchers must also be able to account for the fact that some children show all three, some combine these problems in pairs, and others suffer from a single disorder or difficulty.

A third problem with causal models of the etiology of specific psychiatric disorders is created by the fact that research designs often make it difficult to distinguish between simple correlations (*A* predicts *B*) and causal relationships (*A* causes *B*). Compounding this problem is the fact that mental health researchers have persisted in making a simple but fatal mistake in drawing causal conclusions from their empirical studies. Until recently, these studies almost always began with participants diagnosed in a category of mental illness or psychological disorder, or displaying a range from low to high levels of the problematic behavior in question. Investigators attempted to identify the antecedents or causes of the disorder or the behavior, but causality can never be established by reasoning backward from its presumed effects. Even if *A* causes *B*, our observation of *B* does not prove that *A* was the cause; another variable, *C*, may also cause *B*.

Three common research designs, each increasingly sophisticated, have failed to avoid the causal inference trap. First, through analysis of a single case, or through collecting a sample of patients with the same diagnosis, clinicians attempted to understand the forces that might have created a specific disorder. For example, it was observed that in the families of patients diagnosed as schizophrenic, there was a high incidence of parental psychopathology and very distressed parent–child relationships (e.g., Sullivan, 1962). It is easy to see now that without a control group, the meaning of this observation is ambiguous. It is not known whether the incidence of pathology in the patients' parents is higher than it is in a group of parents whose children have never received the diagnosis. This point seems obvious until we realize how often "backward reasoning" from single cases or samples is accepted as an adequate causal explanation of psychopathology.

To address the flaws of single case and single sample studies, researchers use concurrent or retrospective follow-back designs; in epidemiology these are called *case-control studies*. Two samples are chosen, roughly comparable in demographic characteristics. One sample contains individuals diagnosed as having the disorder, and the other is comprised of individuals described as normal, or at least not disordered. The goal of study is the search for premorbid differences between the two samples. It has been found, for example, that there is a higher incidence of schizophrenia in the biological parents of schizophrenic patients than in parents of controls (Gottesman, McGuffin, & Farmer, 1987). The question is: What can be concluded from such a finding? This chapter is not concerned with the issue of whether the causes of schizophrenia are genetic, environmental, or both. Regardless of one's position on the heredity–environment issue, neither concurrent nor retrospective research studies can be used to establish causal relationships between antecedents and outcomes. If researchers assess the parents and children at the same point in time, we cannot determine whether the parents' pathology presents a risk for their children's development or whether the children's pathology puts their parents' emotional equilibrium at risk.

Even with good data about parents' diagnostic status from prior records, retrospective studies beginning with samples of diagnosed individuals provide a distorted estimate of risk. Suppose all of the schizophrenic children were found to have at least one schizophrenic parent (decidedly not the case). Researchers would still not be able to conclude that parental pathology was a risk factor for the development of schizophrenia. If the study had started prospectively with parents, researchers would find that most schizophrenic parents do not have schizophrenic children. In logic, the fact that A (schizophrenic children) implies B (schizophrenic parents) does not mean that B implies A. Although concurrent and retrospective research designs can be useful in generating hypotheses about antecedents of psychopathology, these hypotheses must be tested in prospective studies that start with an identified risk and follow the subjects forward over time. As will be seen, adopting the prospective risk approach changes the nature of the questions that are asked about psychopathology and alters the conception of psychopathology itself.

Risk Models. A number of risk studies, including adoption studies (Kety, Wender, Jacobsen, & Ingraham, 1994), have used a prospective longitudinal approach, with the outcomes of schizophrenia and antisocial behavior receiving the most attention.[1] In general, this research shows that severe pathology in the parents, or dysfunctional interactions in the family, are associated with greater risk of dysfunction in the children (e.g., Caspi & Elder, 1988; Liem, 1980). However, prospective risk studies often ignore two ideas inherent in the definition of risk. Not all individuals at risk develop the same disorder, and some individuals at risk never develop a disorder at all. A minimum of six risk–outcome pathways should really be examined:

1. Parent schizophrenic → Schizophrenic child
2. Parent schizophrenic → Child with another disorder
3. Parent schizophrenic → Child with no disorder
4. Parent not schizophrenic → Schizophrenic child
5. Parent not schizophrenic → Child with another disorder
6. Parent not schizophrenic → Child with no disorder

---

[1]Technically, not all of these studies actually begin at a point and follow participants forward in time. Many of them identify a risk factor in the past (e.g., a parent's diagnostic status) and assess the current outcome of the child.

Predictions based on risk estimates will inevitably be less than perfect because risk factors occur much more frequently than dysfunctional outcomes do. The traditional psychopathologist is interested in comparing Pathway 1 (high risk → specific dysfunctional outcome) with Pathway 6 (low risk → normal outcome), but studies of Pathways 2 through 5 are equally interesting and equally necessary for a broader understanding of psychopathology. If the links between parents' pathology and schizophrenia in their children are to be traced, it is essential to explain the fact that children of parents with a diagnosis of schizophrenia (Pathway 2) may be at risk for other disorders, and that most children of schizophrenic parents (Pathway 3) will not receive *DSM* diagnoses at all. It is also essential to explain the fact that some children of well-functioning parents receive a variety of clinical diagnoses, and some come to be diagnosed as schizophrenic (Pathways 4 and 5).

When the issue is posed this way, it quickly becomes apparent that the families in Pathways 2 through 5 may represent discontinuity between risk and outcome, but that many of these discontinuities or "exceptions to the rule" are not random. One of the central challenges of developmental psychopathology is to explain the discontinuities by identifying the buffering factors that protect some children from psychological harm in the presence of risk, and the vulnerability factors that lead some children to develop disturbances despite the fact that their circumstances and family environments would lead us to hold more positive expectations. Risk researchers, then, are as interested in understanding why people do not develop disorders as in understanding those who do. A central ingredient of risk research is that it represents a search for both lawful continuity and discontinuity between risks and outcomes.

Risk and Developmental Psychopathology. Another central ingredient of contemporary risk research is its emphasis on moving pictures rather than static snapshots. Single-time studies of psychopathology examine the concurrent correlates of a given diagnostic outcome, or identify risk factors at one time, and follow individuals at a later point to assess the incidence of disease or dysfunction. In both cases, there is a single image of the risk factor and a single image of the outcome. However, in real life, people move in and out of risk status and diagnostic classifications. Although many demographic indicators are fixed (e.g., race) or relatively stable (e.g., social class), psychological risks may fluctuate as life circumstances change. With the exception of very severe mental illness or retardation, an individual's diagnostic status or level of adaptation is also likely to shift over time. Major depressive episodes, fortunately, do not usually last forever. The serious disruption following a divorce often disappears after a substantial period of adjustment and readjustment (Hetherington & Clingempeel, 1992). As time goes on, individuals are increasingly likely to be faced with new risks, to develop new vulnerabilities, and to have new opportunities to develop resilience. Despite risks, severe trauma, and dysfunction at various points in development, there is always the possibility of healing and forward progress, at least for some individuals.

The risk paradigm inevitably leads researchers to search for the regulative processes that determine which of many possible developmental pathways individuals follow in their journeys toward adaptation or dysfunction. At least six alternative pathways are noted:

1. Some individuals and families start off well and stay well.
2. Some start off at risk or in distress and stay that way.
3. Some start off well and then develop a disorder.
4. Some start off at risk or in distress, but function well later on.
5. Some start off with specific problems and remain in distress, but the nature of the problems shifts over time.
6. Some cycle in and out of risk and actual distress.

In contrast with the view that there are specific causes of specific disorders, the risk approach to psychopathology assumes that individuals with similar risk histories may wind up in different diagnostic categories, and individuals may follow very different pathways to the same destination. The key task for a scientist or clinician using the developmental psychopathology risk model is to identify the mechanisms or processes that influence the path linking risks and outcomes at a given point in time. As scientists and clinicians, we are not suggesting that every study of psychopathology must have a prospective longitudinal design, but we do believe that only longitudinal studies allow us to systematically test hypotheses about the origins and development of psychopathology.

Risk–outcome research provides a fresh perspective on psychopathology that is quintessentially developmental. The identification of risk factors may begin with concurrent or follow-back studies, but, ultimately, it must follow individuals over time to examine the impact of shifting risks on changing levels of adaptation. In contrast with traditional approaches to psychopathology, risk researchers are as concerned with the mechanisms that account for coping, competence, and resilience as they are with the processes that explain the links between risks or stressors and vulnerability or psychopathology.

The frequent finding that a large proportion of the population develops relatively well despite severe risks raises a challenge to traditional trauma-based theories of psychopathology. The notion of trauma put forward early in Freud's formulations remains increasingly popular, although still controversial today, and assumes that all forms of psychopathology are precipitated by specific traumas (risks) and that all severe traumas are followed inevitably by psychopathology. The automatic linkage in both directions is questioned by risk researchers: Traumas, like other risks, do not inevitably lead to dysfunctional outcomes, and psychopathology cannot always be traced back to specific traumas. Risk research leads to a new paradigm because it forces us to transform our conception of mental illness from a stable and automatic categorical outcome of specific forces to a dynamic process of moving toward or away from states of psychological adaptation.

In sum, the risk paradigm changes the way research on psychopathology is conducted and alters the way that psychopathology is defined. Even if researchers have a specific disorder in mind, rather than beginning by selecting identified patients, they start with people in certain risk categories. Rather than reasoning backward from effects to causes, the investigator traces the linkage forward from risk status to both expected and unexpected outcomes. In this research paradigm, psychopathology is not a static category but an ever-evolving set of processes that lead to pathways in and out of adaptation.

DEFINING RISK, VULNERABILITY, BUFFER, RESILIENCE, AND ASSET

Risk

The concept of risk has been used thus far without defining it, trying to build a reservoir of connotative meanings inductively. Excellent articles by Rutter (1987), Masten and Garmezy (1985), Sameroff and Seifer (1990), and Richters and Weintraub (1990) are relied on to create more specific definitions.

Risks predispose individuals and populations (identifiable groups of people) to specific negative or undesirable outcomes. As noted earlier, a negative or undesirable outcome in the field of mental health and illness is defined and measured in different ways that include the onset of a disorder, its severity and duration, and the frequency or intensity of one or more behaviors or symptoms, regardless of whether these symptoms constitute a clinical syndrome. The magnitude of risk is measured as the probability of a specific negative outcome in a population when the risk is present, compared with the probability when it is absent, or as a correlation between risk and outcomes measured as continuous rather than categorical variables.

Traditionally, risk was conceived in static terms as a marker, a stressor, or a "factor" predicting undesirable outcomes. Poverty, marital conflict, and child abuse are presumed to place children at risk for negative developmental outcomes because a number of studies have found that more children in these risk groups are identified as having more psychological difficulties or behavior problems than children not in these groups. Rutter (1987) argued that researchers cannot stop with the identification of risk groups or markers. Risks should be thought of as processes. The active ingredients of a risk do not lie in the variable itself, but in the set of processes that flow from the variable, linking risk conditions with specific dysfunctional outcomes. For example, researchers have shown that socially withdrawn or shy children are at greater risk for developing depression than their more outgoing peers (Kellam et al., 1983; Rutter, 1987). The risk should not be attributed to traits of social withdrawal or shyness, as it resides in the processes associated with social withdrawal (e.g., lack of positive feedback from others) that increase the probability of the child developing an internalizing disorder like depression.

Rutter's analysis leads to a related point that is frequently misunderstood in discussions of risk research. Risk processes must be defined by their links with specific outcomes. The same variable in the same child (e.g., shyness) may function as a risk with respect to one outcome (depression), may be neutral with respect to another outcome (perhaps academic achievement), and may function as a protective factor with respect to a third outcome, in the sense that shy children are much less likely to become highly aggressive or delinquent (Kellam et al., 1983; Rutter, 1987). Risk must always be defined with reference to a specific negative outcome. That is, risk is not simply an accumulation of life stressors in which negative life events are associated with any manner of diseases or disorders. "Children at risk" or "families at risk" should not be talked about without specifying what they are at risk for. Although it is known that poverty, marital conflict, and child abuse are not good for children, whether they constitute risk factors depends on the outcomes in mind, and on the mechanisms by which risk processes work their negative effects on the child. How do researchers know whether X is a risk factor for Y? Unfortunately, researchers must conduct a systematic study of the pathways linking measures of assumed risk with specific outcomes to find out whether our assumptions about the risk–outcome connection are justified.

In place of a causal mechanistic model, risk research substitutes a highly contextual, functionalist model of psychopathology. The definition of risk is particular to the specific conceptual and empirical analysis undertaken by the investigator. Even the distinction between risk and outcome is determined by when and where investigators take their research snapshots. For one researcher, ineffective parenting may be an outcome of parents' depression (Radke-Yarrow, Cummings, Kuczynski, & Chapman, 1985), whereas for others it is a process that places children at risk for delays in the development of cognitive and social competence (Baumrind, 1978; Blechman, 1991; Patterson & Capaldi, 1991).

Vulnerability

As has been indicated, even in populations defined by the presence of a common risk, some individuals are more likely to develop a disorder, others are much less likely to be diagnosed or develop the disorder in less severe form, and still others will do surprisingly well despite their at-risk status. The concepts of vulnerability, buffering, and resilience have been used to explain these various departures from what researchers expect on the basis of group statistics.

Vulnerability increases the probability of a specific negative or undesirable outcome in the presence of a risk. Vulnerability operates only when risk is present; without the risk, vulnerability has no effect. A physical analogy may make the distinction between risk and vulnerability clearer. A sailboat is returned to the water after a brief time in drydock, during which a crack in the hull has been hurriedly patched. As long as the weather is reasonably good and the waves are moderate, the boat is fine and will probably remain so indefinitely. If a violent storm springs up, all sailboats in the vicinity are at risk for damage, but this sailboat is particularly vulnerable to severe damage as soon as the storm begins.

The concept of vulnerability should be familiar to those adopting a "diathesis-stress" model of psychopathology (e.g., Rosenthal, 1970). Why is it that only a small number of children who are genetically at risk for schizophrenia develop the disorder? A frequent answer is that, strictly speaking, genetic factors are not risks but diatheses or inherited vulnerabilities that result in psychopathology only when stressors are very high.

Vulnerability does not refer only to genetic predispositions to disorder. The term *vulnerability* generally connotes an inner weakness or an internal locus of a problem, but it is not limited to the genetic predispositions that are a focus of the diathesis-stress model. In addition to genetic or constitutional factors, conditions such as low self-esteem, personality traits, and depression are often described as vulnerabilities. The criteria for the definition of vulnerability, however, lie squarely in the pattern of functional relationships. External conditions can function as vulnerabilities; for example when ineffective parenting makes children more vulnerable to externalizing problems when family stressors are high (Patterson & Capaldi, 1991).

In a study of nonclinic families with either 3½-year-olds or preadolescents, we found marital conflict was correlated with preschoolers' or preadolescents' externalizing (aggressive) behavior, but parents' symptoms of depression were not (Miller, Cowan, Cowan, Hetherington, & Clingempeel, 1993). Parents' depressive symptoms did not constitute a risk factor with reference to the child's aggressive behavior in these nonclinic families.[2] However, when the nonclinic parents had high levels of marital conflict (reported and observed), their children were more likely to be rated by observers and their parents as aggressive. In this case, the marital conflict can be considered a risk factor with respect to preschoolers' and preadolescents' aggressive behavior. When parents with many depressive symptoms (a vulnerability in this context) were also in high-conflict marital relationships (a risk for children's externalizing), the children were more likely to be described as aggressive. That is, depression amplified the risk associated with marital conflict. If the parents with high levels of depressive symptoms were not in high-conflict marriages, their children were not described as aggressive. Depression in isolation did not increase the level of aggressive behavior. Note that in this example, parents' depression as a family vulnerability was internal to the parents, but external to the child.

In the statistical language of analysis of variance, the influence of a risk is a main effect, whereas the influence of a vulnerability depends on an interaction with another variable—it makes a difference to outcomes only at high levels of risk.

---

[2]When parents receive clinical diagnoses of depression, their children are at risk for a variety of disorders and problems, including aggression (e.g., Sameroff, Seifer, & Zax, 1982).

According to the definitions given here, a variable having a negative effect when risks are low, even if the effect is small, should be thought of as an additional risk factor, not a vulnerability. The distinction between risk and vulnerability may be difficult to make in practice, because what constitutes a statistically significant interaction effect may vary with the size of the sample. Nevertheless, the concept of vulnerability is useful in that it reminds psychologists that we will only be able to observe the potential negative effects of some variables if we have assessed individuals and families experiencing some degree of risk.

Buffer

A buffer, protection, or immunization decreases the probability of a negative or undesirable outcome in the presence of a risk. The idea that certain mechanisms buffer or protect us from harm is not new in the fields of medicine or psychopathology. And yet, in an attempt to define the expected pathway between stressors and problematic outcomes in mental health, cases that do not turn out the expected way tend to be disregarded. Any theory of psychological adaptation must account for the fact that many people who experience high risks do not show negative or undesirable problematic effects. They show them in reduced or modified form, or adapt well in spite of these risks.

Using data from the Becoming a Family Project (C. P. Cowan & P. A. Cowan 1992; C. P. Cowan, Cowan, Heming, & Miller, 1991), Cohn found a buffering effect of the quality of couples' marital relationships on the quality of women's relationships with their children (Cohn, Cowan, Cowan, & Pearson, 1992). Parents of 3½-year-old children were interviewed with George, Kaplan, and Main's (1984) Adult Attachment Interview, in which they described their memories of their early relationships with their own parents. Men and women who remembered positive early experiences and recounted them clearly, or who remembered negative early experiences but recounted them in a coherent manner that placed the relationship in perspective were classified as having secure working models of early attachment relationships. Men and women who had difficulty describing the early relationships with their parents or placing their experiences in a coherent perspective were classified as having insecure working models of attachment relationships. In a 40-minute parent–child laboratory interaction session, with raters blind to all other family data, parents who had been classified as having insecure working models were rated as significantly less warm and less structuring with their 3½-year-old children than were parents with secure working models. It can be said, then, that their own insecure working models of attachment placed parents (and their children) at risk for less effective parenting of their children.

Taking a more family systemic approach to risk research on attachment, Cohn and colleagues also examined the attachment classifications for both spouses. Women with insecure working models of attachment who married men with secure working models were found to be as warm and structuring with their children as women with secure working models.[3] In spite of her insecure working model of early attachment, then, something about a woman's relationship with a husband with a secure working model protected her from carrying over ineffective parenting to her relationship with her child. Further analysis of this data set suggests a potential mechanism that may underlie the buffering process. In the nonconcordant couples (wives with insecure models, husbands with secure models), the quality of marital interaction in front of the child was more positive and less negative than that of couples in which both partners were classified as having insecure working models of attachment (Cohn, Silver, Cowan, Cowan, & Pearson, 1992). Perhaps the women with insecure working models of attachment who were in more nurturant marital relationships were able to develop new working models of intimate family relationships to guide their interactions with their children.

Rutter (1987) warned researchers not to equate buffering or protective factors with conditions of low risk. The concept of buffering is meant to describe what happens to reduce the incidence or severity of the anticipated negative outcomes under risk conditions. For example, in their impressive study of the children of Kauai, Werner and Smith (1982) were interested in tracing the long-term impact of biological risks associated with low birthweight and other manifestations of perinatal stress and complications. They found that perinatal complications were consistently related to later impaired physical and psychological development only when combined with persistently poor environmental circumstances such as chronic poverty, family instability, or maternal mental health problems. Children raised in more affluent homes in intact families with well-educated parents showed few, if any, negative effects from the early perinatal complications. The environmental contrasts showed that, without the protection provided by many psychological and physical aspects of the intact, middle-class homes, the early negative consequences of birth-related difficulties persisted into young adulthood.

Richters and Weintraub (1990) noted the difficulty of distinguishing between protective factors and risk reducers. In the Werner and Smith example, the distinction can be kept clear because nothing in the middle-class homes of the children with early perinatal risk could erase what happened to them during pregnancy and birth. In other examples, it may be more difficult to decide whether children did well because their risks were reduced or because external or internal protective factors enabled them to cope with stressful events or conditions.

Resilience

So far, risk has been defined as a predisposer to negative or undesirable outcomes, vulnerability as an amplifier of the probability of negative outcomes in the pres-

---

[3]In 9 of the 11 pairs with differing security of attachment classifications, insecurely attached women were married to securely attached men. The same ratio occurs in Mary Main's samples (personal communication, 1992). With only two couples in which insecurely attached men were married to securely attached women, we could not examine the couple relationship as a buffer for insecure men's parenting behavior.

ence of risk, and buffering as a reducer of the probability of negative outcomes despite risks. All of these concepts refer to the stimulus side of the equation—the set of conditions or mechanisms that predict, or perhaps shape, mental health outcomes. All of them imply that risks produce negative or undesirable effects, although some of these effects may be reduced or minimized by processes that protect the individual from harm. However, if researchers focus in more detail on the outcome side of the equation, we find an important consequence of risk noted by Masten and Garmezy (1985), Anthony (1974), and Werner and Smith (1982), and elaborated on in a special issue of *Development and Psychopathology* (Cicchetti & Garmezy, 1993): Some individuals seem to thrive on the challenges that adversity sets in motion. These children have been described as "invulnerable" or "invincible" but it is now more common to refer to them as *resilient* or *stress-resistant* (Masten & Garmezy, 1985). In one of the few conceptual divergences between Rutter and Garmezy, Rutter minimized the utility of the resilience concept, whereas Garmezy emphasized it. Rutter's primary concern is that resilience is viewed as a static trait or capacity of the individual, and not the outcome of a set of processes or mechanisms.

We share Rutter's concern, but we believe that clearer definitions of resilience can be useful both for the understanding of developmental psychopathology and for the planning of preventive interventions. How is it possible for individuals to do well in the face of risk? There are three alternatives, only the last of which is associated with resilience. First, as has been seen, protective factors can reduce the impact of risk (e.g., active and warm parenting can mitigate the effect of a parent's incapacity); care needs to be taken to distinguish between buffering processes and resilience. Second, Richters and Weintraub (1990) have noted that researchers can define a risk group (e.g., children of parents who have been diagnosed as schizophrenic), but individuals in a risk category may not have experienced many of the stressful experiences that tend to be associated with the risk; care must be taken to avoid concluding that these individuals are resilient until we have verified that they have indeed been subjected to adversity. Third, individuals may develop coping skills to counteract risk and respond to challenges that "cancel" the negative impact of risk, or even advance the individual to new levels of adaptation. It is this last alternative that leads us to the resilience.

Resilience, stress resistance, or *invulnerability* refer to processes that operate in the presence of risk to produce outcomes as good or better than those obtained in the absence of risk. In this definition, resilient individuals are those who do not simply avoid the most negative outcomes associated with risk, but demonstrate adequate or more than adequate adaptation in the face of adversity. Children born of schizophrenic parents often become notably competent and successful individuals (Garmezy, Masten, & Tellegen, 1984). These children are not invulnerable in the sense that they are absolutely impervious to stress or catastrophe. Resilience may be a better descriptive term for the idea that some individuals or families possess physiological strengths, psychological resourcefulness, and interpersonal skills that enable them to respond successfully to major challenges and to grow from the experience.

The Adult Attachment Interview developed by Main and her colleagues (Main & Goldwyn, in press) has been previously referred to. In a subset of couples from the Becoming a Family Project sample (Pearson, Cohn, Cowan, & Cowan, 1994), approximately 75% of the fathers and mothers of preschoolers were categorized as having secure working models of attachment, based on their responses to the hour-long interview describing past and present relationships with both parents. Nevertheless, two thirds of those with secure working models recounted negative experiences with their family of origin during their formative years. Yet, somehow, by the time these men and women had become parents themselves, they managed not only to place those early experiences in perspective, but to develop warm and effective relationships with their children. Compared with the "continuous secure" individuals who presented convincing and detailed accounts of very positive family relationships throughout childhood, the "earned secures" did not emerge unscathed. Men and women with secure working models achieved despite negative family histories described significantly more symptoms of depression on the Center for Epidemiological Studies in Depression Scale (Radloff, 1977) than those with more positive family histories. They were resilient in that their painful experiences did not appear to color the quality of relationships they developed with their husbands, wives, or children.[4]

Garmezy (1985) suggested that it is necessary to test three different hypotheses about the mechanisms that could account for stress resistance or resilience in the face of risk: (a) the child is "immune" to particular stressors, (b) the child compensates under stress to maintain his or her level of competence, and (c) the child is challenged to achieve enhanced competence levels. In a metaphorical analogy with the field of medicine, the questions here are directed to determining whether resilience results from some kind of "natural" immunity, an acquired immunity, or a combination of the two.

Both Rutter and Garmezy come down squarely on the side of acquisition. Resilience, Rutter (1987) argued, is an end product of buffering processes that do not eliminate risk, but encourage the individual to engage with risk effectively. Like medical immunizations, buffers expose individuals to small doses of the disease agent and help them develop the means to fight off illness. Masten and Garmezy (1984) argued that repeated experiences with active coping and stress buffering can build or enhance resilience. Not a fixed, magical Teflon coating that effortlessly repels noxious agents, resilience can be enhanced by mastery experiences that develop and refine new coping skills, or can be eroded by cumulative adverse circumstances or developmental failures. Resilience, then, is

---

[4]Strictly speaking, the quality of their early experience, positive or negative, cannot be determined from an interview obtained during adulthood. The trends described here are consistent with the authors' interpretation of the findings in terms of resilience, but do not provide proof of the resilience hypothesis.

important in risk analysis not because it represents a stable trait, but because it reminds us that there are positive and optimistic outcomes that occur in spite of, or even because of, the individual's exposure to risk.

This conception of resilience helps to determine priorities for preventive intervention programs. If Rutter and Garmezy are correct about the cumulative nature of buffering and resistance to stress, clinicians who are interested in preventive intervention might consider spending less time focusing on how people become dysfunctional, and spend the bulk of their efforts learning how to nurture and foster mechanisms that lead to resilience in the face of ongoing and antici- pated stressors and risks.

Mechanisms

The issue of specifying what is meant by *mechanisms* that connect independent variables and outcomes is actually very complex, and is dealt with only briefly here. An investigator says, "I have discovered a link—a correlation—between parents' marital quality and their children's adaptation. When two parents are in conflict frequently, their children tend to have more difficulties getting along with their peers." It is asked, "What are the mechanisms that link the marital system and the peer system?"

Mechanisms are processes linking risks and outcomes that add to our under- standing of the variance in the outcomes:

$$\text{Risk} \rightarrow \text{Mechanism} \rightarrow \text{Outcome}$$

If we find that marital distress (risk) affects children's adaptation (outcome) through its impact on mothers' and fathers' parenting behavior:

$$\text{Marital distress} \rightarrow \text{Parenting behavior} \rightarrow \text{Children's adaptation}$$

we are saying that individual differences in marital distress are correlated with individual differences in parenting behavior, individual differences in parenting behavior account for variations in the children's adaptation over and above marital distress, and therefore the quality of parenting may be a mechanism by which the conflict in the marriage has a direct impact on the child.

Mechanisms can operate in two ways to link risks and outcomes—as mediators or moderators. A mediating mechanism is a dynamic process that creates a link that is not observable directly from the covariation between risk and outcome. In the study by Miller et al. (1993), briefly described earlier, parents' symptoms of depression were not correlated with preschoolers' aggression, but depressive symptoms were correlated with marital and parenting mediators, which, in turn, were correlated with children's aggression.

By contrast, a moderating mechanism amplifies, reduces, or changes the direction of the correlation between risks and outcomes. For example, Schulz (1994) found that in families with preschool-age children, husbands' job stress (the risk) was more likely to spill over into negative marital interactions during the evening (the outcome) if the husbands were unhappily married, whereas wives' job stress was more likely to spill over into family life if they were happily married. In this case, both marital quality and gender functioned as moderator variables in that they changed the nature of the correlation between risk and outcome; the results force researchers to be more differentiated about defining what is a risk and for whom.

The authors realize that the question of mechanisms is one that could lead to an infinite regress: Each time a link is found between risks and outcomes, it is possible to ask about the links between the links.

"What are the mechanisms linking marriage and parenting?" students ask.

"Patterns of regulating emotion in intimate relationships," the researcher replies (cf. Gottman & Katz, 1989).

"What are the mechanisms mediating intimacy in relationships and affect regulation?" students ask. It is difficult to specify where to stop. Usually it depends on the researcher's theoretical preference, the kinds of questions he or she is asking, and the purposes of the investigation; for example, the need to discover variables that can be manipulated if the research results are going to be used to plan strategies of intervention.

RISK RESEARCH IN A FAMILY CONTEXT

Many of the risk examples that we have given involve family dynamics and processes. Yet, the study of psychopathology is still largely the study of individuals. Although family theorists and therapists are concerned about dysfunctional relationships and family systems (e.g., Minuchin & Fishman, 1981), widely accepted concepts of relational and systemic pathology have yet to be developed. Most family-oriented research using the risk paradigm includes family factors as independent variables to predict the adaptation of individual family members. The size of the family, the organization of the relationships within it, and the processes of interaction among family members can all function as risks, vulnerabilities, buffers, and sources of resilience for individual family members.

Until recently, except for studies of the antecedents of marital distress, risk researchers have not devoted much effort to tracing the links between risk factors and dyadic or triadic relationship outcomes. As Parke and Tinsley (1982) pointed out, the characteristics and behaviors of individuals in a family affect other family members and shape the quality of their dyadic relationships. Relationships in one family domain (e.g., the marriage) have an impact on individuals and on relationships in other family domains (e.g., the parent–child relationship—cf. C. P. Cowan

& P. A. Cowan, 1992). The sum of all these interacting effects can alter the functioning of the family system, just as the system can affect the individuals and relationships within it. Thus, a "complete" family risk model could be schematically represented in a three-dimensional diagram containing 36 ($3 \times 4 \times 3$) cells. The investigator can choose from independent variables in three domains or levels of family analysis (individual, dyadic, and family system), four types of processes (risks, vulnerabilities, buffers, and assets), and dependent variables in three domains of outcome (individual, dyadic, and family system). The complexity of this analysis might be increased by pointing out that the individual level of analysis contains biological, social, and psychological markers of risk (genetic makeup and physical characteristics vs. self-esteem and depression), and so there may be 48, or even more categories of risk-process-outcome. No single study can manage to approximate more than a small portion of this conceptual matrix, but it is important to be clear about the complex array from which research focus is selected.

What happens when families rather than individuals are considered as the unit of analysis in the risk paradigm? Are risks for families merely the sum of risks for individuals and relationships within them? Can the same models be used to identify individuals and families at risk for maladaptation? What constitutes family vulnerability? What buffers families? What would a resilient family look like? The answers are far from obvious and clear, and constitute one of the important agenda items for the future of family risk research (P. A. Cowan, Hansen, Swanson, Field, & Skolnick, 1993).

A central problem in assessing family-level risks and outcomes is the dearth of appropriate measuring instruments. Most self-report measures describe each individual's perceptions of and satisfaction with family life.[5] Most observational measures focus on individual and dyadic behavior. Only a few observational systems attempt to create family-level measures of adaptation (Grotevant & Carlson, 1989; Notarius & Markman, 1989; Reiss, 1981; Walsh, 1982). As researchers develop more complex and sophisticated measures, it will be possible to test more differentiated models that specify how risks, vulnerabilities, buffers, and resilience in various levels of the family system combine to produce various levels of adaptive and maladaptive functioning.

It should be noted that recent emphasis on risk, vulnerability, and resilience evident in clinical psychology, developmental psychology, and mental health was actually preceded by a sociological tradition of family stress theory initiated by Hill (1949, 1958). His ABCX family crisis model, emerging from studies of families separated by war, states that A (the stressor event) interacting with B (the family's resources for meeting crisis) interacting with C (the definition the family makes of the event) produces X (the crisis). This model has been expanded to the double-ABCX model by McCubbin and Patterson (1983; McCubbin & McCubbin, 1989) to include postcrisis-event processes of adaptation, and expanded again by Patterson (1988) as the Family Adjustment and Adaptation Response Model to include

---

[5]An interesting exception is the FAM developed by Skinner, Steinhauer, and Santa-Barbara (1983).

individual, family, and community levels of analysis. With each expansion, terms from the risk literature, such as buffering and vulnerability, have assumed a more prominent place in family stress formulations.

On a conceptual level, family stress theory emphasizes the interaction among various forces both inside and outside the family, an idea consistent with Rutter and Garmezy's formulation of risk research. When the investigators using family stress theory put theory into practice, however, they tend to fall back either on case studies or on large equations summarizing group data that represent responses to specific stressors. These studies tend to catalog the factors associated with family crisis (often measured at the individual level) without tracing the pathways by which some families wind up at Crisis X, others end up at Crisis Y, and still others manage to do reasonably well.

Despite criticism of the present applications of the family stress paradigm, we hope that more family researchers within psychology, psychiatry, and mental health will read and apply the sophisticated theoretical formulations of the ABCX model to individual and family psychopathology. We simply recognize here that no one has yet been able to combine conceptual, measurement, and statistical techniques to investigate the operation of multiple risks, vulnerabilities, buffers, and resilience as they interact within the family to determine pathways to adaptation and dysfunction. Despite the magnitude of the project, this awesome goal seems somehow appropriate for family researchers, who have always claimed that we need ever more complex systemic models to account for the complexity of family adaptation and development.

MULTIPLE RISKS, MULTIPLE BUFFERS: THE LIMITATIONS OF ADDITIVE MODELS

Ideas about risk and resilience have benefited greatly from Garmezy and Rutter's talents at explicating very clear examples. Almost invariably, they describe a three- or four-variable situation—one outcome, one risk, and one vulnerability, protective factor, or buffer as they combine to affect one outcome. Two examples have been cited extensively.

First, Quinton, Rutter, and Liddle (1984) found that girls who had been reared in institutions (the risk factor), and who later married a nonsupportive spouse (the vulnerability factor) tended to be described as ineffective parents (the outcome). However, institutionally reared girls who eventually married supportive husbands (the protective factor) showed about the same incidence of effective parenting as comparison women who did not grow up in institutions and married supportive husbands.

Second, Rutter's (1978) study showed that about 70% of children in homes with marital discord (the risk factor) were diagnosed as having a conduct disorder (the outcome) if they had difficult relationships with all family members (the vulnerability factor). However, if the children had one harmonious family relationship (the protective factor) the incidence of conduct disorder was low even if they experienced discord in the home.[6]

Note that in both of these examples, Rutter is not saying that the protective factor is merely the absence of the vulnerability. Supportive husbands are doing something more than avoiding being unsupportive. A harmonious family relationship is much more than the absence of severe difficulties between parent and child.

Rutter has made an important conceptual contribution by describing protective or buffering effects, but he is quite clear that he cannot yet explain the mechanisms or processes by which they operate. His examples, perhaps chosen to facilitate comprehension, focus on only a few variables and clearly specified outcomes. It seems obvious from our brief discussion of the individual, dyadic, and systemic levels of family risk that a host of variables that affect parenting behavior intervene between the girls' experience of being institutionalized as children, marrying, and having children. What processes associated with their marital relationships buffer their relationships with their children? What processes inherent in untroubled family relationships reduce the incidence of aggression in children whose parents' marriages are in serious conflict? A differentiated and integrated model with many variables at different levels of analysis is needed if the mechanisms linking family risks and outcomes in the children's development are to be mapped.

In one of the seminal articles in this field, Sameroff and Chandler (1975) argued that simple linear causal models (early negative experience X causes later outcome Y) are based on mechanistic theories of development. By contrast, organismic models are not linear. They assume that whatever continuity exists between early experiences and later outcomes results from the fact that early events and regulatory systems continue over time. In Sameroff and Chandler's view, risk must be conceptualized in the context of a transactional model of development in which a "continuum of reproductive casualty" (e.g., prenatal and birth difficulties) has an effect on the child only when considered in combination with a "continuum of caretaking casualty" (e.g., ineffective parenting or mental illness in the parents). For example, parent factors, socioeconomic status, and child characteristics combine over time to determine which child will be abused and how damaging the abuse will be.

Cicchetti and his colleagues (Cicchetti, Toth, Bush, & Gillespie, 1988), also adopting a transactional model, assume that long-term and transient risks and buffers combine to explain variations in the developmental status of children with Down syndrome, nonorganic failure-to-thrive syndrome, and children whose parents are depressed or maltreat them. So far, though, the sophistication of these biosocial family system theories has not been matched by the complexity of statistical models used to examine combinations of risk and buffers or resilience in studies of clinical and nonclinical populations.

---

[6]We should be cautious in accepting some of these examples. This widely cited conclusion is based on a study with only eight children in the high-discord, ineffective parenting cell.

Statistical Models of Multiple Risk

Most researchers use statistical models that assume risks are additive. That is, the effects of each risk are independent of the other and separate risk effects can be summed to estimate an overall probability of dysfunction or distress.

The "Megarisk" Index. Some researchers cope with the vast array of possible risk variables in their studies by creating a high-risk/low-risk score for each variable—using a category system (e.g., minority/nonminority; patient/nonpatient) or a cutoff score (e.g., high depression = high risk) to determine risk status. The megarisk score is the sum of the high risk scores assigned to each individual or family. For example, Sameroff, Seifer, Barocas, Zax, and Greenspan (1987) obtained impressive relationships between 4-year-olds' IQ scores and 10 caretaking casualty factors including minority status, family size, mother's education and occupation; mothers' anxiety, mental health, parenting beliefs, and behavior; and stressful life events and social supports relevant to child development and family life.

Sameroff's approach looks at risks as having independent effects. The results could be used to construct an early screening protocol to identify children at risk for low intelligence scores, but they do not provide us with information about the mechanisms that link the risks and outcomes. Furthermore, this approach does not tell us whether the buffers, vulnerabilities, or resilience factors interact with risk. For example, in Rutter's (1978) study cited earlier, the additive risk could be computed:

Marital discord + difficult family relationships = children's high aggression
(1 risk unit) + (1 risk unit)   = (2 units of aggression)

But the risk effect was canceled out if one family relationship was positive. For example, if either the mother or the father developed an effective relationship with the child, there were no units of negative outcome despite marital uproar in the home. This interactive effect is better represented in the following equation:

Marital discord × 1 good family relationship = children's low aggression
(1 risk unit) × (1 buffering unit, score 0) = (0 units of aggression)

In this case, the multiplicative model of buffering predicts no elevated risk for aggression in the child, whereas the additive model predicts a mildly elevated risk.

The strategy chosen by Sameroff and his colleagues suggests that it is the total number of risks rather than any specific risk that is associated with children's low IQ. But if they had investigated potential buffering effects, they might have found that their risk index would work even more effectively. In some studies, a "risk score of 10" affecting children's school performance could be completely offset by very supportive family environments, whereas a "risk score of 2" could be the last straw for children who are already physically or psychologically vulnerable.

Multiple Regressions.   Some researchers investigating risks or buffers use multiple regression analyses to show how each independent variable contributes to variance in the outcome. For example, Crnic and his colleagues (Crnic, Greenberg, Ragozin, Robinson, & Basham, 1983) used regression analyses to show that social support (a buffer) reduced the adverse effects of stress on mothers' life satisfaction at 1 month postpartum, and also enhanced the effectiveness of mothers' behavior with their infants at 4 months postpartum. However, multiple regression analyses, even with two-way interaction terms entered into the equation, do not allow us to examine the connections (pathways) that link all of the independent variables; they tell us only how these variables combine to predict variance in the outcome. We learn that a combination of mothers' stress, social support, and life satisfaction predicts the quality of their parenting behavior, but this analytic technique does not allow us to identify the mechanism by which social support buffers the effect of stress on mothers' life satisfaction. Thus, multiple regression equations do not allow us to examine the effects of vulnerability and buffers on risk and resilience.

Path Models.   Processes that flow from risk situations can affect individuals directly (e.g., the emotional atmosphere from marital conflict can upset a child) or indirectly by their influence on mediating variables (e.g., marital conflict can disrupt the parents' quality of interaction with the child, which, in turn, can upset the child). Recently, structural equation modeling (path analysis) has become increasingly popular as a technique for describing both direct and indirect effects in child development research (e.g., *Child Development* Special Issue, 1984) and family studies (e.g., Falk & Miller, 1991).

Sigel (1982) and his colleague McGillicuddy-DeLisi (1990) used path models to demonstrate how parents' beliefs about children's learning and parenting behavior combine to predict children's representational competence. Patterson and Capaldi (1991) used path models to show how parents' personality characteristics, socioeconomic status, and discipline practices combine to predict their adolescents' peer status and antisocial behavior outside the family. Hetherington and Clingempeel (1992) used path models to trace the impact of divorce and remarriage on adolescents' personal and social adaptation. In Gottman and Katz's (1989) study of parents and their early school-aged children, path models show that lower physiological arousal in the parents during a family play session is associated with higher marital conflict and less effective parenting, which, in turn, is linked with the children's poorer health and less successful interaction with their peers.

In the authors' own study of early family development (P. A. Cowan, Cowan, Schulz, & Heming 1994), path models reveal that mothers' and fathers' recalled negative relationships with their own parents, marital dissatisfaction in pregnancy, symptoms of depression at 18 months postpartum, and conflictful marital interaction and ineffective parenting when the child is 3½, combine in specific patterns to predict about 50% of the variance in children's academic competence on a standardized achievement test, and 20% to 28% of the variance in their social adaptation as assessed by their kindergarten teacher (see Wampler, Halverson, & Deal, chap. 5, this volume, for additional examples).

The way in which these path models begin to approximate the complexity of clinically based family system theories is exciting; multiple measures of risks, vulnerabilities, buffers, and resilience in different aspects of family life combine to account for variance in children's adaptation or dysfunction. Even with all their advantages in organizing large quantities of longitudinal data, however, path models do not provide a fully differentiated account of the relationships among the variables they describe. First, even in path models that include data from more than one time period, it is difficult to establish the direction of influence between one latent variable and another. If, for example as in most studies, parenting is measured at Time 1 and children's aggressive behavior at Time 2, a correlation between parenting style and aggressive behavior does not prove that the parents have caused the child's aggression. Both parenting behavior and children's aggression are usually stable over time; the results may reflect the fact that the two are reciprocally interacting, or perhaps that they are simply correlated with no implied direction of effects. Investigators might consider using simpler cross-lagged regressions or partial correlations (cf. Hetherington & Clingempeel, 1992) as a way of assessing both independent and dependent variables at more than one time period. Or, they may wish to consider autoregressive and growth curve structural models (Falk & Miller, 1991) that also include measures of consistency and change in the same variables across time.

A second serious limitation of structural equation models is that they are usually limited to the analysis of additive effects.[7] What path diagrams show are the linear regression weights for direct and indirect paths, and the proportion of unique variance that each latent variable contributes to the understanding of variations in the specified outcome. In their focus on group trends and their ignoring of lawful exceptions, path models miss an essential aspect of the risk paradigm. They do not reveal the sources of variance attributable to interactive buffering or vulnerability effects. Structural models include as "error" the outcomes that are not predicted by direct and indirect main effects. They do not, for example, account for the children who are accepted by their peers despite ineffective parenting, or who do well in school despite having parents who are depressed and maritally distressed.

---

[7]It is possible to include interaction terms in the construction of latent variables, but this is rarely done.

The Lack of Dynamic Statistical Models.   Despite the fact that theoretical models of risk assume that bidirectional, transactional processes link risks and outcomes, statistical models are more consistent with assumptions of more traditional, linear, causal models of psychopathology. New ways of analyzing data to handle dynamic interactions among risks, buffers, vulnerabilities, assets, and outcomes are needed.

In this discussion of how statistical models are used to examine hypotheses about risk and resilience, it is easier to criticize than it is to propose solutions, but a number of procedures could help to clarify our understanding of multiple risk even before new statistical models are developed. First, if more than one risk variable is included in a study, it should be examined whether the combined effects are additive or multiplicative. Second, we should do similar tests for additive or multiplicative effects if more than one vulnerability or buffer is included in the study. Third, we should examine the combined effects of risk, vulnerability, and buffers on negative outcomes and on resilience, again testing whether their effects operate independently (additively), or whether some buffers simply cancel the effects of risk (multiplicatively). Fourth, whatever statistical technique is used to organize the data, there should be a comparison of high-risk and low-risk subjects to determine whether potential vulnerability, buffering, or resilience occur under high-risk but not low-risk conditions, as the definitions require. Finally, in longitudinal studies, autoregression effects should be examined by assessing both independent and dependent variables at more than one time period, so that researchers can be more precise in inferences about the direction of effects from risks to outcomes.

Multiple Risk and Cumulative Risk: Time and Development

This discussion of multiple risk has so far focused on the complexity involved in aggregating the number and quality of risks, vulnerabilities, and protective factors into a comprehensive model linking risks and outcomes. Unfortunately, there are additional theoretical and methodological complications involved in the fact that the links between risk and outcomes unfold over time. The severity of a parent's psychopathology or the intensity of the couple's marital conflict may derive power to affect the child not from the present, but from the fact that these conditions have a torturous, cumulative effect over the years of the child's life. Disentangling the impact of multiple current risk and multiple cumulative risk is no easy task.

The assumption that early experience is a primary determinant of later adaptation is at the bedrock of both developmental theory and developmental psychopathology (Bowlby, Freud, Piaget, Werner, Cicchetti). Risk research has benefited from the results of a number of longitudinal projects demonstrating impressive continuity from early childhood into adolescence, including high-risk samples in Rochester

(Sameroff et al., 1982) and Minnesota (Egeland, Carson, & Sroufe, 1993) and relatively low-risk samples in California (Baumrind, 1991; Block & Gjerde, 1990). Assessments of risks associated with early socioeconomic status, parents' characteristics and behavior, and children's characteristics during the preschool years all predict a variety of both normal developmental and pathological outcomes more than a decade later. These findings are often taken as support for the thesis that early developmental status predicts later developmental status, and that early risks play a major role in determining later developmental outcomes.

New data from the Rochester Longitudinal Study (Sameroff, Seifer, Baldwin, & Baldwin, 1993) illustrate some problems with these inferences and provide welcome information about the cumulative developmental effects of risk. The mega-risk index of 10 factors created by Sameroff and his colleagues has been described as highly correlated with the average IQ of the children at 4 ($r = -.58$). Their subsequent follow-up of the children at age 13 showed substantial correlation of IQ scores across time from age 4 to 13 ($r = .72$), and substantial predictive association between early risk and later IQ ($r = -.62$). Do these findings prove that early developmental status and risk affect later development? Not on the basis of the results that have been described so far, because not enough is known about what happened to the early risks and whether they are continuing to affect the child's adaptation.

What is most noteworthy about this study is that the investigators reassessed multiple risk at age 13 and found that the magnitude of stability in multiple risk ($r = .77$) was about the same as that for child IQ. "Those children [who] had poor family and social environments when they were born still had them when they were 13, and probably would continue to have them for the foreseeable future" (Sameroff et al., 1987, p. 95). Thus, one factor determining continuity between early and late assessments of children is that risks continue and cumulate over time. When the early IQ scores were partialled out of the correlation between early risk and later IQ, the risk–outcome correlation remained statistically significant ($r = -.35$). This finding supports the hypothesis that cumulative risk further undermines the child's initially low potential for achieving intellectual competence.

The results of this intriguing report, especially if they are replicated with studies of other risk factors and other outcomes, begin to help us think through the problems involved in understanding the combined effects of early and cumulative risk. In a very different kind of longitudinal study focused more on peer relationships, Sroufe and colleagues (Sroufe, Egeland, & Kreutzer, 1990) found that both early (30 months old) and later (6 years old) risk factors contribute to understanding variations in children's peer competence at age 10 to 11. These kinds of studies are providing a more dynamic model of how the interaction between risks and outcomes plays out in shaping individual developmental trajectories over time.

The notion of transactional risk effects put forth by Rutter (1987) may be relevant to this discussion. The effect of cumulative risk may not always lie in the impact of the same risk sustained over time, but in the fact that some risks lead to a higher probability of other risks occurring. For example, divorce often brings with it poverty, poor discipline, multiple household moves, depression in mothers, and other negative consequences (Hetherington, 1989). Perhaps, then, we should be looking for the effects of cumulative risk in "trajectories of risk sequences."[8]

Multiple Risks and Family Dynamics

In trying to understand more about which parents and children are at risk for later distress, we and our colleagues (Cowan et al., 1985; Cowan et al., 1991) have been examining five major aspects of family life—each at a different level of analysis: the parents' and children's well being or distress as individuals, the quality of the parents' relationship as a couple, the quality of the relationships between each of the parents and their child, the environment in each of the parents' families of origin, and the balance between life stresses and social supports outside the family as they are experienced by each family member. It is assumed that a combination of risks, buffers, and vulnerabilities from each domain, assessed over time, will predict individual and family adaptation better than any single factor taken alone.

This model raises yet another issue in the conceptualization of multiple risk. In many of the authors' previously published reports, we have followed what seems to be the common practice of assessing risk models for mothers and fathers separately—for example, showing how fathers' or mothers' symptoms of depression combine with assessments of the quality of their marital relationship to account for individual differences in their child's behavior (Miller et al., 1993). The five-domain family system model proposed by the authors, however, suggests that the combined effect of maternal and paternal depression needs to be examined to understand the mechanisms underlying how marital conflict and depression affect parenting behavior and children's adaptation. It is in different patterns of connection for women and men that we need to look for evidence of the mechanisms or dynamics that might explain how risk and resilience work on a family level.

Here we present new analyses based on information from the 44 intact families in our study with complete data available on the measures of interest at all time periods (see P. A. Cowan et al., 1994, for details). The measures come from independent sources obtained at different times. Symptoms of depression are assessed by parents' self reports (CES–D; Radloff, 1977), and marital conflict is based on clinical researchers' ratings of the couple during a triadic interaction with the child in the preschool period. Parenting style ratings are based on researchers' ratings of dyadic interaction 2 years later. The quality of mothers' or fathers' parenting style was summarized by a composite of ratings made by two trained observers as each parent interacted with their child in our laboratory

---

[8]An idea suggested by Mavis Hetherington (personal communication).

playroom. Together, family members engaged in some tasks that were difficult for children that age (arranging objects in a matrix by size, shape, and color) and in some tasks that were fun (building a "world" together in a sandtray). A set of ratings in which 17 items were combined in five scales assessed parents' warmth, responsiveness, limit-setting, structure, and engagement. More authoritative parents (cf. Baumrind, 1978) were those who combined warmth, responsiveness, and engagement with limit-setting and structure. This was chosen as an index of "effective parenting" because children of parents with this style have been shown to be more instrumentally and socially competent.

Using median splits of the parents' risk data gathered when the children were 3½ years old, the mothers' and fathers' depression scores and observational ratings of their interaction as a couple when they were working with the children in the playroom laboratory were dichotomized. Parents reporting the greatest number of symptoms of depression and couples who were seen as least warm and most competitive, hostile, and angry with one another constituted the high depression and high marital conflict groups. This typology analysis examines the extent to which individual and dyadic factors in the parents when the children are 3½ years old explain the quality of their parenting 2 years later. An additive risk hypothesis suggests that parenting style would be most effective (i.e., authoritative) when both marital conflict and depression were low. Conversely, parenting should be least effective when both marital conflict and depression were high during the preschool period.

Authoritative parenting ratings are presented here in terms of z scores. A mean of 0 indicates that the parents in that cell were at the average of the whole sample. Positive z scores represent above-average authoritative parenting expressed in standard deviation units above the mean, and negative z scores represent below-average combinations of warmth and structure. We first looked at the fathers' authoritative parenting scores in relation to marital conflict and their wives' symptoms of depression (Table 1.1).

When marital conflict between partners was low, wives' depression during the preschool period was not related to their husbands' parenting behavior 2 years later. However, when marital distress was high, husbands' parenting behavior was vulnerable to their wives' depression: Ratings of fathers' level of authoritative parenting were more than 2½ standard deviations below the mean of the sample.

In the case of their husbands' depression, however, a different pattern is seen, in which wives of depressed men show highly effective (authoritative) parenting 2 years later, but only if marital distress is low. It is known from kindergarten teachers' ratings of the child's academic competence that children whose parents show high conflict and whose fathers are depressed are doing better academically than the children with high-conflict parents whose mothers are depressed. Our data hint at a buffering process in which a better marital relationship allows women to step in authoritatively when their husbands are depressed—thus

TABLE 1.1
Marital Conflict, Spouse Depression, and Authoritative Parenting

1a. Fathers' authoritative parenting as a function of marital conflict and mothers' depression

	Mothers' Depression	
Marital Conflict	Low	High
Low	.09	−2.78
High	.11	−.07

1b. Mothers' authoritative parenting as a function of marital conflict and fathers' depression

	Fathers' Depression	
Marital Conflict	Low	High
Low	−.01	−.04
High	−.66	2.65

Note. $N = 44$ in each analysis.

protecting the children from the most negative effects of having a depressed father.[9] By contrast, men whose marriages are going well, but whose wives are depressed, do not seem to be more effective parents. If the marriage is not going well, these fathers tend to be much less warm, responsive, and structuring with their preschoolers, who, in turn, are not adapting as well to the academic demands of kindergarten.

Gender-linked differences in how men's and women's patterns of depression play out in the family system have been mentioned by a number of investigators. Hinchcliffe, Hooper, and Roberts (1978, in Teichman & Teichman, 1990) observed that marital interaction when husbands are depressed is calmer than interaction in marriages with depressed wives. Similarly, Teichman and Teichman (1990) summarized the findings of several studies that indicate that when men are depressed, their wives tend toward overprotection, but when women are depressed, their husbands are more likely to be hostile and rejecting.

In the pattern of results described here, another illustration of the complexity of multiple risk analysis in families is seen. What are assumed to be "the same" risks by virtue of the fact that they are obtained by the same measuring instruments

---

[9]It is of interest that even though mothers' quality of parenting may be facilitating the children's ability to cope with the academic challenges of early elementary school, there is some evidence that the children may be experiencing some of the effects of their fathers' symptoms in other realms. Although they do well academically, the children whose fathers were depressed 2 years earlier, are described by their teachers as more shy and withdrawn and having more complaints of physical symptoms than the children in any of the three other groups in the fall of kindergarten year, despite the fact that their mothers have an authoritative parenting style.

(e.g., symptoms of depression) may function differently in interaction with other family conditions, depending on whether the mother or the father is the focus of the risk analysis.

THE MEANING OF RISK IN NORMAL FAMILIES

Recent interest in risk analysis has been stimulated by increasing societal concern about individuals and families in the most serious high-risk groups. It is clear that high risk, as marked by severe psychopathology, social disorganization, and poverty, is associated with a frightening incidence of negative social and mental health outcomes—delinquency, teenage pregnancy, dropping out of school, depression, and suicide (Mrazek & Haggerty, 1994). In this attempt to discuss risk and resilience in a family context, we have deliberately shifted back and forth between studies of high-risk populations or families with an already-diagnosed member, and supposedly low-risk populations in which clinical diagnosis has not been raised as an issue. A concern is that, in the understandable focus of policymakers, public officials, clinicians, and researchers on the highest of high-risk groups, the risks associated with the normally occurring circumstances of daily life are being ignored both in research studies and in the availability of services for individuals and families.

In samples of families not defined by their diagnostic and risk status, there are often serious biological, psychological, and social difficulties existing in one or more of the individual and family subsystems. These difficulties constitute risks for later maladaptation. Furthermore, during both normative and non-normative life transitions, normal and adaptive developmental progress may be compromised as new challenges call for coping strategies that are not in the repertoires of the family members or the family group (P. A. Cowan, 1991).

In our own longitudinal study of couples becoming families, we followed the families until their first child completed kindergarten (C. P. Cowan et al., 1985; C. P. Cowan, 1988). In the early phase of the study, begun in 1979, we found that the transition to parenthood, as welcome as it was for most couples, also created significant challenges and disequilibration for the parents. Compared with childless couples, new parents showed increased conflict and decreased satisfaction with marriage over a 2-year period. It was proposed that professionally led couples groups meeting weekly for 3 months before and 3 months after the birth of a first child might help to strengthen couple relationships and ultimately benefit both parents and their children. In the language of Garmezy and Rutter (1983), couples were at risk for distress and disruption; a couples group, it was believed, might serve as a temporary buffer by which couples could reduce their vulnerability and increase their resilience by learning to cope more effectively with the expectable stresses associated with becoming a family.

The couples in this study were fairly well educated, none had a family member who had been classified as mentally ill, and only 1 of 72 was living in poverty, according to family income statistics in the United States. In 1979 to 1980, the couples joining our longitudinal study reported total family incomes ranging from $7,000 to $72,000, with a mean annual income of $22,500. Approximately 15% of the parents were Black, Asian-American, or Hispanic, and 85% were White. The spouses ranged in age from 21 to 49 years of age at the start of the study, with a mean age of 30 for the men and 29 for the women. All had completed high school, many had completed some years of college, and some had earned postgraduate degrees. Almost all would be described as working or middle class. Given that the couples in this study were not recruited or selected on the basis of specific risk factors, and that they were undergoing a normative transition that is commonly interpreted as positive (P. A. Cowan, 1991), the results led to a concern that the risks and dysfunctional outcomes encountered by a substantial number of ordinary people trying to create well-functioning families have been minimized or overlooked. In interviews, questionnaires, and visits to the laboratory playroom at five points between late pregnancy and their first child's completion of kindergarten, these men and women shared a great deal about their backgrounds, their dreams of being a couple and a family, their struggles, their successes, and what they see as their development and their failures. Many of them were surprised at how many serious stressors and how much unexpected strain they have been contending with and, frankly, so were we.

- From 20% to 34% of the new mothers and fathers had scores above the cutoff on the Center for Epidemiology of Depression Scale (CES–D, Radloff, 1977).
- From 9% to 35% of the new mothers and fathers at different assessment points had scores below 100 (the clinical distress range) on the Locke Wallace Short Marital Adjustment Test (Locke & Wallace, 1959). If both marital distress and the 20% of couples with children who divorced are included, 48% of the fathers and 55% of the mothers experienced serious marital distress or dissolution by the time their first child entered elementary school.
- In interviews, 20% of the new mothers and fathers identified themselves as adult children of alcoholics (ACAs), a figure that is consistent with the national estimates of alcoholism in the general population in the United States. Their childhood experiences set processes in motion that placed them and their family at risk for several negative outcomes. The men and women in this study who grew up in an alcoholic family experienced greater difficulty navigating the transition to parenthood, and the women especially showed more variation than non-ACA parents in the quality of their parenting in the preschool years. In turn, the children of ACAs, especially the boys, were rated by their kindergarten teachers as lower in academic competence, and as having more problematic relationships with their peers (C. P. Cowan, Cowan, & Heming, 1988).

Because we did not use epidemiological principles in recruiting this sample, we must be cautious about using these data to make generalizations about the incidence and prevalence of distress in young families across the nation. Nevertheless, this experience, combined with conversations with other researchers exploring the transition to parenthood suggests that it would be tragic if the real difficulties families face as they attempt to raise young children were to be ignored on the assumption that help is needed only by those in more traditionally high-risk samples. We believe that the frequency of distress in nonclinical families is (unfortunately) large enough to justify concerted attempts to apply risk paradigms to studies of normal family adaptation.

One set of findings is of particular concern. Seeking to understand the early roots of differential treatment of boys and girls, Kerig carefully examined dyadic interactions between fathers or mothers and their preschool-age sons or daughters (Kerig, Cowan, & Cowan, 1993). She found a tendency for both parents to be more negating (rejecting, critical, challenging, reprimanding, controlling) of daughters than sons. The differentially negative treatment of girls was amplified when the parents were maritally dissatisfied. This moderator effect was even more marked for maritally dissatisfied fathers: Those with girls tended to treat their daughters the way they treated their wives; those with boys tended to avoid the negative spillover from their marriage into the relationship with their sons. In sum, being a female child functioned as a risk factor with respect to the quality of parenting these young children received. Marital dissatisfaction in these two-parent nonclinical families was a vulnerability factor amplifying the negative impact of the risk on the girls.

Furthermore, we learned that the marital conflict and differential treatment of preschool boys and girls was predictable from the increasing gender differentiation that many parents experienced as they made their transition to parenthood (P. A. Cowan, Cowan, & Kerig, 1993). That is, a normative life transition, with processes that tend to increase differences between husbands and wives, can amplify marital discord, and reduce parenting effectiveness in ways that may place young girls at risk for intellectual and social developmental difficulties.

RISK RESEARCH AND PREVENTION

It was noted at the beginning of this chapter that a concern with intervention is inherent in the definition and operationalization of risk. Gathering data on what predisposes individuals and families to negative or positive outcomes is not simply an exercise in the construction of statistical tables and more precise betting odds. Although many risk researchers may not themselves be concerned with provision of services, the information they provide has implications for those who aim to reduce risk, vulnerability, and psychopathology, and to enhance buffering and resilience processes that promote adaptation—in short to engage in preventive intervention.

Two influential reports on prevention have emerged recently, one sponsored by the National Institute of Mental Health National Prevention Conference (Coie et al., 1993) and one by the National Academy of Science Institute of Medicine (Mrazek & Haggerty, 1994). Differing in size, scope, and focus, the reports make similar points. Consistent with the political climate of the 1960s, the ideology of prevention emerged at the forefront of community psychiatry and community psychology. The explosion of interest in risk and protective factors during the 1980s has begun to provide a solid foundation for a renewed focus on prevention by health service providers and mental health researchers. Because prevention efforts, by definition, occur before severe illness is fully manifested, their activities are designed to "counteract risk factors and reinforce protective factors in order to disrupt processes that contribute to human dysfunction" (Coie et al., 1993, p. 1013). The Mrazek and Haggerty (1994) volume not only chronicles what is known about the risk and protective factors associated with the onset of a number of mental disorders (e.g., Alzheimer's disease, schizophrenia, alcohol abuse, depressive and conduct disorders), but also summarizes a number of preventive intervention research programs targeted to major developmental periods along the life span.

Both reports emphasize the importance of studies of normal development and risk for the design and evaluation of preventive intervention programs. They describe the necessity of identifying "distal" social context variables (social class, ethnicity, neighborhood) to identify populations at risk, but they recommend that intervention efforts focus on the proximal contexts (family, school, peers) that link high levels of risk with the most severe negative outcomes.

Coie and his colleagues also made a strong argument for the importance of intervention research for testing models of risk. Even the most careful and comprehensive longitudinal study yields only correlational statements about the relations between risks and outcomes. In our own study, for example, we found that marital relationship qualities and parenting styles assessed during the preschool period combine to predict children's adaptation to elementary school. This finding suggests, but does not prove, the hypothesis that positive changes in parents' marital relationships and parenting effectiveness will have a positive effect on their children. We are now in the process of testing this hypothesis in a new intervention study with parents of 4-year-olds in the year before their first child makes the transition to kindergarten (C. P. Cowan, Heming, & Boxer, 1995). If we can show that intervention-induced changes in marital and parenting effectiveness have positive effects on the children, a powerful test of the risk model that was developed using correlational methods will be provided.

Multiple risk studies have provided the basis for intervention with high-risk populations, with some of the most comprehensive new research and prevention projects occurring in the area of child and adolescent conduct disorders (e.g., Conduct Problems Prevention Research Group, 1992; Reid, 1993). Consistent with the multiple risk perspective, and guided by a theoretical framework drawing heavily on developmental psychopathology (Cicchetti & Toth, 1992), researcher-clinicians are designing programs to help aggressive boys by reducing risks and building buffers to create resilience in individual, family, peer, school, and neighborhood domains. The developmental psychopathology perspective is also being applied in new ways to create and evaluate preventive interventions for youngsters with Attention Deficit Disorder, and the multiple cognitive, academic, and social problems that these children display (Hinshaw, 1992b).

The public health ideal of eliminating risks at the source (e.g., eliminating swamps that breed malaria-infested mosquitoes) is attractive, but rarely, if ever, possible in psychology. There are two caveats here. First, prevention programs cannot completely avoid problematic outcomes, but they can help to reduce the incidence, severity, or duration of the problems that normally occur. Second, even if it could be done, it may not be wise to eliminate risk altogether. Rutter (1987) suggested that the best protection for individuals at risk is to help them cope with small doses of the potential risks so that they can become more resilient by dint of their own efforts. That is, the best preventive effort may involve some degree of "inoculation" with a "live risk virus."

Another way of reducing the impact of risk is to change its meaning. In the theory of emotion developed by Lazarus and his colleagues (Lazarus, 1991; Lazarus & Folkman, 1984), one's appraisal of a situation plays a large role in determining its potential to evoke stress. By preparing children for hospital visits, or by preparing men and women during the transition to parenthood for the inevitability of stress and disenchantment, these negative events may not be so unexpected, which may moderate their noxious effects (C. P. Cowan, 1988).

Throughout this chapter, we have followed Rutter and Garmezy's lead in arguing that risks have their effects through a chain of processes connecting risks and outcomes. The chains can be very elaborate and complex, with some links difficult to discern. An increasing number of studies, however, suggest that the chains by which negative events elicit inadequate coping processes and produce negative outcomes can be described clearly, even if their entire structure cannot be discovered. These chains tend to extend over long periods of time in the life of an individual and to repeat themselves across generations (Caspi & Elder, 1988; Jacobvitz, Morgan, Kretchmer, & Morgan, 1991; Main & Goldwyn, in press). For identifying the chains that link risks and negative outcomes, risk analysis is essential. In turn, the science and practice of prevention must rely ultimately on risk and resilience analysis to help individuals and families find ways to break the chains that bind them.

ACKNOWLEDGMENTS

This study has been supported throughout by NIMH grant MH 31109. We also want to acknowledge major contributions to the longitudinal study by members of the research team: Gertrude Heming served as data manager throughout the study, and Dena Cowan, Barbara Epperson, and Beth Schoenberger processed the immense data set. Ellen Garrett, William S. Coysh, Harriet Curtis-Boles, and Abner Boles III were the other two couples who followed the families over time and led intervention groups; Laura Mason Gordon and David Gordon interviewed couples in the last 3 years. Sacha Bunge, Michael Blum, Julia Levine, David Chavez, and Joanna Cowan worked with the children in the study; Linda Kastelowitz, Victor Lieberman, Marsha Kline, and Charles Soulé worked with the parents and children together. Laurie Leventhal-Belfer and Elaine Ransom collected the teachers' ratings; and Rachel Conrad, Juanita Dimas, Patricia Kerig, Julia Levine, Nancy Miller, Joanna Self, and Kristina Whitney rated videotaped family interaction. We are indebted to Michael Pratt for his comments on an earlier draft.

REFERENCES

American Psychiatric Association. (1994). *Diagnostic and statistical manual of mental disorders* (4th ed.). Washington, DC: Author.

Anthony, E. J. (1974). The syndrome of the psychologically invulnerable child. In E. J. Anthony & C. Koupernik (Eds.), *The child in his family: Children at psychiatric risk* (pp. 529–544). New York: Wiley.

Baldwin, A. L., Baldwin, C. P., Kasser, T., Zax, M., Sameroff, A., & Seifer, R. (1993). Contextual risk and resiliency during late adolescence. *Development and Psychopathology, 5,* 741–762.

Baldwin, A. L., Cole, R. E., & Baldwin, C. P. (Eds.). (1982). Parental pathology, family interaction, and the competence of the child in school. *Monographs of the Society for Research in Child Development, 47* (5, Serial No. 197).

Baumrind, D. (1978). Parental disciplinary patterns and social competence in children. *American Psychologist, 35,* 639–652.

Baumrind, D. (1991). Effective parenting during the early adolescent transition. In P. A. Cowan & M. E. Hetherington (Eds.), *Family transitions. Advances in family research* (Vol. 2, pp. 111–164). Hillsdale, NJ: Lawrence Erlbaum Associates.

Blechman, E. (1991). Effective communication: Enabling multiproblem families to change. In P. A. Cowan & M. E. Hetherington (Eds.), *Family transitions. Advances in family research* (Vol. 2, pp. 219–245). Hillsdale, NJ: Lawrence Erlbaum Associates.

Block, J., & Gjerde, P. (1990). Depressive symptoms in late adolescence: A longitudinal perspective on personality antecedents. In J. Rolf, A. S. Masten, D. Cicchetti, K. H. Nuechterlein, & S. Weintraub (Eds.), *Risk and protective factors in the development of psychopathology* (pp. 334–360). Cambridge, UK: Cambridge University Press.

Caspi, A., & Elder, G. H., Jr. (1988). Emergent family patterns: The intergenerational construction of problem behavior and relationships. In R. A. Hinde & J. Stevenson-Hinde (Eds.), *Relationships within families: Mutual influences* (pp. 218–240). Oxford, UK: Clarendon Press.

Cicchetti, D., & Garmezy, N. (1993). Prospects and promises in the study of resilience. *Development and Psychopathology, 5,* 497–502.

Cicchetti, D., & Toth, S. L. (1992). The role of developmental theory in prevention and intervention. *Development and Psychopathology, 4,* 489–493.

Cicchetti, D., Toth, S. L., Bush, M. A., & Gillespie, J. (1988). Stage-salient issues: A transactional model of intervention. In E. Nannis & P. Cowan (Eds.), *Developmental psychopathology and its treatment: New directions for child development* (No. 39, pp. 123–146). San Francisco: Jossey-Bass.

Cohn, D. A., Cowan, P. A., Cowan, C. P., & Pearson, J. (1992). Mothers' and fathers' working models of childhood attachment relationships, parenting styles, and child behavior. *Development and Psychopathology, 4,* 417–431.

Cohn, D. A., Silver, D. H., Cowan, C. P., Cowan, P. A., & Pearson, W. (1992). Working models of childhood attachment and couple relationships. *Journal of Family Issues, 13*, 432–449.

Conduct Problems Prevention Research Group. (1992). A developmental and clinical model for the prevention of conduct disorder: The FAST Track Program. *Development and Psychopathology, 4*, 509–528.

Coie, J. D., Watt, N. F., West, S. G., Hawkins, D., Asarnow, J. R., Markman, H. J., Ramey, S. L., Shure, M. B., & Long, B. (1993). The science of prevention: A conceptual framework and some directions for a National Research Program. *American Psychologist, 48*, 1013–1022.

Costello, E. J., & Angold, A. (1993). Toward a developmental epidemiology of the disruptive behavior disorders. *Development and Psychopathology, 5*, 91–102.

Cowan, C. P. (1988). Working with men becoming fathers: The impact of a couples group intervention. In P. Bronstein & C. P. Cowan (Eds.), *Fatherhood today: Men's changing role in the family* (pp. 276–298). New York: Wiley.

Cowan, C. P., & Cowan, P. A. (1992). *When partners become parents: The big life change for couples.* New York: Basic Books.

Cowan, C. P., Cowan, P. A., & Heming, G. (1988, November). *Adult children of alcoholics: What happens when they form new families?* Paper presented to the National Council on Family Relations, Philadelphia, PA.

Cowan, C. P., Cowan, P. A., Heming, G., Garrett, E., Coysh, W. S., Curtis-Boles, H., & Boles, A. J. (1985). Transitions to parenthood: His, hers, and theirs. *Journal of Family Issues, 6*, 451–481.

Cowan, C. P., Cowan, P. A., Heming, G., & Miller, N. B. (1991). Becoming a family: Marriage, parenting, and child development. In P. A. Cowan & E. M. Hetherington (Eds.), *Family transitions. Advances in family research* (Vol. 2, pp. 79–110). Hillsdale, NJ: Lawrence Erlbaum Associates.

Cowan, C. P., Heming, G., & Boxer, C. (1995, March). *Preventive interventions with parents of preschoolers: Effects on marriage, parenting, and children's adaptation to school.* Paper presented at the meeting of the Society for Research in Child Development, Indianapolis, IN.

Cowan, P. A. (1991). Individual and family life transitions: A proposal for a new definition. In P. A. Cowan & E. M. Hetherington (Eds.), *Family transitions* (pp. 3–30). Hillsdale, NJ: Lawrence Erlbaum Associates.

Cowan, P. A., Cowan, C. P., & Kerig, P. (1993). Mothers, fathers, sons, and daughters: Gender differences in family formation and parenting style. In P. A. Cowan, D. Field, D. Hansen, A. Skolnick, & G. E. Swanson (Eds.), *Family, self, and society: Toward a new agenda for family research* (pp. 165–196). Hillsdale, NJ: Lawrence Erlbaum Associates.

Cowan, P. A., Cowan, C. P., Schulz, M., & Heming, G. (1994). Prebirth to preschool family factors predicting children's adaptation to kindergarten. In R. D. Parke & S. Kellam (Eds.), *Exploring family relationships with other social contexts. Advances in family research* (Vol. 4, pp. 75–114). Hillsdale, NJ: Lawrence Erlbaum Associates.

Cowan, P. A., Hansen, D. A., Swanson, G. E., Field, D., & Skolnick, A. (1993). Issues in defining a research agenda. In P. A. Cowan, D. Field, D. Hansen, A. Skolnick, & G. E. Swanson (Eds.), *Family, self, and society: Toward a new agenda for family research* (pp. 465–482). Hillsdale, NJ: Lawrence Erlbaum Associates.

Crnic, K. A., Greenberg, M. T., Ragozin, A. S., Robinson, N. M. & Basham, R. B. (1983). Effects of stress and social support on mothers and premature and full-term infants. *Child Development, 54*, 209–217.

Egeland, B., Carlson, E., & Sroufe, L. A. (1993). Resilience as process. *Development and Psychopathology, 5*, 517–528.

Falk, R. R., & Miller, N. B. (1991). A soft models approach to family transitions. In P. A. Cowan & E. M. Hetherington (Eds.), *Family transitions. Advances in family research* (Vol. 2, pp. 273–301). Hillsdale, NJ: Lawrence Erlbaum Associates.

Fincham, F., Grych, J. H., & Osborne, L. N. (1994). Does marital conflict cause child maladjustment? Directions and challenges for longitudinal research. *Journal of Family Psychology, 8*, 128–140.

Garmezy, N. (1985). Broadening research on developmental risk. In W. K. Frankenburg, R. N. Emde, & J. W. Sullivan (Eds.), *Early identification of children at risk: An international perspective* (pp. 289–303). New York: Plenum.

Garmezy, N., Masten, A. S., & Tellegen, A. (1984). The study of stress and competence in children: A building block for developmental psychopathology. *Child Development, 55*, 97–111.

Garmezy, N., & Rutter, M. (Eds.). (1983). *Stress, coping, and development in children.* New York: McGraw-Hill.

George, C., Kaplan, N., & Main, M. (1984). *Attachment Interview for Adults.* Unpublished manuscript, University of California, Berkeley.

Goldstein, M. (1990). Family relations as risk factors for the onset and course of schizophrenia. In J. Rolf, A. S. Masten, D. Cicchetti, K. H. Nuechterlein, & S. Weintraub (Eds.), *Risk and protective factors in the development of psychopathology* (pp. 408–423). Cambridge, UK: Cambridge University Press.

Gottesman, I. I., McGuffin, P., & Farmer, A. E. (1987). Clinical genetics as clues to the "real" genetics of schizophrenia. *Schizophrenia Bulletin, 13*, 23–47.

Gottman, J. M., & Katz, L. (1989). The effects of marital discord on young children's peer interactions and health. *Developmental Psychology, 25*, 373–381.

Grotevant, H. D., & Carlson, C. I. (1989). *Family assessment: A guide to methods and measures.* New York: Guilford.

Gruenberg, E. (1980). Risk factor research methods. In D. A. Regler & G. Allen (Eds.), *Risk factor research in the major mental disorders* (pp. 8–19). Rockville, MD: U.S. National Institute of Mental Health.

Hetherington, E. M. (1989). Coping with family transitions: Winners, losers, and survivors. *Child Development, 60*, 1–14.

Hetherington E. M., & Clingempeel, G. (1992). *Coping with marital transitions. Society for Research in Child Development Monograph, 57* (No. 2–3).

Hill, R. (1949). *Families under stress.* New York: Harper & Row.

Hill, R. (1958). Generic features of families under stress. *Social Casework, 49*, 139–150.

Hinchcliffe, M. K., Hooper, D., & Roberts, F. J. (1978). *The melancholy marriage: Depression in marriage and psychosocial approaches to therapy.* New York: Wiley.

Hinshaw, S. P. (1992a). Academic underachievement. Attention deficits, and aggression: Comorbidity and implications for intervention. *Journal of Consulting and Clinical Psychology, 60*, 893–903.

Hinshaw, S. P. (1992b). Externalizing behavior problems and academic achievement in childhood and adolescence: Causal relationships and underlying mechanisms. *Psychological Bulletin, 11*, 127–155.

Jacobvitz, D. B., Morgan, E., Kretchmar, M. D., & Morgan, Y. (1991). The transmission of mother-child boundary disturbances across generations. *Development and Psychopathology, 3*, 513–528.

Kellam, S. G., Brown, C. H., Rubin, B. R., & Ensminger, M. E. (1983). Paths leading to teenage psychiatric symptoms and substance use: Developmental epidemiological studies in Woodlawn. In S. B. Guze, F. J. Earls, & J. E. Barrett (Eds.), *Childhood psychopathology and development* (pp. 17–51). New York: Raven Press.

Kerig, P. K., Cowan, P. A., & Cowan, C. P. (1993). Marital quality and gender differences in parent–child interaction. *Developmental Psychology, 29*, 931–939.

Kety, S. S., Wender, P. H., Jacobsen, B., & Ingraham, L. J. (1994). Mental illness in the biological and adoptive relatives of schizophrenic adoptees: Replication of the Copenhagen study in the rest of Denmark. *Archives of General Psychiatry, 51*, 442–455.

Kleinbaum, D. G., Kupper, L., & Morgenstern, H. (1982). *Epidemiologic research: Principles and quantitative methods.* New York: Van Nostrand Reinhold.

Lambert, N. (1988). Adolescent outcomes for hyperactive children: Perspectives on general and specific patterns of childhood risk for adolescent education, social, and mental health problems. *American Psychologist, 43*, 786–799.

Lazarus, R. (1991). *Emotion and adaptation*. Oxford, UK: Oxford University Press.

Lazarus, R., & Folkman, S. (1984). *Stress, appraisal, and coping*. New York: Springer.

Liem, J. (1980). Family studies of schizophrenia: An update and commentary. *Schizophrenia Bulletin, 6*, 429–455.

Locke, H., & Wallace, K. (1959). Short marital adjustment and prediction tests: Their reliability and validity. *Marriage and Family Living, 21*, 251–255.

Main, M., & Goldwyn, R. (in press). Adult attachment classification system. In M. Main (Ed.), *A typology of human attachment organization: Assessed in discourse, drawings and interviews*. New York: Cambridge University Press.

Masten, A. S., & Garmezy, N. (1985). Risk, vulnerability, and protective factors in developmental psychopathology. In B. B. Lahey & A. E. Kazdin (Eds.), *Advances in clinical child psychology* (Vol. 8, pp. 1–52). New York: Plenum.

McCubbin, H. I., & Patterson, J. M. (1983). The family stress process: The double ABCX model of family behavior. *Marriage and Family Review, 6*, 7–37.

McCubbin, M. A., & McCubbin, H. I. (1989). Theoretical orientations to family stress and coping. In C. R. Figley (Ed.), *Treating stress in families* (pp. 3–43). New York: Brunner/Mazel.

McGillicuddy-DeLisi, A. V. (1990). Parental beliefs within the family context: Development of a research program. In I. Sigel & G. Brody (Eds.), *Family research* (Vol. I, pp. 53–85). Hillsdale, NJ: Lawrence Erlbaum Associates.

Mednick, S. A., & Schulsinger, F. (1968). Some premorbid characteristics related to breakdown in children with schizophrenic mothers. *Journal of Psychiatric Research, 6*(Suppl. 1), 354–362.

Miller, N. B., Cowan, P. A., Cowan, C. P., Hetherington, E. M., & Clingempeel, G. (1993). Externalizing in preschoolers and early adolescents: A cross-study replication of a family model. *Developmental Psychology, 29*, 3–18.

Minuchin, S., & Fishman, H. C. (1981). *Family therapy techniques*. Cambridge, MA: Harvard University Press.

Mrazek, P. J., & Haggerty, R. (Eds.). (1994). *Reducing risks for mental disorders: Frontiers for preventive intervention research*. Washington, DC: National Academy Press.

Notarius, C. J., & Markman, H. J. (1989). Coding marital interaction: A sampling and discussion of current issues. *Behavioral Assessment, 11*, 1–11.

Parke, R. D., & Tinsley, B. (1982). The early environment of the at-risk infant: Expanding the social context. In D. D. Bricker (Ed.), *Intervention with at-risk and handicapped infants* (pp. 153–177). Baltimore, MD: University Park Press.

Patterson, G. R., & Capaldi, D. (1991). Antisocial parents: Unskilled and vulnerable. In P. A. Cowan & M. E. Hetherington (Eds.), *Family transitions. Advances in family research* (Vol. 2, pp. 195–218). Hillsdale, NJ: Lawrence Erlbaum Associates.

Patterson, G. R., & Dishion, T. J. (1988). Multilevel family process models: Traits, interactions, and relationships. In R. A. Hinde & J. Stevenson-Hinde (Eds.), *Relationships within families: Mutual influences* (pp. 283–310). Oxford, UK: Clarendon.

Patterson, J. M. (1988). Families experiencing stress. *Family Systems Medicine, 6*, 202–237.

Pearson, J. L., Cohn, D. A., Cowan, P. A., & Cowan, C. P. (1994). Earned and continuous security in adult attachment: Relation to depression and parenting style. *Developmental Psychopathology, 6*, 359–373.

Quinton, D., Rutter, M., & Liddle, C. (1984). Institutional rearing, parenting difficulties and marital support. *Psychological Medicine, 14*, 107–124.

Radke-Yarrow, M., Cummings, E. M., Kuczynski, L., & Chapman, M. (1985). Patterns of attachment in two- and three-year-olds in normal families and families with parental depression. *Child Development, 56*, 884–893.

Radke-Yarrow, M., & Zahn-Waxler, C. (1990). Research on children of affectively ill parents: Some considerations for theory and research on normal development. *Development and Psychopathology, 2*, 349–366.

Radloff, L. (1977). Sex differences in depression: The effects of occupation and marital status. *Sex Roles, 1*, 249–265.

Reid, J. B. (1993). Prevention of conduct disorder before and after school entry: Relating interventions to developmental findings. *Development and Psychopathology, 5*, 243–262.

Reiss, D. (1981). *The family's construction of reality*. Cambridge, MA: Harvard University Press.

Richters, J., & Cicchetti, D. (1993). Editorial: Toward a developmental perspective on conduct disorder. *Development and Psychopathology, 5*, 1–4.

Richters, J., & Weintraub, S. (1990). Beyond diathesis: Toward an understanding of high risk environments. In J. Rolf, A. S. Masten, D. Cicchetti, K. H. Nuechterlein, & S. Weintraub (Eds.), *Risk and protective factors in the development of psychopathology* (pp. 67–96). Cambridge, UK: Cambridge University Press.

Rolf, J., Masten, A. S., Cicchetti, D., Nuechterlein, K. H., & Weintraub, S. (Eds.). (1990). *Risk and protective factors in the development of psychopathology*. Cambridge, UK: Cambridge University Press.

Rosenthal, D. (1970). *Genetic theory and abnormal behavior*. New York: McGraw-Hill.

Rutter, M. (1987). Psychosocial resilience and protective mechanisms. *American Journal of Orthopsychiatry, 57*, 316–331.

Rutter, M. (1989). Isle of Wight revisited: Twenty-five years of child psychiatric epidemiology. *Journal of the American Academy of Child and Adolescent Psychiatry, 28*, 633–653.

Sameroff, A. J., & Chandler, M. J. (1975). Reproductive risk and the continuum of caretaking casualty. In F. D. Horowitz (Ed.), *Review of child development research* (Vol. 4, pp. 187–244). Chicago, IL: University of Chicago Press.

Sameroff, A. J., & Seifer, R. (1990). Early contributors to developmental risk. In J. Rolf, A. S. Masten, D. Cicchetti, K. H. Nuechterlein, & S. Weintraub (Eds.), *Risk and protective factors in the development of psychopathology* (pp. 52–66). Cambridge, UK: Cambridge University Press.

Sameroff, A. J., Seifer, R., Baldwin, A., & Baldwin, C. (1993). Stability of intelligence from preschool to adolescence: The influence of social and family risk factors. *Child Development, 64*, 80–97.

Sameroff, A. J., Seifer, R., Barocas, R., Zax, M., & Greenspan, S. (1987). IQ scores of 4-year-old children: Social environmental risk factors. *Pediatrics, 79*, 343–350.

Sameroff, A. J., Seifer, R., & Zax, M. (1982). Early development of children at risk for emotional disorder. *Monographs of the Society for Research in Child Development, 47* (No. 199).

Schulz, M. S. (1994). *Coping with negative emotional arousal: The daily spillover of work stress into marital interactions*. Unpublished doctoral dissertation, University of California, Berkeley.

Sigel, I. (1982). The relationship between parents' distancing strategies and the child's cognitive behavior. In L. M. Laosa & I. E. Sigel (Eds.), *Families as learning environments for children* (pp. 47–86). New York: Plenum.

Skinner, H. A., Steinhauer, P. D., & Santa-Barbara, J. (1983). The Family Assessment Measure. *Canadian Journal of Community Mental Health, 2*, 91–105.

Sroufe, L. A., Egeland, B., & Kreutzer, T. (1990). The fate of early experience following developmental change: Longitudinal approaches to individual adaptation in childhood. *Child Development, 61*, 1363–1373.

Steinglass, P. (1987). A systems view of family interaction and psychopathology. In T. Jacob (Ed.), *Family interaction and psychopathology: Theories, methods, and findings* (pp. 25–74). New York: Plenum.

Sullivan, H. S. (1962). *Schizophrenia as a human process*. New York: Norton.

Teichman, Y., & Teichman, M. (1990). Interpersonal view of depression: Review and integration. *Journal of Family Psychology, 3*, 349–367.

Walsh, F. (Ed.). (1982). *Normal family processes*. New York: Guilford.

Werner, E. E., & Smith, R. S. (1982). *Vulnerable but invincible: A longitudinal study of resilient children and youth*. New York: McGraw-Hill.

2

▼▼▼▼▼▼▼

Stress, Parenting, and Adolescent Psychopathology in Nondivorced and Stepfamilies: A Within-Family Perspective

Sandra H. Henderson
E. Mavis Hetherington
Debra Mekos
University of Virginia

David Reiss
George Washington University

For the past decade, researchers studying stress and coping have examined factors that either place children at risk or protect them from developing various forms of psychopathology. This research has successfully detailed some of the diverse conditions and pathways associated with the development of internalizing and externalizing behavior in children. In response to stressful life experiences and adverse family circumstances, many children exhibit psychopathology, whereas others survive despite risk and emerge as competent, well-functioning, even enhanced individuals. Currently, many questions concerning the wide variations in adjustment that occur in at-risk children, and the complexity of processes that influence them, have yet to be addressed empirically. Most researchers have concluded that there is no single pathway associated with the development of psychopathology; rather, different experiences will place children at risk, depending on the characteristics of the individual and the larger context in which they live and grow (Bronfenbrenner, 1986; Masten, Best, & Garmezy, 1990; Rutter, 1990; Sameroff & Seifer, 1990).

To date, the primary models for investigating the processes of risk and resilience have focused on between-family factors that are associated with adolescent psychopathology. Yet, given the systemic complexity present in most families, a potential source of risk or resilience may come from within families as well. That is, one sibling's ability to adapt and cope positively under stressful family circumstances is not necessarily related to another sibling's adjustment. For example, if a parent displays more affection and emotional support to one sibling than to another, it is likely that the favored child, but not his or her sibling, would be buffered from the effects of family stress. Thus, differential parental treatment may serve to protect one sibling, at the same time placing the other sibling at risk. Currently, little research has considered how processes of risk and resilience operate within families. However, such a strategy offers a unique opportunity to examine how differential experiences and characteristics of children limit the ability of one sibling to adapt successfully to stressors, simultaneously increasing the ability of another sibling to overcome those same adversities.

The Within-Family Perspective

The within-family approach to psychopathology has its roots in two vastly different theoretical traditions—family systems theory and quantitative behavioral genetics. From family systems theory comes the notion that an understanding of the development of psychopathology for a single individual requires an examination of the network of interdependent relationships among family members (Minuchin, 1985). From the behavioral genetics literature comes the conclusion that the environmental influences important in development are those that are unique, rather than shared, by siblings in the same family (Plomin & Daniels, 1987). In other words, the critical environmental processes are those that operate within the family to make siblings different, rather than similar, to each other. Together, these two theoretical traditions point to the importance of examining processes within the family that result in differential experiences and differential outcomes.

A small group of researchers have begun to examine differences in siblings' experiences within the family. Studies of toddler, school-age, and adolescent siblings show that children living in the same family often receive different treatment from parents (Baker & Daniels, 1990; Brody, Stoneman, & Burke, 1987; Daniels, 1986; Dunn, Stocker, & Plomin, 1990; Reiss et al., in press). Furthermore, evidence indicates that children as young as 3 years of age are sensitive to differences in maternal behavior toward them and their siblings (Dunn & Plomin, 1990). Finally, there is increasing evidence that differential parental treatment, either real or perceived, is related to differences in siblings' adjustment (Daniels, Dunn, Furstenberg, & Plomin, 1985; McHale & Pawletko, 1992; Tejerina-Allen, Wagner, & Cohen, 1994).

OVERVIEW OF THE STUDY

In this chapter, we address several questions about risk and resilience from a within-family perspective. We focus first on factors that contribute to parents' differential treatment of siblings, then on how these differences in treatment lead to differences in sibling psychopathology. The analytic strategy used here is based on Rutter's (1987) argument that risks should be examined as processes, rather than as simple markers or variables. More importantly, Rutter proposed that these processes must be examined under contrasting conditions of both high and low stress to determine if and how risks operate differently under the two stress levels. His underlying premise was that an interaction, or catalytic, effect occurs when certain processes combine with exposure to stress. In effect, high stress intensifies the effect of risks in producing maladjustment, whereas low stress combined with the same risks does not. In the analyses in this chapter, high stress and low stress families were compared to determine whether potential vulnerability, buffering, or resiliency effects operate under high-risk but not low-risk conditions.

All of the following hypotheses were analyzed for high- and low-stress families. Although these hypotheses are of interest in and of themselves, the critical question posed in this chapter is: Do processes operate similarly in all families or do they operate differently depending on level of family stress?

The following are the three major issues addressed herein and the relevant analyses that were run:

1. First, to what extent do differences in parental treatment exist within families and what are the sources of these differences?
   a. Do parents treat siblings differently?
   b. Do family stressors such as economic stress, marital conflict, and parent depression contribute to greater differences in parental warmth, control, or negativity?
   c. Do differences in siblings' characteristics, particularly temperament, influence parents' differential treatment? Are these differences more influential in families experiencing high stress?
   d. Does biological relatedness of siblings to parents create differences in how parents treat siblings, and does this interact with family stress?

2. Second, we address whether differences in parental treatment are systematically related to differences in sibling depression and conduct disorder.
   a. Are there differences in siblings' depression and conduct disorder?
   b. Do differences in the degree of parental warmth, control, and negativity predict differences in sibling depression and conduct disorder? Does level of family stress influence the relationship between differences in parenting and differences in outcome?
   c. Do child characteristics, particularly positive self-concept, mediate the effects of differential treatment on sibling outcome in high-stress families?

3. Finally, because within-family models are fairly new to the field of developmental psychology, we also analyzed identical between-family models for each sibling separately for comparison purposes. In the following sections, we present a brief overview of the sample and measures examined in this chapter. We then present a series of models designed to explicate the processes that link family stress, differential treatment, and differences in sibling psychopathology.

METHOD

Sample

The data used in this project are part of a national study on the role of differential experience in adolescent development (Reiss et al., 1994). The study involved a subsample of 516 families, made up of a male and female head of household and two same-sex adolescent siblings (ages 10–18) who were no more than 4 years apart in age. The sample consisted of approximately equal numbers of boy ($N = 267$) and girl ($N = 249$) sibling pairs.

Families were recruited for the study through national market surveys and random digit dialing. Thus, the families represented a wide range of geographic regions from the 48 contiguous states except South Dakota, 16% in urban areas, 26% in suburban areas, 29% in small towns, and 29% in rural areas. Ethnic composition of the families was 95% Caucasian, 4% African American, and 1% Hispanic. The socioeconomic status of the families ranged from lower working class to upper middle class, with the mean family income falling between $25,000 and $35,000.

The sample included 95 nondivorced families and 421 remarried families. All of the remarried families had been together for at least 5 years prior to the study and were thus well past the initial crisis period in adapting to a marital transition. The families could be further classified in terms of the siblings' biological relationship to each other and to the male and female head of household as follows. In 95 families, both siblings were the biological child of the mother and father (full sibling, nondivorced); in 181 families, both siblings were biological children of the mother and stepchildren of the father (full sibling, stepfamily); in 110 families, the younger sibling was the biological child of both the mother and father and the older sibling was the biological child of the mother and stepchild of the father (half sibling); and in 130 families, one sibling was the biological child of the mother only and the other sibling was the biological child of the father only (blended sibling).

Procedure and Measures

Data were collected in two 2½-hour sessions in the family's home, with a 1-week interim between the two sessions. Mothers, fathers, and the two siblings each independently completed a battery of questionnaires dealing with family relations, family stressors, and parent and child characteristics and behavior. Family members were also given a take-home booklet containing several measures, which they completed independently between sessions one and two. In addition, parents and adolescents were videotaped in a structured problem-solving situation in dyadic, triadic, and tetradic combinations with other family members. In the study presented here, the questionnaire data and observations from the dyadic interactions were used. For dyadic interactions, participants were asked to discuss two areas of conflict previously identified as problematic areas within the relation, and to come to some solution, if possible. Dyadic interactions were videotaped for 10 minutes.

Family Stress. Three domains of family stressors were assessed—economic stress, parent depression, and marital conflict. Economic stress was measured using Elder's calculation of economic pressure as a combination of the family's income-to-needs ratio, financial instability, and worries about finances (Elder, Conger, Foster, & Ardelt, 1992). Parents' symptoms of depression were assessed using mothers' and fathers' self-reports from the Center for Epidemiological Studies Depression Scale (Radloff & Teri, 1986). Two assessments, separated by a week's time, were averaged together to create a total depression score for mothers and a total score for fathers. Marital conflict was assessed using mothers' and fathers' reports on the Locke–Wallace disagreement subscale (Locke & Wallace, 1987) and the symbolic aggression subscale from the Conflict Tactics Scale (Straus, 1979). Mothers' and fathers' reports on these two subscales were correlated; thus, a composite score was constructed by converting mothers' and fathers' reports on each subscale to z scores and averaging them together to create a total marital conflict score. The mean and standard deviation for mothers' Locke–Wallace disagreement subscale were $M = 8.74$, $SD = 2.43$, and for Conflict Tactics symbolic aggression were $M = 30.09$, $SD = 4.97$. For fathers, means and standard deviations were $M = 8.96$, $SD = 3.15$; and $M = 29.65$, $SD = 4.98$, respectively, for the Locke–Wallace and Conflict Tactics subscales.

Parenting. Parents' behavior toward the two siblings was assessed across three general domains of parenting—warmth and support, negativity and coerciveness, and monitoring and control of the adolescent's behavior, employing a multimethod multiagent measurement strategy. Composite scores were created on the basis of factor analyses.

The degree of warmth and support in mother–child and father–child relationships was measured using parents' and adolescents' reports on the closeness/rapport subscale of the Parent–Child Relationship Scale (Hetherington et al., 1992), the expressive affection and instrumental affection subscales of the Expression of Affection Scale (Hetherington et al., 1992), and an observational measure of parents' warmth/support to each sibling, which included individual measures of warmth, communication, assertiveness, and involvement.

Parents' negativity and coerciveness toward each sibling was assessed using parents' and adolescents' reports on the conflict subscale of the Parent–Child Relationship Scale (Hetherington et al., 1992), the symbolic aggression subscale of the Conflict Tactics Scale (Straus, 1979), the total conflict and punitive discipline subscales of the Childrearing Issues Scale (Hetherington et al., 1992), and an observational measure of parents' negativity to each sibling, which included individual measures of coerciveness, hostility, and transactional conflict.

Parents' monitoring and control of the siblings' behavior was assessed using parents' and adolescents' reports on the knowledge, attempted control, and actual control subscales of the Child Monitoring and Control Scale (Hetherington et al., 1992), and an observational measure of parents' monitoring/control, which included individual measures of monitoring, parental influence, and successful control.

In previous research, 2-month test–retest reliabilities for these parenting dimensions ranged from .76 to .91 for warmth/support, .63 to .88 for negativity/coercion, and .68 to .81 for monitoring/control (Hetherington et al., 1992). Exact agreement on observational codes ranged from .69 to 86. Parenting composite measures were created by converting all scales within a construct to z scores and averaging these scores across respondent and measure. The internal consistencies for the composite measures fell within an acceptable range, with Cronbach alpha coefficients varying from .68 to .77.

Adolescent Psychopathology. Measures of adolescent psychopathology were constructed from parent, adolescent, and observer reports. Adolescent depression was measured using parent and adolescent reports on the Child Depression Inventory (Kovacs, 1980–1981), the depression subscale of the Behavior Problem Index (Zill, 1985), the depression subscale of the Behavior Events Inventory (Hetherington et al., 1992), and an observational measure of internalized negativity derived from observer ratings of the adolescent's depressed mood when interacting with mother, father, and sibling. Assessments of conduct disorder were constructed using parents' and adolescents' reports on the antisocial subscale of the Zill's Behavior Problem Index (Zill, 1985), the coercion subscale of the Behavior Events Inventory, and an observational measure derived from observer ratings of the adolescent's antisocial behavior when interacting with mother, father, and sibling.

The composite measures of adolescent depression and conduct disorder were constructed by converting all scales to z scores and averaging across respondent and measure. To increase reliability, parents' and adolescents' reports on the CDI, BPI, and BEI from both assessment sessions were used. Cronbach alphas for conduct disorder were .75 for the older sibling and .71 for the younger sibling. For depression, alphas were .77 for the older sibling and .73 for the younger sibling.

Adolescent Positive Self-Concept. Three indices of adolescents' positive self-concept were assessed for each child. One index was the adolescent's self-report of global self-worth, a subscale taken from the Harter Self-Perception Profile for Adolescents (Harter, 1982). A second index was the adolescent's self-report of physical attractiveness, also a subscale from the Harter (Harter, 1982). The final index was an optimism scale from the Life Orientation Test (Scheier & Carver, 1985). The three indices were used as indicators on a latent variable of positive self-concept.

Adolescent Temperament. Each sibling's temperament was assessed using mother's and father's reports on the emotionality subscale of the EAS temperament scale (Buss & Plomin, 1986). This subscale contains items reflecting emotional difficulty in children, for example "I frequently get distressed," and "I am known as hotblooded and quick-tempered."

Relative difference scores were constructed for all of the parenting and adolescent temperament and psychopathology composites by subtracting the younger sibling's score on a particular construct from the older sibling's score on that construct (i.e., older sibling – younger sibling). Relative differences, rather than absolute differences, were used because of the added information of knowing which sibling (older or younger) is scoring higher, provided by the sign of the relative difference score.

It should be noted that we chose to examine difference scores to assess the effect of parenting on child outcome, following the lead of many others who have explored within-family environments (Daniels et al., 1985; Tejerina-Allen et al., 1994). This is one means of testing a nonshared hypothesis, but there are several other important alternatives in the field, such as sibling covariance models (see Reiss et al., in press; Rovine, 1994).

There has been some criticism in the literature concerning the use of difference scores because of confusion surrounding the issue of reliability (Rovine, 1994). Contrary to the common misconception that difference scores are inherently unreliable, difference scores are nearly as reliable as the individual scores they are constructed from, provided there is adequate variability and low to moderate correlations in the individual scores (Willett, 1987). It is also important to bear in mind that, in this chapter, the difference scores were constructed from multiple measure composites with high internal consistency, comprised of scales with demonstrated reliability from previous research. Although unreliability of the difference score is always an issue to be concerned with, it poses less of a problem in this study because of the increased reliability gained from a multiple measurement strategy.

DETERMINANTS OF DIFFERENTIAL PARENTING

Are There Within-Family Differences in Parenting?

This section addresses the degree to which parents treat their adolescent children differently. Table 2.1 presents the means, standard deviations, and range of differences in parenting within families. Means reflect relative differences scores, with a zero indicating no differences in treatment of older and younger children. All of the parenting dimensions tended to be distributed around zero and had an adequate range of differences. These numbers reveal that some parents prefer the older child and some the younger, but there is no systematic significant older/younger birth order effect.

TABLE 2.1
Summary Statistics for Relative Differences in Parental Treatment

Differences in Parenting (Older Child–Younger Child)	M	SD	Range
Mother warmth	−.01	.52	−2.19–1.88
Mother negativity	.01	.58	−2.42–1.89
Mother control	−.04	.54	−1.60–1.56
Father warmth	−.03	.56	−2.29–1.64
Father negativity	.02	.57	−2.20–1.94
Father control	−.04	.52	−1.52–1.31

The correlations among the dimensions of differential parenting are presented in Table 2.2, and indicate that negativity is modestly correlated with control and warmth. In addition, there are no significant differences in correlations between fathers' and mothers' parenting. All other correlations suggest that differential experiences may, to some extent, operate independently of each other in their association with differences in adolescent psychopathology.

Predictors of Differential Parenting

Having established that although some parents treat siblings similarly, some parents do, indeed, treat their children differently, we now turn to the exploration of factors that might produce differences in parenting. As noted previously, several studies have implicated differential treatment as a source of risk to children's development (Daniels et al., 1985; McHale & Pawletko, 1992; Tejerina-Allen et al., 1994). Clearly, the origins of such treatment warrant careful examination. Some studies have identified an effect of birth order in which parents treat siblings differently based on each child's developmental level (Brody, Stoneman, McCoy, & Forehand, 1992; Hetherington, 1987); however, as yet, no studies have explored other processes that may help to explain why parents discriminate in their treatment of siblings. In this study, three potential sources of differential parenting were examined—family stress effects, child effects, and relationship effects.

TABLE 2.2
Correlations Among Differential Parenting Dimensions

Differences in:	Warmth	Negativity	Control
Warmth	1.00	−.16*	.08
Negativity	−.31*	1.00	.27*
Control	.00	.41*	1.00

Note. Top half of the matrix are correlations for mother's parenting, and bottom half are correlations for father's parenting.
*$p \leq .01$.

Family Stress Effects.   One characteristic of the family that may have direct bearing on parenting is the amount of stress experienced by the family as a whole. Developmental psychologists have become increasingly aware of the importance of examining how external environmental stressors affect the capacity of families to foster healthy development in their children (Bronfenbrenner, 1986). Factors such as poverty, financial instability, and concerns about family finances have been found to be related to increases in parental depression and marital conflict (Conger, McCarty, Yang, Lahey, & Kropp, 1984; Elder & Ardelt, 1992; Elder et al., 1992; Elder, Van Nyugen, & Caspi, 1985; Furstenberg, 1990; McLoyd, 1990). Furthermore, in families in which higher levels of such stressors occur, parents are more coercive and inconsistent in their parenting, and adolescents exhibit more problems in adjustment, including higher levels of depression and conduct disorder (Conger, Conger, & Simons, 1992; Conger et al., 1991; Elder et al., 1992; Forgatch, Patterson, & Ray, in press; Hetherington, Lindner, Miller, & Clingempeel, 1991).

The general conclusion is that mounting economic pressures seriously tax the family's ability to function in an adaptive manner. Disruptions in marital and parent–child relationships are commonplace responses to such stress, and these breakdowns within the family heighten the risk of aversive and inconsistent parenting. Given this set of findings, it was hypothesized that parents experiencing higher levels of stress would also be less consistent in their treatment of the two siblings. The underlying notion is that parents have a finite amount of resources in terms of time, attention, patience, and support to give their children. In families in which most of these resources are devoted to coping with economic stress, depression, and/or marital conflict, parents may become less consciously or intentionally equitable and more driven by preferences or child characteristics in their childrearing efforts.

The proposed model is illustrated in Fig. 2.1. As shown, economic stress is presumed to increase the level of parents' depression, which in turn is presumed to lead to increases in marital conflict and differences in parenting. Additional models were run with direct paths from economic stress to differential parenting; however, the goodness of fit for those models was significantly reduced. Results are summarized in Figs. 2.2 and 2.3.

The results for the model of differential parenting did not confirm the hypotheses. Clearly, as low path coefficients indicate, there was no relation between parent depression, marital conflict, and differences in parental warmth, negativity, or control.

For comparison purposes, the same model was run with parents' individual treatment toward each sibling as the outcome measure. This is a more traditional model of stress and parenting of a single child. As can be seen in Figs. 2.2 and 2.3, for both the older and younger sibling (Child 1 and Child 2), there was a significant relation between family stress and parents' negativity, indicating that parents who had more marital conflicts tended to show more negativity/coercion

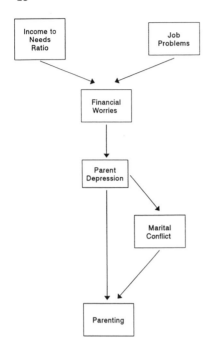

FIG. 2.1. Family stress effects on differential parenting.

and less warmth toward their children, whereas those who were more depressed showed only more negativity. This result replicates the findings of other studies (Conger et al., 1992; Forgatch et al., in press), and assures researchers that the absence of findings for the within-family models is not due to factors unique to this dataset. Furthermore, this finding suggests that the processes involved in differential parenting are clearly different from those found to underlie parenting in between-family studies. Thus, parents who experience higher levels of economic stress and, in turn, higher levels of depression and marital conflict, may treat both siblings poorly, but they are not more likely to treat one child better or worse than the other.

Child and Relationship Effects. Although an effect of family stress on differential treatment was not found, differences in characteristics of the siblings, such as temperament, or in the parents' relationship to the siblings, may be important predictors of differential parenting. Several studies have identified child temperament as a factor that influences parent–child relationships (Garmezy, 1983; Gordon, 1983; Hetherington, 1991; Maccoby, Snow, & Jacklin, 1984; Rutter, 1987). In addition to the direct effects of children's temperament on parents' behavior, some studies have found an interaction between children's temperament and level of family discord as it affects parenting (Hetherington, 1991). These researchers have come to the general conclusion that, in distressed families, children with adverse temperamental characteristics are more likely to

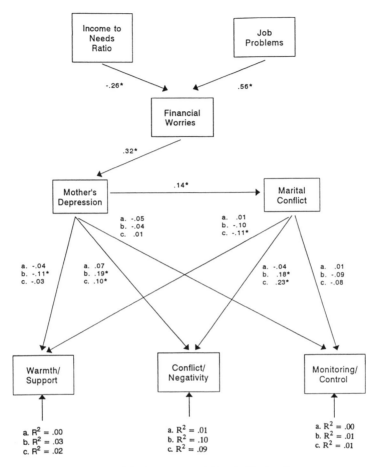

a=difference score model   Chisquare=43.92, df=20, G of F=.975
b=absolute treatment of C1 Chisquare=43.87, df=20, G of F=.975
c=absolute treatment of C2 Chisquare=33.26, df=20, G of F=.982

FIG. 2.2.   Family stress effects on mother's differential parenting.

elicit and be the targets—or scapegoats—of parental hostility, coercion, and irritability. These difficult children seem to bring out the worst in parents who are already burdened with economic and marital problems, and who may suffer from depression as well.

To date, research investigating the relations between child temperament and family processes has focused on between-family differences, with few exceptions (Brody & Stoneman, 1994; Brody, Stoneman, & McCoy, 1992). Although in our sample siblings share up to 50% of their genetic make-up, their personalities may vary greatly (Plomin, 1986). In addition, a one-way analysis of variance (ANOVA) indicated that there were no significant mean Child 1 – Child 2

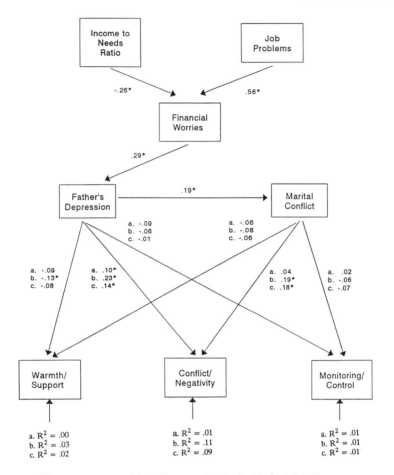

a=difference score model   Chisquare=41.29, df=20, G of F=.974
b=absolute treatment of C1   Chisquare=25.35, df=20, G of F=.986
c=absolute treatment of C2   Chisquare=38.62, df=20, G of F=.979

FIG. 2.3.   Family stress effects on father's differential parenting.

absolute differences in temperament across sibling type, $F(3, 504) = .651$. Thus, in families in which there are differences in sibling temperament, it might be expected that under conditions of high family stress, the emotionally difficult child would receive more overall negativity from parents than would the less difficult child.

A third factor underlying differential parenting could be the nature of the biological relationship between the parent and child. Specifically, it is possible that parents might treat their biological child more positively than their stepchild, especially in families marked by higher levels of stress. In this study, families differed in terms of whether both siblings were the biological child of the parent, neither was the biological child, or one sibling was the biological child and the other was a stepchild. Given previous research concerning the effects of "own-ness" on parenting in remarried families (Brand, Clingempeel, & Bowen-Wood-ward, 1988), it was expected that parents would show preferential treatment toward their biological child. The proposed model is presented in Fig. 2.4.

In order to examine if effects of child temperament or ownness would be intensified under conditions of adversity, families were divided into high- and low-stress groups using a popular strategy in stress and coping research (Garmezy & Masten, 1994; Kolvin, Miller, Fleeting, & Kolvin, 1988; Rutter & Quinton, 1987; Sameroff, Seifer, Barocas, Zax, & Greenspan, 1987). Each family was assigned a cumulative stress score based on five different indices: income, financial worries, job problems, parent depression, and marital conflict. The cutoffs for the risk indices were: at or below the poverty line, 1 standard deviation above the mean on financial worries, 1 standard deviation above the mean on job problems, 1 standard deviation above the mean on marital conflict, and either parent above the clinical cutoff for depression. Families who met the risk cutoff on at least three of the five indices were classified as high stress ($N = 83$) and the remainder of the families were classified as low stress ($N = 433$).

Models of invariance were run with differences in sibling temperament and differences in "ownness" to that parent predicting differential treatment in high- and low-stress families. Separate models were run for mothers' and fathers' differential parenting. For comparison purposes, traditional between-family mod-els were also run using parents' absolute level of treatment to each sibling as the outcome variable. Thus, three models for each parent were run in all: a differential model, a traditional model for the older sibling (Child 1), and a traditional model for the younger sibling (Child 2). Results of the best fitting models are summarized in Table 2.3.

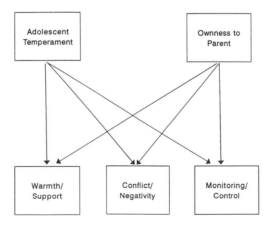

FIG. 2.4. Determinants of differential parenting.

TABLE 2.3

Effects of Child Temperament and Ownness on Mother's
Parenting in High- and Low-Stress Families

	Mother's Parenting		Father's Parenting	
Differential Parenting (Child 1–Child 2)	Differences in Ownness	Differences in Temperament	Differences in Ownness	Differences in Temperament
Warmth/support	−.44*	−.06	−.38*	−.13*
Conflict/negativity	−.20*	.32*	.14*	.26*
Monitoring/control	−.02	.04	−.25*	.00
χ^2		16.32		8.09
df		11		11
GOF		.930		.952
Parenting to Child 1	Ownness	Temperament	Ownness	Temperament
Warmth/support	−.28*	−.09	−.26*	−.10
Conflict/negativity	−.13*	.26*	.12*	.34*
Monitoring/control	−.12*	.01	−.13	.00
χ^2		3.53		4.77
df		11		11
GOF		.985		.975
Parenting to Child 2	Ownness	Temperament	Ownness	Temperament
Warmth/support	−.31*	−.11*	−.12*	−.03
Conflict/negativity	−.11*	.29*	−.02	.29*
Monitoring/control	−.14*	.15*	−.02	.08
χ^2		9.90		11.45
df		11		11
GOF		.960		.946

Note. High- vs. low-stress models were invariant, thus numbers presented are for the entire sample.
*$p \leq .01$.

RESULTS

Interaction With Family Stress

Interestingly, and contrary to what other researchers have suggested (Engfer, 1988; Hetherington, 1991; Rutter, 1990), there were no differences between high- and low-stress families in the amount of differential negativity, warmth, or control that parents directed toward their emotionally difficult versus less difficult child. Further, parents experiencing higher levels of stress did not treat their own child better, or their stepchild worse, than parents who were less stressed. Neither differences in adolescent temperament nor ownness interacted with family stress in any of the models. Instead, the models indicated invariance between low- and high-stress families; specifically, the same pattern and relative magnitude among the variables were evident in both low- and high-stress families.

Main Effects

However, there were main effects of differences in adolescent temperament and ownness on differential treatment, regardless of level of stress in the family. Results were fairly similar for mothers and fathers, and for both the within-family and between-family analyses. In the within-family models, mothers and fathers were more negative to the child who was temperamentally more difficult relative to their sibling. Similarly, the between-family models indicated that adolescent temperament was associated with parents' negativity, with emotionally difficult children receiving higher levels of negativity.

These findings cast a new light on Rutter's "scapegoat" hypothesis. First, these data suggest that adolescent temperament is salient enough to elicit negative behavior from parents without the additional impact of family stress. In addition, not only do difficult children get treated with higher levels of parental negativity between families, but within families, children who are more difficult relative to their sibling receive more negativity from parents than their sibling does. This is important because it suggests that parents are responding quite strongly to personality differences in their children.

The relationship factor, ownness, was also related to differences in parenting. Note that in terms of difference scores for ownness, a 0 represented no differences in ownness between siblings; a 1 indicated that the younger sibling is a biological child and the older sibling is a stepchild; and a −1 indicated that the older sibling is a biological child and the younger sibling is a stepchild. For traditional models, a 0 represented biological children and a 1 represented stepchildren. Results from the difference score model reveal that mothers were more supportive and affectionate with their own child than with their stepchild. Interestingly, mothers were also more negative and coercive with their biological children. The model for fathers indicated that fathers were more warm and more controlling with their biological children. The between-family results reflected a similar pattern of results as the within-family models.

Discussion of Determinants of Differential Parenting

A striking finding from the previously discussed sets of analyses is that parents' differential treatment was more influenced by characteristics of the adolescents and the parent–child relationship than by stressors present in the family. This raises several issues. First, it is clear that parents display different levels of warmth, negativity, and control with their biological children than with their stepchildren. In addition, this differs according to sex of the parent, in that mothers are more affectionate and more negative with biological children, whereas fathers are more affectionate and controlling with biological children. Although it was expected that parents would prefer their biological child, biological mothers were not expected to be more negative than stepmothers. This result may reflect moth-

ers' greater willingess to engage and confront conflict with biological children, whereas with stepchildren, mothers may remove themselves from the issues that create conflict. Such areas may be the domain of the biological father as stepmothers remain "polite" strangers. Additionally, this may be related to the findings reported by Hetherington (1989) that biological parents are more involved with their own children and are more distant and disengaged with stepchildren. Although knowledge of stepfamilies has increased substantially over the past years (see Hetherington et al., 1992), the issue of shifting role expectations of stepfamily members during the adolescent period has not been fully explored.

Second, as previously mentioned, the lack of findings for family stress as a source of differential parenting are in marked contrast to those from previous between-family studies (Conger et al., 1991; Simons, Lorenz, Conger, & Wu, 1992), as well as from our own results of between-family models for both older and younger siblings. Clearly, factors that underlie risk and resilience processes in between-family studies, such as the relationship between family stress and parenting, are different from those that govern such processes within families. It appears that although the absolute level of parenting is affected by family environment and the larger context in which families are embedded, differences in parenting are affected primarily by characteristics of the siblings and the parent–child relationship.

OUTCOMES OF DIFFERENTIAL PARENTING: DEPRESSION AND CONDUCT DISORDER

Are There Within-Family Differences in Depression and Conduct Disorder?

The next question addressed was the degree to which adolescent siblings differ in terms of depression and conduct disorder and whether differences in sibling psychopathology are similar for boy and girl sibling pairs. An examination of sibling correlations for depression and conduct disorder showed a moderate relation between sibling scores, with a correlation of $r = .26$ for depression and $r = .43$ for conduct disorder. The means and standard deviations for the relative difference scores are presented in Table 2.4.

As shown, the distributions for sibling differences tend to be centered at zero, yet there was also a moderate amount of variance in the difference scores and a good range of differences for both girl and boy siblings. Recall that all sibling pairs are same-sex pairs. Additionally, the similar means and ranges for boys and girls indicate that parents are not more liable to treat one pair of siblings more differently than the other, based on child sex. It is also important to note that the percentage of families with no differences in sibling outcome is quite small.

TABLE 2.4
Summary Statistics for Relative Differences in Sibling Psychopathology

Differences in Sibling Psychopathology (Older Child–Younger Child)	M	SD	Range
Boys—Depression	−.02	.72	−2.61–2.24
Girls—Depression	.09	.80	−2.47–2.88
Boys—Conduct Disorder	.03	.66	−2.25–1.90
Girls—Conduct Disorder	.02	.68	−2.87–2.20

Effects of Differential Treatment on Adolescent Psychopathology

The final set of analyses were designed to identify the aspects of differential parenting associated with differences in sibling depression and conduct disorder. First, we discuss why parenting may be critical in explaining within-family differences in psychopathology. The following section is a discussion of models of invariance we ran that examine the effects of differential parenting under conditions of high and low family stress. We also examine how adolescents' positive self-concept may serve as a mediator of negative family experiences. Finally, identical traditional between-family models are analyzed for comparison purposes.

What kinds of family processes are important in understanding sibling differences in depression and conduct disorder? Between-family research and a handful of within-family studies suggest some potentially critical parenting dimensions.

One dimension is parents' warmth, support, and affection toward their children. Many studies have found warm and supportive parental behavior to exert a positive influence on adolescent development (Baumrind, 1991; Hetherington et al., 1992; Maccoby & Martin, 1983; Patterson, DeBaryshe & Ramsey, 1989). In addition, a warm, positive relationship with at least one parent has been found to act as a buffer against the negative effects of family discord on children's adjustment (Rutter, 1978; Werner, 1984). Furthermore, within-family differences in parental warmth and affection may be a risk factor for psychopathology. For example, in a study of differential parenting and differences in siblings' internalizing and externalizing behavior, Dunn and her colleagues (Dunn et al., 1990) found that when mothers were less affectionate to older siblings than to younger ones, older siblings showed greater internalizing problems.

Another important dimension of parenting is parents' use of rejecting and coercive, rather than supportive and assertive, means to control their child's behavior. A number of studies, both cross-sectional and longitudinal, have identified this parenting dimension as a critical factor in the development of depression and antisocial behavior in adolescence (Capaldi, 1991; Conger et al., 1991; Forgatch, 1991; Hetherington et al., 1992; Hirschi, 1969; Laub & Sampson, 1988; Lazerle & Patterson, 1990; Loeber & Dishion, 1983; Patterson, 1982; Patterson & Bank, 1989; Patterson, Reid, & Dishion, 1992; Patterson & Stouthamer-Loeber, 1984; Rutter, 1989).

This set of differential experiences within the family is presumed to have direct effects on differences in sibling psychopathology. Within-family studies have demonstrated that when parents differ in the degree to which they effectively nurture, support, monitor, and control their children's behavior, such differences in treatment lead to internalizing and externalizing problems in children (Dunn & Plomin, 1990). However, little is known about what kinds of circumstances may exacerbate or ameliorate the effects of differential parenting on adolescent adjustment.

In our models, we included a latent variable representing adolescents' positive self-concept as a mediator of within-family experiences. Many studies have identified the importance of positive self-esteem and high self-worth during adolescence (Attie, Brooks-Gunn, & Peterson, 1991; Harter, 1990; Renouf & Harter, 1990) and its role in buffering children from negative outcomes. It is expected that some of the negative effects of differential experiences will be mediated by adolescents' positive self-concept.

In the following section, a special concern was determining whether the effects of differential experiences were intensified when the family was experiencing high levels of stress. The model is pictured in Fig. 2.5. For the first set of models, families were grouped in terms of high and low stress and tests of invariance were run with differential treatment predicting differences in sibling psychopathology. Models were run separately for differences in sibling depression and conduct disorder.

Model Testing

All models were tested using a procedure outlined by Loehlin (1987) to test the improvement in fit for a series of nested models. According to this procedure, a baseline model and its associated goodness of fit is established by constraining the predictor variances, covariances, and betas to be equal for the groups. In the next three models, the predictor variances, covariances, and betas, each in turn, are allowed to differ for the groups, and their associated goodness of fits are compared to the baseline model to determine if groups differ from each other and where that difference lies. If a particular model provides a significant improvement in fit over a previous model, it becomes the baseline model from which all subsequent models are compared. Only results from the best fitting models are presented; thus degrees of freedom may vary from model to model.

Within-Family Differential Treatment and Outcome. Table 2.5 presents the results of the best fitting models for predicting the relation between differential parenting and differences in sibling conduct disorder. (Note: Path coefficients are also pictured in Fig. 2.5 for this model only to help readers understand the overall flow of the variables in the model and how they relate to the tables.)

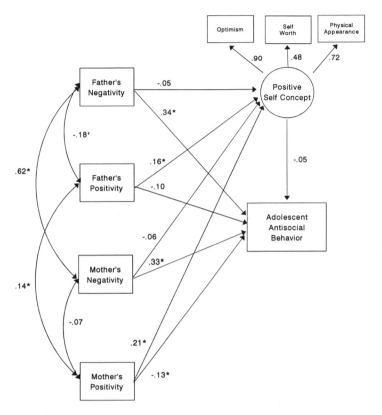

FIG. 2.5. Direct and indirect effects of differential parenting on children's antisocial behavior.

For both low- and high-stress families, the primary predictor of differences in conduct disorder was differences in mothers' and fathers' coercive discipline (β = .33 and .34, respectively), with parents acting more coercively toward the sibling with more problems. In addition, differences in mothers' and fathers' positivity predicted differences in siblings' positive self-concept (β = .16 and .21, respectively), with greater parental positivity leading to adolescents' positive self-concept. The hypothesized mediator effect of adolescents' positive self-concept was not apparent—notice the −.05 beta weight representing the direct path from self-concept to antisocial behavior.

The results for differences in sibling depression are presented in Table 2.6. Mothers were more coercive toward the sibling with higher levels of depression (β = .22), with the same pattern evident in both low- and high-stress families. Again, parents' positivity predicted adolescent self-concept (β = .16 and .22, respectively); however, unlike the conduct disorder models, differences in adolescent self-concept were strongly related to differences in adolescent depression, as noted by the −.40 beta weight. Not surprisingly, as other research has dem-

TABLE 2.5
Mother's and Father's Parenting → Child Antisocial Behavior and Self-Concept, Differential and Absolute Treatment

Betas	Difference Score (Child 1–Child 2)				Absolute Treatment of Child 1				Absolute Treatment of Child 2			
	Antisocial		Self-Concept		Antisocial		Self-Concept		Antisocial		Self-Concept	
	Lo	Hi	Lo	Hi	Lo	Hi	Lo	Hi	Lo	Hi	Lo	Hi
Father's neg →	.34*	=	-.05	=	.34*	=	-.07	.03	.26*	=	-.07	=
Father's pos →	-.10	=	.16*	=	.05	=	-.02	.03	-.05	=	.08	=
Mother's neg →	.33*	=	-.06	=	.34*	=	-.22*	-.11	.39*	=	-.06	=
Mother's pos →	-.13	=	.21*	=	.17*	=	.14*	.13	-.14*	=	.17*	=
	Lo			Hi	Lo			Hi	Lo			Hi
Self-Concept → Antisocial	-.05			=	-.06			=	.01			=
R^2	.42			.48	.46			.45	.38			
χ^2	60.72				51.04				65.23			
df	35				35				48			
GOF	.924				.921				.905			

Note. Standardized estimates are given. Lo = low-stress families (N = 400), Hi = high-risk families (N = 75). "=" denotes a parameter constrained to be equal across groups.

*Beta coefficients and correlations significant at $p < .05$.

TABLE 2.6

Mother's and Father's Parenting and Child Depression and Self-Concept, Differential and Absolute Treatment

Betas	Difference Score (Child 1–Child 2)				Absolute Treatment of Child 1				Absolute Treatment of Child 2			
	Depression		Self-Concept		Depression		Self-Concept		Depression		Self-Concept	
	Lo	Hi	Lo	Hi	Lo	Hi	Lo	Hi	Lo	Hi	Lo	Hi
Father's neg →	.12	=	-.02	=	.34*	=	-.07	-.06	.22*	=	-.06	=
Father's pos →	-.06	=	.16*	=	-.02	=	-.04	.13	.01	=	.07	=
Mother's neg →	.22*	=	-.10	=	.03	=	-.21*	.07	.20*	=	-.08	=
Mother's pos →	-.07	=	.21*	=	-.10	=	.15*	.11	-.04	=	.19*	=
	Lo		Hi		Lo		Hi		Lo		Hi	
Self-Concept → Depression	-.40*	=			-.45*	=			-.24*	=		
R^2	.37		.32		.43		.30		.22		.24	
χ^2	72.51				45.98				74.57			
df	35				31				35			
GOF	.925				.944				.947			

Note. Standardized estimates are given. Lo = low-stress families ($N = 400$), Hi = high-risk families ($N = 75$). "=" denotes a parameter constrained to be equal across groups.

*Beta coefficients and correlations significant at $p < .05$.

onstrated (Harter, 1990), siblings with lower self-esteem tended to have higher levels of depression.

Between-Family Treatment and Outcome. Results from comparative between-family models reflect the pattern of results found within families. Models were run separately for older and younger children. Table 2.5 summarizes results for the best fitting models for conduct disorder. For the most part, the high- and low-stress models were invariant, with one exception. Mothers' negativity predicted self-concept for older siblings in low-stress families only.

Results for models analyzing depression were very similar. Again, there were differences in high- and low-risk families for older children, wherein mothers' negativity and positivity appear to predict adolescents' self-concept in low-risk, but not high-risk, families. It may be that in high-risk families where parents are distressed and may not be functioning competently, older adolescents have the ability to seek out other outlets, such as peers, relatives, or other adults to derive self-esteem, whereas in low-risk families where parents are more stable and consistent, parental behavior continues to be an important influence on how adolescents feel about themselves. Fathers' negativity was related to older children's depression in both high- and low-risk families.

Models run for younger children indicated that mothers and fathers who were more negative had children with higher levels of depression. Additionally, mothers' positivity predicted adolescents' positive self-concept. There were no differences between high- and low-stress families for younger children.

DISCUSSION

It was surprising to find that the effects of differential parental negativity on adolescent psychopathology were, for the most part, not intensified in high-stress families. This finding is open to several interpretations. Family-wide stressors, such as economic stress and parent depression, to which each sibling, presumably, would be equally exposed were purposely chosen. Traditional models of stress and coping commonly analyze stressors that have a direct impact on the child and may differ for each sibling (e.g., stressful life events), but in a nonshared model that employs difference scores, stressors must be identified that affect both children. In this study more distal stressors that are generally hypothesized to affect the entire family system, for example, parental depression, economic problems, and marital conflict, were chosen, rather than more proximal stressors specific to an individual child. Similarly, this may be why few intensification effects of stress in between-family models were seen as well (see Lindner, 1988, for further discussion of this issue).

It is possible that these results did not discriminate between high- and low-stress families because the siblings experienced different degrees of family stress despite the fact that they resided in the same family. In other words, two siblings might live in a high-stress family according to parents' reports, but only one sibling may actually perceive it to be so. As others have demonstrated, children's perceptions of the stressfulness of their environment may be more salient in predicting antisocial behavior and feelings of depression than more "objective" measures of stress (Buchanan, Maccoby, & Dornbusch, 1991). Thus, reliance on distal stressors may account in part for the noticable lack of differences in findings between high- and low-stress families.

An additional point also concerns the chosen criteria for identifying high-stress families. The measure of cumulative family stress used here assumes that stressors are additive and operate independently of each other, but in a cumulative way. The model was tested with each of the chosen five stress indicators separately, and very small variation was noted. However, it may be that some combinations of different stressors constitute a greater risk than others. For example, it may be that stressors such as parental depression, marital conflict, and chronic poverty, when combined together, place parents at risk for differential treatment and siblings at risk for psychopathology, whereas the combination of job problems, financial worries, and marital conflict may not exert such an effect. Thus, in future studies, it may be important to examine the cumulative effect of different combinations of stressors.

In contrast to the first set of analyses that identified some different determinants of differential parenting and absolute parenting, there were few meaningful differences among the within- and between-family models in this set of analyses. Overall, negative parenting was associated with adolescent psychopathology and positive parenting was associated with adolescent's positive self-concept. These findings are consistent with other research that has found that hostile, coercive parenting leads to negative outcomes, whereas warm, involved parenting leads to positive outcomes (Hetherington et al., 1992).

It should be noted that the processes identified in the models tested specified the direction of effects as differential treatment predicting differences in sibling outcome. However, as Forgatch, Patterson, and Ray (chap. 3, this volume) demonstrate, children with problems are likely to become part of a mutually influential system, with children eliciting certain behaviors from parents at the same time that parents are attempting to behave proactively with children. Because of the cross-sectional nature of this study, the question of direction of effects could not be explicitly tested, although a second wave of data currently being collected will allow researchers to explore this further. Thus, it is important to bear in mind that the associations between differential parenting and differences in sibling psychopathology are more likely to reflect a reciprocal, rather than a unidirectional, process (see Hetherington et al., 1992, for further discussion of this issue).

IMPLICATIONS

The results of this study demonstrate that the origins of differential treatment appear to stem more from characteristics of the adolescents and their relationship with parents than from stressors placed on parents and the family as a whole. This departs from results reported in between-family research that document a relationship between stress and absolute level of parenting (Conger et al., 1992) and from this chapter's between-family findings on stress and parenting. Given parents' apparent sensitivity to differences in the characteristics of their children, further investigation in this area is warranted.

In addition, it was found that siblings differ in psychopathology, despite the fact that they live in the same household with the same set of parents. Moreover, this difference is due in part to the differential treatment they receive from parents. Put in terms of risk and resilience, when parents direct their positive and negative behavior differentially to their children, one sibling is buffered at the expense of the other. That is, siblings who receive higher levels of negativity from parents suffer greater psychopathology than their siblings who experience less parental negativity. However, this pattern does not seem to be exacerbated in high-stress families.

The similarities of within-family models and between-family models in predicting adolescent psychopathology suggest that, although the variables are different—difference scores versus absolute scores—similar processes are occurring. Differential treatment may be one more aspect of incompetent parenting, like coerciveness and hostility, that adds to the risk that inept parenting poses to adolescents' development of psychopathology.

Finally, a note about the limitations of this study are in order. Research on within-family differences is still quite new, and the statistical problems posed by including two siblings in an analysis are considerable. Given this, these analyses used only one of the methods available for addressing the questions of differences in parenting and adolescent psychopathology (see Reiss et al., in press; Rovine, 1994; for other alternatives).

What are some alternatives for examining processes within families? One possibility is a categorical approach to measuring differences in treatment, where families are classified in terms of whether, for example, both siblings receive a high score on support, both siblings receive a low score on support, or one sibling receives a high score and the other does not (Anderson, Hetherington, Reiss, & Plomin, 1994). This approach addresses an important variable not considered in this study—level of treatment toward each sibling. It is quite possible that differences in treatment are more salient and exert stronger effects when the level of treatment of each sibling is high or low, suggesting an interaction between difference and level.

In conclusion, this study provided some preliminary clues about the processes that link family stress, differential parenting, and sibling differences in psychopathology. These findings demonstrated some differences occurring between families that do not also occur within families, specifically the relationship between stress and parenting; and some similarities, specifically the relationship between parenting and adolescent depression and conduct disorder. This study has tapped some, but clearly not all, of the critical processes that place an adolescent at risk, and continued attention to differences in siblings' experiences within the family will increase understanding of the development of psychopathology in adolescence.

ACKNOWLEDGMENTS

Data used in this report are from the Nonshared Environment and Adolescent Development Project, supported by the National Institute of Mental Health (MH-43373) and the William T. Grant Foundation. Preparation of the manuscript was supported by the National Institute of Mental Health Research Training Grant (5 T32 MH18387-06 in Child Mental Health—Primary Prevention).

REFERENCES

Anderson, E. A., Hetherington, E. M., Reiss, D., & Plomin, R. (1994). Parent's nonshared treatment of siblings and the development of social competence during adolescence. *Journal of Family Psychology, 8*, 303–320.

Attie, I., Brooks-Gunn, J., & Peterson, A. C. (1991). A developmental perspective on eating disorders and eating problems. In M. Lewis & S. M. Miller (Eds.), *Handbook of developmental psychopathology* (pp. 409–420). New York: Plenum.

Baker, L. A., & Daniels, D. (1990). Nonshared environmental influences and personality differences in adult twins. *Journal of Personality and Social Psychology, 58*, 103–110.

Baumrind, D. (1991). Effective parenting during the early adolescent transition. In P. A. Cowan & E. M. Hetherington (Eds.), *Family transitions* (pp. 111–164). Hillsdale, NJ: Lawrence Erlbaum Associates.

Brand, E., Clingempeel, W. G., & Bowen-Woodward, K. (1988). Family relationships and children's psychological adjustment in stepmother and stepfather families: Findings and conclusions from the Philadelphia Stepfamily Research Project. In E. M. Hetherington & J. D. Arasteh (Eds.), *Impact of divorce, single parenting and stepparenting on children* (pp. 299–324). Hillsdale, NJ: Lawrence Erlbaum Associates.

Brody, G. H., & Stoneman, Z. (1994). Sibling temperaments and family relationships: Between- and within-family analyses. In D. Reiss, E. M. Hetherington, & R. Plomin (Eds.), *Separate worlds of siblings: The impact of nonshared environment on development* (pp. 129–142). Hillsdale, NJ: Lawrence Erlbaum Associates.

Brody, G. H., Stoneman, Z., & Burke, M. (1987). Child temperaments, maternal differential behavior, and sibling relationships. *Developmental Psychology, 23*, 354–362.

Brody, G. H., Stoneman, Z., & McCoy, J. K. (1992). Parental differential treatment of siblings and sibling differences in negative emotionality. *Journal of Marriage and the Family, 54*, 643–651.

Brody, G. H., Stoneman, Z., McCoy, J. K., & Forehand, R. (1992). Contemporaneous and longitudinal associations of sibling conflict with family relationship assessments and family discussions about sibling problems. *Child Development, 63*, 391–400.

Bronfenbrenner, U. (1986). Ecology of the family as a context for human development: Research perspectives. *Developmental Psychology, 22*, 723–742.

Buchanan, C. M., Maccoby, E. E., & Dornbusch, S. M. (1991). Caught between parents: Adolescents' experience in divorced homes. *Child Development, 62*, 1008–1029.

Buss, A. H., & Plomin, R. (1986). The EAS approach to temperament. In R. Plomin & J. Dunn (Eds.), *The study of temperament: Changes, continuities, and challenges* (pp. 41–67). Hillsdale, NJ: Lawrence Erlbaum Associates.

Capaldi, D. M. (1991). Co-occurrence of conduct problems and depressive symptoms in early adolescent boys: I. Familial factors and general adjustment at Grade 6. *Developmental and Psychopathology, 3*, 277–300.

Conger, R. D., Conger, K. J., Elder, G. H., Lorenz, F. O., Simons, R. L., & Witbeck, L. B. (1992). A family process model of economic hardship and adjustment of early adolescent boys. *Child Development, 63*, 526–541.

Conger, R. D., Conger, K. J., & Simons, R. L. (1992, June). *Family economic stress, parenting behavior, and adolescent drinking.* Paper presented at the biennial meetings of the Society for Research on Adolescence, Washington, DC.

Conger, R. D., Lorenz, F. O., Elder, G. H., Jr., Melby, J. N., Simons, R. L., & Conger, K. J. (1991). A process model of family economic pressure and early adolescent alcohol use. *Journal of Early Adolescence, 11*, 430–449.

Conger, R. D., McCarty, J. A., Yang, R. K., Lahey, B. B., & Kropp, J. P. (1984). Perceptions of child, child-rearing values, and emotional distress as mediating links between environmental stressors and observed maternal behavior. *Child Development, 55*, 2234–2247.

Daniels, D. (1986). Differential experiences of siblings in the same family as predictors of adolescent sibling personality differences. *Journal of Personality and Social Psychology, 51*, 339–346.

Daniels, D., Dunn, J., Furstenberg, F. F., & Plomin, R. (1985). Environmental differences within the family and adjustment differences within pairs of adolescent siblings. *Child Development, 56*, 764–774.

Dunn, J., & Plomin, R. (1990). *Separate lives: Why siblings are so different.* New York: Basic Books.

Dunn, J., Stocker, C., & Plomin, R. (1990). Nonshared experiences within the family: Correlates of behavioral problems in middle childhood. *Development and Psychopathology, 2*, 113–126.

Elder, G. H., & Ardelt, M. (1992, June). *Families adapting to economic pressure: Some consequences for parents and adolescents.* Paper presented at the biennial meetings of the Society for Research on Adolescence, Washington, DC.

Elder, G. H., Conger, R. D., Foster, E. M., & Ardelt, M. (1992). Families under economic pressure. *Journal of Family Issues, 13*, 5–37.

Elder, G. H., Jr., Van Nyugen, T., & Caspi, A. (1985). Linking family hardship to children's lives. *Child Development, 56*, 361–375.

Engfer, A. (1988). The interrelatedness of marriage and the mother-child relationships. In R. A. Hinde & J. Stevenson-Hinde (Eds.), *Relationships within families* (pp. 104–118). Oxford, UK: Clarendon.

Forgatch, M. S. (1991). The clinical science vortex: Treatment as an experimental manipulation. In D. Pepler & K. H. Rubin (Eds.), *The development and treatment of childhood aggression* (pp. 291–315). Hillsdale, NJ: Lawrence Erlbaum Associates.

Furstenberg, F. F. (1990). *How families manage risk and opportunity in dangerous neighborhoods.* Unpublished manuscript.

Garmezy, N. (1983). Stressors of childhood. In N. Garmezy & M. Rutter (Eds.), *Stress, coping and development in children* (pp. 43–84). New York: McGraw-Hill.

Garmezy, N., & Masten, A. S. (1994). Chronic adversities. In M. Rutter, L. Herzov, & E. Taylor (Eds.), *Child and adolescent psychiatry* (3rd ed., pp. 191–208). Oxford, UK: Blackwell.

Gordon, B. N. (1983). Maternal perception of child temperament and observed mother–child interaction. *Child Psychiatry and Human Development, 13*, 153–167.

Harter, S. (1982). The perceived competence scale for children. *Child Development, 53*, 87–97.

Harter, S. (1990). Causes, correlates and the functional role of global self-worth: A life-span perspective. In R. Sternberg & J. Kolligian (Eds.), *Competence considered* (pp. 68–97). New Haven, CT: Yale University Press.

Hetherington, E. M. (1987). Six years after divorce: Mothers, children, and siblings. In R. A. Hinde & J. Stevenson-Hinde (Eds.), *Relations among relationships* (pp. 311–331). Cambridge: Cambridge University Press.

Hetherington, E. M. (1989). Coping with family transitions: Winners, losers, and survivors. *Child Development, 60*, 1–15.

Hetherington, E. M. (1991). The role of individual differences and family relationships in children's coping with divorce and remarriage. In P. A. Cowan & E. M. Hetherington (Eds.), *Family transitions* (pp. 165–194). Hillsdale, NJ: Lawrence Erlbaum Associates.

Hetherington, E. M., & Clingempeel, W. G., in collaboration with Anderson, E. R., Deal, J. E., Stanley Hagan, M., Hollier, E. A., & Lindner, M. S. (1992). Coping with marital transitions: A family systems perspective. *Monographs of the Society for Research in Child Development, 57*(2–3, Serial No. 227).

Hetherington, E. M., Lindner, M. S., Miller, N. B., & Clingempeel, W. G. (1991, April). *Work, marriage, and parenting in non-divorced and remarried families.* Paper presented at the 59th biennial meeting of the Society for Research in Child Development, Seattle, WA.

Hirschi, T. (1969). *Causes of delinquency.* Berkeley, CA: University of California Press.

Kolvin, I., Miller, F. J. W., Fleeting, M., & Kolvin, P. A. (1988). Social and parenting factors affecting criminal offense rates (findings from the Newcastle Thousand Families Study, 1947–1980). *British Journal of Psychiatry, 152,* 80–90.

Kovacs, M. (1980–1981). Rating scales to assess depression in school-aged children. *Acta Paedopsychiatrica, 46,* 437–457.

Laub, J. H., & Sampson, R. J. (1988). Unraveling families and delinquency: A reanalysis of the Gluecks' data. *Criminology, 26,* 355–380.

Lazelere, R. E., & Patterson, G. R. (1990). Parental management: Mediator of the effect of socioeconomic status on early delinquency. *Criminology, 28,* 301–323.

Lindner, M. S. (1988). *Family background and family process stressors as predictors of adolescent adjustment.* Unpublished master's thesis, University of Virginia.

Locke, H., & Wallace, K. (1987). Marital adjustment test. In N. Fredman & R. Sheman (Eds.), *Handbook of measurement for marriage and family therapy* (pp. 46–50). New York: Brunner/Mazel.

Loeber, R., & Dishion, T. J. (1983). Early predictors of male delinquency: A review. *Psychological Bulletin, 94,* 68–99.

Loehlin, J. C. (1987). *Latent variable models: An introduction to factor, path, and structural analysis.* Hillsdale, NJ: Lawrence Erlbaum Associates.

Maccoby, E. E., & Martin, J. A. (1983). Socialization in the context of the family: Parent–child interaction. In P. H. Mussen (Series Ed.) & E. M. Hetherington (Vol. Ed.), *Handbook of child psychology: Vol. 4. Socialization, personality, and social development* (4th ed., pp. 1–101). New York: Wiley.

Maccoby, E. E., Snow, M. E., & Jacklin, C. N. (1984). Children's dispositions and mother–child interaction at 12 and 18 months: A short-term longitudinal study. *Developmental Psychology, 20,* 459–472.

Masten, A. S., Best, K. M., & Garmezy, N. (1990). Resilience and development: Contributions from the study of children who overcome adversity. *Development and Psychopathology, 2,* 425–444.

McHale, S. M., & Pawletko, T. M. (1992). Differential treatment of siblings in two family contexts. *Child Development, 63,* 68–81.

McLoyd, V. C. (1990). The impact of economic hardship on Black families and children: Psychological distress, parenting, and socioemotional development. *Child Development, 61,* 311–346.

Minuchin, P. (1985). Families and individual development: Provocations from the field of family therapy. *Child Development, 56,* 289–302.

Patterson, G. R. (1982). *Coercive family process.* Eugene, OR: Castalia.

Patterson, G. R., & Bank, L. (1989). Some amplifying mechanisms for pathologic processes in families. In M. R. Gunnar & E. Thelan (Eds.), *Systems and development: Minnesota symposium on child psychology, Vol. 22* (pp. 167–210). Hillsdale, NJ: Lawrence Erlbaum Associates.

Patterson, G. R., DeBaryshe, B. D., & Ramsey, E. (1989). A developmental perspective on antisocial behavior. *American Psychologist, 44,* 329–335.

Patterson, G. R., & Stouthamer-Loeber, M. (1984). The correlation of family management practices and delinquency. *Child Development, 55,* 1299–1307.

Plomin, R. (1986). *Development, genetics, and psychology.* Hillsdale, NJ: Lawrence Erlbaum Associates.

Plomin, R., & Daniels, D. (1987). Why are children in the same family so different from each other? *Behavioral and Brain Sciences, 10,* 1–16.

Radloff, L. S., & Teri, L. (1986). Use of the center for epidemiological studies-depression scale with older adults. *Clinical Gerontologist, 5,* 119–136.

Reiss, D., Hetherington, E. M., Plomin, R., Howe, G., Simmens, S. Henderson, S. H., O'Connor, T., Bussell, D., & Anderson, E. (in press). Genetic questions for environmental studies: Differential parenting of siblings and its association with depression and antisocial behavior in adolescents. *Archives of General Psychiatry.*

Reiss, D., Plomin, R., Hetherington, E. M., Howe, G. W., Rovine, M., Tryon, A., & Hagan, M. S. (1994). The separate worlds of teenage siblings: An introduction to the study of the nonshared environment and adolescent development. In E. M. Hetherington, D. Reiss, & R. Plomin (Eds.), *Separate worlds of siblings: The impact of nonshared environment on development* (pp. 63–110). Hillsdale, NJ: Lawrence Erlbaum Associates.

Renouf, A. G., & Harter, S. (1990). Low self-worth and anger as components of the depressive experience in young adolescents. *Development and Psychopathology, 2,* 293–310.

Rovine, M. J. (1994). Estimating non-shared environment using sibling discrepancy scores. In E. M. Hetherington, D. Reiss, & R. Plomin (Eds.), *Separate worlds of siblings: The impact of nonshared environment on development* (pp. 33–62). Hillsdale, NJ: Lawrence Erlbaum Associates.

Rutter, M. (1978). Early sources of security and competence. In J. S. Bruner & A. Garton (Eds.), *Human growth and development* (pp. 33–61). Oxford: Clarendon Press.

Rutter, M. (1987). Psychosocial resilience and protective mechanisms. *American Journal of Orthopsychiatry, 57,* 316–331.

Rutter, M. (1989). Pathways from childhood to adult life. *Journal of Child Psychology and Psychiatry, 30,* 23–51.

Rutter, M. (1990). Psychosocial resilience and protective mechanisms. In J. Rolf, A. S. Masten, D. Cicchetti, K. H. Nuechterlein, & S. Weintraub (Eds.), *Risk and protective factors in the development of psychopathology* (pp. 181–214). New York: Cambridge University Press.

Rutter, M., & Quinton, D. (1987). Parent mental illness as a risk factor for psychiatric disorders in childhood. In D. Magnusson & A. Ohman (Eds.), *Psychopathology: An interaction perspective* (pp. 199–219). Orlando, FL: Academic Press.

Sameroff, A. J., & Seifer, R. (1990). Early contributors to developmental risk. In J. Rolf, A. S. Masten, D. Cicchetti, K. H. Nuechterlein, & S. Weintraub (Eds.), *Risk and protective factors in the development of psychopathology* (pp. 52–66). New York: Cambridge University Press.

Sameroff, A. J., Seifer, R., Barocas, R., Zax, M., & Greenspan, S. (1987). Intelligence quotient scores of 4-year-old children: Social-environmental risk factors. *Pediatrics, 79,* 343–350.

Scheier, M. F., & Carver, C. S. (1985). Optimism, coping, and health: Assessment and implication of generalized outcome expectancies. *Health Psychology, 4,* 219–247.

Simons, R. L., Lorenz, F. O., Conger, R. D., & Wu, C. (1992). Support from spouse as mediator and moderator of the disruptive influence of economic strain on parenting. *Child Development, 63,* 1282–1301.

Straus, M. A. (1979). Measuring intrafamily conflict and violence: The conflict tactics (CT) scales. *Journal of Marriage and the Family, 41,* 75–85.

Tejerina-Allen, M., Wagner, B. M., & Cohen, P. (1994). A comparison of across-family and within-family parenting predictors of adoelscent psychopathology and suicidal ideation. In E. M. Hetherington, D. Reiss, & R. Plomin (Eds.), *Separate social worlds of siblings: Impact of nonshared environment on development* (pp. 143–158). Hillsdale, NJ: Lawrence Erlbaum Associates.

Werner, E. E. (1984). Resilient children. *Young Children, 40,* 68–72.

Willett, J. B. (1987). Questions and answers in the measurement of change. *Review of Research in Education, 15,* 345–422.

Zill, N. (1985). *Behavior problems scales developed from the 1981 Child Health supplement to the National Health Interview Survey.* Washington, DC: Child Trends, Inc.

3

▼▼▼▼▼▼▼

Divorce and Boys' Adjustment Problems: Two Paths With a Single Model

Marion S. Forgatch
Gerald R. Patterson
Judy A. Ray
Oregon Social Learning Center

A significant proportion of boys whose parents divorce display elevated rates of externalizing and antisocial behaviors (Hetherington, 1988; Rutter, Tizard, & Whitmore, 1970; Wallerstein & Kelly, 1980; Peterson & Zill, 1986). Although many investigators have interpreted this to mean that some aspect of divorce causes these problems, two prospective studies implicate conditions present prior to divorce (Block, Block, & Gjerde, 1986; Cherlin et al., 1991). To understand the effects of divorce on children's adjustment, a means must be found for estimating how many children had adjustment problems while their families were intact and how many children developed problems subsequent to separation. Second, it must be determined why some youngsters in each group are negatively affected. To keep this chapter within manageable limits, we focus on externalizing and antisocial problems for boys, even though we know that the range of problem behaviors is wider than this, and girls as well as boys are affected by this process (Hetherington, Cox, & Cox, 1982, 1985; Wallerstein & Kelly, 1980).

A MEDIATIONAL MODEL

All families operate in ever-changing contexts. In the normal course of events, there may be serious or long-term illness, occasional unemployment, economic hardship, and sporadic cycles of stress and depression. Although these episodes may be accompanied by mood shifts or lowered self-esteem for children, a long-standing disorder is not likely to develop as an inevitable outcome. Within

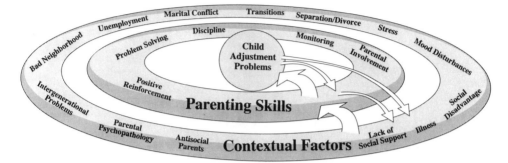

FIG. 3.1.   Parenting skills mediational model.

the parenting skills mediational model displayed in Fig. 3.1, harsh contextual factors place children at risk for adjustment problems only when such contexts interfere with parents' ability to carry out effective family management practices.

Within this model, five parenting skills are identified a priori as crucial to child adjustment (Patterson, 1982). These include *monitoring* children's behavior and supervising their activities, discouraging problem behaviors with effective *discipline*, resolving conflict and managing practical problems with *family problem solving*, support for prosocial behavior with contingent *positive reinforcement*, and *parental involvement* in youngsters' activities. Patterson and his colleagues conducted tests for the status of parenting skills as mechanisms of child adjustment problems in a series of investigations using multimethod, multiagent methodology (Forgatch, 1991; Patterson & Bank, 1989; Patterson, Reid, & Dishion, 1992). These studies have demonstrated that monitoring and discipline account for significant variance in measures of child antisocial behavior for samples of children at varying levels of risk. It is important to note that monitoring and discipline account for current levels of antisocial behavior problems, but measures of problem solving are related to changes in antisocial behavior problems (Forgatch & Ray, 1991).

Of course, these correlational studies do not establish a causal status for parenting practices vis-à-vis child adjustment. Experimental designs are required in which the independent variables are manipulated and changes in these are accompanied by commensurate changes in the dependent variables. Behavioral intervention procedures can be used in random assignment designs to test the causal status of variables such as parenting practices (Forgatch, 1991). It has taken several attempts to achieve an experimental test of the parenting skills model. An early study in this effort was conducted with normal, but mildly noncompliant, preschool children (Forgatch & Toobert, 1979). Mothers were taught to be consistent in the use of time out, a mild disciplinary tactic, with an audiotape that explained the procedure and provided examples of its appropriate and inappropriate use. Noncompliance for the intervention group decreased significantly, whereas control children showed no change. However, data were not collected to show that the amount of improvement in parenting skills was associated with the magnitude of improvement in noncompliance.

To fill this gap, a clinical sample of families with elementary-school-aged children referred for serious antisocial behavior problems was tested before and after treatment. During individual family sessions, parents learned to consistently employ the set of parenting skills described in Patterson and Forgatch (1987) and Forgatch and Patterson (1989). As expected, the greater the changes in parental monitoring and discipline practices, the greater the reductions in antisocial child behavior (Forgatch, 1991). Dishion, Patterson, and Kavanagh (1992) refined the quasi-experimental design in the Forgatch (1991) study with random assignment to groups. The sample consisted of families with middle-school-aged boys and girls at risk for substance abuse. There were four conditions: parent groups teaching parenting skills, adolescent groups teaching social skills, the combination of parent and adolescent skills groups, and self-administered information. The findings supported the parent skills model. Youngsters who showed reductions in antisocial behavior were those whose parents had participated in parent training and had improved their discipline practices. Changes in adolescent social skills did not result in diminished antisocial behavior. The more effective parent discipline was at termination, the greater the reduction in teacher ratings of antisocial behavior. As a group, these studies illustrate how intervention can be used as an experimental manipulation to assess causal relationships. As such, they provide strong support for the parent skills model. Three additional studies are now underway.

Figure 3.1 shows that child adjustment is insulated from contextual variables by parenting practices, but parents are not so insulated. They must struggle with the harsh contexts encompassing the family. Certainly, parents are not absolutely consistent from one day to the next, nor do they treat all members of the family in the same way (Patterson, 1983; Snyder, 1991). We hypothesize that contextual factors such as stress, depression, or family transitions may explain a good portion of this variability. Some mothers become inconsistent and ineffective in their parenting when they are highly stressed or depressed (Beardslee, Bemporad, Keller, & Klerman, 1983; Downey & Coyne, 1990; Forgatch, Patterson, & Skinner, 1988; Longfellow, Zelkowitz, & Saunders, 1982). Others are at risk for disrupted parenting because of their personality traits (e.g., antisocial; Capaldi & Patterson, 1991; Brody, Neubaum, & Forehand, 1988). Such mothers may vacillate between irritable and explosive reactions to their children and general disengagement. Within the mediational model, different contextual variables serve to identify which families are at significant risk for parenting problems. The relationships are probabilistic ones; there is nothing inevitable about them. For example, Wilson (1980) documented the manner in which socially disadvantaged parents living in ghettos protected their children from delinquent activities by redoubling their supervision.

The mediational model postulates bidirectional relationships between parent and child variables. Problematic parenting is expected to produce children with problems, but difficult youngsters are also presumed to be difficult to parent (Hetherington, 1989; Patterson & Bank, 1989; Patterson, Bank, & Stoolmiller, 1990). The general model is a dynamic one in which variables generated by the process can feed back into it and exacerbate the situation. Data presented in a later section demonstrate that children's adjustment problems produced by ineffective parenting practices determine future levels of parent stress, which further disrupts parent practices.

In the discussions that follow, the mediational model is used as a given; what varies is the contextual factor thought to be associated with increased risk for disruption. We make a general case for disrupted parenting skills as direct determinants for boys' externalizing and antisocial behavior problems. Typically, the parents' failure to use effective discipline, monitoring, or problem solving places children at risk. Nevertheless, it is the context in which the family functions that determines when parenting skills will be affected. The implicit assumption is that contextual variables such as maternal depression, social disadvantage, or stress will have an impact on child adjustment only if parenting practices are disrupted. We propose that contextual factors associated with boys' adjustment problems before divorce differ from those associated with boys' adjustment problems that develop after divorce.

In the following section, we provide a brief overview of the demographic characteristics of the samples and the procedures used in testing the divorce models. Then, the parent skills mediational model is outlined. Following that, we review models with contextual variables thought to be relevant for boys who develop problems prior to their parents' separation. The final and major section is a discussion of the contextual variables and parenting practices involved in boys' postseparation adjustment problems.

METHODS

Sample

Oregon Divorce Study (ODS-1).   Subjects were from the Oregon Divorce Study (ODS-1), a passive longitudinal study started in 1984 to test models relevant to separation and divorce.[1] Families were recruited through divorce application records, advertisements in local newspapers, and flyers distributed throughout the community. To be eligible, mothers were required to have separated from a long-term relationship in the prior 3 to 12 months and to have a son between kindergarten (K) and Grade 6. The sample was primarily European American (91%), reflecting the area's ethnic makeup. Multiagent assessment took place three

---

[1]A new sample is currently being assessed in the second phase of the study, which involves an experimental longitudinal study. That sample, which is not included in the present chapter, is ODS-2.

times over a 4-year period. The first assessment (T1) was extensive, including mother, child, and teacher report, as well as observational data in two settings. The second assessment (T2) took place approximately 1 year after T1 and included mother, child, and teacher report data. Approximately 4 years after T1, there was another extensive assessment (T3) with mother, child, and teacher reports, and observational data. At (T1), there were 196 mothers and their sons; 40 of the boys had female siblings. The study's design called for assessing all subject families at T2; there was 97% retention at T2. At T3, the design called for reassessing only 150 families of the original sample; 151 families participated in this assessment. The retention from T1 to T3 was 77%. The strategy used to select the subjects assessed at T3 was affected by practical concerns. Families who lived nearby were chosen first. There were 13 families (6.6%) who refused further participation, 11 families (5.6%) with custody changes, 11 families (5.6%) who had moved from the area, 8 families (4.1%) who could not be located, and 2 families (1%) who were not assessed for miscellaneous reasons. None of the analyses in this chapter employed the full sample of 196. There was only one significant difference for the variables displayed in Table 3.1 between the 45 attrited families and the 151 who were assessed at all three times: Boys in the attrited sample had significantly higher T scores at T1 on the externalizing scale of the teacher-rated Child Behavior Checklist (CBCL; Achenbach & Edelbrock, 1986) (Attrition group $M = 60.17$, $SD = 10.41$; Nonattrited $M = 55.42$, $SD = 9.50$) $F(1, 186 = 7.76, p < .01)$. Although it is impossible to say for certain what effect this condition might have on these analyses, one likely effect is that the estimate of the prevalence of boys with chronic externalizing problems is conservative.

Table 3.1 summarizes the demographic details of the ODS-1 sample that was assessed at T1, T2, and T3, as well as subsamples that are employed in analyses in this chapter. Analyses of variance (ANOVAs) and chi-squares were used to test for differences in the subsamples and significant differences are indicated in Table 3.1.

Younger/Older Subsample.   Families were grouped according to the target boy's grade in school. Younger boys were in kindergarten (K) through Grade 2. Older boys were in Grades 3 through 6. Families with boys in the lower grades differed significantly from the older boys in these variables: The boys were younger, their mothers were younger, and at T3 the younger boys had significantly higher scores on the externalizing scale of the teacher-rated CBCL (Achenbach & Edelbrock, 1986).

Repartnered/Remained Single Subsample.   Families were assigned to these two groups based on whether the mother reported being either remarried or in a live-in intimate relationship at the T3 assessment. Unfortunately, it is not known how many transitions in terms of repartnering may have taken place between T1 and T3, nor how long the mothers had been living with the new

TABLE 3.1
Demographic Characteristics of ODS-1

	n at T3	Boys' age at T1		Mothers' age at T1	
		Range	Mean	Range	Mean
Full Sample	151	5–13	8.6	24–53	33.2
Younger boys	67	5–9	6.7_a	24–46	31.1_c
Older boys	84	6–13	10.1_a	26–53	34.9_c
Repartnered	67	6–12	8.2_b	24–46	32.2_d
Remained single	83	5–13	8.9_b	24–53	34.1_d
Chronic elevated	18	6–12	8.2	25–39	32.4
Never elevated	61	6–13	8.6	24–53	33.2

	Education Levels at T1			
	% Not High School Graduate	% High School Graduate	% Some Post High School	% College Graduate
Full Sample	7.3	19.2	65.0	18.5
Younger boys	9.0	20.9	49.3	20.9
Older boys	6.0	17.9	59.5	16.7
Repartnered	11.9	19.4	52.2	16.4
Remained single	3.6	19.3	57.8	19.3
Chronic elevated	5.6	16.7	66.7	11.1
Never elevated	6.6	19.7	54.1	19.7

	Employment Categories at T1				
	% Unskilled	% Semiskilled	% Clerical	% Med. Business	% Major Business/ Professional
Full Sample	17.2	24.1	11.5	43.2	3.4
Younger boys	15.9	22.7	6.8	50.0	4.5
Older boys	18.6	25.6	16.3	37.2	2.3
Repartnered	22.0	22.0	7.3	46.3	2.4
Remained single	13.3	26.7	15.6	42.2	2.2
Chronic elevated	16.7	41.7	8.3	33.3	0.0
Never elevated	11.1	27.8	13.9	44.4	2.8

	Public Assistance/Unemployment			
	T1 % on P.A.	T3 % on P.A.	T1 % Unemployed	T3 % Unemployed
Full Sample	55.9	57.6	41.6	39.1
Younger boys	52.8	35.8	32.3	41.8
Older boys	58.1	47.6	48.4	36.9
Repartnered	56.9	22.4	37.9	35.8
Remained single	56.0	59.0	45.1	42.2
Chronic elevated	64.7	44.4	33.3	44.4
Never elevated	56.3	42.6	40.0	37.7

(Continued)

TABLE 3.1
(Continued)

| | Family Income | | | | | |
| | T1 | | | T3 | | |
	% Below $10,000	% $10–20,000	% $20,000+	% Below $10,000	% $10–20,000	% $20,000+
Full Sample	66.2	30.4	3.4	38.8	31.3	29.9
Younger boys	62.1	34.8	3.0	30.3	30.3	39.4
Older boys	69.5	26.8	3.7	45.7	32.1	22.2
Repartnered	60.9	37.5	1.6	23.8	23.8	52.4$_c$
Remained single	71.1	24.1	4.8	50.6	37.3	12.0$_c$
Chronic elevated	72.2	27.8	0.0	38.9	44.4	15.7
Never elevated	65.0	30.0	5.0	34.4	32.8	32.8

| | TCBC Externalizing T Scores | | | | | | |
| | | T1 | | T2 | | T3 | |
	n	Mean	SD	Mean	SD	Mean	SD
Full Sample	138	55.3	9.6	56.3	8.8	55.9	11.4
Younger boys	61	54.8	9.6	56.9	8.0	58.4$_h$	10.6
Older boys	77	55.7	8.9	55.8	9.5	53.9$_h$	11.6
Repartnered	62	53.9	9.3	56.3	7.2	56.6	10.6
Remained single	75	56.4	9.8	56.4	10.0	55.3	12.1
Chronic elevated	18	67.4$_f$	4.4	67.4$_g$	4.7	70.4$_i$	5.4
Never elevated	61	48.2$_f$	6.2	50.1$_g$	5.7	47.9$_i$	6.8

Note. Means having the same subscript differ significantly at $p < .05$.

partner. Repartnered families differed significantly from remained single families in that boys and mothers were younger in the repartnered group, and at T3, a greater percentage of mothers who had repartnered were likely to have family incomes of at least $20,000.

Chronically Elevated/Never Elevated Subsample. The chronically elevated sample was made up of those boys who obtained a T score of 60 or more on the externalizing scale of the teacher-rated CBCL (Achenbach & Edelbrock, 1986) at all three assessments. The never-elevated boys were those who never achieved a T score of 60 on that scale at any of the three assessments. There were no other differences between the two groups in terms of Table 3.1 variables.

Oregon Youth Study (OYS). Several sets of analyses in this chapter employed data from the OYS, a long-term longitudinal study designed to test a theory of the development and maintenance of antisocial behavior and delinquency in boys. Families were recruited through schools in high crime-density neighborhoods in a medium-sized metropolitan area (approximately 150,000). There was a 74% participation rate of eligible families, with 98% subject retention over 10 years. At T1 (1984), there were two successive grade cohorts of Grade 4 boys (mean age 10.1, range 9.2 to 11.5), with 102 in the first cohort and 104 in the second. The sample was primarily European American (86%). At least 50% of the families were of working class or low socioeconomic status (SES). The OYS sample and procedures were described more fully in Patterson et al. (1992).

Procedures

Information for ODS-1 and OYS samples, constructs, and analyses presented in this chapter is detailed in the ODS-1 93-11 technical report, obtained by writing Dr. Forgatch. Assessments employed a multiagent, multimethod approach with structured interviews with parent and child, laboratory parent–child problem-solving interactions, home observations, repeated telephone interviews with parent and child, questionnaires from parent and child, and teacher ratings.

Constructs

Constructs were built using a bootstrapping method in which measurement fidelity gradually increases over time (Cronbach & Meehl, 1956; Patterson & Bank, 1986). In practice, several a priori variates were identified for a given construct. Items within each scale were analyzed for internal consistency; scales that produced alphas of less than .6 were excluded, and individual items that generated item-total correlations of less than .2 were dropped. Each indicator represented an aggregate of information, either across items or across behaviors through time. These indicators were required to show convergent validity. Whenever feasible, multiple agents, settings, and methods were used to assess each construct, resulting in several scale (i.e., indicator) scores for each construct.

PRESEPARATION ADJUSTMENT PROBLEMS: CHRONICS

Boys whose parents divorce are at risk for developing problems. Prospective studies suggest that a significant proportion of troubled boys in divorced families developed their problems prior to the separation. For the sake of convenience, this subgroup is labeled *chronic*. Two related questions are addressed in this section: What proportion of boys from separated families fits this chronic status, and what contextual variables are most likely to have been associated with the assumed chronic patterns of disrupted parenting and the concomitant child adjustment problems? Before these issues can be addressed, a method is needed of differentiating families of chronics from those who develop adjustment problems after the separation.

Incidence of Chronics

Cherlin et al. (1991) provided national survey data from Great Britain that identified subsets of intact families and followed them up about 4 years later. There were over 11,000 families available for both the initial assessment when the children were about 7 and again when the children were about 11 years of age. In both assessments, teachers filled out a detailed behavioral assessment, and children were given achievement tests and physical examinations.

During the 4-year interval, there were 239 instances of divorce[2] in first-time marriages. As expected, both parents and teachers perceived the children in the divorced group as showing more adjustment problems than children in intact families. Social class and race were controlled in the analyses. Teachers' ratings identified about 32% more behavior problems for boys in the divorced families. Roughly 12% of these problems were present prior to the divorce. Parents reported 19% more problems for boys in divorced families compared to nondivorced families, but this percentage fell to about 9% after controlling for predivorce problems. Similar comparisons for achievement test scores showed 18% more problems in math after separation; approximately 4% were present beforehand. Reading achievement, on the other hand, could mostly be described as problems existing prior to separation. A second set of findings was based on data from a random sample survey of 1,747 families in the United States. Parents reported 12% more behavior problems for boys in divorced families compared to nondivorced families. About one third of the problems after divorce were viewed by mothers as having been present prior to divorce. In both the Great Britain and the United States datasets, parent ratings corrected for predivorce ratings indicated no difference in problems for boys in divorced and intact families.

The Cherlin et al. (1991) data leave unanswered key questions concerning prevalence of chronic adjustment problems. Means and standard deviations were not given for the measures, and it was not possible to estimate the actual number of children who exceeded some criterion for definition of "problem child." Conservative answers to the prevalence question can be found in studies such as the Ontario Child Health Study (Offord, Boyle, & Racine, 1991). In this carefully crafted investigation, the sample consisted of all of the children born in the Canadian province of Ontario in January 1966 and January 1979. Data from teacher and parent ratings of conduct disorder were combined to identify 7.2% of boys ages 4 through 11 (in urban settings). If about 7% of the boys in the general population can be expected to display conduct problems, then it would be expected that at least that many boys would be found in divorce samples. Offord's sample showed an

---

[2]Separations and legal divorce were both counted as divorce.

odds ratio of 2.2 associated with single-parent status for the occurrence of conduct disorders. This odds ratio leads to the expectation that about 15% of the boys in a divorce sample would be diagnosed as conduct disordered. This is not far off from the teacher-based estimate of a 20% increase in behavior problems (Cherlin et al., 1991). Future studies will no doubt demonstrate that all of these estimates are somewhat off the mark. For example, the prevalence will vary depending on where the threshold value is set and the length of the interval before or after the separation. However, for the present, our best guess is that 15 to 20% of boys from separated families show chronic antisocial problems.

Speculative Models for Boys With Chronic Problems

From the perspective of coercion theory, the chronic problem child develops because inept parenting practices facilitate a rich schedule of reinforcement by family members for coercive and antisocial behaviors (Patterson, 1982; Patterson et al., 1992). Based on several decades of clinical practice in treating families of chronically antisocial boys (see the review in Patterson, Dishion, & Chamberlain, 1993), three primary models are believed to exist. The a priori models are summarized in Fig. 3.2. The parental trait model seems most likely for boys from intact families with chronic problems. Typically, these would be socially disadvantaged families in which one or both of the parents are antisocial. Although the permissive parent model and the disrupter model are believed to occur less frequently among families of boys with chronic problems, no actual data on prevalence for the three models exist.

Parental Traits

We believe social disadvantage and parental antisocial traits often characterize families of chronically antisocial boys.[3] By itself, social disadvantage has been found to be associated with an irritable, commanding, and explosive style of discipline in a number of studies (Bronfenbrenner, 1958; Straus, Gelles, & Steinmetz, 1980). In our own studies, constructs measuring social disadvantage are highly correlated with constructs assessing ineffective discipline practices (Bank, Forgatch, Patterson, & Fetrow, 1993; Bank & Patterson, 1992; Larzelere & Patterson, 1990; Patterson et al., 1992). It is not surprising to find a disproportionate number of antisocial adults who are also socially disadvantaged. Our analyses have shown these two variables to be highly correlated for both mothers and fathers. For example, Patterson and Capaldi (1991) found that a construct assessing parental antisocial behavior (MMPI scales 4 and 9, arrest record, driving license suspension, drug use) and a construct measuring social disadvantage

---

[3]It is also believed that other parental traits are involved (e.g., major adjustment disorders, intense or chronic interparental conflict), but they are not included in this report.

2.a. Parental Trait Model

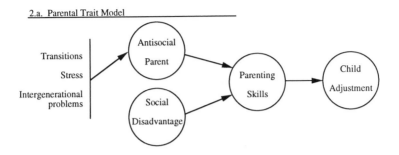

2.b. Permissive Parenting Model

2.c. Disrupted Parenting Model

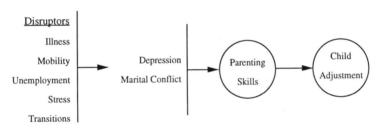

FIG. 3.2.   Three models for chronic adjustment problems.

(education, occupation, and WAIS vocabulary) covaried .33 for mothers and .51 for fathers.

One can well imagine that parents who are socially disadvantaged or antisocial would tend to experience high levels of stress. Poor and poorly educated parents who also lack skills and break society's rules are likely to have lives fraught with stress. According to this model, the effect of stress, social disadvantage, and parental antisocial characteristics on children's antisocial behavior, however, should be mediated through parenting practices. To test this, Patterson and Dishion (1988) conducted structural equation model (SEM) analyses separately for fathers and mothers in the sample of two-parent OYS families (including intact and stepparent families). The hypothesis was that the relationship between parental stress and child antisocial behavior would be doubly mediated, such that stress would impact parental antisocial behavior, which in turn would lead to more ineffective discipline practices, which in turn would impact child antisocial behavior. Stress had the expected relationship with parental antisocial behavior for mothers and fathers, which in turn was associated with ineffective discipline practices, which in turn impacted child antisocial behavior. However, in the model for mothers, there was also a direct path from maternal antisocial behavior to child antisocial behavior.

Patterson and Dishion (1988) also examined the relative contribution of social disadvantage, parent antisocial, and parent depression to irritable discipline practices for the two-parent OYS sample. Multiple regression analyses by parents were performed separately. For mothers, the standard partial betas reflected significant effects on irritable discipline for the maternal antisocial trait (.29) and social disadvantage (.17), with a multiple correlation of .43 ($p < .001$). For fathers, the standard partial betas also were significant for the paternal antisocial trait (.24) and social disadvantage (.40), with a multiple correlation of .50 ($p < .001$). The relative contribution of social disadvantage was the stronger of the two variables for fathers. Depression did not have a significant effect in the models for either parent. It is likely, then, that social disadvantage and antisocial parental traits each make significant and unique contributions to the understanding of disrupted discipline.

There appears to be a group of antisocial parents who are not socially disadvantaged, but are nevertheless at serious risk for having sons with chronic problems. Offord et al. (1991) showed in a simple bivariate analysis that parent arrests contributed significantly to conduct disorders. When multiple variables were considered, however, it was the interaction between arrests and income that made the significant contribution. It was only in high-income families that parental arrests contributed to increased risk for conduct disorders. That study did not assess the parenting practices of these antisocial parents.

As suggested in Fig. 3.2a, variables such as repeated family transitions (i.e., divorce, remarriage) and intergenerational parenting problems are presumed to covary with risk for child adjustment problems. The contribution, however, has been found to be mediated by the parent trait for antisocial behavior for transitions (Capaldi & Patterson, 1991), and for intergenerational effects (Patterson & Dishion, 1988). In each of these cases, the relationship between the parent's antisocial behavior and the child's was mediated by problematic parenting practices.

In an analysis of the OYS, Capaldi and Patterson (1991) demonstrated a linear relationship between the number of marital transitions and adjustment problems for boys (controlling for SES), with boys in intact families experiencing the least number of problems. They also found that a measure of maternal antisocial characteristics was related in a linear fashion to repeated marital transitions, but neither maternal antisocial behavior nor marital transitions had a direct effect on child adjustment when a measure of parenting was included in the model. The relationship was mediated by parental involvement, which included both monitoring and parental participation in child-oriented activities. To determine the precise relationship between maternal antisocial behavior and disrupted parenting in the course of marital transitions, Patterson and Capaldi (1991) conducted a longitudinal analysis of the OYS data set. They showed that of the 24 families involved in a marital transition over a 2-year interval, the majority had antisocial mothers. In keeping with the chronic formulation, the mothers involved in the transitions were characterized by ineffective discipline practices prior to the transition. Monitoring practices declined following the transition.

Permissive Parents

We have carried out no systematic studies of permissive parents, but they have appeared with some regularity in clinical interventions. At one level, these parents give the appearance of unconditional positive regard: No matter what the child does, the parents are warm and accepting. They do not set limits, have few house rules, tend not to monitor their children's whereabouts, and set only occasional sanctions for problem behaviors that cannot be ignored. For some families, this style of parenting is the outcome of carefully considered philosophical positions reminiscent of Rousseau or Carl Rogers. For others, it reflects a lifestyle in which parents are more involved with their own personal states than with childrearing. They find it easier to be accepting and noncontingent than to confront problems and undergo the difficult process of change.

Baumrind (1991) was one of the first to systematically investigate a sample that included such families. Her longitudinal study of middle-class families showed that boys of permissive parents did not differ much from those from authoritarian parents at preschool. At age 9, however, four of the five boys in her sample who had permissive parents tended to be marginal in their adjustment. Given the tiny sample, the findings must be viewed with caution.

Olweus (1980) provided a more comprehensive test for the contribution of permissive parenting to child problem behavior. He used peer nomination data to define antisocial behavior in a sample of 76 boys in Grade 6. Interviews with the parents provided an account of parenting practices. The panel analyses showed a path coefficient of .36 from permissive parenting to child aggression, even after controlling for child temperament, parent power assertion, and maternal negativism. A lax parenting style was significantly associated with greater aggression. A similar effect was obtained for a sample of boys in Grade 9. The Olweus (1980) findings demonstrate that the relationship of permissive parenting to adjustment problems is based on more than just clinical experience. His panel analyses also show that whatever is meant by permissive, it can, in fact, be measured.

Disrupted Parenting

Both research literature and our clinical experience led us to expect the model depicted in Fig. 3.2c to be an easy one to demonstrate. It was surprising, therefore, to find that samples of intact families could not be used to replicate earlier findings (Forgatch et al., 1988), in which the effect of stress on child adjustment was mediated through parental discipline. No matter how hard we tried, no definition of stress for intact families would serve in this role. Consequently, it was more than a little pleasing to learn that Conger (1991) had found a resolution for this problem. In his longitudinal study of intact Iowa families, he had also failed to find a direct correlation between deterioration in economic conditions and disrupted parenting for adolescents. Nevertheless, he went on to demonstrate that the mediating variable that covaried significantly with stress and parenting practices was parental depression.

In an effort to replicate these findings, Patterson (1991) examined the data collected at Grades 4 and 6 in the OYS. During this interval, a drop in income or the advent of a serious illness was found to function as a stressor analogous to those in the Iowa study. The data for OYS intact families showed that a stress risk score covaried significantly with a construct defining parental depression. The findings for the structural equation model are summarized in Fig. 3.3.

The nonsignificant chi-square indicated an acceptable fit of the data to the a priori model postulated by the Iowa researchers. The outcome was consistent with the idea that, under certain conditions, stressors from outside the family would lead to disrupted child adjustment. There was a powerful relation between increased maternal depression and disrupted discipline, which in turn placed the child at risk for adjustment problems (academic failure, antisocial behavior, and peer rejection). Conger, Patterson, and Ge (1995) extended this analysis to demonstrate across-site replications of the stress mediational model for both mothers and fathers.

Although it is not known how prevalent the disruption model is for intact families, in the section that follows, it is demonstrated that the disruption model plays a central role in understanding the postseparation/divorce process.

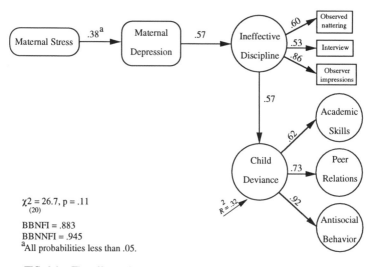

$\chi 2 = 26.7, p = .11$
(20)

BBNFI = .883
BBNNFI = .945
[a]All probabilities less than .05.

FIG. 3.3. The effects of maternal stress on child deviancy: two mediators.

INCIDENCE OF POSTSEPARATION ADJUSTMENT PROBLEMS

Based on the earlier discussion, it seems that a sizable proportion of the boys in a sample of separated and divorced families can be expected to show behavior problems. In our longitudinal analyses, mother reports of child behavior problems were excluded because of concern about introducing systematic bias. Ratings from more distressed mothers (socially disadvantaged, depressed, or clinical samples) have been found to be less likely to converge with ratings made by teachers, observers, or criteria obtained from official records (e.g., the review by Patterson et al., 1993). A significant proportion of the ODS-1 mothers reported experiencing high levels of depressed mood at T1, with diminishing levels over the course of the study (Patterson & Forgatch, 1990). For middle-class families, comparable mother and teacher ratings of child behavior had correlations that were moderate and significant. Other studies reviewed in that report showed that false-positive errors made by mothers in at-risk samples correlated with maternal depression (Patterson, Duncan, Reid, & Bank, 1993). Therefore, teacher ratings were employed when testing levels of child adjustment over time.

In the ODS-1, teachers' ratings on the Child Behavior Checklist (CBCL) (Achenbach & Edelbrock, 1986) were collected within the first year following separation (T1), 12 months later (T2), and approximately 36 months later (T3).[4] The first question addressed was how many boys would be identified with externalizing behavior problems. Problem status was defined by a T score of 60 or above on the externalizing scale of the CBCL. Given this definition, approximately one third of the boys demonstrated problem status at any one of the three assessments. This is very close to the value of 32% of teacher-rated problems described by Cherlin et al. (1991). It is also close to the figure from Zill's (1978) national probability sample, in which 30% of boys in single-mother families were reported as fighting at school in the last week.

Next, a sample of boys with chronic externalizing problems was identified. This status was defined by T scores at or over 60 at each of the assessments; 13% of the boys achieved this status. This may be an underestimate for chronic boys, because a number of the families who dropped out of the study by T3 had boys with elevated scores at T1. However, it is intriguing to note that the figure closely matches the results from teacher ratings in the Cherlin et al. (1991) study, in which 20% of the increased problem behaviors in the divorced sample were present prior to the separation. It also compares well with the 15% of boys with conduct problems in the subsample of single mothers in Offord et al.'s (1991) study.

The questions addressed in the next section concern the explanation for why about 15% of boys will display an increase in antisocial behavior following the separation process. It is assumed that most of these late starters will not be chronic;

---

[4]Teachers were different at each time point.

rather the problems are transient in nature. The study began by testing the possibility that younger boys were differentially at risk for adjustment problems than older boys.

Risk as a Function of Age

There has been some controversy concerning the relevance of children's age at the time of separation to subsequent problems (see Emery, 1982). To test this hypothesis of differential risk, two age groups in the ODS-1 were identified based on their grade in school. "Younger" boys were in the early stages of school (K–2), and "older" boys were in Grades 3 through 6. Again, the data were based on the externalizing scale of teacher-rated CBCL obtained at T1, T2, and T3. Figure 3.4 displays the mean T scores of externalizing behavior for the boys in these groups at each assessment.

At the start of the study, both the older and younger boys were elevated about half a standard deviation on externalizing behavior. During the ensuing 12 months (T1 to T2), there was a slight increase in level for the younger group. It was between 1 and 4 years after the separation that the differentiation became apparent. As perceived by teachers, older boys in separated families became somewhat less externalizing, but younger boys continued their unfortunate growth. The rate of growth for younger boys seems to have been a constant that held through the 4-year interval.

A repeated measures ANOVA revealed a group by time interaction, $F(2, 118) = 7.78$, $p = .006$, indicating that these two trends were distinct. Although the findings strongly supported the hypothesis that the separation process adversely affected younger boys but not older boys, the analysis leaves unanswered the question of whether the contribution of age is manifest only after the second assessment, or whether it is operative throughout the time interval. A latent growth curve (LGC) analysis (McArdle & Epstein, 1987; Tisak & Meredith, 1990) was used to examine not only this hypothesis, but also the possibility that the growth for younger boys was nonlinear. Because latent growth analysis requires the use of nonstandardized scores, a modified externalizing scale was constructed by removing eight items that did not appear to measure externalizing problems, and then taking the mean of the remaining items. Age at time of separation was used as the predictor for the intraindividual growth curves. The first step in the analysis involved developing a model to describe the form of growth of externalizing behavior. A three-factor model (i.e., average level, linear growth, and quadratic effects) provided the best fit.[5] The next step in the analysis was to add the predictor variable, age.

---

[5]A single-factor growth model (which can be viewed as nested within two- or three-factor models) is the most parsimonious solution and is therefore preferred. However, a single-factor model requires that there be no change in rank order of observations over time (except due to measurement error) and that growth rate and initial status be perfectly correlated and strictly proportional (Tisak & Meredith, 1990).

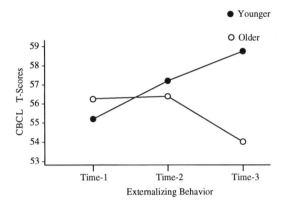

FIG. 3.4.   Changing levels of teacher-rated externalizing behavior.

As can be seen in Fig. 3.5, the nonsignificant chi-square indicated that the model fit the data. The main question addressed by the analysis concerned the extent to which age at separation would account for individual differences in growth of externalizing behavior over time. As shown, age was not related to either the average level or quadratric trends in the data for externalizing behavior. Age did predict intraindividual patterns of linear change in externalizing behavior over the ensuing 4 years. The highly significant path coefficient (–.46) accounted for 21% of the variance in linear changes in level, evidence that younger age was associated with increasing problems over time.

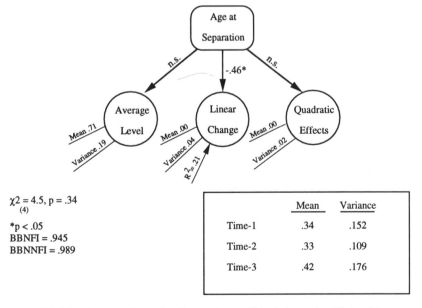

FIG. 3.5.   Age as predictor of teacher-rated externalizing behavior (modified scale).

These two analyses suggest that younger boys were more vulnerable to growth in problem behaviors in the separation and divorce process. These findings are useful because they focus the investigator's attention on another critical question: Under what conditions are young boys in recently separated families at risk for developing adjustment problems? In the sections that follow, the most promising alternatives, the stress-depression models, the repartnering model, and the social disadvantage and maternal antisocial models are explored.

POSTSEPARATION: THE STRESS/DEPRESSION MODELS

Many studies of divorce have emphasized the fact that single parents experienced very high levels of stress, which in turn correlated with diminished parenting (Forgatch et al., 1988; Hess & Camara, 1979; Hetherington, Cox, & Cox, 1979, 1982, 1985; Wallerstein & Kelly, 1980). Forgatch et al. (1988) showed that recently separated single mothers experienced significantly more major life event stressors and almost twice the number of daily hassles as did mothers from intact families. One of the prime stressors reported by mothers in the ODS-1 was the dramatic drop in income. This source of stress has also been reported in the data from a national representative sample by Duncan and Hoffman (1985). They found that separation or divorce was accompanied by significant drops in income and that remarriage improved women's financial situation to levels roughly equivalent to those who remained married.

As noted earlier, stressors were included as a component in a disrupter model thought to be associated with a small but significant number of two-parent families of boys with chronic adjustment problems. For postseparation models, the disrupter model is thought to play a major role. The key difference in the disrupter model for the two types of families would be in the higher levels of stress experienced by the single mothers as compared to mothers in intact families. One apparent effect of this difference is that for single mothers, stress relates directly to disrupted parenting. The Conger et al. (1995) study pointed to the importance of introducing depression as a mediating construct for intact families. It may be that stress and depression operate in functionally distinct manners in single-mother and two-parent families.

Stress and Parenting Practices

Patterson (1982) conducted a series of extended baseline home observation studies with six mother–preschooler dyads. On days that mothers reported high levels of stress, they were also observed to be highly irritable. These studies of microprocesses generated the hypothesis that high levels of stress are directly related to disruptions in discipline practices and that these, in turn, are related to children's adjustment problems. The two modeling studies discussed here directly tested this hypothesis using data from single-mother families. In both studies, maternal discipline was the mediating parent skill for measures of antisocial child behavior. Both studies employed multiagent methods with families of young boys.

In a SEM analysis of the ODS-1 sample, Forgatch et al. (1988) compared two competing models assessing stress effects on the younger sample of boys (K–2). Maternal stress was defined by self-report, discipline was based on observations in the home, and child antisocial behavior was a multiagent construct employing mother, child, and teacher reports. In the fully mediated model, it was hypothesized that the relationship between maternal stress and child antisocial behavior would be mediated by ineffective discipline. In this analysis, the chi-square indicated an adequate fit between the model and the data, and 27% of the variance in child antisocial behavior was explained by ineffective discipline practices. Only 17% of the variance in discipline was accounted for by stress, suggesting that other factors were involved in disrupting this aspect of parenting. Efforts to develop a similar model for single-parent families of older boys were not successful.

Snyder (1991) replicated these findings using EQS (Bentler, 1989) with a sample of preschool boys with conduct problems and their disadvantaged single mothers. In this meticulously designed study, Snyder tested models similar to those described in the preceding study, adding a direct path from maternal distress to child conduct problems. The distress measure was based on maternal self-report, discipline was observation based, and the measure of conduct problems combined observations and daily maternal report. The chi-squares indicated that the model fit the data. In the mediated model, maternal distress (mood and stress) accounted for 57% of the variance in discipline, and maternal discipline in turn accounted for 66% of the variance in the daily fluctuations of conduct problems displayed by the boys. A powerful component of Snyder's study was his use of a within subject, time series approach to study process. Each subject was assessed 10 to 15 times within a 1-month period. The analyses showed that daily fluctuations in maternal stress and negative mood states were accompanied by more ineffective discipline practices. Snyder interpreted the findings as underscoring the importance of the accumulation of "seemingly minute, temporally fleeting but frequent events" (p. 274) on the long-term development and maintenance of child conduct problems.

Both sets of findings offer solid support for the hypothesis that stress may disrupt discipline practices and that this disruption leads to child adjustment problems. In a separate section, we examine the possibility that child adjustment problems contribute to both immediate and future levels of maternal stress. The implication is that the stress-discipline mediational model may be a key component in a feedback loop that keeps some single-parent families in a state of chronic stress.

Effects of Depressed Mood

It seems reasonable to believe that a model that includes not only mother's stress, but also her reactions to it, would provide an easily generalized base for tracing out the effects of single parenting. The Snyder (1991) study obtained considerable power by building a construct that contained both stress and distress. Perhaps a more general stress-depression model would also relate to a wider variety of parenting skills than just discipline practices. The primary concern in this study of divorce is with the question of how things change over time for the mother and boy. Could a stress-depression model explain how parenting skills change over time?

Forgatch and Stoolmiller (1991) used the ODS-1 sample to test for the long-term effects of changes in maternal depressed mood on changes in harsh discipline and changes in uninvolved monitoring. A replication design was employed that permitted a comparison between the ODS-1 sample and the OYS sample of at-risk intact families. With the use of LGC modeling (Tisak & Meredith, 1990), the covariations of changes occurring over a 4-year interval between maternal depressed mood and each of the two parenting skills were examined.

The construct measuring depressed mood was based entirely on mothers' self-report using the CES-D (Radloff, 1977) and ratings collected by repeated telephone interviews for both samples. Diary mood ratings were included in the ODS-1 sample as well. Harsh discipline and uninvolved monitoring were based on maternal self-report and ratings made by interviewers following interviews with mothers. In the ODS-1, mood assessments were obtained at T1, T2, and T3, and harsh discipline and uninvolved monitoring were assessed at T1 and T3. In the OYS, assessments for all constructs were obtained three times, every other year when boys were in Grades 4, 6, and 8. The model and findings are summarized in Fig. 3.6. The model was tested for the full ODS-1 sample and the subset of 65 families in the OYS in which boys were living with both biological parents at each assessment. Data in the figure are organized such that the top number represents ODS-1 findings and the bottom number reflects findings for the OYS intact families.

In examining changes over time, it is possible to study the contributions to intercept (initial level) as well as both linear and nonlinear changes in slope. However, given that the estimates of slope and intercept are highly correlated (see footnote 5), it is possible to use the single-parameter model summarized in Fig. 3.6. The first set of questions concerned changes in mean levels for the constructs. Because the measures of depressed mood were not exactly the same for the two samples, it was not possible to directly compare mean levels in changes. It can be seen, however, that the pattern of change was somewhat dissimilar for the two samples. Maternal depressed mood diminished over time for the sample of single mothers, but there were nonsignificant variations for the mothers in intact families. In order to provide a more exact comparison between the two samples, a repeated measures ANOVA was conducted using the CES-D measure at the three times. The data are presented in Table 3.2. The interaction term for the linear trend in CES-D scores for the two groups was highly significant, $F(1, 204) = 12.68$, $p < .001$. The ODS-1 mothers decreased in depression level more rapidly and steadily than the OYS intact sample.

Harsh discipline showed nonsignificant increases over time for single mothers, but there were significant decreases for mothers of boys from intact families. In both samples, the parents showed less monitoring as the boys grew older.

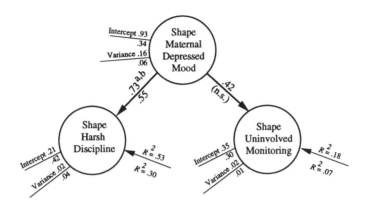

Oregon Divorce Sample
$\chi^2_{(19)} = 24.49$, p = .18

BBNFI = .889
BBNNFI = .970

Oregon Youth Sample: Intact Families
$\chi^2_{(35)} = 48.71$, p = .06

BBNFI = .623
BBNNFI = .849

Maternal Depressed Mood

	Oregon Divorce Sample		Oregon Youth Study Intact Families	
	Mean	Variance	Mean	Variance
Time-1	.94	.28	.33	.15
Time-2	.84	.26	.42	.20
Time-3	.70	.20	.31	.17

Harsh Discipline

	Oregon Divorce Sample		Oregon Youth Study Intact Families	
	Mean	Variance	Mean	Variance
Time-1	.52	.07	.60	.13
Time-2	—	—	.52	.09
Time-3	.56	.09	.42	.13

Uninvolved Monitoring

	Oregon Divorce Sample		Oregon Youth Study Intact Families	
	Mean	Variance	Mean	Variance
Time-1	.50	.05	.32	.08
Time-2	—	—	.51	.06
Time-3	.66	.09	.53	.06

[a] Numbers on top represent Oregon Divorce Sample ($n = 141$); numbers below represent Oregon Youth Study, Intact Family ($n = 65$) scores.

[b] All probabilities less than .05 unless otherwise noted.

FIG. 3.6. Covariations in changes in maternal depressed mood and parenting practices (for two samples; from Forgatch & Stoolmiller, 1991).

TABLE 3.2
CESD Scores for Two Samples

	Mean	SD
ODS (*n* = 141)		
CESD T1	18.84	11.64
CESD T2	15.74	11.52
CESD T3	13.11	8.68
LO intact (*n* = 65)		
CESD T1	9.45	7.48
CESD T2	10.23	6.97
CESD T3	9.26	7.22

The key test of the model concerned the extent to which changes in maternal depressed mood covaried with changes in the two parenting practices at issue. For both samples, the path from depressed mood was substantial and significant for changes in discipline; the path coefficient for the single-mother sample was .73; for mothers of intact families it was .55. As depressed mood increased, discipline practices became harsher. For the single-mother sample, increases in depression covaried with moderate and significant increases in uninvolved monitoring. The comparable path for the mothers in intact families, however, was nonsignificant.

One of the advantages of the LGC analysis is that it enables a test of association of individual differences in changes for independent and dependent variables. The findings here implicate increases in mood disturbance in a pattern of chronically poor parenting. The generalizability of the depressed mood and parenting model must be considered somewhat questionable, however, because maternal self-report data were included as indicators for each of the three constructs. To provide a more conservative test of the relation between depressed mood and maternal discipline practices, Forgatch and Stoolmiller (1991) employed observational data from distinct settings in the ODS-1 sample. In this case, if a relationship between mothers' mood and discipline practices were to be found, it would not reflect distortion inherent in self-report bias. Mothers were observed in two problem-solving settings, one with their child and one with their confidant. Significant levels of sad affect observed in mothers at T1 in problem-solving interactions with their confidants predicted increasing levels of hostile and aversive styles while discussing conflict topics with their sons over a 4-year interval. The path coefficient from T1 sad affect to the measure of changes observed in discipline from T1 to T3 was significant, but modest (.22).

Snyder (1991) showed that maternal distress covaried on a day-by-day basis with discipline practices. Forgatch and Stoolmiller (1991) showed that depressed mood covaried with disrupted discipline over a 4-year period and that sad affect predicted deterioration in discipline practices over the same time interval. Taken together, these studies provide evidence that mood disruptions, which frequently accompany high stress, are an important contextual factor for disrupted parenting practices.

Stress: Maintenance and Future Levels

It seems that the management of stress and accompanying mood disturbances may be one of the key components that determines child adjustment outcomes through their influence on discipline and monitoring practices. In a section that follows, a condition (repartnering) that produces dramatic reductions in some types of stress levels is examined. In the present discussion, the concern is with a variable that has repeatedly been found to be associated with maintenance and future increases in stress: child deviancy. In the preceding discussion and in the discussion that follows, items describing conflict with the child and other family members have been eliminated from the measures of stress to provide a conservative test of the models.

Parenting skills may ameliorate the effect of stressful circumstances on children's adjustment, but difficult children present a challenge for the best of parents in the best of circumstances. This bidirectional relation between child adjustment and parenting is indicated in Fig. 3.1. Furthermore, child maladjustment is thought to make a direct contribution to parental stress. There is now a series of findings lending support to this idea.

In the analyses of ODS-1 by Forgatch et al. (1988) described previously, the effect of stress on child adjustment seemed to be both indirect (mediated through discipline) and direct. The fact that there was a modest but significant covariation between stress and adjustment, even after the discipline mediator was partialled out, posed a conceptual problem. Patterson and Forgatch (1990) clarified the situation in a subsequent analysis of the same sample. They demonstrated modest support for the contribution of antisocial child behavior problems to maternal stress 1 year later.

Neither of the preceding analyses was specifically designed to test for the effects of a broad measure of child deviancy on later levels of stress. An analysis was designed that would directly address several key issues. First, would measures of child adjustment significantly predict later measures of maternal stress? If so, then would this contribution remain significant even after the prior levels of stress were partialled out? An SEM analysis was conducted to assess the strength of T1 stress and T1 child adjustment problems in predicting stress 4 years later. The findings are shown in Fig. 3.7.

The measure of Child Adjustment Problems was a second-order factor defined by four multiagent indicators that were themselves latent constructs: antisocial behavior, depressed mood, academic skills, and peer relationships. Maternal Stress at T1 was defined as a latent construct based on three self-report indicators: daily hassles, life events, and financial problems. In an effort to reduce problems of shared method variance, the stress indicators at T3 were mismatched for T1 and reports provided by agents other than the mother were added.

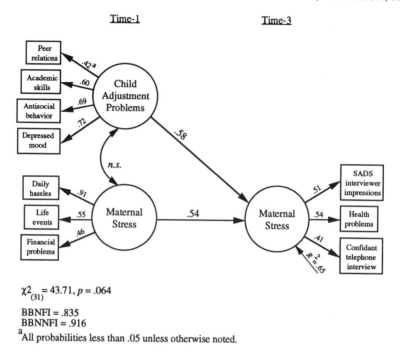

$\chi^2_{(31)} = 43.71, p = .064$

BBNFI = .835
BBNNFI = .916
[a] All probabilities less than .05 unless otherwise noted.

FIG. 3.7.   Predicting maternal stress.

The nonsignificant chi-square showed an adequate fit of the data to the a priori model. The hypothesis tested was that Child Adjustment Problems would predict later levels of maternal stress. The highly significant path coefficient of .58 provided support for this hypothesis. T1 levels of child adjustment predicted later levels of stress even after T1 levels of stress were partialled out. Given the conservative manner in which definitions of stress excluded conflict with family members, the findings can be said to provide a strong test for the model. Maternal stressors may be increased by struggles with the problem child.

POSTSEPARATION: THE REPARTNERING MODEL

In the first year or two following separation, the ODS-1 data showed continued and significant reductions in various kinds of stressors (Patterson & Forgatch, 1990). As might be expected, the reductions in stress seemed to be accompanied by reductions in maternal depression. This naturally led to a search for "coping" techniques that might be associated with the reductions in stress. The search led to paradoxical findings. On the one hand, one of the most effective means for reducing stress was to repartner. However, on the other hand, the process of repartnering exposes the child to new risks for adjustment problems that may not be related to stress per se.

Changing Stress Levels

In keeping with findings of other investigators (e.g., Bloom, Asher, & White, 1978; Hetherington et al., 1979, 1982, 1985; Wallerstein & Kelly, 1980), we expected to find diminishing stress levels over time for the ODS-1 sample as a whole. Self-report data were collected at T1, T2, and T3 for negative life events (Sarason, Johnson, & Siegel, 1978), daily hassles (Patterson, 1982), and financial problems (Fetrow, Dishion, & Viken, 1987). Figure 3.8 displays the levels of each measure over the 4-year period for the two subsamples, mothers who repartnered by T3 and mothers who remained single.

Repeated measures ANOVAs were conducted for each measure of stress. There were significant main effects for time for each type of stress, indicating abated stress for the whole sample over time. There were significant main effects for groups for finances and family events, signifying that mothers in the repartnered group were reporting lower levels of stress in general than mothers who remained single. There was a trend ($p = .08$) for a similar group effect with respect to negative life events. Because repartnering might provide its own set of problems, it was not certain whether it would lead to differential reductions for the two groups in terms of family events or negative life events. The group-by-time interaction term was marginally significant ($p = .09$) for family events and was not significant for negative life events.

In a national representative sample, Duncan and Hoffman (1985) found that separation or divorce was accompanied by significant drops in income and that

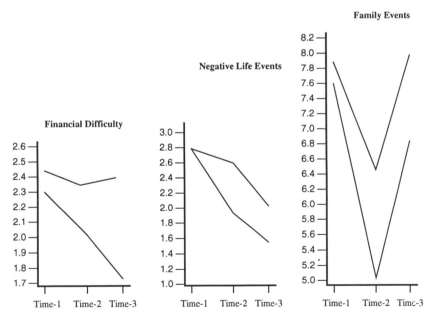

FIG. 3.8.   Changes in stressors for repartnered and for remained-single mothers.

remarriage improved women's financial situation to levels similar to those who remained married. The financial problems of repartnered mothers were expected to show considerable improvement relative to their counterparts who remained single. In Fig. 3.8, the significant interaction term for group-by-time for the financial difficulty variable supported this hypothesis.

The findings suggest that one way to reduce stress would be to join forces with a new partner. In line with Bumpass and Sweet's (1989) position that "cohabitation may represent a clearer transition in intimate relationships than marriage—at least it marks the establishment of a joint household" (p. 615), the focus centered on repartnering (cohabitation) in the ODS-1 sample. In the section that follows, we evaluate a series of hypotheses about those who repartner, the impact of repartnering on levels of stress and child adjustment, and the salient aspects of the parent skills model when mothers repartner or remain single.

Who Is Likely to Repartner?

European American women have a much higher likelihood of remarriage than African American or Hispanic women (Bumpass, Sweet, & Castro-Martin, 1990; Duncan & Hoffman, 1985). Because more than 90% of our sample was European American, predictions were based on data from similar samples. According to rates measured in two current population surveys for 5-year intervals (1975–1980; 1980–1985), 75% of European American women eventually remarry (Bumpass et al., 1990). Twenty-five percent of these do so within about 3 years of separation. Of women who remarry, about 50% of those with one or two children do so within 7 years of separation. In the ODS-1 sample, approximately 40% were repartnered at 4 to 5 years following separation. The fact that the mothers' repartnering patterns were similar to data from the representative samples suggests our crude measure of repartnering was within reasonable bounds.

Other investigators have identified mothers' age, number of children, and mothers' education levels as predictors of repartnering (see review by Bumpass et al., 1990). Nine possible predictors of repartnering, including some that were based on our own hunches, were selected: mothers' age at separation, boys' age, number of children, mother's education, maternal depression at T1, maternal antisocial characteristics, child adjustment at T1, maternal discipline, and mother–child problem-solving outcome at T1. The first two variables were so highly correlated that removal of one became imperative, so boys' age was eliminated. Eight variables were then entered into a stepwise discriminant function analysis; variables that did not make a significant contribution were eliminated. Child adjustment, maternal antisocial qualities, and maternal discipline were eliminated. A single function containing five variables was formed. The findings are summarized in Table 3.3. The first column displays the standardized discriminant function coefficients; the second column describes the extent to which these variables correlated with the function. In descending order of importance to repartnering were: good outcome in problem solving between mother and child,

TABLE 3.3
Discriminant Function Coefficients Predicting Repartnering Status

	Standardized df Coefficients	Correlation Within the Function
Problem-solving outcome	.566	−.277
Number of children	−.519	.371
T1 maternal depression	−.494	.505
Mother's age at separation	−.425	.542
Mother's education	−.389	.441

fewer children, low maternal depression, lower age at separation, and lower education level.

Younger age at separation for women has been identified as "the most important individual characteristic with respect to remarriage rates" (Bumpass et al., 1990, p. 751). Consistent with Bumpass, this study's variable showed the highest correlation within the function. Teachman and Heckart (1985) found no effect for number of children; Bumpass et al. (1990) found women with children to be much less likely to remarry, especially if they had three or more. In this sample, as in the Bumpass et al. study, fewer children was relevant to repartnering. Mothers' education level was negatively associated with remarriage in the Teachman and Heckart (1985) study, but Bumpass et al. (1990) found no effect. In this sample, it had a modest negative relationship to repartnering.

The average function scores for the repartnered group and the remained-single group were .371 and −.290, respectively. Although the Wilks' Lambda F statistic of 3.06 was significant ($p = .01$), the canonical correlation of .313 suggested that the contribution of this array of variables was quite modest. The marginality was also reflected in the fact that the function successfully classified only 62.4% of the cases.

The effort to predict repartnered status was only partially successful. This may be due to the fact that the time interval was too restricted, or the measure was weak. If one accepts the Bumpass et al. (1990) finding of 75% remarriage, the finding of 40% repartnered in the ODS-1 sample indicates that a little more than half of the women who were likely to repartner had done so. Another 3-year follow-up might pick up many of the false positive errors in these prediction tables. As things now stand, it seems that younger, less educated, nondepressed mothers with smaller families and good problem-solving skills are better prospects for repartnering during the first 4 years of separation.

Repartnered Status and Child Adjustment

The literature is quite consistent in showing transitions to be related to increased problems for children (Bray, 1988; Brody et al., 1988; Capaldi & Patterson, 1991; Forgatch & Ray, 1991; Hetherington & Clingempeel, 1992). Studies suggest that the impact of transitions on children may be spurious: Transitions are correlated with parent antisocial traits, which interfere with parenting practices, which in turn affect child adjustment problems (Capaldi & Patterson, 1991). In two independent samples of single mothers, Bank et al. (1993) found antisocial parent characteristics to relate to children's antisocial behavior to the extent that they influenced parenting practices. Another explanation for the troubling influence of transitions is the need for families to adjust to the changes that accompany the introduction of a new parent figure. Hetherington (1988, 1989) and her colleagues studied the entry of stepfathers into the family and then compared the adjustment of children in stepfather and two-biological parent families. The findings were mixed. With a middle-class sample of young children, Hetherington (1988, 1989) found that bringing a stepparent into the family was associated with increased problems for boys at first. However, 2 years later, the children's adjustment improved. In a second study of remarriage with adolescent youngsters, there were more adjustment problems for the children in stepfather compared to intact families both shortly after remarriage and more than 2 years later (Hetherington & Clingempeel, 1992). These findings implicate the age of the children at the time of repartnering as an important factor.

In this study's data, boys of mothers who repartnered showed significant increases in externalizing behaviors compared to boys whose mothers remained single 5 years following marital separation. Forgatch and Ray (1991) assessed externalizing behaviors from the Child Behavior Checklist (CBCL; Achenbach & Edelbrock, 1986) as rated by teachers using all but eight of the items from the externalizing scale. This measure was employed at T1, T2, and T3 in a repeated measures two-way ANOVA for boys in the repartnered and remained single groups. The findings are displayed in Fig. 3.9.

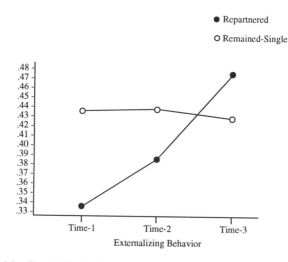

FIG. 3.9.   Changing levels of teacher-rated externalizing behavior (modified scale).

There was a significant interaction term, which indicated that boys in repart-nered families displayed greater growth in externalizing problems than boys living with mothers who remained single. Boys whose mothers would later repartner had somewhat lower levels of externalizing behavior at T1, $F(1, 143) = 2.86$, $p = .09$. This suggests that something in the repartnering process itself produced the negative outcome. The ODS-1 dataset did not have information about duration of repartnered status, and therefore did not allow for a test of the effect of the new partner's time in the family. However, it was possible to conduct a test for differences in repartnering effects based on the boys' ages.

As noted earlier, mothers with younger boys were more likely to repartner and younger boys were more likely than older boys to show increasing levels of teacher-rated externalizing behaviors. These two findings suggested an interaction. To test for this effect, the boys were separated into four subsets—the younger and older groups, and families in which mothers had repartnered or remained single—and we conducted a chi-square analysis. By T3, 54% of the mothers of younger boys had repartnered, and only 37% of the mothers of older boys had done so. The chi-square was significant ($p = .045$). The age-by-repartnering relationship was further explored by conducting separate repeated-measures ANOVAs for the younger and older boys. Repartnering status had no effect on adjustment for older boys. For younger boys, however, there was a marginal effect for group ($p = .09$); boys whose mothers repartnered showed somewhat higher levels of externalizing behavior. The term for main effects of time was significant; younger boys were getting worse. There was no interaction effect. These data support Hetherington's (1988, 1989) findings that younger children may be at risk to respond to repartner-ing with increased levels of adjustment problems.

In keeping with the model in Fig. 3.1, in which parenting skills mediate transitions, parenting skills should account for intraindividual differences in growth in boys' problem behaviors subsequent to repartnering. The importance of ineffective discipline to externalizing and antisocial behavior has been shown in several studies, reviewed earlier. Forgatch and Ray (1991) hypothesized that problem-solving ability would be particularly relevant in future family transitions because of the need to resolve the accompanying misunderstandings and conflicts likely to accompany the introduction of a new partner into the family. Therefore, measures of discipline and problem solving obtained at T1 were tested for their influence on growth in externalizing behavior over 4 years in an LGC analysis (Meredith & Tisak, 1990). Two constructs were formed for the parenting skills: Ineffective Discipline and Poor Mother/Child Problem Solving. Discipline was assessed from a set of three observations conducted in the home. The nattering indicator measured the conditional probability that the mother responded with an aversive behavior regardless of the child's behavior. Explosive discipline measured the mother's rate of extremely negative behaviors, such as humiliate, hit, and threaten. The overall rating was a scale formed from ratings made following each observation with items tapping the extent to which mothers were inconsistent and ineffective in their use of disciplinary tactics. Problem solving was scored from videotaped discussions obtained in the laboratory. Mothers and children each selected the hottest, most frequently occurring conflict between them to discuss in two 10-minute interactions. Two indicators were measures of the outcome of the discussion as rated by observers. Items included ratings of the extent of resolution, quality of solutions proposed, and apparent satisfaction of the participants for the outcome of the discussion. Solutions was a measure of the number of positive solutions that were proposed by mother and child. The microvariable was the conditional probability that the mother would respond to the child with problem-solving behavior regardless of the child's behavior. The measure of externalizing behavior employed the modified externalizing behavior measure as rated by teachers using the CBCL (Achenbach & Edelbrock, 1986) assessed at T1, T2, and T3.

Because of the differences in pattern of growth in externalizing behavior for the two samples, the analyses were run separately for repartnered and remained single families. The models for the two samples are shown in Figs. 3.10a and 3.10b.

The first difference in the two samples was the form that externalizing behavior took over the 4-year interval. In the sample of repartnered mothers, a single factor (Shape Externalizing Behavior) described growth. In the sample of re-

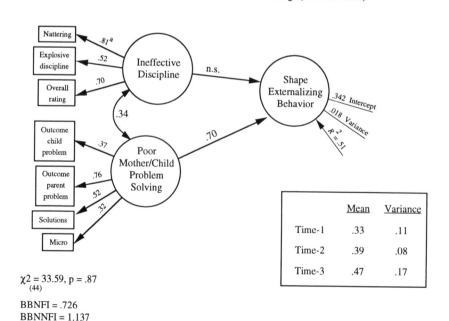

χ2 = 33.59, p = .87
(44)

BBNFI = .726
BBNNFI = 1.137
[a]All probabilities less than .05 unless otherwise noted.

FIG. 3.10a.   Impact of parenting on externalizing behavior.

Time-1   Teacher Ratings (modified scale)

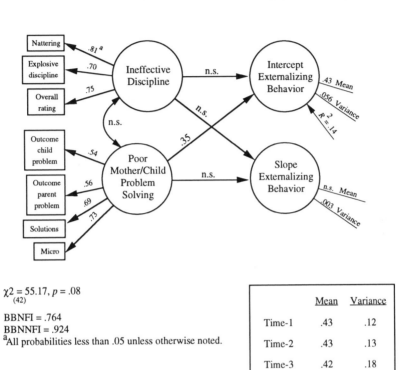

$\chi^2 = 55.17, p = .08$
    (42)

BBNFI = .764
BBNNFI = .924
[a]All probabilities less than .05 unless otherwise noted.

	Mean	Variance
Time-1	.43	.12
Time-2	.43	.13
Time-3	.42	.18

FIG. 3.10b.   Impact of parenting on externalizing behavior.

mained-single mothers, there were no changes in mean levels of externalizing behavior over the 4-year period, which may explain the fact that two factors (Intercept and Slope Externalizing Behavior) were required to describe boys' problem behavior over time.

There was a good fit between the models and the data for both samples. It should be noted, however, that given the small sample sizes, the chi-square provides a somewhat inflated estimate of the goodness of fit. In the repartnered sample, mother/child problem solving was a powerful predictor of changes in individual levels of externalizing-type behavior in the 4 years following separation, accounting for 51% of the variance. Ineffective Discipline did not predict growth in externalizing behavior. The model suggests the importance of problem-solving skill as a means of preventing boys' adjustment problems that may develop in the repartnering process.

In the remained-single sample, 14% of the variance in average levels of child behavior was explained. The path coefficient of .35 from poor problem solving to the intercept for externalizing behavior was significant. It did not account for

changing levels. Ineffective Discipline had no impact on teacher-rated externalizing behavior.

Child Adjustment and Repartnering

As shown in Fig. 3.7, Child Adjustment Problems exhibited shortly after separation were associated with increased levels of Maternal Stress 4 years later. In
Fig. 3.8, it could be seen that mothers who repartnered reported more improve-
ments in stress levels than mothers who remained single, particularly with respect
to financial problems. Figure 3.9 showed that repartnering was associated with
deteriorating child adjustment. In order to determine the relative contribution of
these factors, T1 Child Adjustment Problems and T3 Repartnered Status were
combined in an SEM analysis. The hypothesis tested was that Child Adjustment
Problems at T1 would predict future Maternal Stress, and Repartner Status at
Time 3 would be associated with diminished Maternal Stress. The model is
displayed in Fig. 3.11.

The findings were consistent with the hypothesis. The nonsignificant chi-
square indicated an adequate fit between the model and the data. The paths from
the two independent variables were moderate and of about equal value. The path
coefficient was .32 from Child Adjustment Problems to Maternal Stress even
after the measure of repartnering was partialled out. In a similar vein, the path
coefficient from Repartner Status to Maternal Stress was −.37. Together, the two

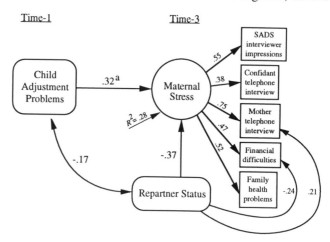

$\chi^2_{(9)} = 12.9, p = .16$

BBNFI = .934

BBNNFI = .945

[a] All probabilities less than .05 unless otherwise noted.

FIG. 3.11.   Two predictors for maternal stress.

variables accounted for 28% of the variance in reports of maternal stress assessed 4 to 5 years after separation.

POSTSEPARATION: THE SOCIALLY DISADVANTAGED AND ANTISOCIAL MOTHER

As noted in a previous section, parental social disadvantage and antisocial traits were assumed to be prime contextual contributors to boys' chronic adjustment problems. Presumably, the risk is most acute when both parents are equally at risk or when the at-risk parent is the dominant figure in charge of childrearing. When the family is intact, it may be that a lack of skills for socially disadvantaged or antisocial mothers is partially offset by a more skilled father, or by members of the extended family. Following a separation, this tenuous balance is disrupted.

Bank et al. (1993) tested this model with single-mother samples. They found that the contribution of the social disadvantage and antisocial variables varied as a function of the child's age. Figure 3.12 shows the findings from their replication design in which they conducted SEM analyses with the younger and older samples from ODS-1 and the single-mother sample from OYS. For the younger sample (K–2), it was the socially disadvantaged mother who was significantly at risk for disrupted discipline (path .63) and for child antisocial problems (path .58). There was an adequate fit for a model in which the construct for Maternal Antisocial Qualities was not included, but addition of that construct led to a fit in the model shown ($p = .03$ for the chi-square value).

The models for older boys from both samples showed a stronger fit. In both instances, the maternal antisocial variable made a direct contribution to disrupted parenting practices, whereas social disadvantage made only an indirect contribution. Disrupted parenting, in turn, had a direct effect on boys' adjustment problems. For the recently separated ODS-1 sample, the mothers' antisocial behavior was also associated with disrupted monitoring practices. This replicates the findings reported by Patterson and Capaldi (1991) that the effect of a transition for antisocial mothers was to significantly increase disruptions in monitoring. The OYS sample was primarily composed of mothers who had long-standing status as single parents.

It is interesting to compare the findings for the OYS single-mother sample with the findings for the OYS two-parent sample described earlier. For two-parent families, social disadvantage had a greater impact on discipline practices than did maternal antisocial behavior. This is parallel to the findings for recently separated single mothers of younger boys (see Fig. 3.12). It seems clear that socially disadvantaged parents are at significant risk for disrupted discipline. It also seems clear that it is the recently separated, socially disadvantaged mother of a younger boy who would profit the most from prevention procedures designed to strengthen her parenting skills. In fact, Forgatch is currently testing this model

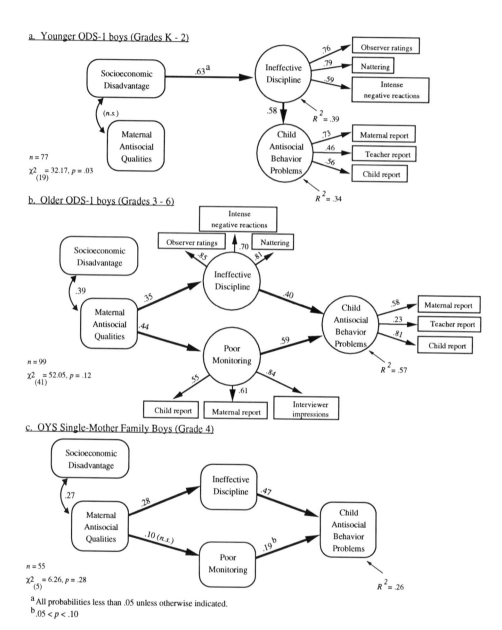

a. Younger ODS-1 boys (Grades K - 2)

b. Older ODS-1 boys (Grades 3 - 6)

c. OYS Single-Mother Family Boys (Grade 4)

[a] All probabilities less than .05 unless otherwise indicated.
[b] .05 < p < .10

FIG. 3.12. Models of social disadvantage and maternal antisocial qualities (from Bank, Forgatch, Patterson, & Fetrow, 1993).

100

in a randomized longitudinal experiment with a new sample of recently separated mothers and their young sons (ODS-2).

In single-parent families of older boys, antisocial mothers seem particularly at risk for disrupted parenting. The key variables appear to be both monitoring and discipline.

IMPLICATIONS

An effort was made to develop a set of contextual models that would be appropriate to the study of families who undergo the family disruption of separation or divorce. The models represent an attempt to deal with the question of why only a minority of families who undergo the experience produce children with adjustment problems. To reduce the magnitude of the problem, we followed Cherlin's and Block's lead in acknowledging that a substantial number of parents who will be divorced have boys who already have adjustment problems. It is estimated that this might be true for about 12 to 15% of the boys. We also made an educated guess that another 20% of the boys in separated families would develop adjustment problems following separation, and that the majority of these problems would be transient.

Making a distinction in when the boys' problems began requires that a theory specify the variables explaining why some boys start their problem behaviors prior to the separation and others start them afterwards. We put forward a mediational model that specified conditions under which contextual variables such as stress, social disadvantage, and parental traits would produce child adjustment problems. Boys with chronic problems seemed to have come from intact families in which at least one parent was socially disadvantaged and antisocial. The high risk for antisocial problem children in these families was due to ineffective discipline and, to a lesser extent, ineffective monitoring practices. Findings showing that disrupted discipline practices were in a sense handed down from one generation to another were reviewed (Patterson & Capaldi, 1991), and a guess was hazarded that disadvantaged/antisocial parents with a concomitant lack of skills in parenting practices would most frequently produce chronically antisocial boys. Alternative models—permissive and stressed/depressed parents—made significant, albeit lesser, contributions to the chronic problem.

The data showed that the majority of the boys who developed antisocial problems after a separation tended to be in the early stages of school (K–2). For these children, the hypothesis was the stressed/depressed mother would be most likely to have disrupted discipline practices and concomitant child adjustment problems. Several of the models showed that antisocial problems were related to a cascade of qualitatively new problems (e.g., school failure, rejection by normal peers, depressed mood). Indicators that measured these problems all loaded significantly on the same second-order deviancy factor (i.e., there was a ripple of effects). It was fascinating to find that as those problems grew, they apparently contributed directly to future levels of maternal stress. Child deviancy, itself a product, seemed to function as a positive feedback loop that kept the process going.

The second group of families at significant risk for increasing problems following separation were those in which the single mother repartnered within 4 years. Although this group showed reduced levels of stress, if they exhibited disrupted family problem-solving processes, their children were more likely to display increases in externalizing behaviors.

The central idea in all of these models is that contextual variables affect child adjustment only under conditions in which the social exchanges among family members are affected, particularly those associated with parenting practices. Under extremely trying circumstances, high levels of parenting skills may still suffice. It should be noted that as the contextual factors increase in difficulty, so do the requirements for successful parenting under those conditions (i.e., there are fewer and fewer families in which parents have the requisite high order of parenting skills). Sampson (1987) described conditions for inner-city families that are so extreme, very few parents would have the necessary skills to overcome the context. Under these conditions, the context wins. The number of parents sufficiently skillful is so small as to be of only academic interest. Society cannot afford to allow the context to win for large numbers of children.

ACKNOWLEDGMENTS

Support for this project was provided by the following NIMH grants: MH38318 from the Prevention Research Branch, Division of Epidemiology and Services Research; MH37940 from the Center for Studies of Violent Behavior and Traumatic Stress; and MH46690 from the Prevention Research Branch, Division of Applied and Services Research. We would also like to acknowledge L. Bank for his thoughtful review and W. Mayer for his creative graphics.

REFERENCES

Achenbach, T. M., & Edelbrock, C. S. (1986). *Manual for the Teacher's Report Form and Teacher Version of the Child Behavior Profile*. Burlington: University of Vermont.

Bank, L., Forgatch, M. S., Patterson, G. R., & Fetrow, R. A. (1993). Parenting practices of single mothers: Mediators of negative contextual factors. *Journal of Marriage and the Family, 55*, 371–384.

Bank, L., & Patterson, G. R. (1992). The use of structural equation modeling in combining data from different types of assessment. In J. C. Rosen & P. McReynolds (Eds.), *Advances in psychological assessment* (Vol. 8, pp. 41–74). New York: Plenum.

Baumrind, D. (1991). Effective parenting during the early adolescent transition. In P. A. Cowan & M. Hetherington (Eds.), *Family transitions* (pp. 111–163). Hillsdale, NJ: Lawrence Erlbaum Associates.

Beardslee, W., Bemporad, J., Keller, M. B., & Klerman, G. L. (1983). Children of parents with a major affective disorder: A review. *American Journal of Psychiatry, 140*, 825–832.

Bentler, P. M. (1989). *EQS structural equations program manual.* Los Angeles: BMDP Statistical Software, Inc.

Block, J. H., Block, J., & Gjerde, P. F. (1986). The personality of children prior to divorce: A prospective study. *Child Development, 57*, 827–840.

Bloom, B. L., Asher, S. J., & White, S. W. (1978). Marital disruption as a stressor: A review and analysis. *Psychological Bulletin, 85*(4), 867–894.

Bray, J. H. (1988). Children's development during early remarriage. In E. M. Hetherington & J. D. Arasteh (Eds.), *Impact of divorce, single parenting, and stepparenting on children* (pp. 279–299). Hillsdale, NJ: Lawrence Erlbaum Associates.

Brody, G. H., Neubaum, E., & Forehand, R. (1988). Serial marriage: A heuristic analysis of an emerging family form. *Psychological Bulletin, 103*(2), 211–222.

Bronfenbrenner, U. (1958). Socialization and social class through time and space. In E. E. Maccoby, T. M. Newcomb, & E. L. Hartley (Eds.), *Readings in social psychology* (pp. 400–424). New York: Holt, Rinehart & Winston.

Bumpass, L. L., & Sweet, J. A. (1989). National estimates of cohabitation. *Demography, 26*(4), 615–625.

Bumpass, L., Sweet, J., & Martin, T. C. (1990). Changing patterns of remarriage. *Journal of Marriage and the Family, 52*, 747–756.

Capaldi, D. M., & Patterson, G. R. (1991). Relation of parental transitions to boys' adjustment problems: I. A linear hypothesis. II. Mothers at risk for transitions and unskilled parenting. *Developmental Psychology, 27*, 489–504.

Cherlin, A. J., Furstenberg, F. F., Chase-Lansdale, P. L., Kiernan, K. E., Robins, P. K., Morrison, D. R., & Teitler, J. O. (1991). Longitudinal studies of effects of divorce on children in Great Britain and the United States. *Science, 252*, 1386–1389.

Conger, R. (1991, April). *Impact of life stressors on adult relationships and adolescent adjustment.* Paper presented at the meeting of the Society for Research in Child Development, Seattle, WA.

Conger, R. D., Patterson, G. R., Ge, X. (1995). It takes two to replicate: A mediational model for the impact of stress on adolescent adjustment. *Child Development, 66*, 80–97.

Cronbach, L. J., & Meehl, P. E. (1956). Construct validity in psychological tests. In H. Feigl & M. Scriven (Eds.), *Minnesota studies in the philosophy of science: Vol 1. The foundations of science and concepts of psychology and psychoanalysis* (pp. 174–204). Minneapolis: University of Minnesota Press.

Dishion, T. J., Patterson, G. R., & Kavanagh, K. (1992). An experimental test of the coercion model: Linking theory, measurement, and intervention. In J. McCord & R. Tremblay (Eds.), *The interaction of theory and practice: Experimental studies of interventions* (pp. 253–282). New York: Guilford.

Downey, G., & Coyne, J. C. (1990). Children of depressed parents: An integrative review. *Psychological Bulletin, 108*(1), 50–76.

Duncan, G. J., & Hoffman, S. D. (1985). A reconsideration of the economic consequences of marital dissolution. *Demography, 22*(4), 485–497.

Emery, R. E. (1982). Interparental conflict and the children of discord and divorce. *Psychological Bulletin, 92*, 310–330.

Fetrow, B., Dishion, T., & Viken, R. (1987). *Stress: OSLC technical report for completed analyses* (Tech. Rep. No. L109). Eugene, OR: Oregon Social Learning Center.

Forgatch, M. S. (1991). The clinical science vortex: Developing a theory for antisocial behavior. In D. Pepler & K. Rubin (Eds.), *The development and treatment of childhood aggression* (pp. 291–315). Hillsdale, NJ: Lawrence Erlbaum Associates.

Forgatch, M. S., & Patterson, G. R. (1989). *Parents and adolescents living together: II. Family problem solving.* Eugene, OR: Castalia.

Forgatch, M. S., Patterson, G. R., & Skinner, M. L. (1988). A mediational model for the effect of divorce on antisocial behavior in boys. In E. M. Hetherington & J. D. Aresteh (Eds.), *Impact of divorce, single parenting, and step-parenting on children* (pp. 135–154). Hillsdale, NJ: Lawrence Erlbaum Associates.

Forgatch, M. S., & Ray, J. (1991, April). *Stress in divorce: Repartnering, parenting, and child adjustment.* Paper presented at the biennial meeting of the Society for Research in Child Development, Seattle, WA.

Forgatch, M. S., & Stoolmiller, M. (1991, April). *The relationship between maternal depression and parenting practices.* Paper presented at the biennial meeting of the Society for Research in Child Development, Seattle, WA.

Forgatch, M. S., & Toobert, D. J. (1979). A cost-effective parent training program for use with normal preschool children. *Journal of Pediatric Psychology, 4*(2), 129–145.

Hess, R. D., & Camara, K. A. (1979). Post-divorce family relationships as mediating factors in the consequences of divorce for children. *Journal of Social Issues, 35*(4), 79–96.

Hetherington, E. M. (1988). Parents, children, and siblings six years after divorce. In R. A. Hinde & J. Stevenson-Hinde (Eds.), *Relationships within families: Mutual influences* (pp. 311–333). Oxford, UK: Clarendon.

Hetherington, E. M. (1989). Coping with family transitions: Winners, losers, and survivors. *Child Development, 60,* 1–14.

Hetherington, E. M., & Clingempeel, W. G. (1992). Coping with marital transitions. *Monographs of the Society for Research in Child Development, 57,* (2–3, Serial No. 227).

Hetherington, E. M., Cox, M., & Cox, R. (1979). Family interaction and the social, emotional, and cognitive development of children following divorce. In V. Vaughn & T. Brazelton (Eds.), *The family: Setting priorities* (pp. 89–128). New York: Science and Medicine.

Hetherington, E. M., Cox, M., & Cox, R. (1982). Effects of divorce on parents and children. In M. Lamb (Ed.), *Nontraditional families* (pp. 233–287). Hillsdale, NJ: Lawrence Erlbaum Associates.

Hetherington, E. M., Cox, M., & Cox, R. (1985). Long-term effects of divorce and remarriage on the adjustment of children. *Journal of the American Academy of Child Psychiatry, 24,* 518–530.

Larzelere, R. E., & Patterson, G. R. (1990). Parental management: Mediator of the effect of socioeconomic status on early delinquency. *Criminology, 28,* 301–324.

Longfellow, C., Zelkowitz, P., & Saunders, E. (1982). The quality of mother-child relationships. In D. Belle (Ed.), *Lives in stress: Women and depression* (pp. 163–176). Beverly Hills, CA: Sage.

McArdle, J. J., & Epstein, D. (1987). Latent growth curves within developmental structural equation models. *Child Development, 58,* 110–133.

Meredith, W., & Tisak, J. (1990). Latent curve analysis. *Psychometrika, 55,* 107–122.

Offord, D. R., Boyle, M. C., & Racine, Y. A. (1991). The epidemiology of antisocial behavior in childhood and adolescence. In D. J. Pepler & K. H. Rubin (Eds.), *The development and treatment of childhood aggression* (pp. 31–54). Hillsdale, NJ: Lawrence Erlbaum Associates.

Olweus, D. (1980). Familial and temperamental determinants of aggressive behavior in adolescent boys: A causal analysis. *Developmental Psychology, 16,* 644–660.

Patterson, G. R. (1982). *A social learning approach to family intervention: III. Coercive family process.* Eugene, OR: Castalia.

Patterson, G. R. (1983). Stress: A change agent for family process. In N. Garmezy & M. Rutter (Eds.), *Stress, coping, and development in children* (pp. 235–264). New York: McGraw-Hill.

Patterson, G. R. (1991, April). *Interaction of stress and family structure and their relation to child adjustment: An example of across-site collaboration.* Paper presented at the meeting of the Society for Research in Child Development, Seattle, WA.

Patterson, G. R., & Bank, L. (1986). Bootstrapping your way in the nomological thicket. *Behavioral Assessment, 8,* 49–73.

Patterson, G. R., & Bank, L. (1989). Some amplifying mechanisms for pathologic processes in families. In M. R. Gunnar & E. Thelan (Eds.), *Systems and development: Minnesota symposium on child psychology* (Vol. 22, pp. 167–210). Hillsdale, NJ: Lawrence Erlbaum Associates.

Patterson, G. R., Bank, L., & Stoolmiller, M. L. (1990). The preadolescent's contributions to disrupted family process. In R. Montemayor, G. R. Adams, & T. P. Gullotta (Eds.), *From childhood to adolescence: A transitional period?* (pp. 107–133). Newbury Park, CA: Sage.

Patterson, G. R., & Capaldi, D. (1991). Antisocial parents: Unskilled and vulnerable. In P. A. Cowan & M. Hetherington (Eds.), *Family transitions* (pp. 195–218). Hillsdale, NJ: Lawrence Erlbaum Associates.

Patterson, G. R., & Dishion, T. J. (1988). Multilevel family process models: Traits, interactions, and relationships. In R. A. Hinde & J. Stevenson-Hinde (Eds.), *Relationships within families: Mutual influences* (pp. 283–310). Oxford, UK: Clarendon.

Patterson, G. R., Dishion, T. J., & Chamberlain, P. (1993). Outcomes and methodological issues relating to treatment of antisocial children. In T. R. Giles (Ed.), *Effective psychotherapy: A handbook of comparative research* (pp. 43–86). New York: Plenum.

Patterson, G. R., Duncan, T. E., Reid, J. B., & Bank, L. (1993, July). Systematic maternal errors in predicting sons' future arrests. In D. Hann (Chair), *Conceptual and methodological modes for understanding family processes related to child mental health.* Workshop conducted at a meeting at the National Institute of Mental Health, Bethesda, MD.

Patterson, G. R., & Forgatch, M. S. (1987). *Parents and adolescents living together: Part I: The basics.* Eugene, OR: Castalia.

Patterson, G. R., & Forgatch, M. S. (1990). Initiation and maintenance of process disrupting single-mother families. In G. R. Patterson (Ed.), *Depression and aggression in family interaction* (pp. 209–245). Hillsdale, NJ: Lawrence Erlbaum Associates.

Patterson, G. R., Reid, J. B., & Dishion, T. J. (1992). *A social learning approach: IV. Antisocial boys.* Eugene, OR: Castalia.

Peterson, J. L., & Zill, N. (1986). Marital disruption, parent–child relationships, and behavior problems in children. *Journal of Marriage and the Family, 48,* 295–307.

Radloff, L. S. (1977). The CES-D Scale: A self-report depression scale for researchin the general population. *Applied Psychological Measurement, 1,* 385–401.

Rutter, M., Tizard, J., & Whitmore, K. (1970). *Education, health, and behaviour.* New York: Wiley.

Sampson, R. (1987). Urban Black violence: The effect of male joblessness and family disruption. *American Journal of Sociology, 93*(2), 348–382.

Sarason, I. G., Johnson, J. H., & Siegel, J. M. (1978). Assessing the impact of life changes: Development of the Life Experiences Survey. *Journal of Consulting and Clinical Psychology, 46,* 932–946.

Snyder, J. J. (1991). Discipline as a mediator of the impact of maternal stress and mood on child conduct problems. *Development and Psychopathology, 3,* 263–276.

Straus, M., Gelles, R., & Steinmetz, S. (1980). *Behind closed doors: Violence in the American family.* Garden City, NY: Anchor.

Teachman, J., & Heckert, A. (1985). The impact of age and children on remarriage: Further evidence. *Journal of Family Issues, 6,* 185–203.

Tisak, J., & Meredith, W. (1990). Descriptive and associative developmental models. In A. von Eye (Ed.), *Statistical methods in longitudinal research* (Vol. 2, pp. 387–407). New York: Academic Press.

Wallerstein, J. S., & Kelly, J. B. (1980). *Surviving the breakup: How children and parents cope with divorce.* New York: Basic Books.

Wilson, H. (1980). Parental supervision: A neglected aspect of delinquency. *The British Journal of Criminology, 20*(3), 203–235.

Zill, N. (1978, February). *Divorce, marital happiness, and the mental health of children: Findings from the F. C. D. national survey of children.* Paper presented at the NIMH Workshop on Divorce and Children, Bethesda, MD.

4

▼▼▼▼▼▼▼

Family Support, Coping, and Competence

Thomas Ashby Wills
Ferkauf Graduate School of Psychology
Albert Einstein College of Medicine

Elaine A. Blechman
University of Colorado at Boulder

Grace McNamara
Ferkauf Graduate School of Psychology

In this chapter, we consider how family support may contribute to coping and competence among children and adolescents. We base our presentation on a developmental model of family relationships, with the following assumptions:

1. Supportive families are those characterized by effective communication.
2. Supportive families contribute to children's adaptive ability through development of coping skills and relevant competencies.
3. Supportive families may also contribute to adaptation through averting the occurrence of negative life events, hence shielding children from experiencing developmentally inappropriate challenges.
4. Participation in effective family communication teaches children strategies for coping with developmentally appropriate affective, social, and achievement challenges.
5. Families with effective communication may enable youth to cope successfully even with developmentally inappropriate challenges.

We outline herein the background for the developmental model and present data from our research on how family support and family structure are associated with coping and outcomes. The developmental model presented joins two lines of empirical and theoretical work. One is research by Blechman and colleagues on family communication, competence, and psychopathology (Blechman, 1990, 1991; Blechman, McEnroe, & Carella, 1986; Blechman, Tinsley, Carella, & McEnroe, 1985; Blechman & Wills, 1992). The other is research by Wills and colleagues on social support, coping, and substance use (Cohen & Wills, 1985; Wills, 1985, 1986, 1990a, 1990b, 1991; Wills, Vaccaro, & McNamara, 1992; Wills & Vaughan, 1989). The former research program is based on the approach of clinical psychology, studying pathologic outcomes in samples of high-risk children and families. The latter research program is based on the approach of social epidemiology, studying the distribution of adjustment in the general population of adolescents. The purpose of this chapter is to show convergence of findings from these two approaches and from studies of resiliency (Garmezy & Masten, 1991; Garmezy & Rutter, 1983; Hetherington, 1989; Hetherington, Cox, & Cox, 1982; Masten, Morison, Pellegrini, & Tegellen, 1990; Rutter, 1985, 1990; Werner, 1986, 1989; Werner & Smith, 1982). The suggestion is made that resiliency effects are based on the development of coping skills among children.

In the following sections the concepts of challenges, support, coping, communication, and competence are defined, and the basis for the developmental model is presented. Then we present findings on family support.

CHALLENGES

A challenge is an event or circumstance that threatens a child's self-esteem, mood, interpersonal relationships, or accomplishment of achievement tasks. Challenges include events and circumstances variously labeled as developmental tasks, problems, dilemmas, transitions, stressors, daily hassles, crises, or life events. A developmentally appropriate challenge requires skills, most of which the young person possesses. A challenge is developmentally inappropriate if most youth of the same chronological age would lack the skills to cope with the challenge. For example, having a parent incapacitated through illness or substance abuse could be coped with effectively by most 16-year-olds but would be difficult for a 6-year-old. No person's life is without challenges and transitions. However, appropriately timed and supported encounters with developmentally appropriate challenges may be a prerequisite for the acquisition of coping skills. In Vygotsky's (1978) terms, youth are in the zone of proximal development when they use their existing skills as "coping scaffolds" to surmount developmentally appropriate challenges. In our model, youth may be at risk for deviant behavior and adverse life outcomes when they are both overexposed to developmentally inappropriate challenges and lack social support for the gradual and timely acquisition of coping skills. This is similar to the Lazarus and Folkman (1984) model of coping, as it considers how available resources are matched to the number and nature of environmental challenges, but it also considers the developmental condition of the young person and the particular role of supportive family relationships for fostering effective coping efforts.

SOCIAL SUPPORT

This definition of family support derives from a functional model of social support. The functional model proposes that interpersonal relationships enhance adaptation through provision of supportive functions that are of direct or indirect assistance for the coping process. These functions have been classified into several domains (Cutrona & Russell, 1987; Vaux, 1988; Wills, 1985), of which three seem most relevant for adolescents. *Emotional support* means the availability of a person with whom one can discuss problems, share feelings, and disclose worries when necessary. It is assumed that emotional support depends on a confidant who can listen effectively, who cares about the respondent as a person, and can reflect about problems without engaging in blaming and criticizing. The latter aspect is particularly emphasized by adolescents, who perceive (rightly or wrongly) that when they try to talk with a parent about one of their problems, they may be blamed for having caused the problem (Burke & Weir, 1978, 1979). *Instrumental support* means having a person available who can provide assistance with important instrumental tasks. For an adolescent, this could mean assistance with transportation, with school work, and last but not least, with financial assistance. *Informational support* means the availability of advice, guidance, and information about community resources (e.g., sports team, medical clinic). Other functions that have been distinguished in the social support literature include social companionship and feedback or "validation" (i.e., providing social comparison feedback about appropriateness or commonness of behavior).

This model proposes that supportive functions from interpersonal relationships should be most relevant for adolescents with high levels of life stress, for whom the functions will be of particular value for assisting the coping effort, and less relevant for adolescents with a low level of stress. This is termed the *buffering effect* because support "buffers" persons from the otherwise adverse impact of negative experiences. A number of studies have shown social integration is related prospectively to health, and buffering effects of functional support have been observed for outcomes including psychological distress and physical morbidity (Cohen & Wills, 1985; House, Landis, & Umberson, 1988; Wills, 1991).

Family Support and Outcomes

Recent research has tested several aspects of functional support for children (cf. Sandler, Miller, Short, & Wolchik, 1989). For example, Burke and Weir (1978, 1979) studied a sample of adolescents and found that measures termed Emotional Support and Concrete (i.e., informational) Support were related to greater well-being among the adolescents. In contrast, measures indexing parents' tendency either to deny the existence of adolescents' problems, or to blame and criticize them for the problem, were related to lower levels of well-being. Another interesting feature is that the investigators obtained parallel measures for parent and peer support. They found that with respect to criterion measures of anxiety and depressive symptomatology, the effects of parent and peer support were approximately the same. Buffering was specifically tested in a study of adolescents by Greenberg, Siegel, and Leitch (1983) in relation to outcome measures of self-concept and life satisfaction. An emotional support measure tapped the adolescent's perception that peers or parents were understanding of one's problems and could be trusted to talk with. Main-effect results showed parent and peer support made independent contributions to well-being, but the effect size was considerably stronger for parent support. These investigators tested whether support from parents or peers buffered the impact of negative life events. They found a significant buffering effect for parental support, but not for peer support.

The effect of family support for a deviant outcome has been tested in several previous studies (Fondacaro & Heller, 1983; Wills, 1986; Wills & Vaughan, 1989) with respect to criterion measures of tobacco and alcohol use. With samples of middle-school students in New York City, Wills and Vaughan (1989) found parent support was inversely related to substance use, whereas peer support was positively related to substance use, particularly when there were several peers who used. Stress × Support interactions were tested (Wills, 1986) and a buffering effect was found for parent support, but not for peer support. Fondacaro and Heller (1983) found with a college student sample that functional support measures (emotional support, problem-solving support) were inversely related to heavy alcohol use, as was inclusion of family members in the student's social network. These data are consistent with other research on adolescent populations, which finds parental support consistently related to positive outcomes, whereas peer-group support is often unrelated to outcomes and, in some instances, related to more deviant outcomes (cf. Hoelter & Harper, 1987; Larson, 1983; Steinberg, Dornbusch, & Brown, 1992).

Socioeconomic Status and Family Support

While family support is expected to have beneficial effects for children at all levels of socioeconomic status, the ability of parents to provide support may not be equal across socioeconomic levels. Specifically, research has linked economic stress to decrements in marital quality and parenting behavior (e.g., Conger et al., 1990; Elder, Nguyen, & Caspi, 1985; Takeuchi, Williams, & Adair, 1991). Thus it is possible that a parent's socioeconomic status has a pervasive effect on his or her ability to be supportive; when a father or mother is tired out by workload, worried about economic uncertainty, and unable to provide some things that children need, the supportiveness of the family environment may be affected.

COPING

The term *coping* is used here to describe the collection of overt and covert strategies that youth use during confrontation with a challenge. These include individual problem-solving responses, such as getting information, considering alternatives, and making a decision about a course of action; observable communication behaviors, such as discussing situations and cooperating with other persons; and unobservable cognitive operations, such as minimizing distress or focusing on positive aspects of the situation. This definition shares elements with models of self-control (e.g., Kendall & Williams, 1980), social competence (e.g., Dodge, Pettit, McClaskey, & Brown, 1986), and means–ends problem solving (e.g., Spivack, Platt, & Shure, 1976). As in other models of coping (Compas, 1987; Lazarus & Folkman, 1984), it is not assumed that any given type of coping is inherently good or bad for all situations or age groups, but rather an attempt has been made to try to define a set of coping dimensions that may either facilitate or detract from adaptation among adolescents. Thus other dimensions are measured, such as whether a youth deals with situations through avoidance of the problem (cf. Rohde, Lewinsohn, Tilson, & Seeley, 1990); responds to a problem by blaming and criticizing other persons, and venting anger (cf. Coie, Dodge, & Kupersmidt, 1990); or responds to a challenge situation with an attitude of helplessness (cf. Carver, Scheier, & Weintraub, 1989). We posit that effective strategies succeed in the short or long run because they actually remove the problem situation or alter a person's (or his or her supporters') perception of his or her coping ability. Ineffective strategies are posited to fail because they alienate potential supporters, fail to remove the problematic situation, or lead to development of negative and pessimistic attitudes about one's personal attributes and coping ability.

Coping With Affective Challenges

Affective challenges test a person's capacity to recognize (not deny) unpleasant facts and to achieve emotional balance nonetheless. Both minor daily hassles (e.g., argument with a family member) and major life events (e.g., serious illness of a family member) pose affective challenges to young people. Youth with good affective competence are (relative to age-matched peers) in control of their moods and able to rebound reasonably quickly from emotional setbacks. Such persons evidence relatively stable emotional states, maintain self-control when anger or anxiety is aroused, and refrain from ruminating about fancied slights or wrongs (Blechman & Wills, 1992); they have the attribute of "soothability" (Tarter, Alterman, & Edwards, 1985) because they can recover (or be helped to recover) from negative states. Because a challenge usually has an affective component, affective competence is a prerequisite for dealing with social or achievement challenges.

Coping With Social Challenges

Social challenges are events or circumstances that test a youth's capacity to get along with peers or adults despite differences of background, preference, or competing interests. Youths skilled at dealing with peer social challenges have several close friends, in part because they know how to enter social groups, read social cues accurately, and plan social activities (Cauce, 1987; Dodge et al., 1986). Youths skilled at dealing with adult social challenges have good relationships with a number of adults inside and outside the family, in part because they know how to accept some degree of authority in relationships, to give and receive necessary information, and to accept correction or criticism without getting into retaliation and "fight cycles" that inhibit problem resolution (Hetherington, 1991).

Coping With Achievement Challenges

Achievement challenges are tasks or circumstances that test a youth's ability to identify problems and persistently look for solutions until a satisfactory or correct solution is found. Successful coping with achievement challenges seems to involve more than sheer intellectual capacity (Sternberg & Kolligian, 1990). In addition to appropriate values about achievement, it includes the ability to plan activities so that assignments are completed on time, pay attention in class, and not talk back to teachers. Although most adolescents periodically fail one of these conditions, to be consistently lacking in all three seems likely to pose difficulties for academic achievement. Most achievement challenges also include an affective component and many have a social component; at some point, other people may be required to contribute to or evaluate the solution. Therefore it would be expected that the best coping with achievement challenges results when a young person is also skilled at dealing with affective and social challenges.

COMMUNICATION

We use the term *communication* to refer to any overt verbal or nonverbal behavior that is enacted by one person in the presence of others, and has a discernible impact on those other people. Communication always confronts participants with affective challenges (How does the current interaction affect each one's mood and self-image?), often confronts participants with social challenges (How much does each one like the other participant?), and sometimes faces participants with achievement challenges (How can this interaction help or harm each participant's chances to accomplish important tasks at school or at work?). Observation of communication exchanges, particularly within a family environment, provides an opportunity to gauge the way participants cope with diverse challenges. Imagine a conversation between a father and a 16-year-old daughter. At the same time that the father and daughter are, for example, communicating with each other, they are also, as individuals, coping with important challenges. The father copes with the affective challenge of feeling good despite his daughter's sarcastic comments. The daughter copes with the affective challenge of maintaining a feeling of independence despite her father's advice giving. The daughter, in the same conversation, copes with a social challenge (her boyfriend would like her to stay out later than the curfew her father has set). Her father also copes with an achievement challenge—ruminating about news of imminent layoffs at work.

Information Exchange

Communication depends on messages from a sender that have an impact on at least one receiver. The most basic message (like an infant's cry) transmits information about the sender's feelings to the receiver through nonverbal sounds and gestures (Buck, 1985). More complex messages use both verbal and nonverbal channels to convey information about feelings and other matters such as preferences, experiences, and ideas. Information is exchanged effectively when a sender's message is received and acknowledged by the receiver as intended by the sender. Under ideal circumstances, the sender transmits clear, detailed messages or statements and the receiver responds with probing questions and restatements until the receiver apparently has shown complete understanding of the sender's point of view. When a message is received as intended, the sender can say, "You've got the point! You understand how I feel (how I think, what I've experienced, what I want)." Receiver statements such as "I see what you mean" don't necessarily indicate effective information exchange. Rather, it is the sender who must affirm, "It is clear to me that you understand my point of view."

COMPETENCE

The term *competence* is used to refer to the observable impact of skillful coping. Competent children, in this usage, are those who have been recognized by others (peers, teachers, parents) for their successful coping. The socially competent child has been recognized by peers, on sociometric measures, as a desirable playmate. The academically competent child has been recognized as an accomplished student on school report cards and standardized achievement tests. Several papers have considered how affective, social, and achievement competence promote psychological health and prevent adverse outcomes (Baumrind, 1991; Blechman, 1990, 1991; Blechman & Wills, 1992; Wills, Vaccaro, & McNamara, 1992; Wills, Vaccaro, McNamara, & Spellman, 1991).

Coping skills and externally recognized competence appear to represent two correlated but partly independent constructs. For example, the correlation between social coping skills and social competence, although generally positive, varies in magnitude. Children who have long coped successfully (over a period of years) are likely to be recognized as competent. However, children who have only recently improved their social coping skills may have to wait a year or more before peer recognition of social competence catches up to skills development (Coie, Dodge, & Kupersmidt, 1990). Also, prejudice may produce a disparity between a minority child's coping skills and peer-recognized social competence. Although successful coping brings some rewards (relevant challenges no longer act as irritants or obstacles), externally recognized competence brings with it a substantial, additional bounty. Among other benefits, competent children's past successes may engender a positive halo effect so that observers evaluate them more kindly and challenge them less often than less competent peers.

COPING, COMPETENCE, AND OUTCOMES

Considerable evidence suggests that lack of coping skills and limited competence (affective, social, or achievement) heighten the risk of adjustment problems. Academic failure, rejection by peers, angry reactions to frustration, and poor relationships with adults all have demonstrated relationships to psychological problems and drug use (see, e.g., Dishion, Reid, & Patterson, 1988; Glantz, 1992; Kaplan, Martin, & Robbins, 1984; Kupersmidt, Coie, & Dodge, 1990; Leadbeater, Hellner, Allen, & Aber, 1989; Parker & Asher, 1987; Wills, Vaccaro, & McNamara, 1992; Wills, Vaccaro, McNamara, & DuHamel, 1992).

Coping skills and competence each, independently, reduce a youth's vulnerability to deviant behaviors, such as aggression and substance abuse, and to adverse life outcomes, such as arrest or teenage pregnancy, through multiple pathways. First, successful coping with challenges (e.g., how to make friends at a new school) reduces the future probability of that challenge and of associated challenges (e.g., the affective challenge of loneliness) and gratifies some of the youth's basic needs (e.g., for affection and companionship). The youth has no need to resort to deviant behavior to fulfill needs for perceived competence and self-regard (cf. Kaplan, 1980). Second, successful coping with challenges demands honest confrontation of reality ("This is a new school where I don't know anyone, I'm going to have to take some chances in order to make some friends. Some kids may reject me, but if so, it doesn't matter that much. I'll survive"), preventing maladaptive defense mechanisms, irrational or pessimistic cognitions, and associated mood or anxiety disorders (Barlow & Cerny, 1988). Third, competent youths' continuing access to others' affection and esteem, even when coping skills are insufficient to overcome current challenges, helps protect them against depressive symptoms and may buffer against stress (cf. Hanson, Henggeler, & Burghen, 1987). Finally, competent youths succeed in getting help from members of social networks, increasing their chances of overcoming even developmentally inappropriate challenges.

SUPPORT, COMPETENCE, AND RESILIENCE

Families in which members use effective information exchange promote development of coping skills and competence among children and adolescents. As previously noted, measures that tap emotional support from, and ability to communicate with, parents have been shown to provide buffering effects against accumulated life stressors, which mostly represent developmentally appropriate challenges (Burke & Weir, 1978, 1979; Greenberg et al., 1983; Wills, Vaccaro, & McNamara, 1992). A supportive family skilled at communication and coping, it is believed, can even promote competence in children confronted with developmentally inappropriate challenges. Evidence for this view emerges from the longitudinal research of Werner (1986, 1989, Werner & Smith, 1982), who followed a birth cohort of 698 children born on the Hawaiian island of Kauai. The children were first assessed at age 1 (including parent interview) and were followed up at ages 2, 10, 18, and 32 years. From this sample, Werner (1986) studied a subgroup of 49 youth whose parents had serious problems with alcohol misuse, clearly a developmentally inappropriate challenge because the parental disorder was present from early on. By age 18, 41% of this group of children had developed learning or behavior problems, but 59% had not; the latter were termed the resilient group. The resilient children were found to differ on a number of measures obtained through retrospective self-report or parent interviews. Factors that discriminated the resilient group included smaller family size, less family conflict, child's temperament (perceived by caretaker as cuddly and affectionate), better intellectual development, and female gender. At age 18, persons in the resilient group showed higher self-esteem, a greater degree of self-control, and higher achievement orientation. The author attributed the differential outcomes of the resilient and vulnerable children to constitutional characteristics of the child and qualities of the early caregiving environment. She suggested that effects of risk factors on children can be buffered by the existence of protective factors, such as competencies, communication skills, and social support, which help to reduce the impact of the risk factor of parental alcoholism. This position is consistent with evidence we previously discussed on the operation of family support.

Because this occurs over a long period of time, relevant empirical knowledge on the development of coping and competence is limited (see Blechman, 1990; Cauce, 1986; Patterson, DeBaryshe, & Ramsey, 1989). One assumes that development of competence in the family context would involve modeling, trial and error learning, and reinforcement. An expectation from social learning theory is that supportive parents help children develop competence because they model effective coping, allow children to learn on their own without punishing or criticizing, and provide positive reinforcement for good performances. It is expected that families expert at coping through effective information exchange would be perceived by adolescents as supportive, and would promote development of competence, through the following processes:

1. In a family where emotional support is high, youths participate in communication experiences that boost their sense of self-esteem and validate the acceptability of their feelings. This can be particularly important for adolescents, who may feel that few persons understand (or care about) their feelings.

2. In a family where emotional and other types of support are available, adolescents have functions available to them that are useful for coping with challenges and transitions. When things go wrong with friends, school, or other parts of life, a teen has the knowledge that family members are available and will help out through listening, helping to deal with negative emotions, and providing useful advice.

3. It is believed that a supportive family environment also helps adolescents to be integrated in the community. Parents may provide information about relevant resources in the community, may themselves know persons who are active in the community and provide introductions, and may provide instrumental functions that are useful for such purposes (e.g., buying a sports outfit, giving lessons, providing transportation).

4. Finally, we think that a family with good support and communication skills also models some very important attitudes and expectancies. Specifically, the youth learns an optimistic approach to adversity, observes persons who take an active, rather than helpless, approach to problems, and participates in interpersonal discussions that show that differences can be accepted and resolved. This would help children to develop the attitude that they can cope with problems and that both instrumental and emotional problems are amenable to resolution without acting out, blaming and criticizing, or attacking other people.

FAMILY STRUCTURE AND ADOLESCENT BEHAVIOR

A final issue is how family relationships, and therefore communication and competence, are affected by family structure. With the lifetime risk of family disruption through divorce approximating 50%, there has been considerable interest in outcomes for children in single-parent families (e.g., Emery, 1988; Hetherington, Arnett, & Hollier, 1988). The specific focus of this section is on research on family structure and adolescents' substance use.

Earlier studies found elevated rates of cigarette smoking and illicit drug use among teenagers with one parent in the home (e.g., Bachman, Johnston, & O'Malley, 1981). Other research distinguished between single-parent and remarried families. Blechman, Berberian, and Thompson (1977) entered indices of family structure in analyses that included age, social class, and peer substance use. These investigators found remarriage to have a significant effect for elevated alcohol use among White students, but not among Black students. Kellam, Ensminger, and Turner (1977) studied an urban, largely minority, sample of young children and found behavior problems were elevated for children from mother-only families. These investigators also found children in blended families (one biological parent and one stepparent) to have higher rates of problem behavior.

Subsequent research involved methodological recommendations following from earlier research (Blechman, 1982), distinguishing between intact and blended families, controlling for social class, and testing effects of family disruption for older versus younger students and for male and female children. For example, Dornbusch et al. (1985) studied a national sample 12 to 18 years of age and found an effect of single-parent status for elevated deviant behavior, with control for parental social class. This effect has been replicated for smoking in European samples (e.g., M. Murray, Kiryluk, & Swain, 1985), and a North American study found smoking, heavy drinking, and marijuana use to be elevated among students with single parents (D. M. Murray, Perry, O'Connell, & Schmid, 1987).

These findings were extended in prospective studies. Flewelling and Baumann (1990) found an effect of single-parent families for onset of substance use and sexual intercourse, with statistical control for age, sex, race, and parental education; interactions indicated a greater impact of family disruption for White, compared with Black, adolescents. Newcomb and Bentler (1988) found a prospective effect of family disruption on a composite index of substance use; this effect was mediated through increases in mother's drug use, child's emotional distress, and child's socially deviant attitudes. Finally, Needle, Su, and Doherty (1990) found that divorce had more effect on substance use onset among boys, but remarriage had more effect on substance use onset among girls.

SUMMARY AND PREDICTIONS

A model of family communication has been outlined that suggests how family relationships produce favorable outcomes for children. This model leads to the prediction that parental support will lead to more adaptive coping, less maladaptive coping, and development of academic and social competence. Research on family structure has shown a decremental effect and suggested that this occurs through disruption of support processes. This leads to the prediction that parental support and adolescents' competence will be decreased among single-parent families. These predictions were tested in studies with samples of urban adolescents, described in the following sections.

FAMILY SUPPORT RESEARCH PROGRAM

The group at Ferkauf Graduate School/Albert Einstein College of Medicine has been conducting epidemiologic research with school samples of adolescents in the New York metropolitan area.[1] Data are obtained through self-report questionnaires administered to students in classrooms by project staff, according to a standardized protocol. The questionnaire includes questions on family support,

---

[1]Kate DuHamel, Mark Spellman, Angela Riccobono, Donato Vaccaro, Jody Wallach, and Caroline Zeoli provided assistance with this research.

coping, and competence, together with criterion measures of tobacco, alcohol, and marijuana use. In one study, student reports of competence were supplemented by teacher ratings for the same measures.

Table 4.1 provides a summary of the participants in the research. The samples are multiethnic and are evenly divided between males and females. The completion rate, defined as number of questionnaires obtained divided by total school enrollment in grade, is typically above 90%, with case loss occurring mainly because of student absenteeism (usually in the range of 6% to 8%). Thus the samples are representative of the school population.

In Study 1, the eight participating schools were from the parochial school system in Harlem and the Bronx, New York City. Census data characterized the areas as low income.[2] In Study 2, the schools were from public school systems in the metropolitan area, representing mixed urban-suburban communities. Census-tract information and data on parental education indicated the families in these communities were somewhat better off economically than the inner-city sample; with a mean educational level just above high school graduate, they would be characterized as working class on the average and are representative of the state's population.

Family Support, Competence, and Substance Use

Study 1 tested a functional model of family support with a sample of 1,289 students in sixth through eighth grades. A 15-item scale was developed to index emotional and instrumental support from parents. Subjects were instructed to complete the items to describe their feelings about the parent they talked to the most, hence responses should not be biased by whether the subject is in a single-parent family (which is a realistic concern as can be seen in Table 4.1). Typical items in the emotional support scale were "I feel that I trust my parent as someone to talk to," and "When I feel bad about something, my parent will listen"; typical items for the instrumental scale were "If I need help in getting somewhere, I can ask my parent for a way to get there," and "If I'm having problems with my school work, I can ask my parent about it." Scoring was for a seven-item emotional support scale (Cronbach $\alpha = .81$) and an eight-item instrumental support scale ($\alpha = .74$). The two scales were substantially correlated ($r = .57$), which is typical for functional measures (Wills, 1991). The support measures were administered together with scales for Academic Competence, Peer Social Competence, and Adult Social Competence using measures from Harter's (1985) Perceived Competence Inventory. Also included was a 23-item inventory for major negative life events during the past year, based on previous instruments

---

[2]Comparisons on measures of competence and life events, using data from other samples, also indicated that these students were comparable to those in local and national samples (see Wills, Vaccaro, & McNamara, 1992).

TABLE 4.1
Descriptive Statistics for Samples, Two Studies

	Study 1	*Study 2*
N	1,289	1,702
Grade	6–8	7
Age of subjects	11.7–13.7 yrs.	11.5 yrs.
Gender		
Female	46%	47%
Male	54%	53%
Ethnic background		
Black	25%	29%
Hispanic	51%	23%
White	17%	37%
Family structure		
Intact	na	53%
Single parent	na	34%
Blended	na	13%
Completion rate	91%	92%
Location	Inner city	Metropolitan area
School system	Parochial	Public

(see Wills, 1986). The criterion measures were items indexing frequency of cigarette smoking, alcohol use, marijuana use, and heavy drinking.

Results for this study showed predicted effects (Wills, Vaccaro, & McNamara, 1992). With overall substance use as the criterion variable, multiple regression analyses showed independent effects for emotional support (main effect $p <$ .0001) and instrumental support (main effect $p < .0001$), both inversely related to substance use. This strengthens confidence in the concept that protective aspects of family relationships derive from the provision of supportive functions, and indicates that each function has an independent effect.[3] Also, there were significant Life Events × Family Support interactions with substance use as the criterion ($p < .0001$ for both emotional and instrumental support): There was a strong relationship between negative life events and substance use for students with low support, but the impact of life events was reduced for students with high support. This indicates that supportive functions from family relationships are most relevant for adolescents with a high level of adversity; this is consistent with previous suggestions about the basis of resilience (Werner, 1986).

The competence measures were also tested as predictors of substance use. Main effects for academic competence and adult competence were significant (p < .0001 for both), with these types of competence inversely related to substance

---

[3]All the reported results were replicated with demographic controls, including indices for sex, race, and age in multiple regression together with the predictor variables. Although sex and race differences were found for some of the predictors, the effects reported are independent of demographic characteristics.

use as predicted. Peer competence was positively related to substance use in the multivariate model. There were significant Life Events × Competence interactions for academic competence and adult competence, consistent in form with stress buffering, for the indices of heavy drinking and marijuana use ($p < .01$ for both). Examples are presented in Figs. 4.1a and 4.1b. For both variables, the relationship between life events and substance use was reduced for students with higher

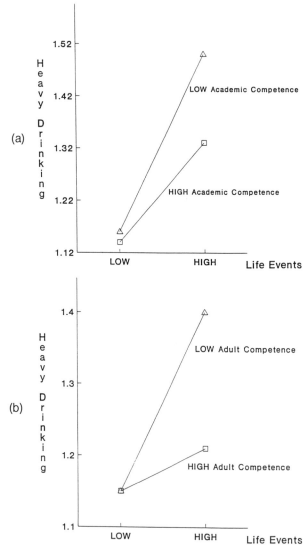

FIG. 4.1.   Interaction of Life Events × Competence for criterion variable of heavy drinking. (a) academic competence. (b) adult competence. Low and high values represent $M \pm 1$ SD for each variable.

higher competence. So there is evidence that these types of competence not only are protective factors, but have a greater effect for adolescents with a high level of life stress. The results for peer competence are more perplexing and suggest that it may be something of a double-edged sword. Although having friends is overall a good thing, adolescents with a high level of peer social activity but a low level of adult support are more vulnerable to modeling effects of peer substance use (cf. Larson, 1983; Wills & Vaughan, 1989).

In this study, there were substantial correlations among the support, competence, and life events variables. Family support was positively correlated with academic, peer, and adult competence (r's ranged from .20 to .53, all significant). The correlations are consistent with the competence model and with the prediction that family support leads to greater competence. Also, both family support and competence were related to lower levels of life events (r's = −.23 to −.27 for support, r's = −.19 to −.36 for competence). The inverse relation between competence and negative events can be viewed as the operation of a preventive process.

Family Support and Coping

Study 2 surveyed a larger sample in the metropolitan area. All subjects were in seventh grade at the outset of the study. This study included teacher ratings of competence in addition to self-report questionnaires completed by students. The questionnaire included an eight-dimensional intention-based coping inventory based on the work of Stone and Neale (1984). Subjects were asked to indicate how often they pursued each of eight coping intentions for each of four types of problems: school work, parents, health, and sadness. The coping dimensions are termed behavioral coping, cognitive coping, and physical exercise (assumed to be adaptive coping mechanisms) and anger, avoidance, "hanging out" with other kids, and helplessness or "giving up" (assumed to be nonadaptive coping mechanisms). Scores aggregating across the four types of problems had good internal consistency, with alphas ranging from .75 to .88. The substance use criterion measures were the same as in the previous study.

This study replicated the previous findings on the protective effect of family support with respect to substance use, showing significant independent effects for parental emotional and instrumental support. Effect size was stronger for emotional support in this sample, suggesting that instrumental support is particularly relevant for lower income children, as in the inner-city sample. The stress-buffering effect of parental support was replicated for indices of more deviant substance use (marijuana and heavy drinking).

The competence data were interesting. Self-reports of academic competence were inversely related to substance use ($p < .0001$), whereas self-reports of peer and adult competence were nonsignificant. Teacher ratings showed adult competence inversely related to substance use, and peer competence positively related ($p < .0001$ for both). When self-report and teacher rating data were entered

TABLE 4.2
Correlations of Family Support and Coping, Seventh Grade Data

	Emotional Support	Instrumental Support
Behavioral Coping	.38****	.39****
Cognitive Coping	.28****	.28****
Physical Exercise Coping	.09***	.08**
Anger Coping	−.24****	−.21****
Avoidance Coping	−.09***	−.12****
Hang Out with Kids Coping	−.08**	−.11****
Helplessness Coping	−.19****	−.18****

Note. N = approximately 1,600 observations.
**$p < .01$. ***$p < .001$. ****$p < .0001$.

together, all the significant effects were maintained; that is, students' self-reported academic competence and teachers' ratings of peer and adult competence each showed unique contributions to substance use in a simultaneous regression model (Wills, Vaccaro, McNamara, & Spellman, 1991). The Life Events × Competence buffer interactions were replicated for academic competence ($p < .0001$) and adult competence ($p < .01$), mainly for the criterion of marijuana use.[4] This indicates that students and teachers have independent but equally useful perspectives on competence (cf. Achenbach, McConaughy, & Howell, 1987).

To test the hypothesis that family support is related to coping mechanisms, zero-order correlations were computed; results are presented in Table 4.2. Notable results are first of all, the symmetric effects: Family support is related to more adaptive coping and less nonadaptive coping. Second, the effect sizes are not trivial; the positive correlations with behavioral and cognitive coping are substantial, and the inverse correlations with anger and helplessness are not negligible either. This provides support for the prediction that family relationships contribute to resilience through the promotion of effective coping.

Is it possible that the correlation between family support and coping is really attributable to a third factor (such as socioeconomic status) that is related to both variables? To address this issue, multiple regression analyses were performed with a coping measure as the criterion and a support measure plus complete demographic controls (sex, race, and parental education) as the predictors. In these analyses, the contribution of family support to coping was essentially unchanged. This strengthens the conclusion that the effect for family support does not simply reflect the operation of a third factor.

---

[4]For overall alcohol use, there was an interaction for peer competence with a positive regression weight; for example, stress had more impact on substance use for students with high peer competence. Again, peer support is a mixed blessing. The fact that this interaction was not found for heavy drinking or marijuana use suggests that it may represent more normative social drinking. Studies of motives for smoking or alcohol often find social use to be an independent motive dimension that is not highly related to addictive motives (see Wills & Cleary, 1995b).

Demographic Effects

The results just discussed were based on analyses for the entire sample. However, do family support or its effects differ across demographic groups? To address this question, two different types of analyses were performed. First, to address differences in absolute level, analysis of variance was performed with gender, ethnicity, family structure, and their two-way interactions as predictors, and $p < .01$ as the criterion for significance. For substance use as the criterion variable, there was no significant gender difference, but a main effect for ethnicity indicated Blacks had lower levels of use than Whites. A significant main effect for family structure indicated subjects from both single-parent families and blended families showed more substance use, compared with those from intact families. For emotional support, a main effect for ethnicity indicated scores for support were lower for Blacks compared with Whites or Hispanics. With regard to family structure, subjects from blended families had lower levels of emotional support compared with subjects from intact or single families. For instrumental support, a main effect for family structure indicated lower support for both single and blended families. Thus there were some significant differences in the absolute levels of support and substance use for different demographic subgroups.

The second question is whether the effect of family support is comparable for all demographic groups. To address this question, multiple regression analyses were performed with substance use score as the criterion variable. The predictor variables were a demographic index (e.g., gender), a family support measure, and the cross-product of the support index and the demographic index (e.g., gender × emotional support). A significant coefficient for the cross-product term in this analysis indicates the strength of effect (i.e., regression slope) for the support measure differs across demographic groups. Some significant interactions were found. There were significant interactions for gender, indicating the relation between parental support and substance use was greater among females ($p < .01$ and $p = .05$ for emotional and instrumental support, respectively), although the effect of parental support was significant in both gender groups. For ethnicity, the relation between parental support and substance use was lower among Blacks, compared with either Whites or Hispanics. This was true for both emotional support ($p < .01$) and instrumental support ($p = .02$), although again the relation between parental support and substance use was significant in all groups. Differential effects were not found as a function of family structure. Thus the hypothesis of comparable effect of family support across demographic subgroups was rejected. The effect of support was greater for females than for males, and for Hispanics and Whites compared with Blacks.

Family Structure and Substance Use

Predictions about the effect of family structure on support, competence, and substance use have been examined with data from Study 2. Family structure was indexed using an item that asked what adult(s) the respondent currently lived with (eight response options). The item indicated a total of 22 different family structures, which is typical for urban samples. This item was recoded into three global categories, as indicated in Table 4.1. The categories were termed *intact family* (subject currently lives with both biological parents), *single-parent family* (subject currently lives with single mother or father, sometimes including relatives), and *blended family* (subject currently lives with one biological parent and one stepparent). A substantial proportion of children were in either single-parent or blended families.

It was hypothesized that family disruption has effects on substance use through a decrement in support from the parent. Disruption may affect a parent's ability to provide support to a child because he or she is preoccupied with financial pressure or emotional problems (Conger et al., 1990; Newcomb & Bentler, 1988; Takeuchi et al., 1991). A decrement in parental support could then relate to lower competence of the child. If the pressures of family disruption reduce the amount of time the parent spends with the child, this could have effects on academic competence as well as social competence. These hypotheses were tested in a path analysis (McNamara, 1992) with a composite score for substance (tobacco, alcohol, marijuana) use as the outcome variable, and including a test of whether effects of competence or family support were mediated through negative affect. The test for negative affect used a 12-item scale ($\alpha = .88$), based on mood adjectives from Zevon and Tellegen (1982), which indexed the adolescent's affect during the previous month.

A path analysis tested the basic model, using data from Study 2. Parallel analyses for family structure were performed, one using a dichotomous index that contrasted adolescents in single-parent families with those in intact families, a second using a dichotomous index that contrasted adolescents in blended families with those in intact families. Sex, race, and number of siblings were unrelated to the variables under study, so these were not included in the path model. It was assumed in the model that family support is antecedent to the development of competence, and that both support and competence are antecedent to development of negative affect.

The findings from this analysis can be summarized as follows: First, rates of substance use were elevated both for adolescents in single-parent families and for adolescents in blended families, consistent with previous research (e.g., Hetherington, 1991). Second, the path models were consistent with the hypothesized process; a typical model, that for academic competence, is presented in Fig. 4.2. Results showed family structure (either singleness or blendedness) was related to lower levels of family support and lower levels of academic competence (but not peer or adult competence). Lower support and lower competence were related to higher levels of negative affect, and negative affect was significantly related to more substance use. Not predicted, but consistent in all models, was a direct effect from family structure to more substance use, not involving any of the other variables in the model. Also, there were direct effects from family

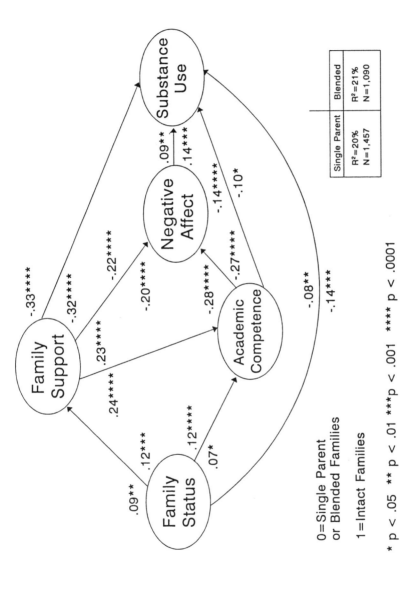

FIG. 4.2. Path analysis for family structure in relation to support, competence, affect, and substance use. Family structure is coded such that 1 = intact family, 0 = single or blended family. Coefficients for single-parent analysis are above line, coefficients for blended-family analysis are below line. Substance use score is equal-weighted composite for tobacco, alcohol, marijuana, and heavy drinking.

125

support to (less) substance use and a direct path from academic competence to (less) substance use. These models accounted for 9% to 11% of the variance in substance use. The limitation of the data is that the path from negative affect to substance use, although significant, is of modest magnitude for a proposed proximal variable, so the indirect effects of family structure, family support, and competence going through this variable are relatively weak. The direct paths in the model may reflect other variables such as parental conflict or lack of supervision (Borrine, Handal, Brown, & Searight, 1991; Patterson et al., 1989). In other analyses, it was shown that the effect of parental support was independent of parental substance use, and a low level of parental support was related to more association with deviant peers (Wills, McNamara, Riccobono, & Vaccaro, 1992; Wills & Cleary, 1995a).

Prospective Effects

In Study 2, students were followed up 1 year subsequent to the baseline survey, and prospective analyses were performed. The analytic model used a Time 2 variable as criterion, and a Time 1 predictor plus the Time 1 level of the criterion (i.e., covariate) as independent variables. This prospective model helps to clarify temporal relationships in the data and resolve ambiguity about direction of effects.

These prospective analyses, performed with a 1-year interval, were consistent with the predictions previously outlined. Parental support was inversely related to substance use over time ($p < .001$), indicating that it is a true protective factor; that is, support is antecedent to change in substance use. In this analysis, emotional support had the unique effect.

Prospective analyses indicated parental support at Time 1 was related to increased competence over time; effects were found for academic competence ($p = .02$), peer competence ($p < .01$), and adult competence ($p < .001$). Support was also related to increased adaptive coping over time ($p < .0001$ for most effects) and decreased nonadaptive coping over time ($p < .001$ for most effects). This is consistent with the prediction that family relationships contribute to increased coping and competence.

Finally, prospective models indicated instrumental support ($p < .0001$) and academic competence ($p < .01$) were inversely related to life events over time. This is consistent with the prediction that support and competence help to prevent the occurrence of negative life events.

SUMMARY AND DIRECTIONS

This chapter has described a model of family communication and support, and proposed the hypothesis that family relationships contribute to resilience through promoting the development of coping and competence in children. Data from research with urban adolescents provide evidence consistent with several tenets of the model. Measures that derive from a functional model of social support are significantly related to lower levels of deviant outcomes, and family support operates as a stress-buffering agent, consistent with suggestions from the literature on resilience (Garmezy & Masten, 1991; Rutter, 1990; Werner, 1986). Emotional support seems to be the function with the most general effect for reducing adverse outcomes, consistent with previous theoretical suggestions on social support (Cohen & Wills, 1985; Wills, 1991). These effects, however, are not the same in all parts of the population. With regard to substance use as an outcome, family support is more relevant for females compared with males, and less relevant for Black teenagers, compared with those of Hispanic or White ethnicity.

The present chapter shows that family support is related to higher levels of coping and competence in children, and demonstrates that this relationship is not attributable to a third factor (socioeconomic status). We find that competence operates as a stress-buffering agent, and we showed how a specific stressor (family disruption) may contribute to adverse outcomes through a detrimental effect on support and competence processes. This provides evidence for several predictions from the chapter's theoretical model, and convergent findings from cross-sectional and prospective analyses provide evidence for the direction of relationships posited in the model. Finally, it was suggested that family support may help to avert the occurrence of negative life events, and this prediction was confirmed in longitudinal data. Together, these data suggest that family support has an important role in resilience effects.

Directions

In the present research, evidence on family support as a protective factor has come from epidemiologic studies that examine the distribution of outcomes in the general population of adolescents. A number of questions are raised by the current evidence and could be pursued to obtain a better understanding of how family support works. One direction would be to obtain direct observation of family members in communication with each other, either in the home or in carefully structured laboratory situations. This would provide data on how supportive families are distinguished from less supportive ones, with respect to specific dimensions of their communication. Analogously, youth from families with different levels of supportiveness could themselves be observed in communication situations with peers or other adults (e.g., teachers, an important element in the lives of children). It would be interesting to find that family background was related to the way children communicate with others, or the way in which they are able to empathize with other teenager's problems (Eisenberg & Fabes, 1992). This type of work could provide evidence to link social support to communication processes.

Another direction is to examine the unfolding of specific coping episodes to determine how particular types of coping contribute to (or detract from) successful adaptation. It is surely unrealistic to expect that a successful coper would simply repeat the same coping mechanism throughout all the stages of dealing with, and resolving, a problematic situation (Lazarus & Folkman, 1984). Beyond this postulate, however, relatively little is known about how successful versus unsuccessful copers (or alternatively, socially competent vs. less competent children) differ in the way they select initial coping mechanisms, the way in which they balance behavioral (problem-focused) coping and cognitive (emotion-focused) coping, or the way in which they involve other persons in the coping process. To do this may well require study of coping on a day-to-day basis.

In research on coping and adjustment, there is also an ongoing question about level of analysis. It is conceivable that outcomes of coping episodes are influenced not so much by the utilization of specific coping mechanisms, but by the person's overall approach to coping. One hypothesis is that an important factor lies in basic attitudinal dimensions that influence the course of the coping effort. There are several good candidates, including optimism (Scheier & Carver, 1987), problem-solving confidence (Heppner, 1989), and perceived control (Wills, 1994). Some evidence for each of these mechanisms is available in retrospective or prospective research, and leads to the prediction that efficacy orientation or generalized outcome expectancies are a crucial factor in predicting the course of the coping effort. An alternative (and not mutually exclusive) concept is that the outcome of coping is strongly influenced by the total number of coping strategies applied over the course of the coping effort (Perri, 1985; Shiffman, 1985).

With respect to social aspects of coping, there are many questions about how basic schemas of the self and social relationships develop. In research on resilience, the ancedotal reports emphasize how some children in adverse life circumstances nevertheless emerge with a sense of trust in interpersonal relationships; the assumption, bordering on a generalized expectancy, is that people (or at least some people) are trustworthy and that being involved with and relying on other people will lead to positive things (Sarason, Pierce, & Sarason, 1990). One has to believe that such orientations, and the allied sense of self-acceptance, are important dimensions of resilience and that longitudinal investigations of relationship orientations will help to deepen understanding of how coping efforts are embedded in an interpersonal matrix (Wills, Mariani, & Filer, in press).

Also, these data indicate that family support helps not only to reduce the impact of negative events but also to prevent the occurrence of such events. This shifts the research question to a focus on why events do not occur, as Sherlock Holmes (in investigating the disappearance of the racehorse Silver Blaze from a guarded barn) emphasized the significance of the dog that did not bark in the night (Doyle, 1927). Attention then focuses on how particular negative events are precipitated, and through comparative studies, on why they occur for some children but not for others with an initially comparable level of risk.

Finally, the present data on family support are derived from studies of children who for the most part are facing normative and developmentally appropriate stressors. Although we believe the findings would also apply for children who face other types of stressors (e.g., war trauma, poverty, or homelessness), this remains to be investigated in work with smaller samples of high-risk children (cf. Seracini, Siegel, Wills, Nunes, & Goldstein, 1995).

ACKNOWLEDGMENTS

This work was supported by grant #R01-DA-05950 from the National Institute on Drug Abuse and #S184A-00035 from the U.S. Department of Education (TAW), and grant #R18-DA-06360 from the National Institute on Drug Abuse and #R18-MH-48018 from the National Institute of Mental Health (EAB). We thank the principals of the participating schools for their support and cooperation.

REFERENCES

Achenbach, T. M., McConaughy, S. H., & Howell, C. T. (1987). Child/adolescent behavioral and emotional problems: Implications of cross-informant correlations for situational specificity. *Psychological Bulletin, 101*, 213–232.

Bachman, J. G., Johnston, L. D., & O'Malley, P. M. (1981). Smoking, drinking, and drug use among American high school students: Correlates and trends 1975–1979. *American Journal of Public Health, 71*, 59–69.

Barlow, D., & Cerny, J. A. (1988). *Psychological treatment of panic.* New York: Guilford.

Baumrind, D. (1991). Effective parenting during the early adolescent transition. In P. A. Cowan & M. Hetherington (Eds.), *Family transitions* (pp. 111–163). Hillsdale, NJ: Lawrence Erlbaum Associates.

Blechman, E. A. (1982). Conventional wisdom about familial contributions to substance abuse. *American Journal of Drug and Alcohol Abuse, 9*, 35–53.

Blechman, E. A. (1990). A model of effective family communication. In E. A. Blechman (Ed.), *Emotions and the family* (pp. 201–224). Hillsdale, NJ: Lawrence Erlbaum Associates.

Blechman, E. A. (1991). Effective communication: Enabling multiproblem families to change. In P. A. Cowan & M. Hetherington (Eds.), *Family transitions* (pp. 219–244). Hillsdale, NJ: Lawrence Erlbaum Associates.

Blechman, E. A., Berberian, R. M., & Thompson, W. D. (1977). How well does number of parents explain unique variance in self-report drug use? *Journal of Consulting and Clinical Psychology, 45*, 1182–1183.

Blechman, E. A., McEnroe, M. J., & Carella, E. T. (1986). Childhood competence and depression. *Journal of Abnormal Psychology, 95*, 223–227.

Blechman, E. A., Tinsley, B., Carella, E. T., & McEnroe, M. J. (1985). Childhood competence and behavior problems. *Journal of Abnormal Psychology, 94*, 70–77.

Blechman, E. A., & Wills, T. A. (1992). Process measures in interventions for drug-abusing women: From coping to competence. In M. M. Kilbey & K. Asghar (Eds.), *Methodological issues in epidemiological, prevention, and treatment research on drug-exposed women and their children* (pp. 314–343). Rockville, MD: National Institute on Drug Abuse.

Borrine, M., Handal, P. J., Brown, N. Y., & Searight, H. R. (1991). Family conflict and adolescent adjustment in intact, divorced, and blended families. *Journal of Consulting and Clinical Psychology, 59*, 753–755.

Buck, R. (1985). Prime theory: An integrated view of motivation and emotion. *Psychological Review*, *92*, 389–413.

Burke, R. J., & Weir, T. (1978). Benefits to adolescents of informal helping relationships with their parents and peers. *Psychological Reports*, *42*, 1175–1184.

Burke, R. J., & Weir, T. (1979). Helping responses of parents and peers and adolescent well-being. *Journal of Psychology*, *102*, 49–62.

Carver, C. S., Scheier, M. F., & Weintraub, J. K. (1989). Assessing coping strategies. *Journal of Personality and Social Psychology*, *56*, 267–283.

Cauce, A. M. (1986). Social networks and social competence: Exploring the effects of early adolescent friendships. *American Journal of Community Psychology*, *14*, 607–628.

Cauce, A. M. (1987). School and peer competence in early adolescence: A test of domain-specific self-perceived competence. *Developmental Psychology*, *23*, 287–291.

Cohen, S., & Wills, T. A. (1985). Stress, social support, and the buffering hypothesis. *Psychological Bulletin*, *98*, 310–357.

Coie, J. D., Dodge, K. A., & Kupersmidt, J. B. (1990). Peer group behavior and social status. In S. R. Asher & J. D. Coie (Eds.), *Peer rejection in childhood* (pp. 17–59). New York: Cambridge University Press.

Compas, B. E. (1987). Coping with stress during childhood and adolescence. *Psychological Bulletin*, *101*, 393–403.

Conger, R. D., Elder, G. H., Jr., Lorenz, F. O., Conger, K. J., Simons, R. L., Whitbeck, L. B., Huck, S., & Melby, J. N. (1990). Linking economic hardship to marital quality and instability. *Journal of Marriage and the Family*, *52*, 643–656.

Cutrona, C. E., & Russell, D. W. (1987). The provisions of social relationships and adaptation to stress. In W. H. Jones & D. Perlman (Eds.), *Advances in personal relationships* (Vol. 1, pp. 37–67). Greenwich, CT: JAI.

Dishion, T. J., Reid, J. B., & Patterson, G. R. (1988). Empirical guidelines for a family intervention for adolescent drug use. In R. H. Coombs (Ed.), *The family context of adolescent drug use* (pp. 189–224). Binghamton, NY: Haworth.

Dodge, K. A., Pettit, G. S., McClaskey, C. L., & Brown, M. M. (1986). Social competence in children. *Monographs of the Society for Research in Child Development*, *51*(2, Serial No. 213).

Dornbusch, S. M., Carlsmith, J. M., Bushwall, S. J., Ritter, P. L., Leiderman, H., Hastorf, A. H., & Gross, R. T. (1985). Single parents and the control of adolescents. *Child Development*, *56*, 326–341.

Doyle, A. C. (1927). The adventure of Silver Blaze. In *The complete Sherlock Holmes* (pp. 383–401). Garden City, NY: Garden City Publishing.

Eisenberg, N., & Fabes, R. A. (1992). Emotion regulation and the development of social competence. In M. S. Clark (Ed.), *Review of personality and social psychology (Vol. 14): Emotion and social behavior* (pp. 119–150). Newbury Park, CA: Sage.

Elder, G. H., Jr., Nguyen, T. V., & Caspi, A. (1985). Linking family hardship to children's lives. *Child Development*, *56*, 361–375.

Emery, R. E. (1988). *Marriage, divorce, and children's adjustment*. Newbury Park, CA: Sage.

Flewelling, R. L., & Bauman, K. E. (1990). Family structure as a predictor of initial substance use and sexual intercourse in early adolescence. *Journal of Marriage and the Family*, *52*, 171–181.

Fondacaro, M. R., & Heller, K. (1983). Social support factors and drinking among college student males. *Journal of Youth and Adolescence*, *12*, 285–299.

Garmezy, N., & Masten, A. S. (1991). The protective role of competence indicators in children at risk. In E. M. Cummings, A. L. Greene, & K. H. Karraker (Eds.), *Life span developmental psychology: Perspectives on stress and coping* (pp. 151–174). Hillsdale, NJ: Lawrence Erlbaum Associates.

Garmezy, N., & Rutter, M. (Eds.). (1983). *Stress, coping, and development in children*. New York: McGraw-Hill.

Glantz, M. D. (1992). A developmental psychopathology model of drug abuse vulnerability. In M. Glantz & R. W. Pickens (Eds.), *Vulnerability to drug abuse* (pp. 389–418). Washington, DC: American Psychological Association.

Greenberg, M. T., Siegel, J. M., & Leitch, C. J. (1983). The nature and importance of attachment relationships to parents and peers during adolescence. *Journal of Youth and Adolescence, 12*, 373–386.

Hanson, C. L., Henggeler, S. W., & Burghen, G. A. (1987). Social competence and parental support as mediators of the link between stress and metabolic control in adolescents with insulin-dependent diabetes mellitus. *Journal of Consulting and Clinical Psychology, 55*, 529–533.

Harter, S. (1985). *Manual for the self-perception profile for children and adolescents.* Denver, CO: University of Denver.

Heppner, P. P. (1989). *Problem solving inventory.* Palo Alto, CA: Consulting Psychologists Press.

Hetherington, M. (1989). Coping with family transitions: Winners, losers, and survivors. *Child Development, 60*, 1–14.

Hetherington, M. (1991). The role of individual differences and family relationships in children's coping with divorce and remarriage. In P. A. Cowan & M. Hetherington (Eds.), *Family transitions* (pp. 165–194). Hillsdale, NJ: Lawrence Erlbaum Associates.

Hetherington, M., Arnett, J., & Hollier, E. A. (1988). Adjustment of parents and children to remarriage. In S. Wolchik & P. Karoly (Eds.), *Children of divorce: Perspectives on adjustment* (pp. 67–107). New York: Gardner.

Hetherington, M., Cox, M., & Cox, R. (1982). Effects of divorce on parents and children. In M. Lamb (Ed.), *Nontraditional families* (pp. 233–288). Hillsdale, NJ: Lawrence Erlbaum Associates.

Hoelter, J., & Harper, L. (1987). Structural and interpersonal family influences on adolescent self-conception. *Journal of Marriage and the Family, 49*, 129–139.

House, J. S., Landis, K. R., & Umberson, D. (1988). Social relationships and health. *Science, 241*, 540–545.

Kaplan, H. B. (1980). *Deviant behavior in defense of self.* New York: Academic Press.

Kaplan, H. B., Martin, S. S., & Robbins, C. (1984). Pathways to adolescent drug use: Self-derogation, peer influence, weakening of social controls, and early substance use. *Journal of Health and Social Behavior, 25*, 270–289.

Kellam, S. G., Ensminger, M. E., & Turner, R. J. (1977). Family structure and the mental health of children. *Archives of General Psychiatry, 34*, 1012–1022.

Kendall, P. C., & Williams, C. L. (1982). Assessing the cognitive and behavioral components of children self-management. In P. Karoly & F. Kanfer (Eds.), *Self-management and behavior change* (pp. 240–284). Elmsford, NY: Pergamon.

Kupersmidt, J. B., Coie, J. D., & Dodge, K. A. (1990). The role of poor peer relationships in the development of disorder. In S. R. Asher & J. D. Coie (Eds.), *Peer rejection in childhood* (pp. 274–305). New York: Cambridge University Press.

Larson, R. W. (1983). Adolescents' daily experience with family and friends: Contrasting opportunity systems. *Journal of Marriage and the Family, 45*, 739–750.

Lazarus, R. S., & Folkman, S. (1984). *Stress, appraisal and coping.* New York: Springer.

Leadbeater, B. J., Hellner, I., Allen, J. P., & Aber, J. L. (1989). Assessment of interpersonal negotiation strategies of youth engaged in problem behaviors. *Developmental Psychology, 25*, 465–472.

Masten, A. S., Morison, P., Pellegrini, D., & Tellegen, A. (1990). Competence under stress: Risk and protective factors. In J. Rolf, A. S. Masten, D. Cicchetti, K. H. Nuechterlein, & S. Weintraub (Eds.), *Risk and protective factors in development of psychopathology* (pp. 236–256). New York: Cambridge University Press.

McNamara, G. (1992). *The relation between family status and adolescent substance use.* Unpublished master's thesis, Ferkauf Graduate School of Psychology, Bronx, New York.

Murray, M., Kiryluk, S., & Swan, A. (1985). Relation between parents' and children's smoking behaviour and attitudes. *Journal of Epidemiology and Community Health, 39*, 169–174.

Murray, D. M., Perry, C. L., O'Connell, C., & Schmid, L. (1987). Seventh-grade cigarette, alcohol, and marijuana use: Distribution in a North Central U.S. metropolitan population. *International Journal of the Addictions, 22*, 357–376.

Needle, R. H., Su, S., & Doherty, W. J. (1990). Divorce, remarriage, and adolescent substance use: A prospective longitudinal study. *Journal of Marriage and the Family, 52*, 157–169.

Newcomb, M. D., & Bentler, P. M. (1988). The impact of family context, deviant attitudes, and emotional distress on adolescent drug use: Longitudinal latent-variable analyses of mothers and their children. *Journal of Research in Personality, 22*, 154–176.

Parker, J. G., & Asher, S. R. (1987). Peer relations and later personal adjustment: Are low-accepted children at risk? *Psychological Bulletin, 102*, 357–389.

Patterson, G. R., DeBaryshe, B. D., & Ramsey, E. (1989). A developmental perspective on antisocial behavior. *American Psychologist, 44*, 329–335.

Perri, M. G. (1985). Self-change strategies for the control of smoking, obesity, and problem drinking. In S. Shiffman & T. A. Wills (Eds.), *Coping and substance use* (pp. 295–318). Orlando, FL: Academic Press.

Rohde, P., Lewinsohn, P. M., Tilson, M., & Seeley, J. R. (1990). Dimensionality of coping and its relation to depression. *Journal of Personality and Social Psychology, 58*, 499–511.

Rutter, M. (1985). Resilience in the face of adversity: Protective factors and resistance to psychiatic disorder. *British Journal of Psychiatry, 147*, 598–611.

Rutter, M. (1990). Psychosocial resilience and protective mechanisms. In J. Rolf, A. S. Masten, D. Cicchetti, K. H. Nuechterlein, & S. Weintraub (Eds.), *Risk and protective factors in development of psychopathology* (pp. 181–214). New York: Cambridge University Press.

Sandler, I. N., Miller, P., Short, J., & Wolchik, S. A. (1989). Social support as a protective factor for children in stress. In D. Belle (Ed.), *Children's social networks and social supports* (pp. 277–307). New York: Wiley.

Sarason, B. R., Pierce, G. R., & Sarason, I. G. (1990). Social support: The sense of acceptance and the role of relationships. In B. R. Sarason, I. G. Sarason, & G. R. Pierce (Eds.), *Social support: An interactional view* (pp. 97–128). New York: Wiley.

Scheier, M. F., & Carver C. S. (1987). Dispositional optimism and physical well-being: The influence of generalized outcome expectancies on health. *Journal of Personality, 55*, 169–210.

Seracini, A. M., Siegel, L. J., Wills, T. A., Nunes, E. V., & Goldstein, R. B. (1995, August). *Coping, social support and adjustment in children of heroin addicts.* Paper presented at the meeting of the American Psychological Association, New York, NY.

Shiffman, S. (1985). Coping with temptations to smoke. In S. Shiffman & T. A. Wills (Eds.), *Coping and substance use* (pp. 223–242). Orlando, FL: Academic Press.

Spivack, G. M., Platt, J. J., & Shure, M. B. (1976). *The problem-solving approach to adjustment: A guide to research and intervention.* San Francisco: Jossey-Bass.

Steinberg, L., Dornbusch, S. M., & Brown, B. B. (1992). Ethnic differences in adolescent achievement: An ecological perspective. *American Psychologist, 47*, 723–729.

Sternberg, R. J., & Kolligian, J., Jr. (Eds.). (1990). *Competence considered.* New Haven, CT: Yale University Press.

Stone, A. A., & Neale, J. M. (1984). A new measure of daily coping. *Journal of Personality and Social Psychology, 46*, 892–906.

Takeuchi, D. T., Williams, D. R., & Adair, R. K. (1991). Economic stress in the family and children's emotional and behavioral problems. *Journal of Marriage and the Family, 53*, 1031–1041.

Tarter, R. E., Alterman, A., & Edwards, K. (1985). Vulnerability to alcoholism: A behavior-genetic perspective. *Journal of Studies on Alcohol, 46*, 329–356.

Vaux, A. (1988). *Social support: Theory, research and intervention.* New York: Praeger.

Vygotsky, L. (1978). *Mind in society.* Cambridge, MA: Cambridge University Press.

Werner, E. E. (1986). Resilient offspring of alcoholics: A longitudinal study from birth to age 18. *Journal of Studies on Alcohol, 47*, 34–40.

Werner, E. E. (1989). High-risk children in young adulthood: A longitudinal study from birth to 32 years. *American Journal of Orthopsychiatry, 59*, 72–81.

Werner, E. E., & Smith, R. S. (1982). *Vulnerable but invincible: A longitudinal study of resilient children and youth.* New York: McGraw-Hill.

Wills, T. A. (1985). Supportive functions of interpersonal relationships. In S. Cohen & S. L. Syme (Eds.), *Social support and health* (pp. 61–82). Orlando, FL: Academic Press.

Wills, T. A. (1986). Stress and coping in early adolescence: Relationships to substance use in urban school samples. *Health Psychology, 5*, 503–529.

Wills, T. A. (1990a). Multiple networks and substance use. *Journal of Social and Clinical Psychology, 9*, 78–90.

Wills, T. A. (1990b). Social support and the family. In E. Blechman (Ed.), *Emotions and the family* (pp. 75–98). Hillsdale, NJ: Lawrence Erlbaum Associates.

Wills, T. A. (1991). Social support and interpersonal relationships. In M. S. Clark (Ed.), *Review of personality and social psychology* (Vol. 12, pp. 265–289). Newbury Park, CA: Sage.

Wills, T. A. (1994). Self-esteem and perceived control in adolescent substance use: Comparative tests in concurrent and prospective analyses. *Psychology of Addictive Behaviors, 8*, 223–234.

Wills, T. A., & Cleary, S. D. (1995a). *How are social support effects mediated: A test for parental support and adolescent substance use.* Manuscript submitted for publication.

Wills, T. A., & Cleary, S. D. (1995b). Stress-coping model for alcohol/tobacco interactions in adolescence. In J. Fertig & J. Allen (Eds.), *Alcohol and tobacco: From basic science to policy* (pp. 107–128). NIAAA Research Monograph.

Wills, T. A., Mariani, J., & Filer, M. (in press). The role of family and peer relationships in adolescent substance use. In G. R. Pierce, B. R. Sarason, & I. G. Sarason (Eds.), *Handbook of social support and the family.* New York: Plenum Press.

Wills, T. A., McNamara, G., Riccobono, A., & Vaccaro, D. (1992, March). *Family support and substance use in urban adolescents: A path model.* Paper presented at the meeting of the Society for Research on Adolescence, Washington, DC.

Wills, T. A., Vaccaro, D., & McNamara, G. (1992). The role of life events, family support, and competence in adolescent substance use: A test of vulnerability and protective factors. *American Journal of Community Psychology, 20*, 349–374.

Wills, T. A., Vaccaro, D., McNamara, G., & DuHamel, D. (1992, August). *Coping and substance use among urban adolescents.* Paper presented at the meeting of the American Psychological Association, Washington, DC.

Wills, T. A., Vaccaro, D., McNamara, G., & Spellman, M. (1991, August). *Three competence domains relate to adolescent substance use.* Paper presented at the American Psychological Assocation, San Francisco.

Wills, T. A., & Vaughan, R. (1989). Social support and substance use in early adolescence. *Journal of Behavioral Medicine, 12*, 321–339.

Zevon, M. A., & Tellegen, A. (1982). The structure of mood change: An idiographic/nomothetic analysis. *Journal of Personality and Social Psychology, 43*, 111–122.

5

▼▼▼▼▼▼▼

Risk and Resiliency in Nonclinical Young Children: The Georgia Longitudinal Study

Karen S. Wampler
Texas Tech University

Charles F. Halverson, Jr.
University of Georgia

James Deal
North Dakota State University

The Georgia Longitudinal Study (GLS) was designed to study the mutual influence of the family context and child functioning over time. Rather than assuming, as in most studies of family factors and child functioning, that the major direction of effect is from the family to the child, the purpose of the GLS was to discover the conditions under which the direction of effect was predominately from the family to the child, as well as the conditions under which the direction of effect was predominately from the child to the family. In order to assess the direction of effect between the family context and child functioning, this research included a longitudinal design with data collection at 1-year intervals over 5 years; an analysis strategy that explicitly examined for effects in the family-to-child direction and the child-to-family direction; a separation of child functioning into externalizing ("acting out" behaviors) and internalizing ("neurotic" or "acting in" behaviors); separate analyses for girls and boys when appropriate; data from multiple sources, specifically teachers, outside observers, mothers, and fathers; separate measures for the important domains of the family context, including the family as a unit, parenting, marriage, and individual parent adjustment; and a measure of congenital risk for child behavior problems, minor physical anomalies (MPAs).

Results on the broad issue of the impact of the family context on child functioning are presented in this chapter, using data from Years 1 through 4 of the GLS. In an analysis of the first 2 years of data (Halverson & Wampler, 1993), evidence supported a child-driven model for boys in that the congenital risk index (MPAs) was the best predictor of child externalizing behavior 1 year later, and boys' temperament had a negative impact on marital quality and parent adjustment. The evidence supported a family-driven model for girls with parenting quality having the most direct effect on girls' externalizing behavior. Combining both boys and girls, the child-driven model was the best fit for the data, suggesting that the family context had little impact on child outcome in terms of externalizing behaviors and that the congenital risk index (MPAs) was the best predictor of child externalizing 1 year later.

In this chapter, both internalizing and externalizing behaviors are considered, and the analyses examine the issue of direction of effect over 3 years (Year 1 to Year 4) instead of just 1 year (Year 1 to Year 2).

REVIEW OF LITERATURE

Although there is considerable research documenting that parenting, marital quality, and whole family functioning are related to child outcome, much of this research is ambiguous as to direction of effects issues. Much of the older research consists of cross-sectional studies of family and child factors based on one child per family that prohibit drawing conclusions about the direction of effects. Child functioning now is more often being conceptualized in the context of the family as a mutual influence system (Gunnar & Thelen, 1989; Hinde & Stevenson-Hinde, 1988; Wampler & Halverson, 1988). As a result, several longitudinal studies have included a consideration of multiple aspects of the family environment as they jointly impact child outcome (cf. Belsky, 1984; Belsky, Rovine, & Fish, 1989; Elder, Caspi, & Downey, 1986; Lambert, 1988; Masten et al., 1988; Patterson & Bank, 1989; Powers, Hauser, & Kilner, 1989; Rutter, 1988; Sameroff, 1989). These studies provide evidence of the impact of parenting quality, marital quality, and parent personality on child outcome. The evidence for the impact of parent personality on parenting, marriage, and child outcome is particularly strong (Belsky et al., 1989; Caspi & Elder, 1988; Lahey et al., 1988; Powers et al., 1989; Rutter, 1988; Sameroff, 1989).

Not all of the studies, however, include measures of child temperament. Some include a measure of child temperament that is retrospective and/or based solely on parental (usually the mother) reports, thus confounding family and child factors (Halverson, 1988). Studies that examine the impact of child temperament appropriately rather consistently find evidence for a child effect (Hetherington, Stanley-Hagan, & Anderson, 1989; Lambert, 1988; Powers et al., 1989). Elder and his colleagues make a convincing case for the impact of child temperament on later relationships, particularly marital and parent–child relationships (Caspi & Elder, 1988; Elder et al., 1986; Liker & Elder, 1983). Lytton (1990), in a comprehensive review, concluded that the evidence supports the "primacy of the child's own contribution to [conduct disorder] within a reciprocal parent-child interactive system" (p. 683).

In spite of strong assumptions of a predominant direction of effect from the family to the child, some researchers have produced evidence of a child effect. For example, in a series of research studies, Patterson and his colleagues (Patterson, 1982; Patterson & Bank, 1989; Patterson & Dishion, 1988), although finding strong relations between parenting practices and child outcome, also discovered that parents are less adept at parenting the child with conduct problems than they are at parenting a sibling. In another study, Patterson (1982) found that decreasing a child's antisocial behavior leads to concomitant decreases in the mother's depression. Both findings suggest a child effect.

Even in longitudinal studies, the direction of effects between the family context and child functioning has been difficult to unravel because the two are always confounded. Adoption studies and transition to parenthood studies are useful ways of addressing this concern. The GLS used a congenital risk factor, the minor physical anomaly index (MPAs), as an indicator of child risk that is most likely not influenced by the family environment. MPAs have been associated with difficult temperament in children (Halverson & Wampler, 1993; Waldrop, Bell, & Goering, 1976; Waldrop, Bell, McLaughlin, & Halverson, 1978; Waldrop & Halverson, 1971), with high MPAs children tending to exhibit behavior problems in interaction with others characterized by impulsivity, distractibility, lack of persistence, and high activity level. The relation between the MPAs and externalizing behavior is especially clear in boys (Halverson & Wampler, 1993; Waldrop et al., 1976; Waldrop & Halverson, 1971). The use of the MPAs index is a rough way of helping untangle family and child effects. Because parents and children exert mutual influences on each other in many ways commencing in the perinatal period, these effects can never really be unambiguously disentangled without longitudinal studies over the transition to parenthood or other approaches such as early adoption studies. The use of the MPAs index, however, is one way of approximating what the child brings to the family in terms of a biological disposition to difficult temperament.

In the research reported here, child functioning has been grouped into two clusters, internalizing and externalizing. *Externalizing* behavior is characterized by a failure to comply with rules, aggression, and impulsivity that involves too little inhibition or control (Achenbach & Edelbrock, 1981, 1983; Block, 1980; Campbell, 1990). In contrast, *internalizing* behavior is characterized by shy, withdrawn behavior, fearfulness, somatic problems, and difficulties in initiating new social behavior that implicate high inhibition and overcontrol (Achenbach & Edelbrock, 1981, 1983; Block, 1980; Campbell, 1990). It should be noted that externalizing and internalizing behaviors are not opposites. Theoretically, a child could be high on one or both or neither.

The purpose of this chapter is to present a set of analyses relevant to the issue of the direction of effects between child functioning and the family context. Two analysis approaches will be used, analysis of variance (ANOVA) and Latent Variable Path Analysis with Partial Least Squares (LVPLS; Falk & Miller, 1991; Lohmoeller, 1984, 1989). LVPLS is a component analysis where composites (latent variables) are created from measured variables in such a way that optimal linear correlations are created among them. This is done by extracting the first principle component from the measured variables so that maximal correlations are obtained. In many respects, this procedure is similar to LISREL, including both a measurement model and a structural model with specified paths among latent variables. LVPLS does not, however, require measurement at an interval level and is not sensitive to departures from multivariate normality and small samples as is LISREL.

In the ANOVAs child externalizing and child internalizing will be predicted over time by the MPAs index and a composite measure of family risk at time one in order to assess the presence of a family effect on the child. In the LVPLS analyses, MPAs and family risk at Year 1 will be entered as predictors of child externalizing and then child internalizing at Years 2, 3, and 4. Based on previous findings from the first 2 years of this data set (Halverson & Wampler, 1993), it is expected that externalizing behavior will be child driven (i.e., affected more by temperament as measured by the MPAs than by family factors) and that internalizing behavior will be family driven (i.e., affected more by family risk than the MPAs).

METHOD

Sample

Families were recruited who had a child between 2½ and 6 years of age, both parents in the home, with neither parent having children from a previous marriage. The child was in an out-of-the-home care setting some time during the week. In Year 1, 136 families completed the study. At the end of Year 4, 103 (74%) of these families remained in study. In Year 3, 50 additional families were added to the sample. The analyses presented here, however, are based on the 77 families with complete data from all 4 years of the study, including complete self-report data from both parents, all teachers, and all observational measures. Families were recruited from preschools, day-care centers, and radio and newspaper announcements. Families and teachers were paid for their participation.

The sample was predominantly White and middle class, with the mean education level for mothers a college degree and for fathers some graduate training. Almost all the fathers were employed full time. The mothers were almost equally divided between full-time employment, part-time employment, and full-time homemaker. The number of children ranged from one to four, with the majority having two children. The mean age of the target child was 4.4 years in Year 1 (range = 3–6) and 7.0 years in Year 4 (range = 5–10). The sample was about equally divided between boys and girls.

Procedures

Families came into the laboratory and completed several videotaped interaction tasks involving the marital dyad, the mother and child, the father and child, and the family consisting of the mother, father, and child together. The parents each completed the Block Childrearing Practices Report Q-Sort (Block, 1980) in the laboratory and were given a questionnaire packet to mail back in Years 1 and 2. In Years 3 and 4, questionnaires were completed in the laboratory. Teacher questionnaires were returned by mail.

Measures

Congenital Risk Index

Minor Physical Anomalies.   Child minor physical anomalies (MPAs) were assessed using the scale developed by Waldrop, Pederson, and Bell (1968) based on earlier work by Goldfarb and Botstein (1964). In this study, the weighted MPAs score for children was based on measures of the total number (out of 18 possible) of minor congenital growth abnormalities observed on the head, hands, and feet. A scoring manual is available from the second author (Waldrop, Halverson, & Shetterly, 1989).

The MPAs are present at birth and are minor developmental deviations most likely resulting from some event occurring in early embryogenesis. The relation of MPAs to difficult behavior is not due to high MPAs children looking strange and thus eliciting negative reactions from others. Several studies have reported no relation between the incidence of MPAs and ratings of attractiveness. Even high MPAs children are within the normal range for attractiveness. Although MPAs are a congenital variable, they may or may not have a genetic basis. The evidence to date shows low to insignificant correlations among siblings and parents on the MPA index, implicating nongenetic (i.e., intrauterine, prenatal, first trimester) modes of transmission.

MPAs for each individual were assessed by from two to eight raters over four periods of data collection. The mean interrater agreement was .87 for mothers, .89 for fathers, and .88 for the target child. The weighted scores ranged from 0 to 9 for mothers ($M = 4.0$), 0 to 10 for fathers ($M = 4.1$), and 0 to 12 for the target child ($M = 5.2$).

Child Functioning

Child Externalizing Behavior.   For the analyses presented in this chapter, child's externalizing behavior was measured by externalizing scores from the teacher. The externalizing score for the teacher is a sum of z scores for the impulsivity subscale of the Preschool Rating Scale (Victor, Halverson, & Montague, 1985), the activity level, emotional intensity, distractibility, and persistence (negatively scored) subscales from the Temperament Assessment Battery (Martin, 1988) and the conduct problem subscale from the preschool version of the Behavior Problem Checklist (Quay & Peterson, 1979). The z scores are based on the mean for this sample at age three. The mean score for externalizing ranged from −2.40 to −2.90 with a standard deviation ranging from 5.36 to 5.86 over the 4 years. The internal consistency for the teacher externalizing score was high with a mean alpha of .85.

Internalizing Behavior. The child's internalizing score from the teacher is the sum of the z scores of the easily upset subscale from the Preschool Rating Scale (Victor et al., 1985), the friendliness, approach/withdrawal, and adaptability (all negatively scored) subscales from the Temperament Assessment Battery (Martin, 1988), and the personality problem subscale from the preschool version of the Behavior Problem Checklist (Quay & Peterson, 1979). The z scores are based on the scores from this sample at age 3. The mean score for each year ranged from .10 in Year 1 to −1.07 in Year 4 with a standard deviation ranging from 3.24 to 4.11 over the 4 years. Mean internal consistency for the internalizing score was .56 over the 4 years.

In this sample, the teacher externalizing and internalizing scores were not significantly correlated with each other. Correlations between externalizing and internalizing over the 4 years ranged from .01 to .17 with a mean correlation of .11.

Family Context

Parent Individual Adjustment. Parent adjustment was assessed using the subscales and Global Severity Index of the revised Symptom Checklist 90 (SCL-90; Derogatis, 1977). The separate male and female norms for nonpatient samples were used.

Marital Quality. The quality of the marital relationship was assessed by the separate husband and wife total scores from the Dyadic Adjustment Scale (DAS; Sharpley & Cross, 1982; Spanier, 1976), the husband and wife separate total scores from the regard and empathy subscales of the Relationship Inventory (RI; Wampler & Powell, 1982), and a sum of the positive affect, respect, and negative affect (negatively scored) clusters from the Marriage Q-Sort (Wampler & Halverson, 1990). Coders observed the couple discussing a disagreement over childrearing and then used the Q-Sort to describe the couple's interaction. Interrater agreement was .76 in Year 1. Internal consistency for the subscales ranged from .75 to .92 in Year 1 (Wampler, 1991).

Parenting. Six variables were used as indicators of positive parenting. The 21 clusters identified by Susman, Trickett, Ianetti, Hollenbeck, and Zahn-Waxler (1985) of the Block Childrearing Practices Report Q-Sort (Block, 1980) were factor analyzed. Two of the resulting seven clusters were summed to form a positive parenting attitudes score for husband and wife (positive parenting – authoritarian control).

Quality of parenting behavior was assessed by coding videotapes of each parent with the target child using the 38-item Q-sort adapted by Buss (1981) from the Teacher Strategy Q-Sort (Block & Block, 1971). Mean interrater agreement was .85 (range = .79–.91). The items were formed into clusters based on factor analyses. The Love and Control (negatively scored) clusters were summed as a measure of positive parenting behavior for husband and wife. Internal consistencies for these two clusters were .75 and .70.

Family Functioning. Family functioning was measured by the sum of the adaptability and cohesion subscales from the Family Adaptability and Cohesion Evaluation Scales (FACES II; Olson et al., 1982) for husband and wife and the sum of the three cohesion scales from the Family Environment Scale (FES; Moos & Moos, 1986) for husband and wife. The cohesion scales on the FES are cohesion, expressiveness, and conflict (negatively scored). Three clusters of the Georgia Family Q-Sort (Wampler, Halverson, Moore, & Walters, 1989) were summed as an observational indicator of family cohesion. These clusters were positive affect, reserved (negatively scored), and negative affect (negatively scored). Coders observed a videotape of the family together building a house out of Lincoln Logs (Year 1). Coders used the Q-sort to describe the family interaction. Mean interrater agreement over the 4 years was .75 (Wampler, Moore, Watson, & Halverson, 1989).

Work Satisfaction. Work satisfaction was measured by the Facet-Free Job Satisfaction questionnaire developed by Quinn and Staines (1979). This five-item scale had an internal consistency in this sample of .80 for husbands and .71 for wives in Year 1.

Agreement. The intraclass correlation was used to obtain levels of agreement between the husband and wife double-standardized scores on four questionnaires: FACES, the FES, the DAS, and the RI. Overall agreement was indicated by the sum of these four scores. Similarity in parental values and behavior has been identified in our earlier research as an important indicator related to positive factors in the family environment (Deal, Halverson, & Wampler, 1989).

Family Risk Index. A composite measure of family risk for husband and wife was obtained by summing extreme scores (no risk, some risk) across 10 areas of family functioning: family self-report measures (FACES and FES), family observation measure (Georgia Family Q-Sort), marriage self-report measures (DAS and RI), marriage observation measure (Georgia Marriage Q-Sort), parenting self-report (Block), parenting observation measure, work satisfaction, parent individual adjustment, agreement (husband–wife agreement on FACES, FES, DAS, and RI), and parent education. For each of the 10 areas, a score in the lowest 25% was considered "risk" and assigned a risk score of 1 with a score in the highest 75% assigned a risk score of 0. Thus, risk scores could range from 0 to 10. The mean risk score for husbands was 2.6 ($SD = 1.9$) and for wives was 2.8 ($SD = 2.0$) in Year 1. The range was 0 to 9 for husbands and 0 to 8 for wives. Wife and husband risk scores were correlated .62 in Year 1. The internal consistency of the family risk score in Year 1 was .61 for both wife and husband family risk scores.

RESULTS

Analyses of Variance

A pattern of mutual influence between child temperament and family functioning was predicted, with healthy families over time helping children with difficult temperament to improve, and less healthy families having a negative impact over time on children with difficult temperament. As a rigorous test of this hypothesis, only teacher scores for child functioning were used. Separate analyses were done for teacher perceptions of the child's internalizing and externalizing behaviors. In addition, the MPAs index was included as a measure of biological risk in each analysis.

The first analysis was a two (child MPAs—high, low) by two (family risk—high, low) by four (time—Years 1, 2, 3, 4) repeated measure ANOVA with the teacher composite score for child externalizing as the dependent variable. Means and standard deviations for the teacher scores on child externalizing can be found in Table 5.1. None of the interaction terms was significant. The only significant effect in this analysis was that of the MPAs, $F(1, 71) = 10.16, p < .002$. Children with higher scores on the MPAs index were more likely to be seen as higher in externalizing behaviors by teachers at all points in the study (Years 1–4).

A second ANOVA was done using the teacher composite score for internalizing behavior as the outcome variable, and the MPAs, family risk at Year 1, and time as the independent factors. Again, the interaction terms were not significant. The effect of the MPAs was significant, $F(1, 71) = 6.18, p < .02$, with high MPAs children indicating higher levels of internalizing behavior (Table 5.1). The main effect for family risk was also significant, $F(1, 71) = 3.98, p < .05$. Children from families with higher levels of risk at Year 1 had higher levels of internalizing (Table 5.1).

These findings are consistent with those based on the first 2 years of the GLS (Halverson & Wampler, 1993). Child externalizing appears to be driven by biological factors, those characteristics the child brings to the family system. In research over 4 years, family factors were not related to child externalizing. Child internalizing also appears to be driven by biological factors, but family factors have an influence as well. The hypothesis of an interaction between child char-

TABLE 5.1

Means and Standard Deviations for Teacher Scores on Child Externalizing Behavior and Child Internalizing Behavior Over 4 Years by MPAs and Family Risk at Year 1

Child Externalizing Behavior

	Time								
	Year 1		Year 2		Year 3		Year 4		
	M	SD	M	SD	M	SD	M	SD	N
Low MPAs									
Low Family Risk	-3.18	5.00	-3.46	5.32	-3.73	5.17	-3.50	4.76	21
High Family Risk	-5.07	3.95	-6.13	2.82	-6.51	2.85	-5.25	3.00	13
High MPAs									
Low Family Risk	-1.40	4.82	-.98	6.56	-.67	5.86	-1.08	6.56	24
High Family Risk	-.78	6.74	-.47	5.81	-2.25	6.14	-1.45	7.10	17

Child Internalizing Behavior

	Time								
	Year 1		Year 2		Year 3		Year 4		
	M	SD	M	SD	M	SD	M	SD	N
Low MPAs									
Low Family Risk	-2.23	2.16	-.35	3.18	-1.26	3.41	-2.21	2.90	21
High Family Risk	.34	4.30	-1.13	1.79	-1.59	2.45	-1.07	2.23	13
High MPAs									
Low Family Risk	.30	4.74	-.36	3.79	-.89	3.13	-1.30	3.44	24
High Family Risk	2.53	3.57	.62	3.47	.60	3.55	.66	4.39	17

acteristics and family functioning was not supported. Separate analyses were completed for boys and girls, with similar results.

Path Models

The same factors were entered into two path models using LVPLS. The MPAs index was entered first, then the composite family risk score at Year 1. Husband and wife scores on family risk were the two manifest variables used as indicators of the latent construct of family risk. The MPAs and family risk at Year 1 were allowed to predict child externalizing at Years 2, 3, and 4 in one analysis, and child internalizing at Years 2, 3, and 4 in the other analysis. Teacher scores for internalizing and externalizing were used. The subscales included in the composite scores in the ANOVAs were considered as separate manifest variables for the LVPLS analyses. See Table 5.2 for the measurement model for both the externalizing and internalizing LVPLS models.

TABLE 5.2
Measurement Models for LVPLS Analyses

| | Child Externalizing Model | | | |
	Year 1	Year 2	Year 3	Year 4
Child MPAs				
Family Risk				
Husband	73			
Wife	99			
Teacher–Child Externalizing				
Conduct Problems		85	84	88
Activity Level		86	87	89
Emotional Intensity		78	77	85
Impulsivity		93	93	88
Persistence		−77	−79	−81
Distractibility		83	85	86
	Child Internalizing Model			
	Year 1	Year 2	Year 3	Year 4
Child MPAs				
Family Risk				
Husband	80			
Wife	97			
Teacher–Child Internalizing				
Personality Problems		23	50	75
Approach/Withdrawal		−39	−91	−85
Friendliness		−92	−44	−28
Easily Upset		09	78	88
Adaptability		19	−81	−84

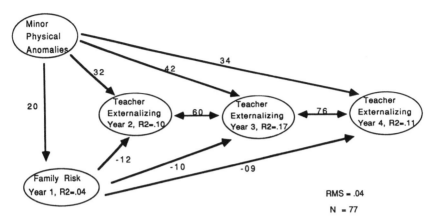

FIG. 5.1. LVPLS model predicting child externalizing.

As can be seen in Fig. 5.1, the model for externalizing is consistent with the ANOVA results. If paths of .20 or greater are considered significant (Falk & Miller, 1991), MPAs are related to child externalizing at Years 2, 3, and 4 with no effect of family risk at Year 1 on child externalizing at any year. The significant path between the MPAs and family risk indicates a modest negative impact of the child on the family. As would be expected, child externalizing was quite stable over time with zero-order correlations of .60 and .76 between Years 2 and 3 and Years 3 and 4. The proportion of variance accounted for is relatively small (11%). The fit of the model is quite high (RMS = .04). Separate boys' and girls' models were run with parallel results in terms of fit and significant paths. The major difference was that the proportion of variance explained was higher in the boys' model ($R = .26$) than in the girls' model ($R = .06$). The only other difference was that the path between MPAs and family risk at Year 1 was significant for boys and not for girls.

In the internalizing model shown in Fig. 5.2, there were significant paths between the MPAs and child internalizing at Years 2 and 4 but these paths were weaker than those in the externalizing model. Family risk at Year 1 was related to child internalizing at Years 2, 3, and 4. The stability of internalizing behavior was lower than that for externalizing with zero-order correlations of .23 and .50 between Years 2 and 3 and Years 3 and 4. The proportion of variance accounted for by the model was modest (10%). The girls' and boys' models for internalizing were parallel with each other.

Correlations Between Family Constructs and Child Constructs

The use of composite indicators of child functioning and family factors was the approach chosen to examine broad direction of effect issues. Moving away from the level of composites allows a more differentiated examination, including a

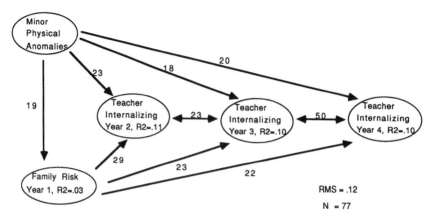

FIG. 5.2.   LVPLS model predicting child internalizing.

consideration of the impact of various aspects of the family on child functioning. Both the ANOVAs and path models indicated no effect of family factors on child externalizing, and a modest impact of family factors on child internalizing. To search for possible relations at a more precise level, the measures that were combined into the composites for child internalizing and child externalizing at Year 4 were correlated with specific family variables at Year 1. The family variables included both husband and wife perceptions of the marriage, family as a unit, their individual adjustment, and their parenting. Again, only the teacher measures for child functioning were used. Because of the large number of zero-order correlations possible, the .01 level and a two-tailed test were used to determine the level of significance.

The significant correlations among the teacher's view of the child at Year 4 and family variables at Year 1 are contained in Table 5.3. Confirming the previous analyses, the correlations between the child externalizing measures at Year 4 and family variables at Year 1 are not significant. Contrary to expectation, only mother perceptions of the family at Year 1 are related to child internalizing at Year 4. Correlations using the husband family scores were not significant.

The teacher's perception of the child in Year 4 as not exhibiting shy, with-drawn, and fearful behavior in new situations (TAB—approach/withdrawal subscale) was significantly correlated with the mother's view of her family, her marriage, her parenting, and her psychological symptoms in Year 1. The number of personality problems on the Behavior Problem Checklist that the teacher saw in Year 4 was related to the mother's view of her marriage in Year 1. The teacher's view of the child as being tense and easily upset (PRS—Upset) was correlated significantly with the mother's psychological symptoms in Year 1 and her view of the family. The teacher's view of the child's sociability (PRS—Friendly) was related to mother's psychological symptoms.

TABLE 5.3

Zero-order Correlations between Family Variables in Year 1 and Teacher
Scores on Child Internalizing Subscales in Year 4 ($n = 81$)

Child Year 4	Family Year 1	
Personality Problems	Wife Dyadic Adjustment Scale	−.24*
Approach/Withdrawal	Wife Positive Parenting	.29*
	Wife Dyadic Adjustment Scale	.25*
	Wife FACES + Family Env. Scale	.24*
	Wife Obsessive-Compul./SCL-90	−.31*
	Wife General Symptoms/SCL-90	−.31*
Easily Upset	Wife FACES + Family Env. Scale	−.30*
	Wife Obsessive-Compul./SCL-90	.30*
	Wife Sensitivity/SCL-90	.30*
	Wife Phobic/SCL-90	.30*
	Wife Paranoid/SCL-90	.35*
	Wife General Symptoms/SCL-90	.27*
Friendly	Wife Obsessive-Compul./SCL-90	−.30*
	Wife Sensitivity/SCL-90	−.40**
	Wife Depression/SCL-90	−.38*
	Wife Anxiety/SCL-90	−.30*
	Wife Paranoid/SCL-90	−.40**
	Wife General Symptoms/SCL-90	−.34*
Adaptability	Wife FACES + Family Env. Scale	.28*
	Wife Obsessive-Compul./SCL-90	−.35*
	Wife Paranoid/SCL-90	−.31*

$*p < .01.$ $**p < .001.$

DISCUSSION

Most of the research examining the relations among family factors and child functioning have used measures from one point in time and one source, usually the mother (Wampler & Halverson, 1993). In the research reported in this chapter, much more stringent methods were used. In this study, relations were examined over 4 years in a nonclinical sample. A relatively narrow range of child behavior and family variables was considered. Whenever possible, multimethod, multisource measures of constructs were used, thus minimizing the problem of confounding single source measures.

Evidence from this study supports the importance of congenital factors in predicting child externalizing behavior. No evidence of a relation between family factors and child externalizing was found in the ANOVAs and path models using 4 years of data, or in the zero-order correlations among family variables at Year 1 and child externalizing at Year 4. The best predictor of child externalizing was the MPAs index, an indicator of the presence of congenital factors associated with difficult temperament in children. There was some evidence for a child effect with respect to externalizing behavior in that MPAs was related to family risk in Year 1, especially for boys.

A relation between family factors and child internalizing behavior was found in the ANOVAs, path models, and zero-order correlations. This relation could be characterized as consistent, but modest in size. The MPAs were also related to child internalizing behavior. The expected differences between boys and girls were not found. In examining the relation of different family variables in Year 1 to child internalizing in Year 4, only the mother's scores were related to child outcome.

Although finding a child effect is supported in the literature (Lytton, 1990), such a finding is inconsistent with much of the literature that provides evidence for family effects (cf. Miller, Cowan, Cowan, Hetherington, & Clingempeel, 1993). In addition, the amount of variance in child externalizing and internalizing accounted for is lower than in other studies. For example, Miller et al. (1993) found an average of 27% (19% for fathers and 34% for mothers) of the variance in child externalizing explained by family factors in the sample with older children. In this study, only 11% of the variance in child externalizing was explained.

There are several reasons for such differences in findings. First, a completely independent outcome measure was used in this study: teacher scores on externalizing and internalizing rather than mother, father, and observer reports. Even ratings of the child by observers may share more variance with family measures than teacher ratings in that many observations of children in studies including family measures are done in the home or in the presence of the parents. Second, the time difference between the family measures and child outcome in this study was 3 years. Most of the evidence for family effects comes from studies using concurrent measures of the child and the family. Third, and most important, variance due to a child biological factor, MPAs, was taken out first, prior to examining the relation between family factors and child outcome. Most research simply assumes no child effect and the possible impact of the child on the family is not examined.

The approach used in the data analyses reported here did lump many factors together. It is possible that if family factors were left separate, more of a family effect would be found. The zero-order correlations, however, do not support this view. The homogeneity of the sample and the relative health of the sample may have enabled a child effect to be seen more clearly. As Dodge (1990) noted, when environmental variation is relatively small, child effects might appear larger than environmental (i.e., family) effects.

Implications

These results have direct implications for the models of child and family effects that motivated this longitudinal study in the first place. Recall that it was predicted that when families were functioning well (here operationalized as low family risk), high-risk children (here, high MPAs) would not develop behavior problems over time—that there would be a positive family effect on children with predispositions to internalizing or externalizing behavior. No evidence was found for this prediction in the analyses of either internalizing or externalizing behavior. In fact, for externalizing, no family effect was found at all. High MPAs children were consistently higher on externalizing and only the MPAs index predicted externalizing over the 4 years analyzed for this study. In general, it appears that externalizing is quite stable and the causal nexus of variability in externalizing behavior seems to be within the child.

It may be that the operationalization of the family variable did not select the right mix of variables, or that family effects on externalizing may take more than 4 years to manifest themselves. Whatever the case, for externalizing, the model has been revised (for preschool children at least) in light of these data. Clearly, if there is a linkage between externalizing and family functioning, the link in this sample is from child to family and not vice versa. This study of these possible linkages began when the children were 3, 4, and 5 years of age. It could be that effective families have, by 3 years of age, already managed to cope with mild tendencies toward externalizing and what was sampled were the more "hard core," resistant children, who were already fairly canalized in externalizing by the time we saw them at 3, 4, or 5 years of age. Whatever the case, mild externalizing represented in this sample of normal, unselected preschoolers, has shown remarkable stability and independence from family effects over 4 years.

The analyses for internalizing behavior show a more complex developmental picture. Both means analyses and structural equation modeling indicate that, for this sample, internalizing has links to both the biological risk variable and the family risk variable. Both make independent and consistent contributions to internalizing over time. The model guiding this research, however, was not completely supported by these findings. No interactions were found. Low family risk did not moderate the expression of internalizing over time. Children higher on the biological risk factor (MPAs) in low-risk families did not improve differentially over time as the models guiding this research would have predicted. An additive model was supported instead with both the congenital variable and family variables having a modest contribution to child internalizing. Mother's variables, especially her psychological functioning, were the aspect of the family context most associated with child internalizing.

The results for internalizing must be interpreted with caution. Unlike externalizing, which had a robust measurement model at each time period, internalizing was fairly unevenly identified in Years 2, 3, and 4. Further, the stability of this construct (especially between Years 2 and 3—probably because of measurement instability) was not very high. For this sample of preschoolers, it appears that the specification of the internalizing construct will take further refinement. This is especially important in light of the empirical findings presented here of a different model explaining each type of child behavior. It may be that analyses at a more molecular level may improve both the internal consistency and relations to both proximal and distal predictors of change over time for the internalizing construct.

In conclusion, although no real support was indicated for the models of a negative or positive synergy between family and child risk variables, analyses did show that the congenital risk variable (MPAs) predicts both externalizing and internalizing child behavior over time, with stronger relations for the externalizing construct. These findings are in complete agreement with the major prediction of a congenital effect on problem behaviors in children and replicate much of our earlier findings of relations between MPAs and problematic outcomes in children. Whatever occurred in pregnancy to elevate the incidence of MPAs, its common effect on behavioral control (either too much or too little) can be traced out over a 7- to 9-year period after birth in this sample of children. The new data in our current longitudinal study is that for externalizing, this congenital effect is surprisingly and robustly independent of family effects, either positive or negative—whereas internalizing is tied additively to two sources: one residing in the individual, and the other in the family. Further follow-up of these children as they enter adolescence will help researchers trace the joint effects of both congenital and family sources to adjustment and coping.

ACKNOWLEDGMENTS

This research was supported by grant MH39899 from the National Institute of Mental Health. The authors wish to thank the families for their participation and the able assistants who have collected the data and coded the videotapes, especially Karen Shetterly, Carol Watson, John Moore, Dominique Gore, Leah Wampler, Jerry Tieman, Cathy Stawarski, Mike Williamson, and Angela Pesce.

REFERENCES

Achenbach, T. M., & Edelbrock, C. (1981). Behavioral problems and competencies reported by parents of normal and disturbed children aged four through sixteen. *Monographs of the Society for Research in Child Development, 46* (Serial No. 188).

Achenbach, T. M., & Edelbrock, C. (1983). *Manual for the Child Behavior Checklist and Revised Child Behavior Profile.* Burlington, VT: University Associates in Psychiatry.

Belsky, J. (1984). The determinants of parenting: A process approach. *Child Development, 55,* 83–96.

Belsky, J., Rovine, M., & Fish, M. (1989). The developing family system. In M. R. Gunnar & E. Thelen (Eds.), *Systems and development, The Minnesota Symposium on Child Psychology* (Vol. 22, pp. 119–166). Hillsdale, NJ: Lawrence Erlbaum Associates.

Block, J. (1980). *The Child-Rearing Practices Report (CRPR): A set of Q items for the description of parental socialization attitudes and values.* Berkeley: Institute of Human Development, University of California.

Block, J., & Block, J. (1971). *Teacher Strategy Q-Sort.* Berkeley: Institute of Human Development, University of California.

Buss, D. (1981). Predicting parent–child interactions from children's activity level. *Developmental Psychology, 17,* 59–65.

Campbell, S. B. (1990). *Behavior problems in preschool children.* New York: Guilford.

Caspi, A., & Elder, G. H., Jr. (1988). Emergent family patterns: The intergenerational construction of problem behaviour and relationships. In R. A. Hinde & J. Stevenson-Hinde (Eds.), *Relationships within families: Mutual influences* (pp. 218–240). Oxford, UK: Clarendon.

Deal, J. E., Halverson, C. F., & Wampler, K. S. (1989). Parental agreement on child-rearing orientations: Relations to parental, marital, family, and child characteristics. *Child Development, 60,* 1025–1034.

Derogatis, L. Q. (1977). *The SCL-90 Manual I: Scoring, administration and procedures for the SCL-90.* Baltimore, MD: Johns Hopkins University Press.

Dodge, K. A. (1990). Nature versus nurture in childhood conduct disorder: It is time to ask a different question. *Developmental Psychology, 26,* 698–701.

Elder, G. H., Jr., Caspi, A., & Downey, G. (1986). Problem behavior and family relationships: Life course and intergenerational themes. In A. B. Sorensen, F. E. Weinert, & L. R. Sherrod (Eds.), *Human development and the life course: Multidisciplinary perspectives* (pp. 293–340). Hillsdale, NJ: Lawrence Erlbaum Associates.

Falk, R. F., & Miller, N. B. (1991). A soft models approach to transitions. In P. A. Cowan & E. M. Hetherington (Eds.), *Advances in family research, Vol. 2: Family transitions* (pp. 273–301). Hillsdale, NJ: Lawrence Erlbaum Associates.

Goldfarb, W., & Botstein, A. (1964). *Physical stigmata in schizophrenic children.* Unpublished manuscript, Henry Ittelson Center for Child Research, Brooklyn, NY.

Gunnar, M. R., & Thelen, E. (1989). *Systems and development. The Minnesota Symposia on Child Psychology* (Vol. 22). Hillsdale, NJ: Lawrence Erlbaum Associates.

Halverson, C. F. (1988). Remembering your parents: Reflections on the retrospective method. *Journal of Personality, 56,* 435–444.

Halverson, C. F., & Wampler, K. W. (1993). The mutual influence of child externalizing behavior and family functioning: The impact of a mild congenital risk factor. In D. Reiss & R. Cole (Eds.), *How do families cope with chronic illness?* (pp. 71–93). Hillsdale, NJ: Lawrence Erlbaum Associates.

Hetherington, E. M., Stanley-Hagan, M., & Anderson, E. R. (1989). Marital transitions: A child's perspective. *American Psychologist, 44,* 303–312.

Hinde, R. A., & Stevenson-Hinde, J. (1988). *Relationships within families.* Oxford: Clarendon Press.

Lahey, B. B., Hartdagen, S. E., Frick, P. J., McBurnett, K., Connor, R., & Hynd, G. W. (1988). Conduct disorder: Parsing the confounded relation to parental divorce and antisocial personality. *Journal of Abnormal Psychology, 97,* 334–337.

Lambert, N. M. (1988). Adolescent outcomes for hyperactive children. *American Psychologist, 43,* 786–799.

Liker, J. K., & Elder, G. H., Jr. (1983). Economic hardship and marital relations in the 1930s. *American Sociological Review, 48,* 343–359.

Lohmoeller, J. B. (1984). *LVLPS 1.6 Program Manual: Latent variable path analysis with partial least-squares estimation.* Cologne: Universitaet zu Koehn, Zentralarchiv fuer Empirische Sozialforschung.

Lohmoeller, J. B. (1989). *Latent variable path modeling with partial least squares.* New York: Springer-Verlag.

Lytton, H. (1990). Child and parent effects in boys' conduct disorder: A reinterpretation. *Developmental Psychology, 26,* 683–697.

Martin, R. P. (1988). *The Temperament Assessment Battery.* Athens, GA: Developmental Metrics.

Masten, A. S., Garmezy, N., Tellegan, A., Pellegrini, D. S., Larkin, K., & Larsen, A. (1988). Competence and stress in school children: The moderating effects of individual and family qualities. *Journal of Child Psychology and Psychiatry, 29,* 745–764.

Miller, N. B., Cowan, P. A., Cowan, C. P., Hetherington, E. M., & Clingempeel, W. G. (1993). Externalizing in preschoolers and early adolescents: A cross-study replication of a family model. *Developmental Psychology, 29*, 3–18.

Moos, R. H., & Moos, B. S. (1986). *Family environment scale manual* (2nd ed.). Palo Alto, CA: Consulting Psychologists Press.

Olson, D., McCubbin, H., Barnes, H., Larsen, A., Muxen, M., & Wilson, M. (1982). *Family inventories*. St. Paul, MN: Family Social Science.

Patterson, G. R. (1982). *A social learning approach to family intervention: III. Coercive family process*. Eugene, OR: Castalia.

Patterson, G. R., & Bank, L. (1989). Some amplifying mechanisms for pathologic processes in families. In M. R. Gunnar & E. Thelen (Eds.), *Systems and development. The Minnesota Symposium on Child Psychology* (Vol. 22, pp. 167–209). Hillsdale, NJ: Lawrence Erlbaum Associates.

Patterson, G. R., & Dishion, T. J. (1988). Multilevel family process models: Traits, interactions, and relationships. In R. A. Hinde & J. Stevenson-Hinde (Eds.), *Relationships within families: Mutual influences* (pp. 283–310). Oxford, UK: Clarendon.

Powers, S. I., Hauser, S. T., & Kilner, L. A. (1989). Adolescent mental health. *American Psychologist, 44*, 200–208.

Quay, H. C., & Peterson, D. R. (1979). *Behavior problem checklist for children 2 to 5*. Unpublished manuscript, University of Miami.

Quinn, R., & Staines, G. (1979). *The 1977 quality of employment survey*. Ann Arbor, MI: Institute for Social Research.

Rutter, M. (1988). Functions and consequences of relationships: Some psychopathological considerations. In R. A. Hinde & J. Stevenson-Hinde (Eds.), *Relationships within families: Mutual influences* (pp. 332–353). Oxford, UK: Clarendon.

Sameroff, A. J. (1989). Commentary: General systems and the regulation of development. In M. R. Gunnar & E. Thelen, *Systems and development: The Minnesota Symposium on Child Psychology* (Vol. 22, pp. 219–235). Hillsdale, NJ: Lawrence Erlbaum Associates.

Sharpley, C., & Cross, D. (1982). A psychometric evaluation of the Spanier Dyadic Adjustment Scale. *Journal of Marriage and the Family, 44*, 739–742.

Spanier, G. B. (1976). Measuring dyadic adjustment. *Journal of Marriage and the Family, 38*, 15–28.

Susman, E. J., Trickett, P. K., Ianetti, R. J., Hollenbeck, B. E., & Zahn-Waxler, C. (1985). Child-rearing patterns in depressed, abusive and normal mothers. *American Journal of Orthopsychiatry, 55*, 237–251.

Victor, J. B., Halverson, C. F., & Montague, R. B. (1985). Relations between reflection-impulsivity and behavioral impulsivity in preschool children. *Developmental Psychology, 21*, 141–148.

Waldrop, M., Bell, R., & Goering, J. (1976). Minor physical anomalies and inhibited behavior in elementary school girls. *Journal of Child Psychology and Psychiatry, 17*, 113–122.

Waldrop, M., Bell, R., McLaughlin, B., & Halverson, C. (1978). Newborn minor physical anomalies predict short attention span, peer aggression and impulsivity at age 3. *Science, 199*, 563–564.

Waldrop, M., & Halverson, C. (1971). Minor physical anomalies and hyperactive behavior in young children. In J. Hellmuth (Ed.), *The exceptional infant* (Vol. 2, pp. 343–381). New York: Brunner/Mazel.

Waldrop, M. F., Halverson, C. F., & Shetterly, K. (1989). *Manual for assessing minor physical anomalies*. Unpublished manuscript, University of Georgia, Athens.

Waldrop, M. F., Pederson, F. A., & Bell, R. Q. (1968). Minor physical anomalies and behavior in preschool children. *Child Development, 39*, 391–400.

Wampler, K. S. (1991). *The Manual for the Georgia Marriage Q-Sort*. Unpublished manuscript, Texas Tech University, Lubbock.

Wampler, K. S., & Halverson, C. F. (1988). Mother and father perceptions of child behavior problems: Relation to teacher perceptions of the child and family context variables. *Family Perspective, 22*, 1–12.

Wampler, K. S., & Halverson, C. F. (1993). Quantitative measurement in family research. In P. G. Boss, W. Doherty, R. LaRossa, W. Schumm, & S. Steinmetz (Eds.), *Sourcebook of family theories and methods: A contextual approach* (pp. 181–194). New York: Plenum.

Wampler, K. S., & Halverson, C. F., Jr. (1990). The Georgia Marriage Q-Sort: An observational measure of marital functioning. *American Journal of Family Therapy, 18,* 156–178.

Wampler, K. S., Halverson, C. F., Jr., Moore, J. J., & Walters, L. H. (1989). The Georgia Family Q-Sort: An observational measure of family functioning. *Family Process, 28,* 223–238.

Wampler, K. S., Moore, J., Watson, C., & Halverson, C. F. (1989). *The Manual for the Georgia Family Q-Sort.* Unpublished manuscript, University of Georgia, Athens.

Wampler, K. S., & Powell, G. (1982). The Barrett–Lennard Relationship Inventory as a measure of marital satisfaction. *Family Relations, 31,* 139–145.

6
▼▼▼▼▼▼▼

The Timing of Childbearing, Family Structure, and the Role Responsibilities of Aging Black Women

Linda M. Burton
Pennsylvania State University

> *My girl and grandgirl had babies young. Now, they keep on rushin' me, expectin' me to do this and that, tryin' to make me old 'fore my time. I ain't got no time for myself. I takes care of babies, grown children, and the old peoples. I work too. I get so tired. I don't know if I'll ever get to do somethin' for myself.* (Julia, a 53-year-old great-grandmother)

> *Yeah, it's true, we had children young. But I don't have to be worried with them now. I'm old and tired and have done my time with my family. Now I can just take it easy and let them take care of me. This is what I waited for all my life.* (Jessie, a 56-year-old great-grandmother)

> *All the women in my family don't have children until they're at least 21. That's what we were taught. It makes it easier for everyone else. All I really have to be concerned with is taking care of my mother. My daughter and granddaughter even help me with that.* (Sarah, a 64-year-old great-grandmother)

Julia, Jessie, and Sarah represent different sides of the same coin. They are all aging Black women, in multigeneration families, who occupy the lineage position of great-grandparent. Despite their common intergenerational family position, however, they have markedly different experiences in their attendant roles.

Julia became a great-grandmother at age 52. By her own definition, she considers herself "too young for the role." Her early ascension to great-grandmotherhood was the "ripple effect" (Hagestad, 1981) of her daughter and granddaughter becoming teenage mothers. Now Julia is "trapped" in a five-tier female lineage in which sne, as a great-grandmother, is responsible for the care of four dependent generations, including her great-granddaughter (age 10 months), adolescent granddaughter (age 17), adult daughter (age 32), and mother (age 80). Julia is overwhelmed.

Jessie, like Julia, became a great-grandmother in her early 50s. Both her daughter and granddaughter were also teenage mothers. Unlike Julia, however, Jessie feels that she became a great-grandmother "at the right time in her life." She is the oldest member in a four-generation lineage that includes her 38-year-old daughter, 17-year-old granddaughter, and 2-year-old great-grandson. Her only "duty" in the family is to let her adolescent granddaughter take care of her. Jessie notes that she has earned that privilege. She is content.

Sarah, on the other hand, entered the role of great-grandmother at age 64. She became a great-grandmother at a much later age than Julia and Jessie because both her daughter and granddaughter did not have children until they were 21 or older. Sarah feels that the timing of her transition to great-grandparenthood was "right on target." Although she, too, is a member of a five-generation lineage, including her 86-year-old mother, 43-year-old daughter, 21-year-old granddaughter, and 5-month-old great-grandson, she does not have the same family responsibilities that Julia has. Everyone in her family "takes care of one another." Sarah, like Jessie, is content.

Why do three women who share the same generational position—great-grand-mother—have such different familial role responsibilities? Are expectations regarding their role tied to family norms that govern the timing of childbearing in their families? Do certain parental timing patterns in families produce family structures that create distinct family role responsibilities for aging Black women?

This chapter examines the questions raised by Julia's, Jessie's, and Sarah's contrasting experiences. It explores the relationship between the timing of child-bearing, family structure, and the role responsibilities of women from an intergenerational perspective. Using data from a study of urban, working-class, Black female lineages and from a qualitative field study of low-income, multigeneration families in a small Black, semirural community, roles in families with patterns of "young adult" parental timing are compared to those in families with cross-generational patterns of adolescent childbearing. Two questions are addressed: What types of multigenerational family stuctures are produced in families with patterns of young adult as compared to teenage parental timing? What are the implications of parental timing and family structure for the family role responsibilities of aging Black women?

CONCEPTUAL FRAMEWORK

Family Roles and an Intergenerational Life Course Perspective

The relationship between the timing of childbearing and family roles has received considerable attention from social science researchers in recent years (Eggebean & Uhlenberg, 1989; Hogan, 1987; Rindfuss, Morgan, & Swicegood, 1988); however, there is little research on the intergenerational consequences of parental timing. Much of the existing research assesses the impact of adolescent (early) and later life (delayed) childbearing on the role performances of mothers (Baldwin & Cain, 1980; Rossi, 1980) and fathers (Gershenson, 1983; Nydegger, 1973). Meager attention has been devoted to exploring how the timing of childbearing affects the familial duties and parenting responsibilities of grandparents and great-grandparents (Hagestad, 1987; Hagestad & Burton, 1986).

The study of the timing of childbearing, family structure, and the roles of aging women reported here is conceptually grounded in an intergenerational life-course perspective (Elder, 1984; Hagestad & Neugarten, 1985). The life-course perspective is a theoretical orientation that focuses on the interlocking pathways that individuals and families follow through the age-differentiated life span (Elder, 1978; Hagestad, 1990; Rossi, 1980). This discussion focuses on two dimensions of the life course—the timing of family transitions and the interdependent life trajectories of family members.

Families, as cultural units, devise timetables for the movement of individuals through predictable phases of development and changing family structures (Hagestad, 1986; Hareven, 1982; Zerubavel, 1981). Family timetables provide prescriptions concerning when and in what order events such as marriage, the birth of a child, and the transition to grandparenthood should occur (Hareven, 1977). They also implicitly provide guidelines as to what constitutes appropriate age- and generationally linked role expectations and behaviors among family members (Plath, 1980).

The aspect of family timetables most salient to this discussion concerns role transitions and definitions of role obligations and behaviors in families when individual members either adhere to or violate timing norms. Life course scholars suggest that when family role transitions occur "on time," that is, in accordance with family timetables, individuals experience less stress during transition and have a clearer sense of what they should be doing in families (Zerubavel, 1981). When role transitions violate family timetables, however, serious stresses often arise for individuals and families because the event upsets the expected cadence of lives (Brim & Ryff, 1980; Elder & Rockwell, 1976; Pearlin, 1982; Seltzer, 1976). Individuals may be "thrown off track" with respect to family obilgations and have to dramatically reframe familial role expectations given the existing circumstances. Neugarten (1970) stated that:

> It is the unanticipated, not the anticipated, which is likely to represent the traumatic event. Major stresses are caused by events that upset the sequence and rhythm of the expected life cycle, as when the death of a parent comes in adolescence rather than in middle age; *when the birth of a child is too early or too late*; ... when the empty nest, *grandparenthood* ... or widowhood *occur off-time*. (p. 86, italics added)

The second component of the life course perspective—interdependent lives—draws attention to the connectedness of family role transitions (Hagestad &

Dixon, 1980; Johnson, 1988; Klein, Jorgensen, & Miller, 1979). Hagestad and Neugarten (1985) identified two dimensions of life course interdependence that are applicable to this discussion. The first is career contingencies. Career contingencies refer to the process by which the expectations that individals have about the trajectories of others influence their own construction of the life course. For example, parents make decisions about their own life course based on the projected life course of their children (Hagestad & Neugarten, 1985).

The second is countertransitions (Riley & Waring, 1976). Countertransitions are those changes in life course that are the "ripple effects" of changes in another person's life. For example, the timing of entry to grandparenthood hinges not only on the ages at which the grandparents themselves became parents, but also on the ages at which their children reproduce for the first time (Sprey & Matthews, 1982). Consequently, the temporal interdependence of these transitions often creates a domino effect in which the role expectations and performances of one family member can redefine the role expectations and performances of an entire kinship network.

Parental Timing and Multigenerational Family Structure

The various forms family structure takes during a woman's lifetime are generated by the timing and sequencing of role transitions (e.g., marriage and parenthood) in the intergenerational system. The timing of childbearing, particularly, has powerful implications for intergenerational family structure and the roles of aging women. To begin, the birth of the first child to a member of the youngest generation of a family changes intergenerational structure by adding another generational tier to the family line (Hagestad, 1981). Also, when those births occur during the young adult years, families are more likely to have distinctly demarcated generations in which developmental life stages, generational positions, and roles are consistent. For example, a four-generation family in which a new generation has arrived every 22 years produces a structure in which there is clearly a child generation (age 1), a young adult parent generation (age 23), a middle-aged grandparent generation (age 45), and an elderly great-grandparent generation (age 67). Within these distinct generational boundaries, family members are more likely to have clear perceptions of their generational position in the family and the roles that accompany that position.

When childbearing is early, however, as in the case of adolescent pregnancy, an age-condensed structure is formed (Bengtson, Rosenthal, & Burton, 1990; Burton, 1990; Burton & Dilworth-Anderson, 1991). The boundaries between generations in these families are not necessarily consistent with age, developmental life stage, and family role status. A case in point is the situation in which a new generation is born every 14 years. This pattern produces a condensed, overlapping intergenerational structure with a child generation comprising both a mother (age 15) and her offspring (age 1), a young adult generation that includes a 29-year-old grandmother, and a middle-aged generation that includes a 43-year-old great-grandmother. In this example, family roles are chronologically and developmentally "out of synch" with generational position. The adolescent mother, as a function of giving birth, is launched into a young adult role status (parenthood); however, she remains legally and developmentally a member of the child generation. Similarly the young adult female has moved to the role status of grandmother—a role typically associated with midlife. Further, the middle-aged woman has been propelled to the status of great-grandmother, a role usually occupied by women in their later years.

In addition to affecting the structure of intergenerational families, the timing of childbearing also influences the types of role responsibilities that emerge for women in the family. For example, patterns of on-time childbearing are more likely to produce grandparental roles for women in which they are not expected to be the primary caregiver for their grandchildren. A 22-year-old woman who wants to be a parent and has planned the birth of her first child would probably not expect her mother to raise her child unless extreme circumstances prevailed (e.g., in the event of the 22-year-old mother's illness or premature death).

In contrast, early childbearing, especially the out-of-wedlock variety, can force a woman to assume grandparental status accompanied by the role function of surrogate parent to her grandchild (Furstenberg, 1979). The potential for "role overload" for young grandmothers in this situation is tremendous (Lehr, 1984). For example, a 29-year-old married woman who becomes a grandmother when her 15-year-old daughter becomes a mother might find herself overwhelmed at attempting to integrate the roles of wife, parent to her own young children, surrogate parent to her grandchild, and, quite possibly, employee on a 9-to-5 job.

Although timing of family transitions does affect intergenerational structure and roles, it is important to note that not all families share the same perceptions of "on-time" and "off-time" role transitions. Hogan (1987) noted that the timing and sequencing of role transitions in families within different population subgroups may vary as a function of the family's social class, community context, and ethnic ancestry. In fact, what has been delineated as an early transition—adolescent childbearing—is in some cultural enclaves considered to be on-time behavior (Burton, 1990; Hamburg, 1986). When adolescent childbearing is consistent with family timetables, what happens to family structure and the roles of aging women?

Empirical data from two exploratory qualitative studies are presented to illustrate the relationships among timing of childbearing, intergenerational family structure, and the roles of aging women. Specific attention is given to examining how variable role outcomes for aging women are dependent on the different sociocultural meanings attached to family timetables. Patterns in three groups of Black families are discussed—urban lineages in which young adult childbearing is defined as being on-time and actual patterns reflect that norm, urban lineages in which adolescents bear children in violation of family norms, and semirural lineages in which teenage parenting is deemed a normal, on-time transition.

METHODS

The Urban Study

In 1984, I conducted an exploratory study (Burton, 1985; Burton & Bengtson, 1985; Elder, Caspi, & Burton, 1987; Hagestad & Burton, 1986) of the effects of timing of childbearing on intergenerational family structure and function. The study involved a sample of four-, five-, and six-generation Black female lineages living in the Los Angeles area. Forty-one lineage units ($n = 120$), each including the new mother, grandmother, and great-grandmother, participated in the study. Eighteen of these lineages were classified as "off-time" units. The age ranges of the respondents in these lineages were 11 to 18 for the young mothers, 25 to 38 for the grandmothers, and 46 to 57 for the great-grandmothers. The median ages for generations represented in the early lineages are: for the young mothers, 16 years; for the grandmothers, 32 years; and for the great-grandmothers, 56 years.

The remaining 23 lineages were classified as on-time units. The age ranges for mothers, grandmothers, and great-grandmothers were 21 to 26, 42 to 57, and 60 to 73, respectively. The median ages for each generation were 21 years for young mothers, 45 years for grandmothers, and 67 years for great-grandmothers.

The "early" and "on-time" transition categories were established in accordance with current demographic inferences concerning the ages at which women become mothers, grandmothers, and great-grandmothers for the first time. The modal age for entry to parenthood for Black females is approximately 20 years (Farley & Allen, 1987). Sprey and Matthews (1982) and Troll (1983) identified the median age of contemporary grandmothers at role entry to be in the range of 42 to 60 years. Current trends in the age at entry to great-grandmotherhood suggest that 65 to 70 years is the modal pattern (Atchley, 1980; Troll & Bengtson, 1979). To be markedly under these ages when entering the role of mother, grandmother, or great-grandmother is defined in this study as being off-time.

Socioeconomic data indicate that, in general, the multigeneration families who participated in this study were upwardly mobile. Less than 15% of the 120 respondents were receiving welfare. In fact, 50% of the respondents were in the workforce and 15% were retired. The monthly median income for respondents in the early lineages was $320 for young mothers, $1,850 for the grandmothers, and $650 for the great-grandmothers. The median income for members of the on-time lineages was $900 for the mothers, $1,525 for the grandmothers, and $450 for the great-grandmothers.

As for education, it was determined that the young mothers, grandmothers, and great-grandmothers in the early lineages had completed a median of 10, 12, and 10 years of school, respectively. In the on-time lineages, the median years of education completed were 13 for the young mothers, 12 for the grandmothers, and 10 for the great-grandmothers.

In the on-time and early lineages, approximately 31% of the total sample ($n = 120$) were married. The highest percentage of marriages (50%) was among the on-time mothers ($n = 23$). The largest proportion of those who had never married was among the early mothers ($n = 18$, 91%), and the on-time grandmothers ($n = 23$) represented the highest percentage (52%) of those divorced.

Data on family norms concerning the timing of role transitions, expectations for intergenerational role responsibilities, and family dependencies were collected from the lineage members in lengthy interviews administered by four indigenous interviewers. Both quantitative data (responses to prestructured scales reflecting family dynamics) and qualitative data (responses to open-ended questions) were collected from the lineage members to illuminate the possible impact of the respondents' sociocultural context on timing, intergenerational family structure, and the familial role responsibilities of aging women.

The Female Lineages of Gospel Hill

In January 1985, I began a 3-year exploratory qualitative study of the effects of adolescent childbearing on multigeneration families in "Gospel Hill," a small Black community in the Northeast region of the United States (Burton, 1990). The primary sample interviewed for this study included 20 low-income, Black, four-generation maternal lineages ($n = 53$). Each lineage unit included a young mother (age 14–26), grandmother (age 35–45), and great-grandmother (age 56–68). The median ages of the generations were 18, 37, and 56, respectively. All but three of the respondents gave birth to their first child as teenagers.

Participants in this community study were qualitatively different from those in the urban study. All of the participants' primary source of income was welfare. The median household income was $750. With the exception of two families, all of the participants lived in multigeneration households comprised of 4 to 9 people and headed by respondents in the grandmother generation.

As for education, the median number of years of school completed by the young mothers was 12, the grandmothers, 10 years, and the great-grandmothers, 7 years. Only one of the respondents, a young mother aged 21, was married. The remainder had never been married (77%), were divorced (19%), or were widowed (2%).

Data were collected from participants using a variety of qualitative field research strategies. The strategies included face-to-face interviews, focus group discussions, and informal participant observation in community and family events (i.e., family reunions, holiday celebrations, and church outings). Three key informants who were members of the Gospel Hill Community also provided valuable insights.

RESULTS

Findings from these studies indicated some striking differences between the urban on-time, urban early, and Gospel Hill lineages. In the urban on-time lineages, 87% ($n = 66$) of the new mothers, grandmothers, and great-grandmothers welcomed the role transitions that created their four-generation families. Lineage members noted that their comfort with their roles was in large part due to consistency across generations in perceptions of the appropriate age to become a mother and the actual age at which the lineage members entered the role. Figure 6.1 indicates that in these lineages, both the perceived timetable for childbearing and the actual timing of childbearing was 20 to 23 years between generations. Consistency of perceptions and behaviors in the timing of marriage (19–21 years of age) and the transition to grandmotherhood (42–45 years of age) was also maintained across generations. The family timetables for childbearing, marriage, and grandparenthood provided clear directives for these women as they moved from one family role to the next. Lineage members who subscribed to these timetables expected their role transitions when they occurred, were prepared for them, moved systematically to their "generational stations," and assumed their attendant role responsibilities willingly. The comments of one 22-year-old mother illustrate: "I became a mother at the right time. . . . I was ready, my husband was ready, my mother was ready, my father was ready, my grandmother couldn't wait."

The role responsibilities for the majority of women in these lineages were as clearly delineated as the norms that governed the timing of childbearing. In 87% ($n = 23$) of the on-time lineages, a system of adjacent generational role responsibilities was in operation. Basically, this system was composed of patterns of mutual assistance where independent generations (the young adult and midlife

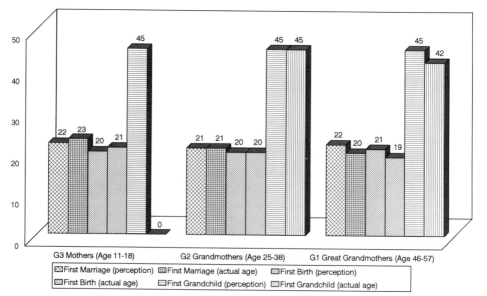

Median Ages Reported

FIG. 6.1. Perceptions of appropriate and actual age at role entry: on-time lineages—urban sample ($N = 23$ lineages).

adult generations) served as primary and secondary caregivers to adjacent dependent generations (the child and older adult generations). This system of mutual assistance is graphically presented in Fig. 6.2.

Figure 6.2 illustrates that in the five-generation structures of the on-time lineages, there were two dependent generations—the children and the great-great-grandmothers. Primary care for the child was the responsibility of the new mother in the lineage. The majority of mothers, however, did receive secondary support for the care of their children from their own mothers and grandmothers, usually in the form of economic assistance or babysitting. One 23-year-old mother noted:

> I had my son because I knew I was ready to take care of a child. My mother and grandmother don't bother me very much about how to raise him. They let me do it on my own. . . . What's nice about them, though, is that they know that I get tired sometimes and need a break. At least three times a week, one of them will take my son for the whole day so that I can get some rest.

The great-grandmothers and grandmothers in the lineage shared the task of taking primary care of the great-great-grandmother generation. In 65% of the cases (*n* = 20) the great-great-grandmother or other elderly relative was physically unable to care for herself. In such cases the grandmothers and great-grandmothers attended to the needs of the oldest generation by performing the daily tasks of bathing, dressing, and feeding them, and also the less regular tasks such as taking them to the doctor. The new mothers in the lineages were backup caregivers for the great-great-grandmother generation. In this role, the new mothers often provided relief services for their mothers and grandmothers. A 45-year-old grandmother commented about the help she received from her daughter: "I don't know what we would do without Sandra. Even though she has a baby, my grandchild, she still helps me and my mother with Granny Bee [great-great-grandmother in the lineage]. . . . Sometimes I take care of my grandchild and Sandra takes care of Granny. . . . It's like we are trading babies."

In the on-time lineages, the timing of childbearing from one generation to the next, coupled with a mutual aid system of adjacent generational role responsibilities, created an intergenerational family context in which the older women were not expected to take care of more than one generation at a time. The early lineages were quite different.

An initial distinction between the early and on-time lineages is the disparity in the early lineages between perceptions of family timetables and the actual timing of transitions to parenthood and grandparenthood particularly. As indicated in Fig. 6.3, the young mothers thought the appropriate time to begin childbearing was age 16, although both the grandmother and great-grandmother generation perceived the appropriate age to be in the early 20s. The young mothers' perceptions challenged the perceptions of their mothers and grandmothers, but were consistent with the median age at which 60% of them and 55% of their mothers

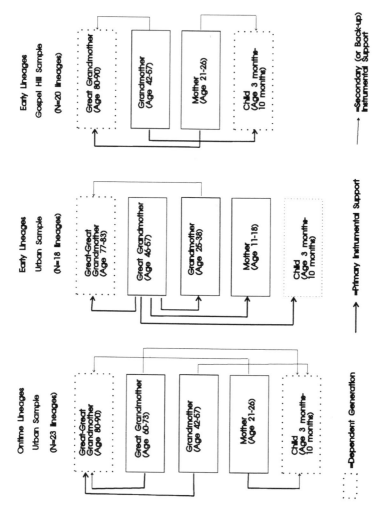

FIG. 6.2. Intergenerational paths of role responsibilities in the on-time and early lineages.

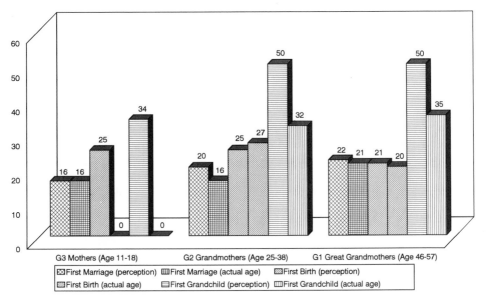

Median Ages Reported

FIG. 6.3. Perceptions of appropriate and actual age at role entry: early
lineages—urban sample (*N* = 18 lineages).

became mothers themselves for the first time. One 17-year-old stated, as did
several of the other young mothers, "I'm only following in my mother's footsteps.
She was a teenage mother too."

Inconsistencies between generations are also noted in timing perceptions and
actual ages at role entry for marriage and grandparenthood. The median age for
marriage that the mother and grandmother generations perceived as appropriate
was 25, whereas the majority of great-grandmothers felt that the appropriate age
for a young woman to marry was 21. It is important to emphasize that this
inconsistency also prevailed in perceptions concerning the sequencing of marriage
in the life course. The two youngest generations felt that marriage should occur
after the birth of the first child, but women of the great-grandmother generation
felt that one should marry before having children.

For entry to grandparenthood, both the grandmother and great-grandmother
generations perceived 50 years of age as timely. The young mother generation,
however, felt that 34 was more appropriate. The young mothers were therefore
satisfied with the actual ages (32–35 years) at which their mothers and grandmothers had become grandparents. The grandmothers and great-grandmothers,
however, were not quite as enthusiastic. What happened in the early lineages
was that accelerated childbearing sparked a series of quickened transitions to
grandmotherhood and great-grandmotherhood that violated family timetables.
These lineages were "thrown off track" because they did not expect, nor were

they prepared for, the roles into which they had been propelled. The reaction to these early transitions, particularly by the two youngest generations, was a behavior that is figuratively known as "passing the buck." This behavior had overwhelming consequences for the role responsibilities of the great-grandmothers in these families.

Essentially, the adolescent mothers in these lineages, although they told me that the appropriate age to become a mother was 16, really wanted to continue their lives as teenagers. Thus they expected their mothers to assume the primary role in the care of their children. Eighty-three percent of the young grandmothers ($n = 18$), however, refused to assume an active surrogate parent role for the baby. For the majority of early grandmothers, the role of grandmotherhood conflicted with their own developmental agenda—an agenda that included a variety of "young adult" roles related to work, education, friendship, romance, and even their own continued childbearing.

When the mother and grandmother abdicated their roles, responsibility for the care of the new family member is pushed up the generational ladder to the great-grandmother in the lineage. Indeed, it was in the role of great-grandmother that the impact of accelerated transitions and dependent generations was most strongly realized. The relinquishing of roles by two generations—the teenage mothers and the young grandmothers—resulted in 57% of the great-grandmothers ($n = 18$) being responsible for their grandchildren and great-grandchildren. Forty-two percent of those great-grandmothers were responsible for primary care of at least three generations: their grandchildren and great-grandchildren, and their own aging mothers or elderly relatives as well. The triple duty of these great-grandmothers is presented in Fig. 6.2, which outlines the paths of intergenerational role responsibilities in the early lineages.

As one might expect, many of the great-grandmothers in the early lineages experienced the strain of role overload. The effects in a number of cases were potentially catastrophic. A particularly profound case is noted in the case of Ann, a 56-year-old great-grandmother. Ann occupies the lineage position of "woman in the middle" in her family. She is flanked upwardly by the 76-year-old great-great-grandmother (her mother) in the lineage and downwardly by a 29-year-old grandmother (her daughter) and 15-year-old (her granddaughter). Here is her story:

> Ann functioned as caregiver to her elderly mother, Erma, and as surrogate parent to her granddaughter, Carla, and great-grandson Steve. Ann had been taking care of Carla for at least 7 months before Steve was born. Diane (Ann's daughter and Carla's mother) had put Carla out because she felt that her daughter's circumstance (teenage motherhood) was interfering with the relationship she was trying to build with her (Diane's) new boyfriend.
>
> Ann was furious with her daughter's attitude. Within 6 months after Carla moved in, the relationship between Ann and Diane had disintegrated.
>
> After Steve was born, Ann went into a serious depression. She was working and taking care of her mother, Carla, and the baby too. Ann was frustrated because, as she states, Carla was "too busy running the streets, acting like a teenager instead

of like a mother." Ann often commented, "My granddaughter and daughter keep making these babies and expect me to take care of them. I ain't no nursemaid; I ain't old; and I ain't dead yet."

When Steve was about 7 months old, Ann found herself a 34-year-old boyfriend. She let him move in with her only 2 days after she met him. This behavior was totally out of character for Ann.

Within 2 weeks after Ann's new romance had begun, she became the victim of a "sweetheart con." Ann's boyfriend apparently recognized her vulnerability, endeared himself to her, and then disappeared with her car and money while she was at work. Shattered, Ann called me, threatening to commit suicide.

I sat with Ann for 12 hours that day. She uttered continuously, "I don't feel like no mother, no grandmother, no woman, no nothing. I'm too old for this. All I wanted was someone to take the pressure off, to help me, to support me. Lord knows I don't get it from my family. Why me, Lord? Why me?"

Ann's circumstances demonstrate not only the effects of role overload, but also the effects of off-time transitions on the creation of a dependent intergenerational family structure. What becomes important, in understanding the dependencies in these families, is that they were the result of the lineage members feeling that their early transitions were not what they "ought" to be doing at a particular time in their lives. For example, Ann's granddaughter had difficulty in responding to her role as a mother because she still wanted to do "teenage things." Ann's daughter did not engage in any grandparental behavior, because she felt that it made her look old to her boyfriend. These feelings, in large part, were based on the women's internalization of urban working-class norms, which dictate, as they did in the on-time lineages, that the birth of a new generation should occur about every 21 years. What happens to family structure and the roles of aging women when early childbearing is the norm? Results from the Gospel Hill Study illustrate.

Gospel Hill Sample

Intergenerational family structure and roles were quite different for the Gospel Hill families as compared to the urban Black lineages. First, in contrast to the preference of the urban respondents for on-time childbearing, there was a family norm in these lineages that required designated females in the family become early childbearers. The basis for this mandate was the lineage members' identification of the association between the timing of childbearing and the transition to grandparenthood. Figure 6.4 indicates that in these families, the perceived timetable for childbearing and the actual timing of childbearing was 15 to 18 years between generations. Consistency of perceptions and behaviors regarding timing of grandparenthood (35–36 years of age) was also maintained across generations.

Early childbearing was considered a necessary activity in these families to ensure that older women would have the opportunity to experience the parental role. The role of parent in these families was not behaviorally experienced until

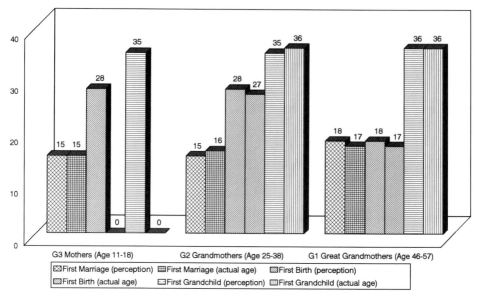

Median Ages Reported

FIG. 6.4. Perceptions of appropriate and actual age at role entry: early lineages—Gospel Hill sample (*N* = 20 lineages).

a woman became a grandmother. Mothers did not raise their children. The tradition is that grandmothers raise the grandchildren. Because of the physical demands rearing young children places on females, these women believed that it was important to become a grandmother as young as possible so that they would have the "energy" to engage in parental behavior. Comments from a 37-year-old grandmother illustrate: "I never really raised a child before until Sharon [her granddaughter] was born. I was 31 when she came. I still had my health. I could chase after her and play with her. I couldn't have done that if I was 40 when she came. You start being old when you're 40."

These lineages' preference for accelerated transitions was in many ways also a product of the sociocultural context in which they lived. Unlike the urban working-class Black families, these women, having lived in limited resource environments, had a very truncated view of the individual life course. Ninety-five percent of the women interviewed (*n* = 53) estimated their life expectancy to be 60 years. The majority of respondents noted that if they were going to live life to the fullest, slower paced role transitions, like those of the on-time urban lineages, made little sense.

Another factor that influenced the perpetuation of accelerated female lineages concerned the shortage of "marriageable" employed Black males in the community. Due to a depressed economy in this community, most of the adult Black males were unemployed. Although the female respondents felt that it was acceptable to date these males, they believed that it was not in their best interest or the interest of their families to marry them. Such beliefs encouraged early patterns of childbearing outside of marriage and promoted the reliance of female family members on each other for emotional and instrumental family support.

A second significant difference between the Gospel Hill lineages and the urban families was indicated in patterns of generational role responsibilities. As noted in the discussion of the urban study, the on-time lineages had a mutual aid system of adjacent role responsibilities, and in the early lineages there was a dependent intergenerational family structure in which the "care of generations" was the responsibility of one woman—the great-grandmother. In the Gospel Hill lineages, however, a pattern of a mutual aid system with nonadjacent role responsibilities emerged.

As indicated in Fig. 6.2, the primary role responsibility for grandmothers in the lineages was the care of their grandchildren, whereas the principal duty for their daughters (the mothers of their grandchildren) was the care of the great-grandmothers. Mary, a 19-year-old mother, provided a summary statement for this system's existence: "My grandmother raised me. Now it's time for me to give her something back. It's O.K. if my mother raised my child for now. If she didn't, I wouldn't be able to take care of my grandmother."

DISCUSSION AND CONCLUSION

Beginning with the profiles of the distinctive life experiences of Julia, Jessie, and Sarah as great-grandmothers in multigenerational Black families, this chapter has discussed the interrelationships among timing of childbearing, intergenerational family structure, and the roles of aging Black women. Three distinct patterns emerged. In the urban on-time lineages, a 20- to 23-year pacing of generational turnovers created a family system of mutual assistance and adjacent generation role responsibilities; older women in the lineage were not saddled with the care of multiple generations. In the early urban lineages, accelerated childbearing in two successive generations created a dependent intergenerational system; great-grandmothers in the lineage became overwhelmed with the care of three and four generations. Finally, in the Gospel Hill study, early childbearing, as an adaptive strategy to a distinct sociocultural environment, created a family system of mutual assistance and nonadjacent role responsibilities. Older women in these lineages did not have to take care of anyone.

Although the two studies reported here yield interesting findings on the relationship between timing of childbearing family structure and the roles of aging women, they are exploratory and thus have a number of limitations. The first limitation concerns generalizability of the findings. In both studies, respondents were not randomly selected from Black populations that are necessarily representative. This limitation is noted particularly in the case of the Gospel Hill respondents. It is important, therefore, in reviewing the findings from these studies that readers do not divorce the data from the context and attribute the life-course patterns of Black families in these two studies to Black families in general.

A second limitation of this research concerns its focus on maternal lineages. Clearly, important elements may be missed when data on family dynamics are not also gathered directly and as intensively from spouses, boyfriends, fathers, siblings, aunts, and other extended family members. The intent of these exploratory studies, however, was not to explore the complexity of extended intergenerational family dynamics. Rather, it was an attempt to examine the roles of aging Black women using a perspective, the life-course/generations approach, that has not been traditionally used in studies of the family roles of Black females.

Despite the limitations of the studies, however, several issues for future research on timing, family structure, and the distribution of roles in families are indicated. First, social science researchers should further examine the mechanisms (i.e., early childbearing) that create intergenerational family structure and the rhythms of family transitions. An important and relatively unexplored component of that mechanism is family timetables. Do Black families create temporal blueprints that direct the life course of individual family members? Do those blueprints have different specifications for the roles of aging men as compared to aging women?

A second path would extend the investigation of time, structure, and roles beyond the lineage to the kinship network. What roles do extended family members play in the design of family timetables? How do the life-course paths of in-laws, uncles, aunts, cousins, and "adopted kinfolks" affect the family roles of men and women in later life?

A third direction for future research would involve an assessment of the relationship among family timetables, family role transitions, and stress. Do family members who make role transitions that are not in accordance with family time tables experience greater stress than those that do?

ACKNOWLEDGMENTS

This research was funded in part by grants from the National Science Foundation (RII-8613960), the Center for the Study of Child and Adolescent Development, the Pennsylvania State University, and the Brookdale National Fellowship Program. Acknowledgment is also given to the American Sociological Association's Minority Fellowship Program and the Randoff Haynes and Dora Haynes Foundation. This chapter was partially completed while the author was a Fellow at the Center for Advanced Study in the Behavioral Sciences. I am grateful for the financial support provided by the John D. & Catherine T. MacArthur Foundation and the Spencer Foundation.

REFERENCES

Atchley, R. (1980). *Social forces in later life*. Belmont, CA: Wadsworth.

Baldwin, W. S., & Cain, V. S. (1980). The children of teenage parents. *Family Planning Perspectives, 12*, 34–43.

Bengtson, V. L., Rosenthal, C., & Burton, L. M. (1990). Families and aging. In R. Binstock & L. George (Eds.), *Handbook on aging and the social sciences* (pp. 263–287). New York: Academic Press.

Brim, O. G., & Ryff, C. D. (1980). On the properties of life events. In P. Baltes & O. G. Brim (Eds.), *Life-span development and behavior* (Vol. 3, pp. 23–45). New York: Academic Press.

Burton, L. M. (1985). *Early and on-time grandmotherhood in multigenerational black families*. Unpublished doctoral dissertation, University of Southern California, Los Angeles.

Burton, L. M. (1990). Teenage childbearing as an alternative life-course strategy in multigeneration black families. *Human Nature, 1*(2), 123–143.

Burton, L. M., & Bengtson, V. L. (1985). Black grandmothers: Issues of timing and continuity of roles. In V. L. Bengtson & J. L. Robertson (Eds.), *Grandparenthood* (pp. 61–77). Beverly Hills, CA: Sage.

Burton, L. M., & Dilworth-Anderson, P. (1991). The intergenerational family roles of aged black Americans. *Marriage and Family Review, 16*(3/4), 311–330.

Eggebeen, D. J., & Uhlenberg, P. (1989). Changes in the age distribution of parents, 1940–1980. *Journal of Family Issues, 10*(2), 169–188.

Elder, G. H., Jr. (1978). Family history and the life course. In T. K. Hareven (Ed.), *Transitions: The family and the life course in historical perspective*. New York: Academic Press.

Elder, G. H. (1984). Families, kin, and the life course: A sociological perspective. In R. Parkes (Ed.), *Advances in child development research and the family*. Chicago: University of Chicago Press.

Elder, G. H., Caspi, A., & Burton, L. M. (1987). Adolescent transitions in developmental perspective: Sociological and historical insights. In M. Gunnar (Ed.), *Minnesota Symposium on Child Psychology* (Vol. 21). Hillsdale, NJ: Lawrence Erlbaum Associates.

Elder, G. H., & Rockwell, R. (1976). Marital timing and women's life patterns. *Journal of Family History, 4*, 34–53.

Farley, R., & Allen, W. R. (1987). *The color line and the quality of life in America*. New York: Russell Sage.

Furstenberg, F. (1979). *Burdens and benefits: The impact of early childbearing on the family*. Washington, DC: George Washington University Press.

Gershenson, H. P. (1983). Redefining fatherhood in families with White adolescent mothers. *Journal of Marriage and the Family, 45*, 591–599.

Hagestad, G. O. (1981). Problems and promises in the social psychology of intergenerational relations. In R. W. Fogel, E. Hatfield, S. B. Kiesler, & E. Shanas (Eds.), *Aging: Stability and change in the family*. New York: Academic Press.

Hagestad, G. O. (1986). The aging society as a context for family life. *Daedalus, 115*, 119–139.

Hagestad, G. O. (1987). Dimensions of time and the family. *American Behavioral Scientist, 29*, 679–694.

Hagestad, G. O. (1990). Social perspectives on the life course. In R. K. Binstock & L. K. George (Eds.), *Handbook of aging and the social sciences* (3rd ed., pp. 151–168). New York: Academic.

Hagestad, G. O., & Burton, L. M. (1986). Grandparenthood, life context, and family development. *American Behavioral Scientist, 29*, 471–481.

Hagestad, G. O., & Dixon, R. (1980, November). *Lineages as units of analysis: New avenues for the study of individual and family careers*. Paper presented at the NCFR Theory Construction and Research Methodology Workshop, Portland, OR.

Hagestad, G. O., & Neugarten, B. L. (1985). Age and the life course. In E. Shanas & R. Binstock (Eds.), *Handbook of aging and the social sciences* (pp. 35–61). New York: Van Nostrand Reinhold.

Hamburg, B. A. (1986). Subsets of adolescent mothers: Developmental, biomedical, and psychosocial issues. In J. Lancaster & B. Hamburg (Eds.), *School-age pregnancy and parenthood* (pp. 115–145). New York: Aldine de Gruyter.

Hareven, T. K. (1977). Family time and historical time. *Daedalus, 107*, 57–70.

Hareven, T. K. (1982). *Family time and industrial time: The relationship between the family and work in a New England industrial community.* New York: Cambridge University Press.

Hogan, D. P. (1987). The demography of life-span transitions: Temporal and gender comparisons. In A. Rossi (Ed.), *Gender and the life course* (pp. 65–78). New York: Aldine.

Johnson, C. L. (1988). Active and latent functions of grandparenting during the divorce process. *The Gerontologist, 28*(2), 185–191.

Klein, D. M., Jorgensen, S. R., & Miller, B. (1979). Research methods and developmental reciprocity in. families. In R. M. Lerner & G. B. Spanier (Eds.), *Child influences on marital and family interactions: A life-span perspective* (pp. 106–131). New York: Academic.

Lehr, U. (1984). The role of the women in the family generation context. In V. Garms-Homolova, E. M. Hoerning, & D. Schaeffer (Eds.), *Intergenerational relationships* (pp. 23–35). New York: C. J. Hogrefe.

Neugarten, B. L. (1970). Dynamics of transition from middle to old age: Adaptation in the life cycle. *Journal of Geriatric Psychology, 4*, 71–87.

Nydegger, C. (1973). *Timing of fatherhood: Role perception and socialization.* Unpublished dissertation, Pennsylvania State University.

Pearlin, L. I. (1982). Discontinuities in the study of aging. In T. K. Hareven & K. J. Adams (Eds.), *Aging the life course transitions: An interdisciplinary perspective* (pp. 32–67). New York: Guilford.

Plath, D. W. (1980). *Long engagements.* Stanford, CA: Stanford University Press.

Riley, M. W., & Waring, J. (1976). Age and aging. In R. K. Merton & R. Nisbet (Eds.), *Comparative social problems* (4th ed., pp. 89–101). New York: Harcourt, Brace, & Jovanovich.

Rindfuss, R. R., Morgan, P. S., & Swicegood, C. G. (1988). *First births in America: Changes in timing of parenthood.* Berkeley: University of California Press.

Rossi, A. (1980). Aging and parenthood in the middle years. In P. B. Baltes & O. G. Brim, Jr. (Eds.), *Life-span development and behavior* (Vol. 3, pp. 137–205). New York: Academic Press.

Seltzer, M. (1976). Suggestions for the examination of time-disordered relationships. In J. Gubrium (Ed.), *Time, roles, and self in old age* (pp. 10–27). New York: Human Sciences.

Sprey, J., & Matthews, S. (1982). Contemporary grandparenthood: A systematic transition. *Annals of American Academy of Political and Social Sciences, 464*, 91–103.

Troll, L. (1983). *Intersections of grandparenting with other life processes.* Paper presented at the Wingspread Conference on Grandparenting and Family Connections, Racine, WI.

Troll, L., & Bengtson, V. L. (1979). Generations in the family. In W. R. Burr, R. Hill, F. I. Nye, & I. L. Reiss (Eds.), *Contemporary theories about the family* (Vol. 1, pp. 144–167). New York: The Free Press.

Zerubavel, E. (1981). *Hidden rhythms: Schedules and calendars in social life.* Chicago: University of Chicago Press.

7

▼▼▼▼▼▼▼

Family Wages, Family Processes, and Youth Competence in Rural Married African American Families

Gene H. Brody
Zolinda Stoneman
Douglas Flor
University of Georgia

In this chapter an ongoing project is described in which rural married African American families were observed and interviewed to identify the family processes that account for academic and socioemotional competence in early adolescence. This project helps to fill the need for research on African American family dynamics, particularly among rural populations. The research also will provide information that can be used in prevention and intervention efforts, by identifying those family processes that sustain parents' functional impact on their children's development.

The difficulties that rural African American families experience have been well documented. Data indicate that, in the South, 1 million of these families are faced with adverse environmental conditions that place them at risk for unemployment, low wages, low educational attainment, substandard housing, and high infant and maternal mortality rates (Coward & Smith, 1983; Orthner, 1986). In the state of Georgia, illiteracy rates are particularly high among African American citizens, and the rural counties with largely African American populations also have the lowest adult education levels (Gabriel, 1986). To date, very little attention has been given to understanding the links between family processes and youth outcomes among rural African Americans. Although half of the 10 million African American households in the United States were headed by a married couple in 1990 (U.S. Bureau of the Census, 1992), with an even higher percentage among those living in rural areas, most research on African American families has focused on single-mother-headed households. Such a focus inadvertently contributes to stereotypic impressions about African American families, without providing information on their diversity and their responses to economic stress. For rural African American families, the challenge of overcoming the obstacles associated with economic stress can be even greater than that faced by urban families, because rural areas often lack the facilities, amenities, health care resources, and other services that are often available to urban families (Orthner, 1986).

DEVELOPMENT OF RESEARCH METHODS AND ASSESSMENTS WITH THE ASSISTANCE OF COMMUNITY MEMBERS

From the beginning of this study, community leaders were involved in the decision-making process to help them feel a part of the project and make them comfortable referring potential participants. The accurate assessment of the population to be studied was a concern, because most instruments used to evaluate family processes and individual outcomes have been developed for use with, and standardized on, White middle-class families. Accordingly, a focus group comprised of rural African American community members was recruited to help develop culturally appropriate measures. Most of the group members served as peer agents for the Energy Education Program and the Expanded Food and Nutrition Program, two state agencies housed on The University of Georgia campus; some of these agents recommended other African American community leaders for participation. The final focus group included 40 people from throughout Georgia who were representative of the population to be studied. The group addressed two measurement issues, the first of which concerned the development of valid self-report instruments. Each group member rated, on a 5-point Likert scale ranging from 1 (*not appropriate*) for rural African American families through 3 (*appropriate*) to 5 (*very appropriate*), each instrument to be used. Those instruments that attained a mean rating of at least 3.5 were retained. Most of the instruments presented no validity problems to the focus group members. Some individual items were reworded for simplicity and clarity according to the group members' suggestions, and a few were eliminated as irrelevant to African Americans.

Another area of concern involved plans to videotape family interactions. The group expressed reservations about subjects' acceptance of videotaping, and suggested that it be made as nonthreatening as possible by recording no interactions involving financial concerns or other sensitive information. From a list of activities in which families have been videotaped in other projects, the group selected game playing and family discussions as videotaping contexts that the subject families would consider most acceptable. Because in past projects the videotaping of family interactions has been found to be essential for close study of the relationships under consideration, the taping proceeded as planned. If the families found the taping to be unacceptably intrusive, however, the procedures would have been changed to accommodate their needs. In order to make it as acceptable as possible, during the first home visit, the project staff clearly explained the videotaping procedure and the reasons for its use, strongly emphasizing its confidentiality. The staff also gave particular attention to establishing rapport and putting the family at ease, a process that was emphasized throughout the entire project. The home visitors were African American graduate and undergraduate students at the University of Georgia, majoring in psychology, sociology, social work, law, education, counseling, and public administration. African American graduate students served as videotape coders, to minimize misinterpretation of verbal and nonverbal behaviors.

EXAMINING A MODEL OF FAMILY WAGES, PARENT PSYCHOLOGICAL FUNCTIONING, PARENT CAREGIVING RELATIONSHIPS, AND COMPETENCE IN RURAL AFRICAN AMERICAN YOUTH

The impact of financial resources on family functioning and developmental outcomes is a central concern in this research project. Financial resources are viewed as a static construct that is best regarded as a proxy for the social and personal processes that covary with it. Rather than assuming that financial resources cause variation in youth outcomes, the links between financial resources and family processes are examined, which in turn are associated with variations in youth outcomes.

In this chapter specific descriptions are given of the role strains that are created by the circumstances in which the families live. In many families, one or both spouses work two jobs, and mothers and fathers often work different shifts. Although this scheduling may make it more likely that at least one parent will be at home with the child, many parents consequently spend a minimal amount of time at home together. Such long working hours are apparently necessary to provide for the families' needs, given the low wages that the parents earn. The annual incomes of the families in this study were computed and compared with the number of hours the husbands and wives worked. Cases emerged in which the number of hours worked differed between families whose incomes were the same. An example from the data illustrates this point. Three families, named, for this illustration, "Jones," "Smith," and "Johnson," each earned $38,000 a year. In the Jones family, only the father is employed, working 40 hours a week. In the Smith family, both parents are employed 40 hours per week, whereas in the Johnson family, the father works 72 and the mother works 50 hours per week. Although these families have the same income, the effort expended to earn it varies greatly among them. In order to capture this difference, a family hourly wage measure was computed.

Relatively few studies have addressed the impact of working for low wages on family processes, and those that have been undertaken support a role strain interpretation. Bolger and associates (Bolger, DeLongis, Kessler, & Wethington, 1989) reported that husbands' reports of overload at work were positively associated with their wives' reports of overload at home the following day. Crouter, Perry-Jenkins, Huston, and Crawford (1989) and Repetti (1987) found that husbands' reports of work overload stress were positively associated with their wives' reports of negative marital interactions later that day. Similarly, husbands' reports of negative marital relations have been associated with wives' overload at work (Billings & Moos, 1982; Repetti, 1987). It seems that parents who work fewer hours will be less stressed than those who work longer hours for the same wages. Longer working hours increase the necessity of cooperation between parents in coordinating schedules and sharing household responsibilities, thus creating more opportunities for dissension and conflict.

The data presented in this chapter were used to examine a conceptual model, using partial least squares modeling techniques (Lohmoeller, 1989), of hypothesized links among family wages, parental depression, parental optimism, quality of parental cocaregiving relationships, children's self-regulatory competencies, children's academic competence, and children's psychological adjustment in a sample of married rural African American families. The chronic stress associated with low pay has been linked with parent-reported depressive symptoms that resulted from work-related anger and frustration (McLoyd, 1990). It was hypothesized, therefore, that low family wages would be directly associated with relatively high levels of maternal and paternal depression (Hypothesis 1), and with less supportive and more conflicted cocaregiving relationships (Hypothesis 2). Elevated levels of parental depression have also been associated with the use of less involved and communicative, and more negative and hostile, interaction styles in family relationships (Conger et al., 1992; Conger et al., 1990; Longfellow, Zelkowitz, & Saunders, 1982). Thus, it was predicted that parental depression would undermine parental cocaregiving relationships (Hypothesis 3).

The potential positive effects of parental optimism as a resilience factor were also examined. Scheier, Carver, and their associates (Scheier & Carver, 1985; Scheier et al., 1989; Scheier, Weintraub, & Carver, 1986) found an optimistic view of life to be linked to effectiveness in coping with stress. Other researchers have found optimism to be associated with feelings of self-worth, empathy, and the ability to nurture others (Taylor & Brown, 1988). In this conceptualization, parental optimism was hypothesized to be positively associated with higher hourly wages (Hypothesis 4) and with more supportive and less conflicted parental cocaregiving relationships (Hypothesis 5).

Although married African American mothers and fathers both contribute to childrearing, the partnership may not always be amiable (cf. Wilson, 1984). Parental cocaregiving functions optimally when parents agree on the developmental goals to be fostered in their children, as well as the childrearing practices to be used to achieve those goals. It is not uncommon for parents to experience conflict because they hold different views on childrearing (Block, Block, & Morrison, 1981; Emery, 1988; Gerber, 1976; Grych & Fincham, 1990; Vogel & Bell, 1968). Contradictory, confusing messages from disagreeing cocaregivers stress the child's loyalties and complicate his or her attempts to discern order and predictability in the world (Block et al., 1981). Accordingly, the family's ability to foster competence in rural African American youths was hypothesized to be enhanced when parental cocaregivers display congruence on childrearing practices, communicate with one another about childrearing, and provide one another with instrumental and emotional support on childrearing tasks (Hypothesis 6).

In this formulation, the development of self-regulatory competence in African American youths serves as a bridge between family processes and academic and adjustment outcomes. Self-regulatory competence includes the ability to set and attain goals, to plan actions and consider their consequences, and to persist. Family processes, such as parental cocaregiving, may be linked with variations in self-regulation, which in turn may be linked with youth developmental outcomes. The work of Greenberg (1982) and of Steinberg, Elmen, and Mounts (1989) supports this hypothesis. They found that differences in self-regulation were associated across time with academic, social, and emotional competence, even when social class and academic ability were controlled statistically. It is also plausible that parental cocaregiving may be linked directly with youth outcomes; the literature examining the association of divorce and interparental conflict with child outcomes suggests this possibility (Emery, 1988). This issue was conceptualized as an empirical question, to determine whether parental cocaregiving is associated directly with variations in academic and adjustment outcomes, whether those links are mediated by variations in self-regulatory competence, or whether both direct and indirect links exist.

PROCEDURES

The subjects participated in a longitudinal study. The Year 1 assessment involved three home visits, each lasting 2 to 3 hours arranged as closely to a week apart as the families' schedules allowed. The home visits included observation of dyadic and triadic parent–child game-playing interactions and triadic parent–child problem-solving discussions, as well as administration of standardized self-report instruments during face-to-face interviews with family members. Teachers' reports of child adjustment were also obtained as part of the Year 1 assessments. The families will be briefly reassessed 18 and 36 months after the Year 1 visit. The reassessments will include the collection of self-report data from the parents and the youth, and further data from the teacher. The data presented in this chapter are derived from the Year 1 assessments; the follow-up assessments are in progress.

Sample

The sample included married African American families with a 9- to 12-year-old child (48 females and 42 males) who resided in nonmetropolitan counties in Georgia and South Carolina. Of the 90 families, 17 had a per capita income (family's annual income divided by the number of people living in the household, indicating the amount of money available to support each person) of $3,300 or less ($M = $1,906$). According to criteria established by the Census Bureau (U.S. Bureau of the Census, 1992), this places them in the first quintile for household income, which the bureau defines as poverty status. The mean total family annual income in this group was $11,882, which was below the poverty line criterion of $12,195 set by the Census Bureau. The largest group, which included 51 families, placed in the Census Bureau's third income quintile with an average per capita income of $5,515. The 21 remaining families' average per capita income of $9,044 placed them in the Census Bureau's fourth income quintile. Total family annual income ranged from $2,500 to $57,500, and per capita income ranged from $357 to $13,500. These data indicate that the sample included an economic cross-section of rural married African American families.

Measures

Family Wage per Hour. Family income was divided by 52 (the number of weeks in a year), then further divided by the combined number of hours mothers and fathers worked per week, to yield the family wage per hour.

Parental Depression. Depression was assessed using the Center for Epidemiologic Studies Depression Scale (CES–D; Radloff, 1977), which is widely used with community samples. The Cronbach alphas for mothers' and fathers' reports were .85 and .84, respectively.

Parental Optimism. Mothers' and fathers' scores on the optimism subscale of the CES–D and on Rosenberg's Self-Esteem Scale (Rosenberg, 1965) were used to measure optimistic outlooks and positive views of the self. The Cronbach alphas for mothers' and fathers' reports exceeded .80 for both scales.

Marital Interaction Quality. The ways in which the couple relate to one another in the child's presence is an important aspect of coparenting. Harmonious and communicative interaction styles promote competence and maturity, whereas conflicted styles often are associated with academic difficulties and adjustment problems (Grych & Fincham, 1990). Accordingly, observations were made of the quality of the parents' interaction.

African American student assistants received 10 hours of training in observational coding, which included study and discussion of the coding category definitions and observation of videotaped family interactions. The coders worked in teams of two, viewing the videotapes and independently rating the interactions on the following dimensions: (a) the Conflict-Harmony scale, ranging from 1 (*conflicted*; relationships among the family members are hostile and tense, with frequent displays of negative verbal and nonverbal behavior) to 7 (*harmonious*; relationships are warmly supportive; dialogue is relaxed; members clearly work together to resolve issues; tone is friendly); (b) the Engagement scale, ranging from 1 (*not engaged*; family members do not speak to one another or interact nonverbally) to 7 (*engaged*; family members frequently talk to each other and interact nonverbally); and (c) the Communication scale, ranging from 1 (*not at all characteristic*; family members rarely explain or clarify their remarks to make themselves understood) to 7 (*highly characteristic*; family members virtually always explain and clarify their remarks to promote understanding). The codes were designed to focus on the interacting couple as a dyad in order that the couple, not the individuals, would be the focus of the analyses. Because couple interactions took place in two task settings (game playing and problem solving), the scores for each setting were averaged across tasks to increase the reliability of the assessments (Epstein, 1979). Coders did not rate any families whose homes they had visited.

Reliability was calculated using Pearson Product–Moment Correlations, computed for each possible pair of observers. Mean agreement scores were calculated across subjects for each pair, and across all pairs, of observers. Average agreement for each code was: conflict-harmony scale = .73; engagement scale = .79; communication scale = .78.

Cocaregiver Support and Conflict. The quality of the cocaregiving relationship was assessed using a revision of Ahrons' (1981) Quality of Coparenting Scales, on which respondents use a Likert-type format to assess communication and conflict. The Cronbach alphas for this sample ranged from .70 to .80 for mothers, and from .65 to .82 for fathers. To assess frequency of interparental conflict in the presence of children, mothers and fathers completed the O'Leary–Porter Scale (OPS; Porter & O'Leary, 1980). Cronbach alphas for both mothers and fathers in this sample exceeded .85.

Youth Self-Regulation. Self-regulation was assessed using the self-control subscale of the Children's Self-Control Scale (Humphrey, 1982). This subscale contains five items that were rated on a 5-point scale by mothers, fathers, and teachers. The items were: thinks ahead of time about the consequences of his or her actions, plans ahead before acting, pays attention to what he or she is doing, works toward goals, and sticks to what he or she is doing, even on long, unpleasant tasks, until finished. The Cronbach alphas for mothers, fathers, and teachers were .80, .71, and .92, respectively.

Reading Competency. Assessments of reading competency included reading grades assigned by teachers (A, B, C, D, F), mothers' and fathers' reading grade expectations (A, B, C, D, F), and the child's score on the vocabulary subscale of the WISC–R. The latter measure was administered individually to the target youth in his or her home.

Mathematics Competency. Mathematics competency was assessed in a manner similar to reading competency. Measures included mathematics grades assigned by teachers, parents' mathematics grade expectations, and the child's score on the mathematics subscale of the WISC–R.

Externalizing Problems. Mothers, fathers, and teachers completed the 10-item conduct disorder subscale from the Revised Behavior Problem Checklist (RBPC; Quay & Peterson, 1987). The Cronbach alphas exceeded .90 for both parents and teachers in this sample. Parents and teachers also completed the antisocial behavior subscale from the Self-Control Inventory (SCI; Humphrey, 1982). Cronbach alphas for parents exceeded .70, and for teachers, .90. The teacher-assigned classroom conduct grade (A, B, C, D, F) was included as an additional indicator.

Internalizing Problems. Mothers, fathers, and teachers completed a revised version of the Children's Depression Inventory (CDI; Kovacs, 1981). This instrument consists of 27 items, each of which allows respondents to select alternatives on a 3-point scale reflecting degrees of particular symptoms. Cronbach alphas for parents and teachers in this sample were .78 and .90, respectively.

Structural Modeling

The hypotheses were analyzed using a partial least squares (PLS) approach to causal modeling. This approach is suited to the analysis of data that do not conform to the highly restrictive assumptions that underlie maximum likelihood techniques such as LISREL (Fornell & Bookstein, 1982). The advantage of PLS over other regression analyses is that it allows the assessment of both direct and indirect effects, both of which are included in the hypotheses.

Several statistics are included in the analysis (see Falk, 1987). First, goodness-of-fit indices assess the extent to which the model reproduces the actual covariance matrix. The coefficient RMS COV (EU), which stands for the root mean square of the covariance between the residuals of the manifest and latent variables, is an index of the overall model's fit with the raw data. This coefficient would be 0 in a model that describes with complete accuracy the relationships between the variables. A coefficient above .20 indicates a poor model, and a coefficient of, for example, .02 indicates a superior one. Each of the two models presented here achieved a coefficient of .07. Second, the mean of the squared multiple correlations of latent variables is the arithmetic average of the multiple R squares for all the endogenous variables. Third, the commonality statistics (h_2) assess the shared variance among all of the latent constructs. Falk (1987) suggested that PLS models attaining a commonality above .30 are considered good. The two models presented here attained commonalities of .57 and .58. The path coefficients assess the strength of the connections between concepts or variables. The test of significance on the R^2s was reported using the degrees of freedom for the full model, thereby reducing the capitalization on chance for the null hypothesis that R^2 equals zero.

Falk (1987) recommended that, following the computation of each model, the paths be examined for suppressor effects. Such effects, which produce spurious relationships, occur when an independent variable is uncorrelated with a dependent variable, but is useful in predicting the dependent variable; this increases the multiple R^2 by virtue of its correlation with other independent variables. Falk (1987) identified two indicators by which these effects can be detected: path coefficients that have different signs than their correlation coefficients, and large discrepancies between the path coefficient and the correlation coefficient. The models were examined for suppressor effects and any that emerged were removed.

Two models were evaluated; one used maternal, and the other used paternal, depression and optimism constructs. The models were not run separately by gender of child because, although these procedures allow for the analysis of relatively small samples, they require an adequate number of subjects for the number of composite variables in the model. The factor loadings of the manifest variables on their respective latent variables are presented in Table 7.1. They may be considered approximations of first principal component loadings because they also take into account the hypothesized relations among the latent variables.

Examination of the loadings, which represent the correlations of the manifest variable with the latent variable, shows the manifest variables to be good indicators of their respective constructs. Note that the latent variables for financial resources and parent depression are comprised of only one manifest variable.

RESULTS

Figure 7.1 presents the relationships for mothers among family hourly wage, depressive symptoms, optimism, marital interaction quality, fathers' cocaregiver support, mothers' cocaregiver support, cocaregiver conflict, youth self-regulation, reading competency, mathematics competency, externalizing problems, and internalizing problems. The analysis indicated that with higher family hourly wages, mothers reported less depression and more optimism. Higher hourly wages were linked with more harmonious, communicative marital interaction quality, more cocaregiving support from fathers, and less cocaregiver conflict. Mothers' reports of depressive symptoms were positively linked with cocaregiver conflict. Associations also emerged between maternal optimism and mothers' and fathers' cocaregiving support. Harmonious, communicative marital interaction and mothers' receipt of more cocaregiver support from fathers were associated with higher youth

TABLE 7.1

Component Loadings on Manifest Variables by Mother and Father Models

Variable	Mothers	Fathers
Family wages		
Family Wages	1.00	1.00
Depression		
Depression Subscale (CES–D)	1.00	1.00
Optimism		
Optimism Subscale (CES–D)	0.66	0.80
Rosenberg Self-Esteem Scale	0.93	0.92
Maternal interaction quality		
Harmony—Behavioral Observation Ratings	0.84	0.82
Engagement—Behavioral Observation Ratings	0.85	0.86
Warmth—Behavioral Observation Ratings	0.55	0.56
Communication—Behavioral Observation Ratings	0.74	0.75
Fathers cocaregiver support received from mothers		
Communication Subscale (Ahron's Quality of Co-Parenting Scales)	0.46	0.87
Support Subscale (Ahron's Quality of Co-Parenting Scales)	0.99	0.76
Mothers cocaregiver support received from fathers		
Communication Subscale (Ahron's Quality of Co-Parenting Scales)	0.71	0.77
Support Subscale (Ahron's Quality of Co-Parenting Scales)	0.91	0.87
Cocaregiver conflict		
Conflict Subscale, Mothers (Ahron's Quality of Co-Parenting Scales)	0.73	0.69
Conflict Subscale, Fathers (Ahron's Quality of Co-Parenting Scales)	0.64	0.73
Conflict Scale, Mothers (O'Leary Porter Scale)	0.74	0.65
Conflict Scale, Fathers (O'Leary Porter Scale)	0.67	0.73
Youth self-regulation		
Self-Control subscale, Mothers (Self-Control Inventory)	0.75	0.75
Self-Control subscale, Fathers (Self-Control Inventory)	0.53	0.53
Self-Control subscale, Teachers (Self-Control Inventory)	0.78	0.78
Reading competency		
Actual school grades	0.77	0.76
(WISC–R) Vocabulary subscale	0.63	0.63
Parental grade expectation, mothers	0.76	0.76
Parental grade expectation, fathers	0.66	0.67
Mathematics competency		
Actual school grades	0.77	0.77
(WISC–R) Arithmetic subscale	0.67	0.68
Parental grade expectation, mothers	0.72	0.71
Parental grade expectation, fathers	0.68	0.68
Externalizing problems		
Conduct Disorder subscale, mothers (Child Behavior Checklist)	0.71	0.71
Conduct Disorder subscale, teachers (Child Behavior Checklist)	0.83	0.83
Antisocial Behavior subscale, mothers (Self-Control Inventory)	0.79	0.79
Antisocial Behavior subscale, teachers (Self-Control Inventory)	0.83	0.83
Socialized Aggression subscale, teachers (Child Behavior Checklist)	0.61	0.60
Conduct grade expectation ratings, teachers	0.69	0.69
Internalizing problems		
Child Depression Inventory ratings, mothers	0.70	0.84
Child Depression Inventory ratings, fathers	0.87	0.74

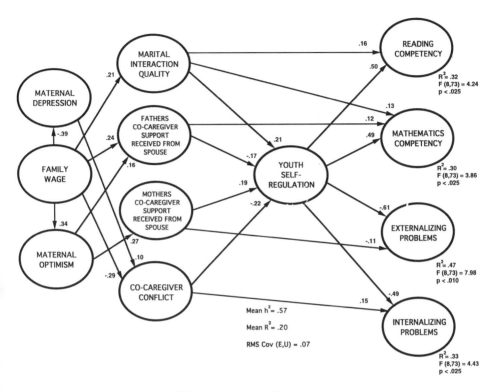

FIG. 7.1. Path model for mothers.

self-regulation ratings. Cocaregiver conflict and fathers' receipt of more co-caregiver support were associated with lower youth self-regulation ratings. The association between fathers' receipt of more cocaregiving support from mothers and lower levels of youth self-regulation was surprising, and suggests that less self-regulated youths may require their fathers to enlist more cocaregiving assistance from mothers. Higher levels of youth self-regulation were linked to greater competency in reading and math, and to fewer externalizing and internalizing problems.

Direct links also emerged between cocaregiving processes and the youth competency processes. Marital interaction quality was positively associated with reading and math competence. Fathers' receipt of cocaregiving support from mothers was positively associated with math competence, and higher levels of cocaregiver conflict were associated with higher levels of internalizing problems.

The path model for fathers is shown in Fig. 7.2. Higher family hourly wages were linked with less paternal depression and more optimism. More depressive symptoms among fathers were associated with lower levels of cocaregiver support that parents provided to one another, and with more cocaregiver conflict about childrearing. Paternal optimism was positively associated with harmonious, communicative marital interactions and with mothers' and fathers' cocaregiver support;

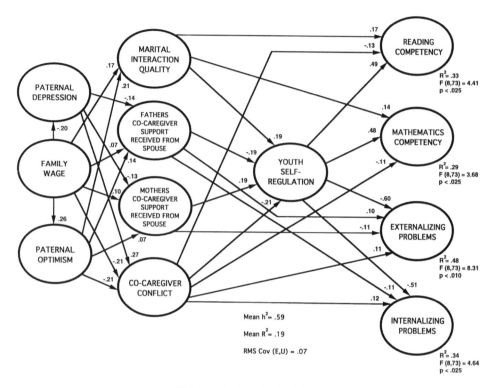

FIG. 7.2. Path model for fathers.

it was negatively associated with cocaregiver conflict. Family wage per hour was positively associated with mothers' and fathers' receipt of cocaregiver support. The paths from cocaregiving to self-regulation and to academic and adjustment outcomes, depicted in Fig. 7.2, are just as they were in the mothers' model. Direct, positive paths again emerged between marital interaction quality and competence in reading and math. Higher levels of cocaregiver conflict were associated with more externalizing and internalizing problems. Fathers' receipt of cocaregiving support from mothers was positively associated with youths' externalizing problems. Again, because the data reported here are contemporaneous, conclusions about direction of effects cannot be drawn; it is possible that youths who display difficult behavior draw their fathers and mothers together in the cocaregiving process.

DISCUSSION

In this chapter analyses were presented that were used to test a model of the linkages between family hourly wages and youth competency in rural married African American families. Rather than focusing only on the amount of money the families earned, the number of hours husbands and wives worked to earn their wages were also considered. Accordingly, a family wage per hour measure was developed to provide a more sensitive assessment of the level of effort that rural married African American parents expended to support their families. Parents in some families worked as much as three times the number of hours as did parents in other families to earn the same amount of money per year. It was hypothesized that family wage per hour would be positively associated with psychological functioning and cocaregiving relationship quality. The analyses supported this hypothesis. For mothers and fathers, higher family wage per hour was linked with reports of fewer depressive symptoms and more optimism. Family wage was also linked positively with harmonious marital interaction and fathers' cocaregiving support, and negatively with cocaregiving conflict. Presumably, the stress associated with earning a low hourly wage takes its toll on the parents' psychological functioning, spilling over into the marital and cocaregiving relationships as well.

The links between parental psychological functioning and cocaregiving relationships were somewhat different from those that were predicted. It was hypothesized that parents' reports of depressive symptoms would be linked with the quality of their cocaregiving relationships. This hypothesis was supported for fathers, but not for mothers. Contrary to expectations, when the family wage per hour measure was included in the analysis, only one path, between maternal depression and cocaregiving conflict, emerged. These data suggest that the link between depression and family processes may be influenced by the number of hours family members must work to earn their income. Overall, the literature suggests that economic hardship is linked to depression, which in turn impacts family processes (McLoyd, 1990). For the mothers in this study, the strains associated with working long hours, such as fatigue and the constant need to coordinate schedules, apparently are more likely than depression per se to impact the provision of instrumental and emotional cocaregiving support.

Parental optimism was included as a resilience factor, which was hypothesized to be positively associated with hourly wages and supportiveness in cocaregiving relationships. These hypotheses were supported. Unlike the findings for depression, parental optimism was positively associated with cocaregiving support when the family wage per hour was considered. This suggests that parental optimism is not simply the "flip side" of depression; it is a unique construct that evinces its own associations with patterns of instrumental and emotional support. These data suggest that optimistic and self-confident parents confront work-related stress by creating supportive family relationships, which in turn act as a protective buffer from the strains of working long hours for low wages.

Supportive marital and cocaregiving relationships were positively associated with self-regulatory competencies in youths. This link was hypothesized based on the assumption that youths internalize the ability to regulate their behavior and anticipate the consequences of their actions from family environments that are emotionally secure and feature supportive parental cocaregiving. Self-regulatory competencies in turn were linked with reading and math competencies, and with lower levels of externalizing and internalizing problems. The inclusion of self-regulatory competencies as a mediator between family processes and youth outcomes suggests that family processes foster a core set of self-competencies in youths that are reflected in their academic competence and psychological adjustment. Although the contemporaneous nature of the data precludes the inference of causality, the data are consistent with this formulation.

The quality of the cocaregiving relationship also contributes uniquely to youth outcomes, independent of its contribution to self-regulatory competence. When family cocaregiving relationships were characterized by higher conflict levels, academic and socioemotional competence were compromised. Harmonious marriages created a context that directly contributed to academic competence. Just as in the findings for self-regulatory competence, mothers' receipt of cocaregiving support was negatively associated with externalizing problems, and fathers' receipt of this support was positively associated with such problems. The findings for fathers suggest that mothers may become more involved in cocaregiving when youths display problems with self-control. Longitudinal data currently are being collected on the families; as these data become available, direction of causality issues will be addressed. Taken together, the data suggest that, when family environments are characterized by interparental teamwork and emotional support, youths develop the ability to regulate and organize their behavior, resulting in academic and socioemotional competence (cf. Hetherington, Cox, & Cox, 1979).

CONCLUSION

Many families in the rural South work long hours in physically demanding jobs for low hourly wages. In a sense, all of the families in this study are resilient, in that they have weathered the transition-to-parenthood years and have remained intact despite seemingly stressful and complicated lives. The data in this chapter indicate that parents who maintain an optimistic view of life foster supportive cocaregiving relationships. Such relationships provide the children in these families with a secure base from which they develop the ability to govern their own behavior. Some caveats must be noted. The proposed model is not intended to be exhaustive. Other family processes and intraparental variables than those included in this model could account for variation in the outcome assessments. In addition, although the paths between the variables in the model may imply causality, at this point only the extent to which the variables can be predicted from the hypothesized model can be tested, without respect to direction of effects.

ACKNOWLEDGMENTS

This study was supported by grants from the Spencer Foundation and the National Reading Research Center.

REFERENCES

Ahrons, C. R. (1981). The continuing coparental relationship between divorced spouses. *American Journal of Orthopsychiatry, 51,* 315–328.

Billings, A. G., & Moos, R. H. (1982). Work stress and the stress-buffering roles of work and family resources. *Journal of Occupational Behavior, 3,* 215–232.

Block, J. H., Block, J., & Morrison, A. (1981). Parental agreement-disagreement on childrearing orientations and gender-related personality correlates in children. *Child Development, 52,* 965–974.

Bolger, N., DeLongis, A., Kessler, R. C., & Wethington, E. (1989). The contagion of stress across multiple roles. *Journal of Marriage and the Family, 51,* 175–183.

Conger, R. D., Conger, K. J., Elder, G., Lorenz, F. O., Simons, R. L., & Whitbeck, L. B. (1992). A family process model of economic hardship and adjustment of early adolescent boys. *Child Development, 63,* 526–541.

Conger, R. D., Elder, G. H., Lorenz, F. O., Conger, K. J., Simons, R. L., Whitbeck, L. B., Huck, S., & Melby, J. N. (1990). Linking economic hardship to marital quality and instability. *Journal of Marriage and the Family, 52,* 643–656.

Coward, R. T., & Smith, W. M. (1983). *Family services: Issues and opportunities in contemporary rural America.* Lincoln: University of Nebraska Press.

Crouter, A. C., Perry-Jenkins, M., Huston, T. L., & Crawford, D. W. (1989). The influence of work-induced psychological states on behavior at home. *Basic and Applied Psychology, 10,* 273–292.

Emery, R. E. (1988). *Marriage, divorce and children's adjustment.* Beverly Hills, CA: Sage.

Epstein, S. (1979). The stability of behavior: I. On predicting most of the people much of the time. *Journal of Personality and Social Psychology, 37,* 1097–1126.

Falk, R. F. (1987). *A primer for soft modeling.* Berkeley: University of California.

Fornell, C., & Bookstein, F. L. (1982). A comparative analysis of two structural equation models: LISREL and PLS applied to market data. In C. Fornell (Ed.), *A second generation of multivariate analysis* (pp. 289–394). New York: Prager.

Gabriel, R. (1986). *Report to the Kellog Task Force on the Learning Society.* Unpublished manuscript, University of Georgia, Athens.

Gerber, G. (1976). Conflicts in values and attitudes between parents of symptomatic and normal children. *Psychological Reports, 38,* 91–98.

Greenberg, E. (1982). Education and the acquisition of psychosocial maturity. In D. McClelland (Ed.), *The development of social maturity* (pp. 155–189). New York: Irvington.

Grych, J. H., & Fincham, F. D. (1990). Marital conflict and children's adjustment: A cognitive-contextual framework. *Psychological Bulletin, 108,* 267–290.

Hetherington, E. M., Cox, M., & Cox, R. (1979). Family interaction and the social, emotional, and cognitive development of children following divorce. In V. Vaughn & T. Brazelton (Eds.), *The family: Setting priorities* (pp. 89–128). New York: Science & Medicine.

Humphrey, L. L. (1982). Children's and teacher's perspectives on children's self-control: The development of two rating scales. *Journal of Consulting and Clinical Psychology, 50,* 624–633.

Kovacs, M. (1981). Rating scales to assess depression in school-aged children. *Acta Paedopsychiatry, 46,* 305–315.

Lohmoeller, J. B. (1989). *Latent variable path modeling with partial least squares.* New York: Springer-Verlag.

Longfellow, C., Zelkowitz, P., & Saunders, E. (1982). The quality of mother–child relationships. In D. Belle (Ed.), *Lives in stress: Women and depression* (pp. 163–179). Beverly Hills, CA: Sage.

McLoyd, V. C. (1990). The impact of economic hardship on Black families and children: Psychological distress, parenting, and socioemotional development. *Child Development, 61,* 311–346.

Orthner, D. (1986, April). *Children and families in the South: Trends in health care, family services, and the rural economy* [Prepared statement for a hearing before the U.S. House of Representatives

Select Committee on Children, Youth, and Families, held in Macon, GA]. Washington, DC: U.S. Government Printing Office.

Porter, B., & O'Leary, K. D. (1980). Marital discord and childhood behavior problems. *Journal of Abnormal Child Psychology, 8*, 287–295.

Quay, H. C., & Peterson, D. R. (1987). *Manual for the Revised Behavior Problem Checklist.* Unpublished manuscript, University of Miami, Coral Gables, FL.

Radloff, L. S. (1977). The CES–D Scale: A self-report depression scale for research in the general population. *Applied Psychological Measurement, 1*, 385–401.

Repetti, R. L. (1987). Linkages between work and family roles. *Applied Social Psychology Annual, 7*, 98–127.

Rosenberg, M. (1965). *Society and the adolescent self-image.* Princeton, NJ: Princeton University Press.

Scheier, M. F., & Carver, C. S. (1985). Optimism, coping, and health: Assessment and implications of generalized outcome expectancies. *Health Psychology, 4*, 219–247.

Scheier, M. F., Matthews, K. A., Owens, J. F., Magovern, G. J., Sr., Lefebvre, R. C., Abbott, R. A., & Carver, C. S. (1989). Dispositional optimism and recovery from coronary artery bypass surgery: The beneficial effects on physical and psychological well-being. *Journal of Personality and Social Psychology, 57*, 1024–1040.

Scheier, M. F., Weintraub, J. K., & Carver, C. S. (1986). Coping with stress: Divergent strategies of optimists and pessimists. *Journal of Personality and Social Psychology, 51*, 1257–1264.

Steinberg, L., Elmen, J. D., & Mounts, N. S. (1989). Authoritative parenting, psychosocial maturity, and academic success among adolescents. *Child Development, 60*, 1424–1436.

Taylor, S. E., & Brown, J. D. (1988). Illusion and well-being: A social psychological perspective on mental health. *Psychological Bulletin, 103*, 193–210.

U. S. Bureau of the Census. (1992, September). *Poverty in the U.S., 1991.* Washington, DC: U.S. Department of Commerce.

Vogel, E. F., & Bell, N. W. (1968). The emotionally disturbed child as the family scapegoat. In N. W. Bell & E. F. Vogel (Eds.), *A modern introduction to the family* (pp. 412–427). New York: The Free Press.

Wilson, M. N. (1984). Mothers' and grandmothers' perspectives of parental behavior in three-generational Black families. *Child Development, 55*, 1333–1339.

Attention—The Shuttle Between Emotion and Cognition: Risk, Resiliency, and Physiological Bases

Beverly J. Wilson
Oregon State University

John M. Gottman
University of Washington

In this chapter we explore the hypothesis that attentional processes mediate between risk and psychopathology in children (Kellam et al., 1991). In fact, we develop the idea that attentional processes play executive roles in organizing both cognition and emotion. We suggest that attentional processes provide a "shuttle" between the cognitive and emotional realms, and that the abilities involved in being able to attend and to shift attentional focus are fundamental to emotion regulatory processes. Furthermore, we suggest that attentional processes not only organize both cognitive and emotional processes, but that there is a *dual physiological basis* for this organization, parasympathetic tone and the ability to self-soothe from sympathetic activation. The evidence suggests that this physiological basis involves both a parasympathetically based capacity of the nervous system for organizing effortful and automatic information processing, and for self-soothing. As such, attentional processes organize cognition, emotion, and the physiological responses that accompany them, acting as a sort of gatekeeper. We also suggest that attentional processes can provide a window on temperament.

We know that attentional processes organize experiences from the earliest moments of life. They play a central role in the establishment of physiological homeostasis and emotion regulation abilities (Rothbart & Derryberry, 1981). It is quite probable that attentional abilities form a necessary precondition for much subsequent cognitive and social advancement. Attentional processes may also affect important sources of socialization and support for infants. This may occur in the caregiver–infant and peer systems as well as academic settings later in life.

To better understand how attentional processes may mediate between risk and psychopathology, we first review relevant literature on stress and resiliency. Of particular interest are factors that serve to protect children from the detrimental effects of stress and the processes and mechanisms that support the development of these protective factors. We discuss the role of attention in a number of psychopathologies. In the next section, we discuss definitions and classical and contemporary issues concerning attention, arousal, and performance from the field of cognitive psychology and suggest that emotion regulation may be the fundamental risk variable linking attention and psychopathology. Evidence concerning cardiovascular physiological processes that support or influence attentional processes is also presented. In the second half of this chapter, we suggest an overview of the influence of attentional processes on crucial developmental milestones during the first 4 to 5 years of life. Milestones during infancy include physiological homeostasis and the acquisition of basic interpersonal skills, such as turn-taking and the communication and regulation of affect. During the toddler and preschool years, we discuss the child's ability to establish and maintain effective peer relationships and the use of language for redirecting attention and regulating emotional states. Also discussed is the role of caregivers in the achievement of these milestones.

STRESS AND RESILIENCY

There are a number of normative and nonnormative events in the lives of children that can be stressful. Changes in family composition due to the birth of a sibling and transitions and challenges in academic and peer settings are typically part of growing up. Unfortunately, many children must also cope with marital conflict and the separation or divorce of parents (Hetherington & Clingempeel, 1992; Patterson, Vaden, & Kupersmidt, 1991). These events may adversely affect the health, social, and psychological well-being of children (Emery, 1982; 1988; Johnson & O'Leary, 1987; Jouriles, Pfiffner, & O'Leary, 1988; Long, Forehand, Fauber, & Brody, 1987; Long, Slater, Forehand, & Fauber, 1988; Rutter, 1971; 1982). On the other hand, there is considerable variability in children's reactions to stressors. Some children are better able to cope and quickly recover from stressful events, whereas others experience more severe and long-lasting effects. As stressful events are inevitable in the lives of children, identifying and understanding factors that differentiate between more and less resilient children is essential.

Studies of children at risk indicate that three broad sets of variables function as protective factors (see Garmezy, 1985, for a review). These variables include certain temperamental characteristics of the child, a supportive family milieu, and external sources of support. Protective factors during infancy include such positive temperamental qualities as being "active" and "socially responsive" (Werner & Smith, 1982), exhibiting "flexibility of response," and "positive mood" (Rutter, Cox, Tupling, Berger, & Yule, 1975a; Rutter, Yule, Quinton, Rolands,

Yule, & Berger, 1975b). In older children, feelings of self-esteem and self-efficacy operate as protective factors (Rutter, 1987). A close, warm, supportive family environment, and support from friends, ministers, and teachers also serve to protect individuals at risk (Garmezy, 1985; Werner & Smith, 1982). These factors have proven to be robust predictors of resiliency.

Despite the fact that these risk and resiliency factors are useful, there is a lack of more fundamental theory that helps us understand how these factors may do their work. In fact, Rutter (1987) proposed that these factors are of limited value for developing appropriate interventions. He suggested that what is needed is a better understanding of the processes and mechanisms that support the development and maintenance of these factors, and how they may affect individual development. We suggest that what is basic to a number of these risk and resiliency factors involves the capacity of the child to manage attention.

Attentional Processes and Risk

There is evidence that attentional processes mediate between risk and psychopathology in children. Kellam et al. (1991) found that problems in concentration played a central role in the development of shy and aggressive behavior and poor achievement in first-grade boys and girls. Problems in concentration also predicted depressive symptoms among the girls. It is known that problems in attention are also associated with disorders such as schizophrenia (Mirsky & Duncan, 1986), phenylketonuria (Anderson, Siegel, Frisch, & Wirt, 1969), epilepsy (Mirsky, Primac, Ajmone Marsan, Rosvold, & Stevens, 1960), and lead intoxication (Needleman et al., 1979). The *Diagnostic and Statistical Manual of Mental Disorders* (4th ed. [DSM-IV]; American Psychiatric Association, 1994) includes difficulties in attention as symptoms for the diagnosis of depression, mania, and bipolar disorder. Because difficulties in attention are so pervasive among pathologies, it may be helpful to examine the relationship between attention and the development of psychopathology.

Impairments in attentional processes are among the most pervasive and least understood problems encountered in educational and neuropsychiatric contexts (Mirsky, Anthony, Duncan, Ahearn, & Kellam, 1991). Estimates are that as many as 20% to 30% of public school students experience problems in attention (Cantwell, 1975; Rutter, 1970). Attention Deficit Hyperactive Disorder (ADHD) is the most severe example of these problems (American Psychiatric Association, 1994). Intrauterine exposure to alcohol and nicotine is also significantly related to attentional problems in preschool-age children (Herman, Kirchner, Streissguth, & Little, 1980; Streissguth, Martin, Barr, & MacGregor Sandman, 1984).

Classical Research on Attention From Cognitive Psychology

What is the mechanism through which attention is linked to psychopathology? We review work on attentional processes from cognitive psychology and then point out that both emotion and physiology need to be considered to suggest a mechanism. Research suggests that there are two separate attentional processes that need to be considered in this discussion of attention.

What processes are involved in attention? Attention at its base involves focusing on some stimuli and not others. The issue of stimulus selection has generated much research in cognitive psychology. During the 1950s and 1960s, several theories were developed to explain this process. In his early work, Broadbent (1958) proposed the filtering model of attention. He suggested that selective attention functions as a filter by allowing in some channels of information and blocking others out. This filtering effect occurs as a result of a shift in the way individuals process information. This shift involves a transition from parallel to serial processing. In parallel processing, many things are processed at the same time, whereas in serial processing only one thing is processed at a time. This transition was called the *attention bottleneck* because of the narrowing of attentional focus.

Broadbent's model was ultimately shown to be inadequate by demonstrations that individuals could switch their attention from one channel to another in order to follow the meaning of a particular message (Treisman, 1960). Eysenck (1982) concluded that the greatest inadequacy of these early theories of attention was their failure to account for the great flexibility of attentional processes. Subsequently, attention was conceptualized as the general limit on a system's capacity for processing information. The limited-capacity model of attention suggested that information may be processed in at least two ways. These are *automatic* and *attention-demanding* processing (Posner & Snyder, 1975a). Automatic processes involve parallel processing of information, whereas attention-demanding processes involve serial processing.

Automatic Versus Attention-Demanding Processes. In a series of priming experiments, Posner and Snyder (1975a, 1975b) were able to demonstrate the difference between automatic and attention-demanding processes. Their results suggested that automatic processes occur without conscious intention or awareness, and develop as a result of prior learning. Posner (1978) suggested that automatic processes are a "set of internal codes and their connections that are activated automatically by the presentation of a stimulus" (p. 90). Hence, automatic processes are not constrained by the limited capacity of the processing system. Other types of information processing may occur simultaneously with automatic processes. Conscious or attention-demanding processes, on the other hand, are characterized by their limited capacity. It is difficult for individuals to perform two attention-demanding tasks simultaneously.

Shiffrin and Schneider (1977) suggested a similar distinction between "automatic" and "controlled processes." They found that automatic processes are rapid but difficult to modify once learned. Once their subjects formed a strong association between pairs of stimuli, they were able to perform simple matching tasks automatically. This led to faster and more accurate performances. However, when the criteria for the matching task was changed, these subjects were significantly slower than other subjects who were learning the modified task for the first time. Thus, it was very difficult to relearn the task after moving to an automatic level of processing the information. The older associations appeared to interfere with processing the new information. In contrast, when subjects used controlled processes on the task, they were able to readily modify their approach when changes in circumstances required it.

In summary, research on automatic and effortful (attention-demanding) processes indicate that they make differential demands on the information processing system. Controlled or effortful processing is more constrained by the capacity of this system. The use of automatic processes may free up attentional capacity that can be used to deal with more novel challenges. Learning or forming associations between certain stimuli play a central role in the development of automatic processes. In some cases, automatic processes may also result in enhanced performance (both faster reaction time and accuracy); however, the cost is a loss in flexibility and the ability to modify these processes should conditions change. Effortful processes are more easily modifiable because they are more consciously controlled and are not based on the acquisition of strong associations.

How are these two processes related to risk for psychopathology? Are both central factors in risk and vulnerability, or is one more important than another, and, if so, what are the implications of these facts for development? We suggest that these important questions cannot be answered without considering the realm of emotion, and the role that attention plays in processes that involve emotion. Laboratory experiments in cognitive psychology typically deal with affectively neutral stimuli, such as letters or numbers. Yet many day-to-day cognitive events are far from being "cold cognitions." Human experiences often elicit strong emotions and increase arousal levels. It is necessary, therefore, to consider how attention is influenced by these arousing experiences. Research also suggests the importance of attentional processes in emotion regulation. It may be that emotion regulation is the fundamental risk variable that is being sought.

Emotion Regulation May Be the Core Risk Variable

Most current theories in cognitive psychology fail to give appropriate consideration to the relationship between emotions, motivation, and attention. How do we know that such a connection exists? We know that the past experiences and present goals of individuals often determine the direction of their attention. In addition, evidence indicates that high levels of anxiety may affect performance. For example, some individuals become distracted from a primary task, such as a test, by negative cognitions revolving around self-doubt and fear of failure (Darke, 1988; Deffenbacher, 1978; Hembree, 1988; Sarason, Sarason, & Pierce, 1990). To examine the relationship between emotions, motivation, and attentional processes, we briefly review the literature on arousal and performance.

Despite the fact that recent theorizing in cognitive psychology has largely ignored emotion, this has not always been the case. The notion that arousal influences task performance has a long history in psychology. The venerable Yerkes–Dodson law (1908) predicts an inverted-U function between arousal and performance. This law proposes that performance should be lowest at very low and very high levels of arousal and increase with moderate levels. Although there have been many methodological critiques of this law, including the difficulty of defining arousal in a unidimensional way, as well as the difficulty of disproving the hypothesis, Kahneman (1973) showed that, in general, physiological arousal increases with task difficulty. He suggested that task difficulty is based on the degree of mental effort or attentional capacity required by the task.

The most famous attempt to explain the Yerkes–Dodson law was undertaken by Easterbrook (1959), who proposed that arousal and states of high emotionality result in a progressive narrowing of attention to cues related to the task. The "attentional narrowing" hypothesis suggests that, initially, mild levels of arousal result in a narrowing of attention that excludes irrelevant cues. This should lead to an increase in performance. However, continued narrowing of attention results in the elimination of relevant cues, which results in a decrement in performance. According to this model, when subjects are engaged in a dual task paradigm (i.e., a primary and secondary task simultaneously), high levels of arousal should increase attention toward the primary task at the expense of the secondary task.

However, arousal produced by anxiety and shock results in quite different effects from arousal produced by incentives. Eysenck (1982) reviewed over 50 studies that examined the effect of arousal on dual task performance. High arousal caused by incentives was associated with increases in performance on the primary task and, in the majority of cases, no decrease in performance on the subsidiary task. High levels of arousal caused by anxiety or shock, on the other hand, typically did not influence performance on the main task, but were associated with decreased performance on secondary tasks. Some indication of factors related to the negative effects caused by aversive arousal may be gleaned from work by Bacon (1974). He found an association between arousal caused by shock and a reduction in the ability to hold information in short-term or working memory.

Thus, the "attentional narrowing" hypothesis does not work very well in explaining the effects of anxiety or heightened emotionality on performance. Instead of an attentional narrowing, in the case of test anxiety, there appears to be an expansion of attention to irrelevant cues, including negative self-evaluation and worry, probably the result of hypervigilance. There also appears to be a decrease in attending to task-relevant cues. Self-report data indicate that, during testing, highly anxious subjects spend only about 60% of the available time actually engaged in the task, engaging in task-irrelevant processing activities the rest of the time (Deffenbacher, 1978). Highly test-anxious children are also easily distracted and exhibit more off-task glances when engaged in difficult anagram problems (Nottelman & Hill, 1977). These situations are roughly equivalent to dual-task or divided attention situations. Some of the limited capacity of working memory is pre-empted by the processing of negative cognitions and subsequent behavioral coping strategies (i.e., self-distraction).

In summary, several theorists have argued that the effects of emotional arousal on performance are mediated, at least in part, by attentional processes. Eysenck (1982) suggested that the curvilinear relationship between arousal and performance has its basis in changes in attentional selectivity, capacity, and the negative effects of distractibility. Moderate and, in some cases, high levels of arousal may lead to increased attentional selectivity. This selectivity may be an active coping response initiated to focus attention on a primary task. In the case of anxiety, high levels of arousal may decrease the ability to use parallel or shared processing. This difficulty may be most evident in tasks that require concurrent cognitive operations such as retrieving information from long-term memory, storing it temporarily, and then actively processing it (Eysenck, 1982). High levels of anxiety may also lead to greater attentional lability and susceptibility to distraction to both internal and external events.

It is likely that the two types of attention are involved in the realm of emotion. Emotional information and experiences are probably processed effortlessly; even newborns are able to take in facial expressions and imitate them reliably (Meltzoff & Moore, 1983). However, the processing of one's own emotional state with respect to organizing oneself for action toward some external goal must require effortful processing. These *executive functions of emotion regulation* require the conscious focusing of attention away from the emotion-arousing event. We suggest that it is precisely these executive functions of attention that require a dual ability with respect to the child's physiology.

The Physiology of Attention

As with anxiety, many emotions have both cognitive and physiological components. A great number of normative and nonnormative life events may potentially generate strong emotions in children. As many of these events are inevitable, individuals must have mechanisms that allow them to cope and *recover physiologically* from these experiences. This raises a number of important questions. What about children who have difficulty accomplishing this recovery? What developmental outcomes might be expected when children are unable to recover physiologically? What other mechanisms might these children utilize? Will these children encounter special problems in development and throughout the life span? To answer these questions, research linking attention and physiology needs to be examined.

Research indicates that a close relationship exists between processing demands and physiological arousal. Kahneman, Tursky, Shapiro, and Crider (1969) found that the greater the processing demands, the larger were the physiological effects. For example, in a digit transformation task, subjects were presented with a series of digits that had to be transformed by adding 0, 1, or 3, after a 2-second pause.

Three physiological measures (pupil diameter, heart rate, and skin conductance) all showed increases during the input and processing of information, followed by a decrease. Pupil diameter also grew steadily as task load (the number of serially presented digits) and task complexity (add 0, 1, or 3) increased (also see Kahneman, 1973, for a review).

There are also EEG correlates of serial or effortful information processing. Posner (1978) suggested that the average evoked potential P300 wave reflects close attention or vigilance to a particular kind of event (it could also reflect the omission of an event). Instructional manipulations (i.e., to watch for and count matches or mismatches) affect the P300 wave. P300, thus, reflects the formation of expectations, which is one of the functions of conscious attention.

The notion of arousal as a unidimensional construct has been challenged. After researchers in the 1960s (e.g., Duffy, 1962) proposed that arousal could be considered unidimensional, there was considerable criticism of this view. In everyday situations, behavioral and cortical arousal (e.g., when an animal moves from a drowsy to a wakeful, attentive state) are not necessarily related to autonomic indices of arousal.[1] Under relatively benign experimental conditions in the laboratory, physiological measures are not well correlated. This is even true in such paradigms as when a snake-phobic subject approaches or picks up a snake. In more everyday situations, many physiological response systems appear to be weakly correlated.

This lack of association between physiological measures may relate to fundamental psychological processes. Sokolov (1963) differentiated between two patterns of response to novel stimuli, the orienting and defense responses. The orienting response facilitates attention to a novel stimulus. Habituation occurs once it is determined that the stimulus poses no threat. The orienting response involves increased sensitivity of the sense organs, increased somatic or muscular tone, a turning of sensory receptors toward the stimulus, gross motor inhibition, and a delay in respiration followed by a decrease in frequency (Stern & Sison, 1990). It is a nonspecific response with regard to the intensity and quality of the stimulus and is ephemeral and easily habituated. In fact, it is common in orienting experiments to include a dishabituation stimulus in the series of habituation stimuli. Research on the orienting response (OR) shows that physiological responses evidence what Lacey (1967) called *directional fractionation*. There is an increase in skin conductance but a decrease in heart rate following orienting.

In contrast, the defense response is elicited by a strong stimulus that may be painful or dangerous. There is no directional fractionation with the defense response. Heart rate increases and so does skin conductance. There is a decrease in sensitivity of the sense organs and muscular changes occur that facilitate moving

---

[1]Of course, if the range of experimental conditions is great (including mild emotion-eliciting stimuli such as films, as well as intense shock, startle stimuli such as unexpected gunshots, etc.) there will be a strong correlation across physiological channels. To observe these effects, one must include in the experiment a strong emotion-arousing situation, such as those used by Ax (1953) to elicit intense anger and fear in his subjects.

or turning away from the stimulus. These adjustments help to protect the organism from high levels of stimulation. Habituation occurs very slowly or not at all with the defense response.

At first, Graham, Lacey and others (Lacey, 1967; Graham & Clifton, 1966) thought that orienting and defense responses constituted physiological examples of sensory "intake" and "rejection" of stimuli. The notion was that the directional heart rate response could be a physiological marker of the perceived aversiveness of the incoming stimuli. In "intake," heart rate decreased and sensory thresholds were lowered, whereas in "rejection," heart rate increased and sensory thresholds were raised. However, subsequent research (e.g., Cacioppo & Sandman, 1978) indicates that *increases or decreases in physiological response were a function of the degree of effort in processing information*, independent of the aversiveness of the stimuli. Increases in physiological response could be obtained by simply increasing the processing demands of the stimulus; for example, heart rate increases with increased mental effort (e.g., mental arithmetic). Also, if the processing demands were small, an orienting response could be created, even in response to aversive slides.

Thus, it is in the area of effortful information processing that physiological arousal is likely to occur. It is in this realm that the executive functions of attention are likely to be most important and related to the child's resiliency to stressful life events. What, if any, are the physiological correlates of reduced resiliency? Two potential areas of research are reviewed that suggest that the physiological correlates of reduced resiliency are *low vagal tone* and *increased cardiovascular reactivity*. How can researchers make use of physiological correlates when a unidimensional view of arousal has been so elusive? The answer may lie in considering two opponent processes, the vagal "brake" and the sympathetic "accelerator." In the following section we discuss how each of these systems influences attentional processes.

Brief Review of Autonomic Physiology

The Vagal "Brake" and the Sympathetic "Accelerator." The autonomic nervous system controls internal organs such as the heart and glands and has what may crudely be considered two antagonistic branches, the sympathetic and parasympathetic nervous systems (SNS and PNS). These branches work together to maintain a state of homeostasis inside the body. Although the two systems are not always antagonistic (e.g., see Berne & Levy, 1987, on the synergistic effects of the PNS and SNS in myocardial contractility), the basic function of the sympathetic branch is to mobilize the body to meet emergency situations, and the parasympathetic's is to conserve and maintain bodily resources. The activity of the parasympathetic branch usually works to counteract that of the sympathetic. The result is a complex and highly interrelated system of control. The chief nerve of the parasympathetic nervous system is the Xth cranial nerve, the vagus nerve, which, among other things, stimulates digestion and acts as a brake on the heart. For example, during initial exercise, rapid heart rate increases of up to 100 beats per minute (BPM) are due to the releasing of this vagal brake. After that, the SNS cuts in and heart rate increases above 100 BPM are obtained. The releasing of PNS inhibition cannot speed the heart beyond its intrinsic pacemaker rhythm, usually about 110 BPM. High levels of cardiovascular arousal indexed by increased heart rate involve "releasing" the vagal brake and "stepping on" the SNS accelerator. Further increases in cardiac output (CO) are obtained by increasing dimensions of myocardial contractility (roughly how hard the heart contracts; e.g., ejection fraction), which is mediated mostly by the SNS (see Berne & Levy, 1987).

Vagal Tone

Under most conditions, the vagus nerve acts tonically on the heart, firing frequently so that the heart beats at a rate below that of the atrial pacemaker cells. So the vagus maintains a basal "tonus," called vagal tone. If the vagus is cut or frozen temporarily, the heart would beat at about 100 to 110 BPM, the intrinsic rhythm of the heart. Vagal input to the heart is interrupted on a rhythmic basis with each successive respiratory cycle. Heart rate increases during inspiration and decreases during exhalation. This repetitive turning off and on of parasympathetic stimulation to the heart due to respiration is known as "respiratory sinus arrhythmia" (RSA). When there are greater parasympathetic influences on the heart, larger transient accelerations in heart rate occur after interruptions of vagal influences. This results in greater amplitude of RSA (Porges, personal communication, 1992). Porges (1985) developed a time-series measure of RSA that he equated with vagal tone. The analyses attempts to partial out variability in heart rate due to RSA from variability due to other factors such as blood pressure, thermoregulatory processes, and movement. Pharmacological, surgical, and electrical stimulation studies confirm that Porges' index of vagal tone provides a reliable index of the parasympathetic nervous system's influence on the heart (McCabe, Yongue, Ackles, & Porges, 1985; McCabe, Yongue, Porges, & Ackles, 1984; Porges, 1986; Yongue et al., 1982).

Vagal Tone, Development, and Risk. We know that, in general, vagal tone increases monotonically during development and then decreases with old age (Gellhorn & Loofbourrow, 1963; Larson & Porges, 1982). The myelination process may account for some of the increase early in development (Sachis, Armstrong, Becker, & Bryan, 1982). Vagal tone also appears to index the integrity of the CNS; high-risk neonates (i.e., preterm infants) have significantly lower vagal tone than full-term infants (Porges, 1992). Furthermore, vagal tone effectively places preterm infants on a continuum of clinical risk; healthier preterms have higher vagal tone (Porges, 1983). Vagal tone begins to show moderate long-term stability by the second half of the first year of life (Fox, 1989).

Unfortunately, at this point in time, researchers know very little about the factors involved in the stabilization process of vagal tone. It is assumed that maturation of PNS areas are involved in this process (Porges, personal communication, 1992). It is also known that vagal tone decreases when physical health is compromised and during periods of stress. Recent work by DiPietro, Larson, and Porges (1987) indicated that at 1 to 2 days of age, breast-fed infants have higher vagal tone than bottle-fed infants. DiPietro et al. suggested that nutrition (i.e., colostrum) may be the key factor in this association.

Heart Rate Variability, Vagal Tone, and Attention.   Research over the past 20 years has consistently found a strong association between heart rate variability and attentional processes. Lacey (1967) noted that heart rate decelerates and stabilizes (periods between beats become more constant) during periods of attention. Although Lacey did not use heart rate variability as a dependent variable, Porges and Raskin (1969) later quantified and re-examined these data. They found that regardless of the direction of the specific heart rate response (i.e., heart rate increases or decreases), heart rate variability was always suppressed during attention. Based on subsequent research, Porges and his colleagues constructed a two-component model of attention (Porges, 1976, 1980). The first component is reactive and involuntary. It consists of an organism's initial reaction to an external stimulus, based on stimulus characteristics such as intensity and novelty. This passive form of attention is associated with directional heart rate responses and may be mediated by either sympathetic excitation or vagal inhibition. The second component consists of an organism's voluntary and sustained response to a stimulus. This active form of attention is characterized by a reduction in heart rate variability, respiration, and motor inhibition (Porges, 1991). This second component is mediated by the parasympathetic nervous system.

Subsequent studies with infants, children, and adults have found a strong association between vagal tone and attentional abilities (Porges, 1972, 1973, 1974). Linnemeyer and Porges (1986) observed the behavior of 6-month-old infants as they engaged in a visual recognition memory task. Infants with high vagal tone looked at novel stimuli longer during test trials and displayed better recognition memory than infants with low vagal tone. Vagal tone has also been associated with sustained attention and faster reaction time during a stimulus-search task in school-aged children. Porges and Humphreys (1977) assessed physiological response patterns related to vagal tone and the allocation of attention in retarded adolescents and nondelayed children of equivalent mental age. The retarded subjects exhibited low resting levels of heart rate variability (suggestive of low vagal tone). Significant group differences in heart rate variability patterns also emerged as subjects engaged in cognitive tasks demanding sustained attention. The retarded adolescents did not suppress heart rate variability during the task. This atypical pattern indicates deficits in parasympathetic control over the heart and suggests a physiological concomitant of developmentally delayed children's attentional difficulties.

A recent study with developmentally delayed 6- to 8-year-old children found that vagal tone differentiated between the attentional abilities of these children (Wilson, 1994). Delayed children with high vagal tone were significantly more accurate in their responses during a sustained attention task than delayed children with low vagal tone. Thus, evidence indicates a clear and reliable relationship between active attention, the suppression of heart rate variability, and vagal tone.

A logical question at this point might be "Why would a system (the PNS) that is associated with maintenance, recovery, and homeostasis be suppressed during attentional processes?" Heart rate variability is a sign of healthy functioning; decreases in heart rate variability and vagal tone occur with illness, stress, and aging (Porges, 1985). Porges (1991) suggested that "heart rate variability is a marker of the efficiency of the neural feedback mechanism and may index the health status of the individual's capacity to organize physiological resources to respond appropriately" (p. 208). The actions of the autonomic nervous system are ergotrophic (related to life support and work) and trophotropic (related to growth). The parasympathetic system is critical for both of these functions. Ergotrophic functions include physical work, stress, and intense emotions. Porges (1991) noted that attentional processes are also ergotrophic and that sustained attention is particularly costly to organisms. Normal homeostatic processes are, therefore, disrupted during these periods. The ability to subjugate homeostatic needs to attend appropriately to relevant aspects of the environment is an adaptive function needed for continued survival (Porges, 1991). The suppression of vagal tone appears to be a necessary physiological state for the promotion of sustained attention. In general, individuals with low vagal tone are less able to suppress or modulate their vagal tone to meet immediate challenges in their environment. For example, the retarded subjects studied by Porges and Humphreys (1977) exhibited low basal vagal tone and an inability to suppress vagal tone during attention-demanding tasks. This general finding has also been replicated with adults and infants (e.g., Porges & Raskin, 1969; Richards, 1985).[2]

---

[2]Researchers have identified two groups that do not fit this general pattern, regulatory-disordered infants and hyperactive children. Regulatory-disordered infants fail to establish normal sleep-wake cycles and are rated as being highly irritable and difficult. Although regulatory disordered infants have high vagal tone, their responses to attention-demanding tasks are extremely heterogeneous (Degangi, DiPietro, Greenspan, & Porges, 1991). Many of these infants have a difficult time regulating their autonomic nervous systems to support attention and information processing. It is interesting that the regulatory-disordered infants studied by Degangi et al. have higher vagal tone than normally developing infants with high vagal tone. At this point, however, it is unclear how this may influence their regulatory and attentional abilities. Hyperactive children have normal resting levels of vagal tone, yet are unable to suppress their vagal tone during attention-demanding tasks. Medication given to these children not only increases their ability to attend, but is paralleled by a suppression in heart rate variability (Porges, Walter, Korb, & Sprague, 1975). Research with these two anomalous groups may further illuminate the precise physiological processes necessary for attention.

Hence, research indicates that the vagal brake is clearly important in attentional processes. What of the sympathetic accelerator? The role of the sympathetic nervous system in the stress response has been recognized for some time (Cannon, 1914). As has already been discussed, high levels of arousal, especially arousal associated with anxiety, have detrimental effects on attentional processes. In the following section we explore the hypothesis that individual differences in cardiovascular reactivity and Type A behavior pattern impact attentional processes and lead to reduced resiliency.

Cardiovascular Reactivity

Cardiovascular reactivity (CVR) appears to be an individual difference variable that emerges early in childhood and is quite stable across time (Matthews, Rakaczky, & Stoney, 1987; Matthews, Woodall, & Stoney, 1990). Exaggerated increases in heart rate and blood pressure following exposure to stressors are demonstrated by about 15% to 20% of primary school children (Murphy, Alpert, Willey, & Somes, 1988). Twin and family research suggests that CVR has a genetic component (Hastrup, Light, & Obrist, 1982; Jorgensen & Houston, 1981). CVR typically persists into adulthood and may influence the risk of heart disease and several other chronic medical problems (Ewart, Harris, Zeger, & Russell, 1986). A behavioral correlate of CVR that may impact attentional processes and resiliency is the Type A behavior pattern.

Type A Behavior Pattern and Risk.   The Type A behavior pattern (TABP) is associated with cardiovascular reactivity and is characterized by a rapid pace of activity, a sense of time urgency, and competitive and aggressive tendencies. The pattern was first identified in adults as a risk factor for coronary heart disease, but recent research has identified similar behavioral patterns in preschool children (Vega-Lahr & Field, 1986).

The Type A behavior pattern may be important to this discussion of attention and resiliency for several reasons. First, TABP is associated with the ability to recover from strong emotion. For example, it is related to high levels of anxiety and physiological arousal during stressful and challenging situations. This arousal may adversely influence attentional processes and consequently interfere with the development of certain emotion regulation strategies. Second, Type As (i.e., individuals who exhibit high levels of TABP) are more likely to use an attentional narrowing strategy in response to stressful tasks (Matthews, 1982). If we think of Easterbrook's hypothesis, this strategy may negatively influence the ability of Type As to successfully accomplish certain tasks if the focus is too narrow. Finally, the interpersonal style of Type A individuals appears to be characterized by issues related to control, such as dominance, competitiveness, and aggressiveness (Glass, 1977). This style may adversely influence the ability of Type As to develop supportive social relationships.

Physiological Responses, TABP, and Attention. Although one might expect that children who focus attention during stress might reduce their heart rate by activating the vagal brake, this is not so. Children who exhibit TABP show exaggerated heart rate and blood pressure responses to mildly stressful and challenging events. Children as young as 1 to 4 years old who exhibit Type A behavior show significant increases in urinary catecholamine secretion after experiencing stress (Lundberg, 1983, 1986). This indicates a heightened reactivity of the sympathetic adrenomedullary system, which is associated with the stress response. Physiological and self-report data indicate that Type A individuals experience significant anxiety and physiological arousal during stressful situations (Haynes, Levine, Scotch, Feinleib, & Kannel, 1978; Siegel, 1982). Research on performance and arousal indicates that attentional processes may be disrupted by these high levels of arousal. This is especially problematic because many emotion regulation strategies are based on attentional processes such as attentional selectivity (Rothbart & Derryberry, 1981). Thus, children who exhibit the TABP may have fewer strategies available to them for regulating their physiological arousal. In fact, Type A children have been reported to react to situations intensely and to have short attention spans (Kurdek & Lillie, 1985). Heightened levels of arousal and the attentional patterns of Type A individuals also influence their performance on a number of tasks.

Type A Behavior Pattern and Attentional Narrowing. Matthews (1982) reviewed the literature on TABP and task performance and found that adult Type As outperformed Type Bs (individuals low on Type B behaviors) on tasks that required speed and persistence. Type A individuals used an attentional narrowing approach when confronted with these challenging tasks. This strategy enabled them to ignore their own fatigue and external distractions. However, they did more poorly than Type Bs on tasks that required slow and careful responses or a broad focus of attention. Similar results have been found with Type A children (Blaney, 1990). Most social situations require attention to subtle cues, shifts in attentional focus, and flexibility in thinking. The ability to accomplish these tasks may be adversely affected by the attentional style of Type As.

Type As and Interpersonal Relations. A major component of the TABP involves attempts to gain and maintain control over their environments (Brunson & Matthews, 1981; Glass, 1977; Matthews, 1979). This tendency extends into the realm of social relationships. If a social situation is seen as challenging to Type A individuals, then they could be expected to utilize a perceptual narrowing strategy. Some interpersonal situations may be similar to the dual task paradigm, with interpersonal control as the primary task for Type As and other interpersonal goals (e.g., giving and receiving support, validation) as secondary tasks. This orientation is reflected in the interpersonal style of individuals who exhibit Type A behavior; they tend to be aggressive, competitive, and controlling (Matthews, 1982).

The relationships of Type A individuals are often negatively influenced by their attempts to control interactions. Research with children suggests that they see Type A peers as being less fun to play with, noisy, and the cause of interpersonal problems (Whalen & Henker, 1986). Observations of their behavior in class and during structured group tasks indicates that they are more likely to talk, make noise, disrupt others, and engage in negative contact with peers. Work by Kurdek and Lillie (1985) also suggest that Type A boys lack a number of social cognitive skills, such as knowledge about the importance of trust in friendships and how to solve conflicts. The social problems of Type As also influence the degree of support and satisfaction they derive from their relationships. Type A adults report dissatisfaction with their work, marriages, and lives (Haynes, Feinleib, & Kannel, 1980; Howard, Cummingham, & Rechnitzer, 1976; 1977; Waldron, 1978). In addition, Type A behavior in children is associated with depression (Heft et al., 1988).

Caregiver variables may be involved in the evolution of TABP in children. Woodall and Matthews (1989) found that Type A children are more likely to come from families who are low in supportiveness and interpersonal involvement. Type A undergraduate males are more likely than Type Bs to describe both parents as establishing high standards for achievement and continually escalating their demands (McCranie & Simpson, 1987). Type A boys (9- to 12-year-olds) tend to have fathers who have high expectations of them, yet perceive that they are not reaching these goals (Kliewer & Weidner, 1987). There is also some evidence that children with Type A parents are more likely than other children to exhibit Type A behavioral patterns (Bortner, Rosenman, & Friedman, 1970; Matthews & Krantz, 1976). Hence, not only might these parents encourage Type A behavior by communicating excessively high goals and dissatisfaction with their children's achievements, but they may serve as role models of this behavioral orientation.

Generalization and Summary

We have been discussing vagal tone and cardiovascular reactivity in terms of specific categories of disorders such as attentional deficit disorders and Type A personality. However, these two factors are likely to be useful in general for discussing dimensions important for emotion regulation in all children. The vagal tone construct concerns the ability of the parasympathetic nervous system to take in and regulate the inflow of stimulation appropriate to a task at hand. Cardiovascular reactivity concerns the sympathetic branch of the autonomic nervous system, which is related to body's ability to gather resources for meeting environmental challenges. Individuals with CRV and TABP experience heightened reactivity to challenge and may be at risk for problems related to internal soothing and the regulation of this autonomic arousal. We suggest that both dimensions are important in the regulation of emotion, part of which is the ability to focus attention.

In summary, research on attentional processes highlights the role of physiological processes. We have discussed two broad classes of opponent physiological processes, those mediated by the PNS and those mediated by the SNS. Research by Porges and his colleagues on the PNS indicates a strong association between high vagal tone and good attentional abilities. The suppression of vagal tone appears to be a necessary physiological state for sustained attention. Research on the SNS indicates that cardiovascular reactivity and Type A behavior pattern also affect attentional processes and the resiliency of children by directing the allocation of these resources. The attentional patterns of children who exhibit the Type A behavior pattern are organized in relation to their interpersonal goals (i.e., the tendency to strive for control and dominance). This narrowing of attentional focus may interfere with the performance of certain tasks and may also limit the ability of these individuals to develop effective and supportive relationships with others. This research suggests that two separate *dual physiological processes* may be important in the ability to mobilize attentional resources: (a) the vagal process, which is related to regulating the intake of stimulation; and (b) cardiovascular reactivity, which may interfere with attentional processes and the ability to internally soothe and regulate sympathetic arousal.

Are these physiological processes related to temperament, in the sense that they are determined and fixed at birth, and unaffected by salient environmental events after birth? We believe that these physiological variables are, in fact, quite malleable, and strongly influenced by the family. At this point we would like to integrate research from cognitive psychology and psychophysiology on attention into a developmental framework.

ATTENTIONAL PROCESSES AND DEVELOPMENT OVER THE FIRST FIVE YEARS OF LIFE

In the following sections, we describe and speculate about how attentional processes influence normal development in the first 5 years of life. We show how attentional processes provide a foundation for the abilities to cope and manage numerous challenges throughout development. To do this we discuss the mediating role of attentional processes in the development of physiological homeostasis, early experiences with caregivers, and the ability to form and maintain successful peer relationships.

Physiological Homeostasis

In this section we describe the infant's first task, that of establishing physiological homeostasis. Attentional processes play a central role in the accomplishment of this task. In fact, caregivers generally soothe distressed neonates by attempting to change the infant's attentional focus. Individual differences exist in attentional abilities and the physiological processes that underlie them. These differences are related to infants' ability to attend appropriately and acquire strategies for regulating physiological arousal.

Successful adaption for the neonate includes the regulation of arousal and physiological states. The infant must be able to regulate sleep and wake cycles, digest food effectively, and modulate arousal levels in response to changing environmental demands. Although most infants initially have difficulty accomplishing these tasks, the majority develop these regulatory abilities by 5 to 6 months of age (Degangi et al., 1991).

Cicchetti described homeostasis as a dynamic process through which the infant achieves stability and internal consistency (Cicchetti, Ganiban, & Barnett, 1991). Homeostatic processes maintain a "set point" for functioning. For the neonate, departure from this set point is tied to changes in physiological states induced by hunger, pain, cold, or fatigue. With development, changes in psychological states, such as anxiety and stress, also cause departures from this set point. Theoretically, a lack of homeostasis introduces tension into the system. This tension then motivates the behavioral system to subsequently act to relieve the tension and return the organism to a physiologically homeostatic state (Cicchetti et al., 1991).

During the first month of life, infants are able to reduce their physiological arousal to some degree by enacting certain reflexive patterns, such as eye blinks, bringing their hands to the mouth, nonnutritive sucking, and by turning their head away from aversive stimuli (Kopp, 1989). The limited behavioral and cognitive repertoire of the neonate necessitates frequent intercession by caregivers.

Cicchetti et al. (1991) proposed that the maturation and development of homeostatic ability may be guided by early experiences with caregivers. The first months of life are known to be a period of rapid neurological growth and maturation. As a result, interactions with caregivers during this period may have long-term effects on the organization and development of the brain. By providing predictable routines, appropriately meeting the needs of and soothing their infants, caregivers support the development of physiological homeostasis. Parents often use rhythmic movements, verbalizations, and the presentation of objects to soothe their infants. Many soothing strategies involve attempts to distract infants. The idea is to calm the negative arousal by shifting the infant's attention away from some internal signal toward a new source of stimulation, often in the external world.

By soothing their distressed infants, caregivers enable them to experience successful transitions from distress back to a homeostatic state before they are able to do this for themselves. This external support may provide a type of scaffolding on which infants can eventually build their own internal control. Infants gain experience in developing their own abilities during those times when caregivers are not readily available to soothe them.[3] Attentional processes play a central role in the development of these self-regulatory abilities.

---

[3]An interesting and important question for future research is "What are the processes from external to self-soothing?" It may be that repeated experiences with external soothing results in the creation of an internal event or representation of it. Certain strategies become "paired with soothing." When an infant is distressed and caregivers are not immediately available, this event is activated.

The Role of Attention in Self-Regulation.   Self-regulation refers to processes that function to increase, maintain, restructure, or decrease reactivity. According to Rothbart and Derryberry (1981), attentional processes play a central role in the modulation of reactivity. An infant's state of reactivity can be maintained by sustaining attention toward a stimulus, reduced somewhat by momentarily redirecting attention away from a stimulus, or terminated by shifting attention to a different event. Individual differences also appear to exist in these abilities (Rothbart & Posner, 1985). Furthermore, an infant's ability to learn these strategies may be influenced by his or her initial reactivity and interactions with caregivers.

Rothbart and Derryberry (1981) reported that some infants are more easily distracted by peripheral stimulation than others. Although attention must be maintained long enough to assimilate a particular stimulus, the ability to shift attentional focus (or self-distractibility) has adaptive functions. As noted earlier, the ability to shift attentional focus helps to regulate arousal. Shifts away from a stimulus may provide infants with time for recovery so that they can continue processing information without becoming too aroused (Stern, 1974). For example, Rothbart, Ziaie, and O'Boyle (1992) found a negative relationship between infants' ability to shift attentional focus and their distress to stressors. It may be that infants who are able to make these attentional shifts are better able to benefit from parental attempts to distract them when they are distressed.

The ability to engage in self-distraction improves with advancements in cognitive, sensory, and motoric development over the first few weeks of life. Infants voluntarily turn away from stimuli that they find aversive or intrusive and actively choose to return their attention to pleasurable events. For example, young infants engage in what Piaget (1952) termed *primary circular reactions*. The repetition of pleasurable behaviors, such as bringing the hands to midline and looking at them, provide infants with a sense of control over their level of arousal. They also provide infants with the means to distract themselves when distressed and caregivers are not immediately available (Kopp, 1989). Individual differences in physiological functioning may also influence the infant's ability to learn these regulatory strategies.

Individual differences in physiological functioning may influence the ability of infants to benefit from early experiences with caregivers and subsequently develop effective regulatory abilities. Rothbart and Derryberry (1981) suggested that individual differences in reactivity and self-regulatory processes underlie much of an infant's affective, cognitive, and social behavior. Reactivity refers to the threshold, intensity, and latency of an infant's reactions to changes in the environment. Individual differences in reactivity may also influence interactions with caregivers (Porges, 1991).

High and Low Reactivity.   Problems may occur during the first few months of life if an infant's physiological system has a very low or very high threshold for reactivity. Some of these difficulties may be mediated by the attentional processes of these infants. For example, an underreactive infant may be at risk because of missed opportunities in the environment. These infants may be less aware of sensory and social input from the world around them than other infants. Parents of these infants must "work harder" to engage and maintain their attention. Down syndrome infants are reported to be at particular risk for difficulties, because they exhibit relatively low physiological reactivity and delayed and weak emotional responses (Bergan, 1990; Cicchetti et al., 1991). These characteristics may influence the ability of caregivers to read the signals of these infants and to effectively engage and soothe them. Infants with low reactivity may also encounter fewer experiences with modulating between affective states. This could influence their ability to acquire more conscious regulatory strategies as they mature.

On the other hand, highly reactive infants may be at risk because they are more irritable, difficult to soothe, and have difficulties establishing regular cycles for feeding and sleeping (Degangi et al., 1991; Porges, 1991). These difficulties place high demands on caregivers to supplement the infant's immature regulatory system. Highly reactive infants who are unable to modulate their reactivity may be at particular risk for later problems because they may spend a large proportion of their time in a state of physiological dysregulation and miss many social and cognitive opportunities.

Latency to Peak Arousal State. An infant's ability to learn to modulate reactivity may also be influenced by individual differences in latency to peak arousal state. For some infants, reactivity builds rapidly after the presentation of a stimulus, whereas for others it builds more slowly (Posner & Rothbart, 1980). An infant whose reactivity builds too rapidly may have less time to practice self-regulatory behaviors. Stern (1985) proposed that coping and regulatory strategies are acquired in the space between the upper threshold for stimulation tolerance and the point at which behavior becomes disorganized (e.g., when the infant cries). In highly reactive infants, this window may be very small. Thus, these infants may have fewer opportunities for learning and practicing these abilities. These infants and their caregivers also experience fewer opportunities to learn the warning signs of forthcoming distress. This decreases the probability that appropriate changes in the level of stimulation can be made before behavioral disorganization occurs. These events may be experienced by young children with cardiovascular reactivity and may interfere with their acquisition of effective regulatory strategies.

Vagal Tone. Another physiological variable that has been associated with both reactivity and self-regulation is vagal tone (Fox, 1989). Newborns with high vagal tone are highly reactive, more irritable, and initially have greater difficulty soothing themselves than those with low vagal tone (Porter & Porges, 1988). Fox (1989) reported that 5-month-old infants with high vagal tone were more likely to employ selective attention strategies to calm themselves when distressed than infants with low vagal tone. These infants diverted their attention to objects or other things in the environment when exposed to stressors. At 14 months they were also more likely to approach novel objects and people with less apparent apprehension or stress.

Recall that Rothbart and Posner (1985) suggested that the ability to attend selectively to stimuli in the environment provides multiple strategies for dealing with physiological arousal. Thus, the attentional abilities of young infants with high vagal tone may provide a protective function for these infants. It may also be that early in life, infants with high vagal tone are more likely to elicit care from their caregivers via their higher reactivity (Porges, 1991). Frequent and effective soothing episodes with caregivers in combination with the high vagal tone of these infants may aid in a more optimal organization of the central nervous system. The resulting system should enable infants to quickly respond to both positive and negative events and return to a less aroused state.

In summary, during the first 2 to 3 months of life the infant's major task is one of achieving physiological homeostasis. Attentional processes play a central role in this process as they provide multiple strategies for self-soothing and increase the ability of infants to be soothed by others. Caregivers play a vital role by helping infants achieve this state before they are able to do this for themselves. In addition, some infants are more physiologically able to accomplish this task. Highly reactive infants who are unable to regulate their reactivity may be at particular risk for later problems. On the other hand, high vagal tone is related to high reactivity and the ability to regulate this reactivity (Fox, 1989). Physiological homeostasis is a crucial task for infants, because it enables them to shift their energy and attention from the inner to the outer world. It also provides an optimal state for the reception of sensory and social information. This state has been referred to as one of alert inactivity (Stern, 1985). During these times infants are physically quiet, yet alert and apparently able to take in information from the social world.

Attention and Early Infant–Caregiver Interactions

In this section we explore the role of attentional processes in the infant's acquisition of the basic skills that underlie communication. These include turn-taking, the mutual regulation of affect, the building of positive expectations concerning social interactions, social referencing, and shared states of attention. These skills are acquired during face-to-face interactions with caregivers during the first year of life. The attentional abilities of the infant and the sensitivity of caregivers to infant signals are particularly important for the accomplishment of these tasks.

At the interpersonal level, attentional patterns are influential in human interactions because they affect the degree of connectedness experienced by participants. Infants who attend appropriately to the signals and cues of others are more rewarding partners in social interactions (Malatesta, Culver, Tesman, & Shepard, 1989). New mothers feel great pleasure when their infants first engage in eye-to-eye contact with them (Robson, 1967). Robson reported that mothers increased their play with their infants after this event. Mothers of infants with attentional difficulties, such as preterm and Down syndrome infants, must work harder to engage their infants (Field, 1987; Jones, 1977; Malatesta et al., 1989; Malatesta-Magai, 1991). These mothers reported feeling less successful and rewarded in interactions with their infants. This may influence future interactions of these dyads and possibly the closeness or bond that they experience. For example, Field and others (Field, 1987; Goldberg, Brachfield, & Divitto, 1980) have reported that caregivers of premature infants spend less time in face-to-face play, touch and smile at their infants less, engage in less body contact, and appear more emotionally withdrawn from their children (even when the children were 2 years old). Attentional processes also play a central role in the ability of infants to benefit from early social experiences with caregivers.

Face-to-Face Interactions. Beginning in the first months of life, infants and their caregivers engage in cycles of attention and withdrawal (Brazelton, Koslowski, & Main, 1974). These interactions are characterized by reciprocal gazes, vocalizations, facial expressions, and body gestures that proceed in a turn-taking manner. It is within the caregiver–infant relationship that infants learn a number of important skills for establishing and maintaining effective social engagement with others. These skills include turn-taking, the regulation of levels of stimulation during engagement, and sharing internal states.

One important skill needed for social interactions is *turn-taking.* During early interactions with their infants, caregivers typically watch for signals, such as eye contact or smiles, before engaging their infants (Brazelton et al., 1974). Caregivers then direct some behavior toward their infants, such as smiles, vocalizations, or physical play. Caregivers typically wait while their infants respond to these behaviors. Pauses in the infant's behaviors serve as a signal for the onset of additional caregiver behaviors. The infant's cycles of attention and inattention form the basis for these judgments. Sensitive caregivers use these states to draw infants into periods of engagement that become more mutually regulated as the weeks pass. Caregivers also make adjustments in these interactions based on the reactivity, tolerance for stimulation, and attentiveness of their infants. For example, mothers of Down syndrome infants talk more rapidly when interacting with their infants (Buckhalt, Rutherford, & Goldberg, 1978). This tendency may be related to the finding that Down syndrome infants vocalize more randomly and leave shorter pauses between their vocalizations (Jones, 1977, 1980). Apparently their mothers adjust their responses to fit into the spaces provided by their infants. As infants mature, parental responsibility for managing states of engagement decreases and infants begin to take a more active role in regulating these interactions.

Mutual Regulation. Tronick (1989) noted that in the first few months of life infants and caregivers begin to mutually regulate the level of stimulation experienced in their interactions. Infants have different tolerance levels for excitement during these interchanges. When they become overstimulated and need to calm down, they engage in what Tronick (1989) called "self-directed" regulatory behaviors. These behaviors include looking away, sucking the thumb, or looking at the hands, and help infants lower the level of stimulation. These behaviors also serve as signals to caregivers that the infant needs a reduction in the level of stimulation. Infants use "other-directed regulatory behaviors," such as smiles or eye contact, to signal their renewed desire to interact (Tronick, 1989).

In normal caregiver–infant interactions, about 30% of the time is spent in coordinated interaction (Tronick, 1989). Transitions from coordinated to miscoordinated states and back again are frequent events. These experiences may help to build stress tolerance in infants; they may learn to maintain interactions with others despite periods of miscoordination. Tronick (1989) suggested that successful transitions from miscoordinated to coordinated states and recovery from negative affect challenge infants to expand and elaborate their regulatory repertoires. Although some conflictual or miscoordinated interactions occur in all infant–caregiver dyads, a high proportion of these states may adversely influence the development of effective regulatory patterns.

Expectations, Attention, and Regulatory Patterns.   Infants who habitually experience miscoordinated states, such as infants with unresponsive caregivers, exhibit difficulties in their regulatory patterns. Researchers have investigated the effects of chronic miscoordinated states by using the "still-face" paradigm (Cohn & Tronick, 1983). In this paradigm, mothers are asked to maintain a frozen yet neutral expression while seated in front of their infants. Most infants initially react to this situation by signaling that they want mother to interact with them. When these attempts fail, infants express distress followed by self-directed regulatory behavior. Infants build up expectancies about the consequences of their behavior in these situations. Thus, previous experiences with success or failure at repairing miscoordinated states influence the regulatory behavior of infants. Infants who have experienced a high degree of success are more likely to use other-directed regulatory behaviors to elicit their mother's attention (Gianino & Tronick, 1988), whereas infants in chronically miscoordinated dyads, such as depressed mothers and their infants, repeatedly engage in self-directed regulatory behavior. Normal interaction patterns are disrupted in these dyads, and infants employ self-regulatory behaviors in an automatic, inflexible, and indiscriminate way. Because this pattern is used defensively in anticipation of negative affect, it may result in a passive, "depressive" pattern of responding. This atypical pattern has been dramatically demonstrated by Field et al. (1988), who reported that the regulatory patterns and interaction style of infants of depressed mothers did not vary with the responsiveness of different social partners. In these cases, the regulation of negative affect becomes the infant's primary goal. In extreme cases, the result may be disengagement from people and objects because these interactions require too much regulatory energy (Tronick, 1980; Tronick & Field, 1986).

Hence, parental psychopathology influences sensitivity to infant signals. The presence of familial stressors, such as marital discord, may also adversely affect this ability (Fendrich, Warner, & Weissman, 1990). Elizabeth Fivaz-Depeursinge (personal communication, 1991) reported that unhappily married couples consistently overstimulated their infants in triadic play situations (i.e., mother, father, and infant). When their infants became distressed, these parents also failed to appropriately soothe them. Consequently, these infants were less able to organize their gaze in the play situation and looked away from their parents more than infants of happily married parents.

Interactions with caregivers present many regulatory challenges and social opportunities for infants. Patterns of attention play a central role in structuring these interactions. Through the use of attention deployment strategies, infants are able to regulate their own levels of arousal. These strategies also serve a communicative function; they communicate to caregivers the need to adjust the level of stimulation. The sensitivity and responsiveness of caregivers to these signals is a key element in the infant's ability to acquire effective regulatory patterns. When infants experience a high proportion of successful transitions from miscoordinated to coordinated states, they may feel a sense of control over their arousal levels in social situations. They are better equipped to engage the world and maintain interactions despite periods of stress.

Sharing States of Attention

During the last half of the first year of life, infants shift from regulating their internal experiences to intentionally sharing them with others. Parents also seem aware of this shift in their infant's abilities and increasingly address the subjective experiences of their infants (see Stern, 1985). Intersubjectivity involves the sharing of internal experiences between the self and others. These early experiences include attempts to share attentional focus, intentions, and affective states.

Early signs of intersubjectivity can be seen in infants' responses to attempts to redirect their attention to various objects and events. In the second half of the first year, infants are able to visually follow the line of their mother's gaze to a particular target (Scaife & Bruner, 1975). At about 9 months they are also able to shift their attention from a pointing hand and follow an imaginary line from the pointing finger to the target with their gaze (Murphy & Messer, 1977). Infants often visually check their mother's face during these encounters to confirm that they have correctly identified the target. Infants also begin to use gestures to redirect the attention of their caregivers at about this same time.

At about 9 months, infants point and use other body gestures to communicate their needs and desires. Many of these early attempts to redirect the attention of caregivers involve a desire for an object or event. An infant who spots her bottle on the kitchen counter may point toward it, alternating her gaze between her mother and the desired object. This type of "intentional communication" (Bates, 1979) by infants suggests that they understand that internal states can be shared with others. The sharing of affective states is often part of these events.

A primary means of communication for preverbal infants is the sharing of affective states. Requests for objects are often accompanied by changes in either the infant's facial expression, tone of voice, or both. Infants also learn to differentiate between the positive and negative affective signals of caregivers. As infants gain the ability to move further away from familiar adults, attention to signals from caregivers provides an important source of emotion regulation. Studies of *social referencing* indicate that by 10 to 12 months, infants actively check their caregivers' emotional responses in ambiguous situations. Infants then modify their own affective responses and behavior based on these signals (Campos & Sternberg, 1981).[4]

Attentional processes play a central role in the early development of intersubjectivity. In fact, intersubjectivity is a complex problem of shared and coordinated attention between two people. Caregivers and infants use their attentional focus to indicate that they understand each other, to communicate their needs and desires, to regulate their emotional responses, and to share the affective states of the other. The development of intersubjectivity enables children and their caregivers to experience a new level of interrelatedness.

In summary, attentional abilities are related to infant characteristics such as social responsiveness. Infants who are attentive during interactions with caregivers are regarded as more rewarding social partners. This may influence the way that caregivers interact with their infants and the affectional bond experienced by the pair. Attentional processes also influence the infant's ability to benefit from early caregiver interactions, especially the ability to learn skills for effective communication, such as turn-taking, mutual regulation of arousal and affect, and to share internal experiences with others. Sensitive and responsive caregiving is critical for the infant's development of positive expectations about the ability to engage and maintain interactions with others. Difficulties in these early interactions will also influence children's ability to gain information necessary for their social, emotional, and cognitive development and to form and maintain relationships with others. Problems associated with attentional deficits may also be expected to extend into another important area for socialization and support, peer relationships.

Attentional Processes and Peer Relations

In this section, we explore the role of attentional processes in establishing and maintaining effective peer relationships. The ability to interact successfully with peers and to form lasting peer relationships are important developmental tasks. Children who fail at these tasks, especially in the making of friends, are at risk for a number of later problems (Parker & Asher, 1987). The peer context presents new opportunities and formidable challenges to children. Interacting with peers pro-

---

[4]It is also interesting to note that an infant's tendency to social reference a caregiver is influenced by the emotional availability or sensitivity of that caregiver. For example, Dickstein and Parke (1988) found that infants do not socially reference their unhappily married fathers.

vides opportunities to learn about more egalitarian relationships, to form friendships with agemates, negotiate conflicts, engage in cooperative and competitive activities, and learn appropriate limits for aggressive impulses. To succeed in the peer context, children must be alert to opportunities for social engagement with others, attend to information that will help them gain entrance into the play of others, watch for cues and feedback from others, and modify their behavior based on this information. Control over attentional processes is critical to the accomplishment of these tasks.

The role of attentional processes in social competence has recently been explored by Eisenberg et al. (1993). They found a positive relationship between the ability of 5-year-old boys to control attentional processes, such as sustained attention and shifts in attentional focus, and their social skills and peer-rated sociometric status. In the following sections, we describe how attentional processes may be implicated in the successful completion of several social tasks.

Early Peer Interactions. At about 4 months of age, infants begin to spend more time attending to objects in their environment. Object play often mediates early social behavior; 88% of interactions between infants from 12 to 24 months involve nonsocial objects (Mueller & Brenner, 1976). What begins as object play often leads to the discovery of interpersonal contingencies. The ability to shift attention from object to object and from objects to potential social partners is a prerequisite skill for play interactions. Those who experience difficulties in shifting attentional focus, such as developmentally delayed children, may miss opportunities for interacting with peers.

Attentional Problems in Developmentally Delayed Children. Developmentally delayed children experience difficulties in their ability to shift attentional focus and to sustain attention. Landry and Chapieski (1989) found that 6- and 12-month-old Down syndrome infants had more difficulty shifting attention between toys and mother than nondelayed infants. When mothers attempted to direct their infant's attention to a toy, Down syndrome infants often became distracted, stopped playing, and looked at their mother instead.

Krakow and Kopp (1983) compared the attentional patterns of normally developing 12- to 18-month-old infants, developmentally delayed infants of unknown etiology (UE), and Down syndrome infants (DS) during free play. They found that delayed UE infants were significantly less likely to engage in sustained attention during play than the normally developing infants. Both delayed groups were less likely than nondelayed infants to visually monitor their mothers and the play environment during play. At 3 years of age, both delayed groups had greater difficulty making transitions from one play activity to another when prompted by the experimenter.

As children mature and their social interactions increase in complexity, difficulties associated with attentional problems would be expected to compound.

One complex but necessary social task faced by children is entry into the ongoing play activities of others.

Successful Entry Into the Play of Others. The ability of children to enter the ongoing activities of others has received much interest over the past 15 years. Successful entry serves as a prerequisite for further social interaction. Young children are frequently presented with the need to enter a new play group, because interactional episodes between young children are typically quite short, averaging less than 5 minutes (Corsaro, 1981). Phillips, Shenker, and Revitz (1951) suggested that the most important task for entering children is one of determining the "frame of reference" common to the groups' members and then establishing themselves as somehow sharing in this frame of reference. For example, children often observe a group's activity briefly to determine the current play theme, then make a comment or engage in a behavior related to this theme. In general, high-status (i.e., popular) children are more successful at these tasks than low-status children. Low-status children are also more likely to redirect the group's attention to themselves (Dodge, Schlundt, Schocken, & Delugach, 1983; Putallaz, 1983; Putallaz & Gottman, 1981; Putallaz & Wasserman, 1989).[5]

Entry also appears to be a difficult and potentially stressful task for children. Dodge, McClaskey, and Feldman (1985) reported that the entry situation is frequently identified by clinicians and teachers as being especially problematic. Because the play interactions of young children are quite fragile and easily disrupted, children tend to protect their interactions by discouraging the initial attempts of others to enter their play (Corsaro, 1979). Consequently, entering children must frequently deal with disputes over access to the group and their activities. They must also handle rejection from the group, because over 50% of all initial attempts fail (Corsaro, 1979).

Thus, at least two tasks are important to successful entry. First, the child must attend to the group's activities to assess their frame of reference and then incorporate this information into the entry attempt. Second, the child must have strategies for handling negative responses to their initial entry requests. These experiences are stressful and may generate negative affective responses in the entering child. An inability to calm oneself after experiencing strong affect may lead to less organized and adaptive behavior. Children may act aggressively toward the group or withdraw completely, responses that will decrease the probability of successful entry.

Children with good attentional abilities should be better able to handle the challenges presented by social tasks such as entry. In our laboratory, Wilson (1994) investigated the relationship between children's ability to sustain attention during a cognitive task and their ability to attend to relevant information in an

---

[5]Children who are unsuccessful at entry may also be calling attention to their own unsatisfied emotional needs, such as a lack of affection and positive interaction with parents. This is a need that most peers are not going to meet.

analogue entry situation. Children were presented with the task of entering the ongoing play of two other children. These two children were confederates of the researcher and followed a predetermined script that required them to change their play activity every 2 minutes. One play theme involved finding a "lost pizza" to feed a robot. The situation was contrived in such a way that the confederates were unable to find the missing pizza. The pizza had been placed close to the entering child at the beginning of the session. This situation presented a social opportunity for the entering child to help the confederates solve the pizza problem. Children who were faster and more accurate in their responses during a sustained attention task were also faster in responding to this social opportunity (i.e., they found the pizza more quickly). It may be that these children are better able to selectively attend to socially relevant information in entry situations.

Emotion Regulation in the Peer Setting. Selective attention also provides a number of avenues for the regulation of positive and negative emotion in the peer context (Rothbart & Posner, 1985). Social tasks, such as entry, often require that children wait or patiently persist at some behavior before they receive a positive response. Children with attentional problems may have a more difficult time regulating their responses to these frustrating events.

Developmentally Delayed Children's Emotion Regulation Strategies. Kopp, Krakow, and Johnson (1983) found that Down syndrome children (with developmental ages between 24 and 40 months) had significantly more difficulty with tasks requiring delay than normally developing children of the same developmental age. Kopp et al. suggested that a primary factor in the difficulties of these children was their lack of attention-distraction strategies. During one task, children were shown an attractive play telephone and told that they could play with it after the experimenter returned from the next room. To cope with the frustration of having to wait, normally developing children looked away from the telephone, watched their hands, and gazed at the ceiling and around the room. The delayed children, on the other hand, rarely turned away from the telephone and engaged in few of these distraction strategies. Similar patterns have also been found in our laboratory with 6- to 8-year-old developmentally delayed children. Wilson (1994) compared developmentally delayed and nondelayed children's responses to having their entry attempts ignored. This was a frustrating event for most children. Developmentally delayed children were less likely than nondelayed children to avert their gaze from the play area after being ignored. They were also more likely than nondelayed children to use disruptive entry bids, such as aggression, after their initial attempts failed.

After initiating play with others, children must continue to attend to relevant social cues and to regulate their emotional responses. The ability to successfully maintain a joint play interaction is a particularly complex task. Children typically negotiate concerning roles, ownership of toys, and changes in activities. Attending to the affective signals of others and modifying behavior appropriately based on these cues enables children to maintain their play activity despite periods of tension and disagreement. Monitoring of the play environment helps children anticipate and prepare for changes in this environment. Children who become engrossed in object play and fail to appropriately monitor the activities of playmates will miss feedback from peers about their behavior. Not only do these children miss opportunities available in extended social play, but their peers may come to perceive them as unpredictable or even unrewarding play partners. Research in our laboratory indicates that children with high vagal tone are better able to maintain a joint play activity with their best friend (Stanley & Katz, 1991). The attentional and emotion regulation abilities of these children may help to explain this association.

To summarize, peer relationships present children with many new challenges. Unlike parent–child interactions, the responsibility for engaging and maintaining peer interactions often rests solely on the children. They must be able to shift their attention from objects to potential social partners to avail themselves of opportunities for social contact. Children must also select from multiple sources of information the information that will enable them to reach their social goals. For example, children must attend to the play themes of peers before they can generate appropriate strategies for joining their play. Monitoring the play environment also enables children to gain feedback from peers regarding their behavior and to modify inappropriate behavior before it disrupts the play session. Failures in the peer context are frequent events. Given adequate resources for regulating the negative arousal associated with these events, moderate levels of failure may lead to greater resiliency in children. Children may build up expectancies for eventual success that will help them cope with future stresses and challenges in the peer context. As children mature they acquire a new tool for redirecting their attention and regulating their arousal in stressful situations; that tool is language.

Language: An Additional Way of Regulating Emotions

In this section we discuss how language provides a new means for redirecting attention and facilitating children's ability to solve problems and regulate their emotional responses in stressful situations. With the development of "*self talk*," children have a new and powerful tool for soothing negative affect at their disposal. Self-talk can be used to direct one's attention toward relevant aspects of a problem and away from irrelevant factors (e.g., negative cognitions). Vygotsky (1962) proposed a developmental progression in children's use of language. Initially, children use language to establish and maintain contact with others. At about 3 or 4 years of age they begin to use egocentric speech, talking to themselves as they engage in activities. Language begins to provide a new means of solving problems at this point. Vygotsky observed that children tend to talk to themselves at a much higher rate (almost double) when confronted with frustrating situations. In the following example, a child is getting ready to draw and finds that there is no paper or pencil of the color he needs:

> The child would try to grasp and to remedy the situation in talking to himself: "Where's the pencil? I need a blue pencil. Never mind, I'll draw with the red one and wet it with water; it will become dark and look like blue" (Vygotsky, 1962, p. 16).

At this point the child uses overt speech, but eventually this will no longer be necessary and language will go "underground." He can then talk to himself as a means of calming down and solving problems more effectively. For example, confronted with an unfamiliar challenging situation, children may tell themselves that everything will be all right and that they can figure things out. Alternately, young children may engage in negative self-talk. As described earlier, negative cognitions about one's ability may distract children from their primary task and subsequently impede their performance. These negative cognitions may compete for the attentional capacities of these children.

Labeling emotions also provides a mechanism for shifting attention away from the physiological arousal associated with some stressor to understanding and coping with it. Sensitive and responsive parenting during the preschool period involves the ability to notice the affective states of children and help them learn to label and cope with these states (Greenberg, Kusche, & Speltz, 1991).

SUMMARY, CONCLUSIONS, AND SUGGESTIONS FOR FUTURE RESEARCH

In this chapter we have explored the hypothesis that attentional processes mediate between risk and psychopathology. Attentional processes provide an executive function by organizing social, cognitive, and affective experiences from the first months of life. To demonstrate how attentional processes might organize these experiences, we first outlined basic research on attentional processes from cognitive psychology and psychophysiology and then attempted to integrate these findings into a developmental framework.

Classical research from cognitive psychology contrasts automatic and effortful (or attention-demanding) information processes. Automatic processing occurs without conscious effort and is not constrained by the limits of the processing system. When strong associations have been formed by overlearning, the automatic processing of information may lead to faster and more accurate responses, but the cost is a loss in flexibility. It is difficult to change a process once it has become automatic. Effortful processes, on the other hand, are under conscious control and are limited by the capacity of the processing system. Individuals may be able to do only one effortful process at a time.

Early in the chapter we made the point that many emotional experiences appear to be processed without conscious effort. Does this mean that emotions are processed at the automatic level? At least some affective responses may be prewired into the brain's circuitry. Affective reactions have their roots in evolutionarily old brain structures, such as the hypothalamus, amygdala, hippocampal formation, and cingulate gyrus. Although there are extensive and direct connections between neocortical areas and some of these structures (e.g., the hippocampal formation and amygdala), some affective responses may be partially independent of the information processing system. Zajonc (1980) reviewed research on impression formation, preference, attitudes, and decision making and found support for the independence of affective judgments. He found that affective responses were made faster and with greater confidence than cognitive judgments. For example, the discrimination of preference ("like" versus "dislike") can be made without the involvement of cognitive processes such as recognition memory. Zajonc suggested that cognition and affect may contribute independently to the information processing system.

We believe it is not necessarily the case that emotions are processed at an automatic level, for several reasons. Automatic processes are not associated with autonomic arousal, whereas emotional experiences, such as facial expressions, are associated with these changes (Ekman, Levenson, & Friesen, 1983; Levenson, 1988; Levenson, Ekman, & Friesen, 1990). Emotional regulatory processes entail dealing with some affective information, such as understanding and coping with one's own emotional experience, and this requires more effortful, conscious information processing. In other words, attentional processes may be expected to play a central role in the ability to manage and cope with many affect-eliciting events. Strategies for regulating emotional responses are likely to be attention-demanding and effortful.

We also know that intense emotions, such as fear and anxiety, may prove disruptive to attentional processes. Under some conditions, negative cognitions may serve as a secondary task and compete for the attentional capacity of individuals. Effortful (attention-demanding) processes are central to coping with the arousal caused by negative cognitions and emotions. These include sustaining attention toward some aspect of the situation until it is understood and shifts in attentional focus. Shifting attention allows individuals to disengage from one aspect of a situation that may be distressing (e.g., mother leaving) to another aspect that may enable them to cope (e.g., her assurances that she will return).

In this chapter we suggested a dual physiological basis for effortful processes. Risk factors in this realm are low vagal tone and cardiovascular reactivity. High vagal tone is associated with good attentional abilities, the use of emotion regulation strategies, and the ability to self-soothe (such as attention deployment). Most infants with high vagal tone are highly reactive, yet they acquire strategies for regulating this reactivity. Thus, infants with high vagal are more responsive to experiences around them and are able to use their attentional processes to soothe themselves and take in information from the social world.

Cardiovascular reactivity (CVR) refers to exaggerated increases in heart rate and blood pressure following exposure to stressors. This pattern of physiological arousal is associated with the Type A behavior pattern, which is characterized by a rapid pace, a sense of time urgency, and competitive and aggressive tendencies. The physiological and cognitive tendencies of Type A individuals place them at risk for problems in regulating their negative arousal. First, Type As experience high levels of arousal in challenging situations. Heightened levels of arousal have been shown to disrupt attentional processes. Second, the negative cognitions of Type As concerning failure may serve as a secondary task that competes for their attentional capacity. In addition, when faced with challenging situations, Type As tend to use an attentional narrowing strategy. This strategy enables them to focus on the current task and ignore external distractions, such as their own fatigue. While this may lead to superior performance on simple tasks, it is less effective on complex tasks and interferes with the ability of Type As to be cognizant of and modulate their level of arousal.

During the first 5 years of life, children move from being largely driven by their emotional states to representing them symbolically. Attentional processes play a central role in the ability to accomplish these tasks. The role of caregivers in children's development of effective attentional and emotion regulation abilities changes with each new advancement in the infant's repertoire. The caregiver's goal is to provide external support for those tasks that infants cannot perform for themselves.

The infant's first task is the establishment of physiological homeostasis. The accomplishment of this task is aided by responsive caregivers who can effectively soothe their infants and assist them in establishing routines. External soothing provides infants with a framework for developing their own self-soothing strategies. Individual differences in reactivity may influence the ability of infants to benefit from and learn these strategies. In the case of highly reactive infants, the brief period between their initial overarousal and behavioral disorganization may limit their ability to learn effective regulatory strategies.

The establishment of a more stable physiological state and the maturation of the central nervous system enables infants to engage the social world in new and potentially beneficial ways by the second and third months of life. Infants who attend responsively to caregivers are perceived as more rewarding social partners. This responsiveness may influence future interactions in these dyads. These interactions also provide a vehicle for infants to learn about turn-taking, mutual regulation, and the emotions of others and themselves, important intra- and interpersonal skills needed throughout development.

During the preschool period, children spend more time with peers and begin to use language to control their behavior. Good attentional abilities assist children in forming and maintaining effective relationships with peers. The ability to shift attentional focus from objects to potential social partners provides an important mechanism for early peer contact. As children mature, they also need to attend to the play themes and responses of peers to gain entry into their play and to maintain these interactions over time. Children also develop the ability to use verbal mediation to regulate their affective states and behavior during this period. Caregivers can assist children with these tasks by helping them label and understand their own feelings and the feelings of others.

With each period of development, the central role of attentional processes can be seen, as can an increasingly complex system of emotion regulation. Former systems for regulation must be integrated with subsequent ones for optimal development. Each system may be subject to different types of stress and subsequently influence the dynamics of the whole. For example, the excessive needs of low- and high-reactive infants may stress the caregiver system. An issue not addressed in this chapter is the resources available to caregivers, which may have a profound affect on the ability of this system to meet the needs of infants.[6]

Recall that protective infant temperamental qualities include being active, socially responsive, and exhibiting a positive mood. In older children, feelings of high self-esteem and self-efficacy also provide protective functions. Rutter (1987) suggested that knowledge of these factors are of limited use for developing appropriate interventions. What is needed is a better understanding of the processes and mechanisms that support the development of these factors. In this chapter we have suggested that attentional processes provide the executive function of organizing the social, emotional, and cognitive experiences of children. We believe that the ability to manage attentional processes supports the development of many of the qualities associated with resiliency. For example, we have shown that social responsiveness in infancy is related to appropriate patterns of attention. In addition, positive mood is influenced by the ability to self-soothe and regulate arousal levels. Research suggests that attentional processes provide mechanisms for accomplishing these tasks. Control of attentional processes, such as sustained attention and attentional shifts, is associated with low levels of negative emotions in infants and preschool children. Children with good attentional abilities are also better able to master basic interpersonal skills acquired in early caregiver settings, such as turn-taking and mutual regulation, and the sharing of internal states. These skills aid children in establishing effective relationships with others. As these children mature, successes in managing emotional and social experiences should lead to feelings of self-efficacy and high self-esteem.

Rutter (1987) has suggested that "stress inoculation" plays an important role in resiliency. Children who encounter stressful situations and are able to successfully negotiate their way through these events become more stress-resistant. These children are more likely to seek out opportunities for growth in the future. For example, recall that Fox (1989) found that at 5 months infants with high vagal tone were more likely to use emotion regulation strategies such as the differential allocation of attention when they were distressed. This increased

---

[6]For example, recent work by Patterson et al. (1991) indicates that children of families experiencing stress are more likely to experience peer rejection.

ability to regulate one's level of arousal in potentially stressful circumstances enabled these children by 14 months to encounter novel situations with less apparent apprehension and stress.

This chapter highlights the role of attention in organizing cognitive, social, and emotional experiences. Much research remains to be done in this area. For example, the relationship between individual differences in physiology, caregiving practices, and resiliency needs to be explored. The strong association between vagal tone and attentional abilities suggests that this should be a fruitful area for study. We need to identify variables that contribute to the stabilization of vagal tone in the first 5 to 6 months of life. It would be beneficial to identify variables (e.g., nutrition, exposure to stress, or caregiver behaviors) that account for some of this variability. In addition, research with regulatory disordered infants and children with attention deficit hyperactivity disorder may eventually help us answer a number of questions concerning the physiological mechanisms needed for attention. These anomalous groups tend to have high or normal vagal tone, yet fail to appropriately modify their vagal tone to meet environmental demands such as sustained attention.

Research on cardiovascular reactivity in children may also help us address some puzzling issues. For example, physiological reactivity in infancy may be associated with CVR in older children (Matthews, personal communication, 1992). Does this initial reactivity place these children at risk at birth? What factors help to mediate this risk? Attentional processes may play a central role, because they provide multiple strategies for regulation. Highly reactive infants may be at particular risk for failing to learn these strategies because of the short duration between their initial overarousal and behavioral organization. Individuals who fail to acquire effective strategies for regulation may be at risk for social problems throughout development. For example, the reactivity and attentional patterns of Type A individuals may make them at risk for emotion regulation difficulties. Children high in TABP have difficulty tolerating frustrating events and controlling their behavior. This adversely affects their social relationships (Whalen & Henker, 1986). Research needs to be directed toward understanding the role of attentional processes and reactivity in the development and utilization of emotion regulation strategies in Type A individuals.

REFERENCES

American Psychiatric Association (1994). *Diagnostic and statistical manual of mental disorders* (4th ed.). Washington, DC: Author.

Anderson, E. V., Siegel, F. S., Frisch, R. O., & Wirt, R. D. (1969). Responses of phenylketonuric children on a continuous performance test. *Journal of Abnormal Psychology, 74*, 358–362.

Ax, A. F. (1953). The physiological differentiation between fear and anger in humans. *Psychosomatic Medicine, 15*, 433–442.

Bacon, S. J. (1974). Arousal and the range of cue utilization. *Journal of Experimental Psychology, 102*, 81–87.

Bates, E. (1979). Intentions, conventions and symbols. In E. Bates (Ed.), *The emergence of symbols: Cognition and communication in infancy* (pp. 33–68). New York: Academic.

Bergan, J. (1990). Interactions between parents and their infants with Down syndrome. In D. Cicchetti & M. Beeghly (Eds.), *Children with Down syndrome: A developmental perspective* (pp. 101–146). New York: Cambridge University Press.

Berne, R. M., & Levy, M. N. (1987). *Cardiovascular physiology* (4th ed.). St. Louis, MO: C. V. Mosby.

Blaney, N. T. (1990). Type A, effect to excel, and attentional style in children: The validity of the MYTH. *Journal of Social Behavior and Personality, 5,* 159–182.

Bortner, R. W., Rosenman, R. H., & Friedman, M. (1970). Familial similarity in pattern A behavior. *Journal of Chronic Disease, 23,* 39–43.

Brazelton, T. B., Koslowski, B., & Main, M. (1974). The origin of reciprocity: The early mother–infant interaction. In M. Lewis & L. A. Rosenblum (Eds.), *The effect of the infant on its caregiver* (pp. 49–76). New York: Wiley.

Broadbent, D. E. (1958). *Perception and communication.* London: Pergamon.

Brunson, B. I., & Matthews, K. A. (1981). The Type A coronary-prone behavior pattern and reactions to uncontrollable events: An analysis of learned helplessness. *Journal of Personality and Social Psychology, 40,* 906–918.

Buckhalt, J. A., Rutherford, R. B., & Goldberg, K. E. (1978). Verbal and nonverbal interaction of mothers with their Down syndrome and nonretarded infants. *American Journal of Mental Deficiency, 82,* 337–343.

Cacioppo, J. T., & Sandman, C. A. (1978). Physiological differentiation of sensory and cognitive tasks as a function of warning, processing demands and reported unpleasantness. *Biological Psychology, 6,* 181–192.

Campos, J. J., & Sternberg, C. R. (1981). Perception, appraisal, and emotion: The onset of social referencing. In M. E. Lamb & L. R. Sherrod (Eds.), *Infants social cognition: Empirical and social considerations* (pp. 273–314). Hillsdale, NJ: Lawrence Erlbaum Associates.

Cannon, W. B. (1914). The interrelations of emotions as suggested by recent physiological research. *American Journal of Psychology, 25,* 256–282.

Cantwell, D. P. (1975). Genetics and hyperactivity. *Journal of Child Psychology and Psychiatry and Allied Disciplines, 16,* 261–264.

Cicchetti, D., Ganiban, J., & Barnett, D. (1991). Contributions from the study of high-risk populations to understanding the development of emotion regulation. In J. Garber & K. Dodge (Eds.), *The development of emotion regulation and dysregulation* (pp. 15–48). New York: Cambridge University Press.

Cohn, J. F., & Tronick, E. Z. (1983). Three-month-old infants' reaction to simulated maternal depression. *Child Development, 54,* 185–193.

Corsaro, W. (1979). We're friends, right?: Children's use of access rituals in a nursery school. *Language in Society, 8,* 315–336.

Corsaro, W. (1981). Friendship in the nursery school: Social organization in the peer environment. In S. Asher & J. M. Gottman (Eds.), *The development of children's friendships* (pp. 207–241). New York: Cambridge University Press.

Darke, S. (1988). Effects of anxiety on inferential reasoning task performance. *Journal of Personality and Social Psychology, 55,* 499–505.

Deffenbacher, J. L. (1978). Worry, emotionality, and task-generated interference in test anxiety: An empirical test of attentional theory. *Journal of Educational Psychology, 70,* 248–254.

Degangi, G. A., DiPietro, J. A., Greenspan, S. I., & Porges, S. W. (1991). Psychophysiological characteristics of the regulatory disordered infant. *Infant Behavior and Development, 14,* 37–50.

Dickstein, S., & Parke, R. D. (1988). Social referencing in infancy: A glance at fathers and marriage. *Child Development, 59,* 506–511.

DiPietro, J. A., Larson, S. K., & Porges, S. W. (1987). Behavioral and heart rate pattern differences between breast-fed and bottle-fed neonates. *Developmental Psychology, 23,* 467–474.

Dodge, K. A., McClaskey, C. L., & Feldman, E. (1985). A situational approach to the assessment of social competence in children. *Journal of Consulting and Clinical Psychology, 53,* 334–353.

Dodge, K. A., Schlundt, D. G., Schocken, I., & Delugach, J. D. (1983). Social competence and children's social status: The role of peer group entry strategies. *Merrill-Palmer Quarterly, 29,* 309–336.

Duffy, E. (1962). *Activation and behavior.* London: Wiley.

Easterbrook, J. A. (1959). The effect of emotion on cue utilization and the organization of behavior. *Psychological Review, 66,* 183–201.

Eisenberg, N., Fabes, R. A., Bernzweig, J., Karbon, M., Poulin, R., & Hanish, L. (1993). The relations of emotionality and regulation to preschoolers' social skills and sociometric status. *Child Development, 64,* 1418–1438.

Ekman, P., Levenson, R. W., & Friesen, W. V. (1983). Autonomic nervous system activity distinguishes among emotions. *Science, 221,* 1208–1210.

Emery, R. E. (1982). Interparental conflict and the children of discord and divorce. *Psychological Bulletin, 92,* 310–330.

Emery, R. E. (1988). *Marriage, divorce and children's adjustment.* Newbury Park, CA: Sage.

Ewart, C. K., Harris, W. L., Zeger, S., & Russell, G. A. (1986). Diminished pulse pressure under mental stress characterizes normotensive adolescents with parent high blood pressure. *Psychosomatic Medicine, 48,* 489–501.

Eysenck, M. W. (1982). *Attention and arousal: Cognition and performance.* New York: Springer-Verlag.

Fendrich, M., Warner, V., & Weissman, M. M. (1990). Family risk factors, parental depression, and psychopathology in offspring. *Developmental Psychology, 26,* 40–50.

Field, T. (1987). Interaction and attachment in normal and atypical infants. *Journal of Consulting and Clinical Psychology, 55,* 853–859.

Field, T. Healy, B., Goldstein, S., Perry, S., Bendell, D., Schanberg, S., Zimmerman, E. A., & Kuhn, C. (1988). Infants of depressed mothers show depressed behavior even with nondepressed adults. *Child Development, 59,* 1569–1579.

Fox, N. A. (1989). Psychological correlates of emotional reactivity during the first year of life. *Developmental Psychology, 25,* 364–372.

Garmezy, N. (1985). Stress resistant children: The search for protective factors. In J. Stevenson (Ed.), *Recent research in developmental psychopathology* (pp. 213–231). Oxford: Pergamon.

Gellhorn, E., & Loofbourrow, G. N. (1963). *Emotion and emotional disorders: A neurophysiological study.* New York: Harper & Row.

Gianino, A., & Tronick, E. Z. (1988). The mutual regulation model: The infant's self and interactive regulation, coping, and defense. In T. Field, P. McCabe, & N. Schneiderman (Eds.), *Stress and coping* (pp. 47–68). Hillsdale, NJ: Lawrence Erlbaum Associates.

Glass, D. C. (1977). *Behavior patterns, stress, and coronary disease.* NJ: Lawrence Erlbaum Associates.

Goldberg, S., Brachfeld, S., & Divitto, B. (1980). Feeding, fussing, and play: Parent-infant interaction in the first year as a function of prematurity and perinatal medical problems. In T. M. Field (Ed.), *High-risk infants and children* (pp. 133–153). New York: Academic Press.

Graham, F. K., & Clifton, R. K. (1966). Heart rate changes as a component of the orienting response. *Psychological Bulletin, 65,* 305–320.

Greenberg, M., Kusche, D. A., & Speltz, M. (1991). Emotion regulation, self-control and psychopathology: The role of relationships in early childhood. In D. Cicchetti & S. Toth (Eds.), *Rochester Symposium on Developmental Psychopathology* (Vol. 2). New York: Cambridge University Press.

Hastrup, J. L., Light, K. C., & Obrist, P. A. (1982). Parental hypertension and cardiovascular response to stress in healthy young adults. *Psychophysiology, 19,* 615–622.

Haynes, S. G., Feinleib, M., & Kannel, W. B. (1980). The relationship of psychosocial factors to coronary heart disease in the Framingham Study. III: 8-year incidence of CHD. *American Journal of Epidemiology, 111,* 37–58.

Haynes, S. G., Levine, S., Scotch, N., Feinleib, M., & Kannel, W. B. (1978). The relationship of psychosocial factors to coronary heart disease in the Framingham study: Part I. Methods and risk factors. *American Journal of Epidemiology, 107*, 362–383.

Heft, L., Thoresen, C. E., Kirmil-Gray, K., Wiedenfeld, S. A., Eagleston, J. R., Bracke, P., & Arnow, B. (1988). Emotional and temperamental correlates of Type A in children and adolescents. *Journal of Youth and Adolescence, 17*, 461–475.

Hembree, R. (1988). Correlates, causes, effects and treatment of test anxiety. *Review of Education Research, 58*, 47–77.

Herman, C. S., Kirchner, G. L., Streissguth, A. P., & Little, R. E. (1980). Vigilance paradigm for preschool children used to relate vigilance behavior to IQ and prenatal exposure to alcohol. *Perceptual and Motor Skills, 50*, 863–867.

Hetherington, E. M., & Clingempeel, W. G. (1992). Coping with marital transitions. *Monographs of the Society for Research in Child Development, 57* (2–3, Serial No. 227).

Howard, J. H., Cunningham, D. A., & Rechnitzer, P. A. (1976). Health patterns associated with Type A behavior: A managerial population. *Journal of Human Stress, 2*, 24–31.

Howard, J., Cunningham, D. A., & Rechnitzer, P. A. (1977). Work patterns associated with Type A behavior: A managerial population. *Human Relation, 30*, 825–836.

Johnson, J. R., & O'Leary, K. D. (1987). Parental behavior patterns and conduct disorders in girls. *Journal of Abnormal Child Psychology, 15*, 573–581.

Jones, O. H. M. (1977). Mother-child communication with pre-linguistic Down syndrome and normal infants. In H. R. Schaffer (Ed.), *Studies in mother-infant interaction*. London: Academic.

Jones, O. H. M. (1980). Prelinguistic communication skills in Down syndrome and normal infants. In T. Field, D. Goldberg, D. Stern, & A. Sostek (Eds.), *High-risk infants and children: Interactions with adults and peers* (pp. 205–285). New York: Academic.

Jorgensen, R. S., & Houston, B. K. (1981). Family history of hypertension, gender, and cardiovascular reactivity and stereotypy during stress. *Journal of Behavioral Medicine, 4*, 175–189.

Jouriles, E. N., Pfiffner, L. J., & O'Leary, S. G. (1988). Marital conflict, parenting, and toddler conduct problems. *Journal of Abnormal Psychology, 16*, 197–206.

Kahneman, D. (1973). *Attention and effort*. Englewood Cliffs, NJ: Prentice-Hall.

Kahneman, D., Tursky, B., Shapiro, D., & Crider, A. (1969). Pupillary, heart rate, and skin resistance changes during a mental task. *Journal of Experimental Psychology, 79*, 164–167.

Kellam, S. G., Wethamer-Larson, L., Dolan, L. J., Hendricks Brown, C., Mayer, L. S., Rebok, G. W., Anthony, J. C., Laudolff, J., & Edelshn, G., (1991). Developmental epidemiologically based preventive trials: Baseline modeling of early target behaviors and depressive symptoms. *American Journal of Community Psychology, 19*, 563–584.

Kliewer, W., & Weidner, G. (1987). Type A behavior and aspirations: A study of parents' and children's goal setting. *Developmental Psychology, 23*, 204–209.

Kopp, C. (1989). Regulation of distress and negative emotions: A developmental view. *Developmental Psychology, 25*, 343–354.

Kopp, C., Krakow, J. B., & Johnson, K. L. (1983). Strategy production by young Down syndrome children. *American Journal of Mental Deficiency, 88*, 164–169.

Krakow, J. B., & Kopp, C. (1983). The effects of developmental delay on sustained attention in young children. *Child Development, 54*, 1143–1155.

Kurdek, L. A., & Lillie, R. (1985). Temperament, classmate likability, and social perspective coordination as correlates of parent-rated Type A behaviors. *Journal of Applied Developmental Psychology, 6*, 73–83.

Lacey, J. I. (1967). Somatic response patterning and stress: Some revisions of activation theory. In M. H. Appley & R. Trumbell (Eds.), *Psychological stress: Issues in research* (pp. 4–44). New York: Academic.

Landry, S. H., & Chapieski, M. L. (1989). Joint attention and infant toy exploration: Effects of Down syndrome and prematurity. *Child Development, 60*, 103–118.

Larson, S. K., & Porges, S. W. (1982). The ontogeny of heart period patterning in the rat. *Developmental Psychobiology, 15*, 519–528.

Levenson, R. W. (1988). Emotion and the autonomic nervous system: A prospectus for research on autonomic specificity. In H. L. Wagner (Ed.), *Social psychophysiology and emotion theory and clinical applications* (pp. 17–42). Chichester, England: John Wiley & Sons.

Levenson, R. W., Ekman, P., & Friesen, W. V. (1990). Voluntary facial action generates emotion-specific autonomic nervous system activity. *Psychophysiology, 27*, 363–384.

Linnemeyer, S. A., & Porges, S. W. (1986). Recognition memory and cardiac vagal tone in 6-month-old infants. *Infant Behavior and Development, 9*, 43–56.

Long, N., Forehand, R., Fauber, R., & Brody, G. (1987). Self-perceived and independently observed competence of young adolescents as a function of parental marital conflict and recent divorce. *Journal of Abnormal Child Psychology, 15*, 15–27.

Long, N., Slater, E., Forehand, R., & Fauber, R. (1988). Continue high or reduced interparental conflict following divorce: Relation to young adolescent adjustment. *Journal of Consulting and Clinical Psychology, 56*, 467–469.

Lundberg, U. (1983). Note on Type A behavior and cardiovascular responses to challenges in 3–6 year old children. *Journal of Psychosomatic Research, 27*, 39–42.

Lundberg, U. (1986). Stress and Type A behavior in children. *Journal of the American Academy of Child Psychiatry, 25*, 771–778.

Malatesta-Magai, C. (1991). Development of emotion expression during infancy: General course and patterns of individual difference. In J. Garber & K. Dodge (Eds.), *The development of emotion regulation and dysregulation* (pp. 49–68). New York: Cambridge University Press.

Malatesta, C. Z., Culver, C., Tesman, J., & Shepard, B. (1989). The development of emotion expression during the first two years of life. *Monographs of the Society for Research in Child Development, 54* (1–2, Serial No. 219, pp. 1–104).

Matthews, K. A. (1979). Efforts to control by children and adults with the Type A coronary-prone behavior pattern. *Child Development, 48*, 1752–1576.

Matthews, K. A. (1982). Psychological perspectives on the Type A behavior pattern. *Psychological Bulletin, 91*, 293–323.

Matthews, K. A., & Krantz, D. S. (1976). Resemblances of twins and their parents in Pattern A behavior. *Psychosomatic Medicine, 28*, 140–144.

Matthews, K. A., Rakaczky, C. J., & Stoney, C. M. (1987). Are cardiovascular responses to behavioral stressors a stable individual difference variable in childhood? *Psychophysiology, 24*, 464–473.

Matthews, K. A., Woodall, K. L., & Stoney, C. M. (1990). Changes in and stability of cardiovascular responses to behavioral stress: Results from a four-year longitudinal study of children. *Child Development, 61*, 1134–1144.

McCabe, P. M., Yongue, B. G., Ackles, P. K., & Porges, S. W. (1985). Changes in heart period, heart period variability, and a spectral analysis estimate of respiratory sinus arrhythmia in response to pharmacological manipulations of the baroreceptor reflex in cats. *Psychophysiology, 22*, 195–203.

McCabe, P. M., Yongue, B. G., Porges, S. W., & Ackles, P. K. (1984). Changes in heart period, heart period variability and a spectral analysis estimate of respiratory sinus arrhythmia during aortic nerve stimulation in rabbits. *Psychophysiology, 21*, 149–158.

McCranie, E. W., & Simpson, M. E. (1987). Parental child-rearing antecedents of Type A behavior. *Personality and Social Psychology Bulletin, 12*, 493–501.

Meltzoff, A. N., & Moore, M. K. (1983). Newborn infants imitate adult facial gestures. *Child Development, 54*, 702–709.

Mirsky, A. F., Anthony, B. J., Duncan, C. C., Ahearn, M. B., & Kellam, S. G. (1991). Analysis of the elements of attention: A neuropsychological approach. *Neuropsychology Review, 2*, 109–145.

Mirsky, A. F., & Duncan, C. C. (1986). Etiology and expression of schizophrenia: Neurobiological and psychosocial factors. *Annual Review of Psychology, 37*, 291–319.

Mirsky, A. F., Primac, D. W., Ajmone Marsan, C., Rosvold, H. E., & Stevens, J. A. (1960). A comparison of the psychological test performance of patients with focal and nonfocal epilepsy. *Experimental Neurology, 2*, 75–89.

Mueller, E., & Brenner, J. (1976). The growth of social interaction in a toddler playgroup: The role of peer experience. *Child Development, 48*, 854–861.

Murphy, J. K., Alpert, B. S., & Willey, E. S., & Somes, G. W. (1988). Cardiovascular reactivity to psychological stress in healthy children. *Psychophysiology, 25*, 144–152.

Murphy, C. M., & Messer, D. J. (1977). Mothers, infants and pointing: A study of a gesture. In H. R. Schaffer (Ed.), *Studies in mother–infant interaction*. London: Academic.

Needleman, H. L., Gunnol, C., Leviton, A., Reed, R., Peresie, H., Maher, C., & Barrett, P. (1979). Deficits in psychologic and classroom performance of children with elevated dentine lead levels. *New England Journal of Medicine, 13*, 689–695.

Nottelman, E. D., & Hill, K. T. (1977). Test anxiety and off-task behavior in evaluative situations. *Child Development, 48*, 225–231.

Parker, J. G., & Asher, S. R. (1987). Peer relations and later personal adjustment: Are low accepted children at risk? *Psychological Bulletin, 102*, 357–389.

Patterson, C. J., Vaden, N. A., & Kupersmidt, J. B. (1991). Family background, recent life events and peer rejection during childhood. *Journal of Social and Personal Relationships, 8*, 347–361.

Phillips, E. L., Shenker, S., & Revitz, P. (1951). The assimilation of the new child into the group. *Psychiatry, 14*, 319–325.

Piaget, J. (1952). *The origin of intelligence in children*. New York: International Universities.

Porges, S. W. (1972). Heart rate variability and deceleration as indices of reaction time. *Journal of Experimental Psychology, 92*, 103–110.

Porges, S. W. (1973). Heart rate variability: An autonomic correlate of reaction time performance. *Bulletin of the Psychonomics Society, 1*, 270–272.

Porges, S. W. (1974). Heart rate indices of newborn attentional responsivity. *Merrill-Palmer Quarterly, 20*, 231–254.

Porges, S. W. (1976). Peripheral and neurochemical parallels of psychopathology: A psychophysiological model relating autonomic imbalance to hyperactivity, psychopathy, and autism. In H. W. Reese (Eds.), *Advances in child development and behavior* (Vol. 11, pp. 35–65). New York: Academic.

Porges, S. W. (1980). Individual differences in attention: A possible physiological substrate. In B. K. Keogph (Ed.), *Advances in special education* (Vol. 2, pp. 111–134). Greenwich, CT: JAI.

Porges, S. W. (1983). Heart rate patterns in neonates: A potential diagnostic window to the brain. In T. M. Field & A. M. Sostek (Eds.), *Infants born at risk: Physiological and perceptual responses* (pp. 3–22). New York: Grune & Stratton.

Porges, S. W. (1985). Spontaneous oscillations in heart rate: Potential index of stress. In P. B. Moberg (Ed.), *Animal stress* (pp. 97–111). Betheseda, MD: The American Physiological Society.

Porges, S. W. (1986). Respiratory sinus arrhythmia: Physiological basis, quantitative methods and clinical implication. In P. Grossman, K. Janssen, & D. Vaitl (Eds.), *Cardiorespiratory and cardiosomatic psychophysiology* (pp. 101–115). New York: Plenum.

Porges, S. W. (1991). Autonomic regulation and attention. In B. A. Campbell, H. Hayne, & R. Richardson (Eds.), *Attention and information processing in infants and adults* (pp. 201–223). Hillsdale, NJ: Lawrence Erlbaum Associates.

Porges, S. W. (1992). Vagal tone: A physiological marker of stress vulnerability. *Pediatrics, 90*, 498–504.

Porges, S. W., & Humphreys, M. M. (1977). Cardiac and respiratory responses during visual search in non-retarded adolescents. *American Journal of Mental Deficiency, 82*, 162–169.

Porges, S. W., & Raskin, D. C. (1969). Respiratory and heart rate components of attention. *Journal of Experimental Psychology, 81*, 497–503.

Porges, S. W., Walter, G. F., Korb, R. J., & Sprague, R. L. (1975). The influence of methylphenidate on heart rate and behavioral measures of attention in hyperactive children. *Child Development, 46*, 727–733.

Porter, F. L., & Porges, S. W. (1988). Newborn pain cries and vagal tone: Parallel changes in response to circumcision. *Child Development, 59,* 495–505.

Posner, M. I. (1978). *Chronometric explorations of mind.* Hillsdale, NJ: Lawrence Erlbaum Associates.

Posner, M. I., & Rothbart, M. K. (1980). The development of attentional mechanisms. *Nebraska Symposium on Motivation, 28,* 1–52.

Posner, M. I., & Snyder, C. R. R. (1975a). Attention and cognitive control. In R. L. Solso (Ed.), *Information processing and cognition: The Loyola symposium* (pp. 55–85). Hillsdale, NJ: Lawrence Erlbaum Associates.

Posner, M. I., & Snyder, C. R. R. (1975b). Facilitation and inhibition in the processing of signals. In P. M. A. Rabbitt & S. Dornic (Eds.), *Attention and performance* (Vol. 5, pp. 669–682). New York: Academic.

Putallaz, M. (1983). Predicting children's sociometric status from their behavior. *Child Development, 54,* 1417–1426.

Putallaz, M., & Gottman, J. M. (1981). An interactional model of children's entry into peer groups. *Child Development, 52,* 986–994.

Putallaz, M., & Wasserman, A. (1989). Children's naturalistic entry behavior and sociometric status: A developmental perspective. *Developmental Psychology, 25,* 1–9.

Richards, J. E. (1985). Respiratory sinus arrhythmia predicts heart rate and visual responses during visual attention in 14- and 20-week-old infants. *Psychophysiology, 22,* 101–109.

Robson, K. S. (1967). The role of eye-to-eye contact in maternal–infant attachment. *Journal of Child Psychology and Psychiatry, 8,* 13–25.

Rothbart, M. K., & Derryberry, D. (1981). Development of individual difference in temperament. In M. E. Lamb & A. L. Brown (Eds.), *Advances in developmental psychology* (Vol. 1, pp. 37–86). Hillsdale, NJ: Lawrence Erlbaum Associates.

Rothbart, M. K., & Posner, M. I. (1985). Temperament and the development of self-regulation. In C. L. Hartledge & C. R. Telzrow (Eds.), *The neuropsychology of individual differences: A developmental perspective* (pp. 93–123). New York: Plenum.

Rothbart, M. K., Ziaie, H., & O'Boyle, C. (1992). Self-regulation and emotion in infancy. In N. Eisenberg & R. A. Fabes (Eds.), *Emotion and self-regulation in early development: New directions in child development* (pp. 7–24). San Francisco: Jossey-Bass.

Rutter, M. (1970). Sex differences in children's responses to family stress. In E. J. Anthony & C. Koupernik (Eds.), *The child in his family* (pp. 165–196). New York: Wiley.

Rutter, M. (1971). Parent–child separation: Psychological effects on children. *Journal of Child Psychology and Psychiatry, 12,* 223–260.

Rutter, M. (1982). Epidemiological-longitudinal approaches to the study of development. In W. A. Collins (Ed.), *The concept of development: Minnesota Symposia on Child Psychology* (Vol. 15, pp. 105–144). Hillsdale, NJ: Lawrence Erlbaum Associates.

Rutter, M. (1987). Psychosocial resilience and protective mechanisms. *American Journal of Orthopsychiatry, 57,* 316–331.

Rutter, M., Cox, A., Tupling, C., Berger, M., & Yule, W. (1975a). Attainment and adjustment in two geographical areas: Part 1. The prevalence of psychiatric disorder. *British Journal of Psychiatry, 126,* 493–509.

Rutter, M., Yule, B., Quinton, D., Rowlands, O., Yule, W., & Berger, M. (1975b). Attainment and adjustment in two geographical areas: Part 3. Some factors accounting for area differences. *British Journal of Psychiatry, 126,* 520–533.

Sachis, P. N., Armstrong, D. L., Becher, L. E., & Bryan, A. C. (1982). Myelination of the human vagus nerve from 24 weeks postconceptional age to adolescence. *Journal of Neuropathology and Experimental Neurology, 41,* 466–472.

Sarason, I. G., Sarason, B. R., & Pierce, G. R. (1990). Anxiety, cognitive interference, and performance. *Journal of Clinical Psychology, 9,* 133–147.

Scaife, M., & Bruner, J. S. (1975). The capacity for joint attention in the infant. *Nature, 253,* 265–266.

Siegel, J. M. (1982). Type A behavior and self reports of cardiovascular arousal in adolescents. *Journal of Human Stress, 8,* 24–30.

Shiffrin, R. M., & Schneider, W. (1977). Controlled and automatic human information processing: Part 2. Perceptual learning, automatic attending, and a general theory. *Psychological Review, 84,* 127–190.

Sokolov, E. N. (1963). *Perception and the conditioned reflex.* Oxford: Pergamon.

Stanley, B. J., & Katz, L. (1991, April). *Vagal tone, gender, and peer relationships of preschool children.* Poster session at The Society for Research in Child Development, Seattle, WA.

Stern, D. N. (1974). Mother and infant at play: The dyadic interaction involving facial, vocal and gaze behaviors. In M. Lewis & L. A. Rosenblum (Eds.), *The effect of the infant on its caregiver.* New York: Wiley.

Stern, D. N. (1985). *The interpersonal world of the infant: A view from psychoanalysis and developmental psychology.* New York: Basic Books.

Stern, R. M., & Sison, C. E. (1990). Response patterning. In J. T. Caccioppo & L. G. Tassinary (Eds.), *Principles of psychophysiology: Physical, social, and inferential elements* (pp. 193–215). Cambridge, UK: Cambridge University Press.

Streissguth, A. P., Martin, D. C., Barr, H. M., & MacGregor Sandman, B. (1984). Intrauterine alcohol and nicotine exposure: Attention and reaction time in 4-year-old children. *Developmental Psychology, 20,* 533–541.

Treisman, A. M. (1960). Verbal cues, language and meaning in selective attention. *American Journal of Psychology, 77,* 206–219.

Tronick, E. Z. (1980). On the primacy of social skills. In D. B. Sawin, L. O. Walker, & J. H. Penticuff (Eds.), *The exceptional infant: Psychosocial risks in infant environment transactions* (pp. 144–158). New York: Brunner/Mazel.

Tronick, E. Z. (1989). Emotions and emotional communication in infants. *American Psychologist, 44,* 112–119.

Tronick, E. Z., & Field, T. (1986). *Maternal depression and infant disturbance: New directions for child development* (Vol. 34). London: Jossey-Bass.

Vega-Lahr, N., & Field, T. (1986). Type A behavior in preschool children. *Child Development, 57,* 1333–1348.

Vygotsky, L. S. (1962). *Thought and language.* Cambridge, MA: MIT Press.

Waldron, I. (1978). The coronary-prone behavior pattern, blood pressure, employment and socio-economic status in women. *Journal of Psychosomatic Research, 22,* 79–87.

Whalen, C. K., & Henker, B. (1986). Type A behavior in normal and hyperactive children: Multisource evidence of overlapping constructs. *Child Development, 57,* 688–699.

Werner, E. E., & Smith, R. S. (1982). *Vulnerable but invincible: A longitudinal study of resilient children and youth.* New York: McGraw-Hill.

Wilson, B. J. (1994). *The entry behavior and emotion regulation abilities of developmentally delayed children.* Unpublished doctoral dissertation, University of Washington.

Woodall, K. L., & Matthews, K. A. (1989). Familial environment associated with type A behaviors and psychophysiological responses to stress in children. *Health Psychology, 8,* 403–426.

Yerkes, R. M., & Dodson, J. D. (1908). The relation of strength of stimulus to rapidity of habit-formation. *Journal of Comparative Neurology of Psychology, 18,* 459–482.

Yongue, B. G., McCabe, P. M., Porges, S. W., Rivera, M., Kelley, S. L., & Ackles, P. K. (1982). The effects of pharmacological manipulations that influence vagal control of the heart on heart period, heart-period variability, and respiration in rats. *Psychophysiology, 19,* 426–432.

Zajonc, R. B. (1980). Feeling and thinking: Preferences need no inferences. *American Psychologist, 35,* 151–175.

Author Index

A

Abbott, R. A., 176, *188*
Aber, J. L., 114, *131*
Achenbach, T. M., 71, 73, 81, 94, 96, *102,*
    122, *129,* 137, *150*
Ackles, P. K., 198, *225, 228*
Adair, R. K., 110, 124, *132*
Ahearn, M. B., 191, *225*
Ahrons, C. R., 179, *187*
Ajmone Marsan, C., 191, *226*
Allen, J. P., 114, *131*
Allen, W. R., 160, *171*
Alpert, B. S., 201, *226*
Alterman, A., 111, *132*
Anderson, E. R., 40, 42, 43, 44, 45, 54, 55,
    61, 62, *63, 65, 66,* 136, *151*
Anderson, E. V., 191, *221*
Angold, A., 3, *35*
Anthony, B. J., 191, *225*
Anthony, E. J., 14, *34*
Anthony, J. C., 189, 191, *224*
Ardelt, M., 43, 47, *64*
Armstrong, D. L., 198, *227*
Arnett, J., 116, *131*
Arnow, B., 203, *224*
Asarnow, J. R., 1, 32, *35*

Asher, S. J., 91, *103*
Asher, S. R., 114, *132,* 212, *226*
Atchley, R., 160, *171*
Attie, I., 56, *63*
Ax, A. F., 196, *221*

B

Bachman, J. G, 116, *129*
Bacon, S. J., 194, *221*
Baker, L. A., 40, *63*
Baldwin, A. L., 3, 25, *34, 38*
Baldwin, C. P., 3, 25, *34, 38*
Baldwin, W. S., 157, *171*
Bank, L., 55, *65,* 68, 70, 74, 76, 81, 94, 99,
    100, *102, 104, 105,* 136, 137, *152*
Barlow, D., 114, *129*
Barnes, H., 141, *152*
Barnett, D., 205, 207, *222*
Barocas, R., 21, 25, *38,* 51, *66*
Barr, H. M., 191, *228*
Barrett, P., 191, *226*
Basham, R. B., 22, *35*
Bates, E., 211, *221*
Baumann, K. E., 117, *130*

Baumrind, D., 10, 25, 27, *34,* 55, *63,* 79, *102,*
    113, *129*
Beardslee, W., 69, *103*
Becher, L. E., 198, *227*
Bell, N. W., 177, *188*
Bell, R. Q., 137, 139, *152*
Belsky, J., 136, *150*
Bemporad, J., 69, *103*
Bendell, D., 210, *223*
Bengtson, V. L., 158, 160, *171, 172*
Bentler, P. M., 85, *103,* 117, 124, *132*
Berberian, R. M., 116, *129*
Bergan, J., 207, *222*
Berger, M., 190, 191, *227*
Berne, R. M., 197, 198, *222*
Bernzweig, J., 213, *223*
Best, K. M., 39, *65*
Billings, A. G., 176, *187*
Blaney, N. T., 202, *222*
Blechman, E. A., 10, *34,* 108, 111, 113, 115,
    116, *129*
Block, J., 25, *34,* 67, *103,* 137, 139, 140, 141,
    150, 177, *187*
Block, J. H., 67, *103,* 141, *150,* 177, *187*
Bloom, B. L., 91, *103*
Boles, A. J., 26, 29, *35*
Bolger, N., 176, *187*
Bookstein, F. L., 180, *187*
Borrine, M., 126, *129*
Bortner, R. W., 203, *222*
Botstein, A., 139, *151*
Bowen-Woodward, K., 51, *63*
Boyle, M. C., 75, 78, 81, *104*
Brachfeld, S., 209, *223*
Bracke, P., 203, *224*
Brand, E., 51, *63*
Bray, J. H., 93, *103*
Brazelton, T. B., 209, *222*
Brenner, J., 213, *226*
Brim, O. G., 157, *171*
Broadbent, D. E., 192, *222*
Brody, G. H., 40, 46, 49, *63,* 69, 93, *103,*
    190, *225*
Bronfenbrenner, U., 39, 47, *63,* 76, *103*
Brooks-Gunn, J., 56, *63*
Brown, B. B., 110, *132*
Brown, C. H., 3, 9, 10, *36*
Brown, J. D., 176, *188*
Brown, M. M., 111, 112, *130*
Brown, N. Y., 126, *129*
Bruner, J. S., 211, *227*
Brunson, B. I., 202, *222*

Bryan, A. C., 198, *227*
Buchanan, C. M., 56, *63*
Buck, R., 113, *130*
Buckhalt, J. A., 209, *222*
Bumpass, L. L., 92, 93, *103*
Burghen, G. A., 114, *131*
Burke, M., 40, *63*
Burke, R. J., 109, 115, *130*
Burton, L. M., 157, 158, 159, 160, 161, *171*
Bush, M. A., 20, *34*
Bushwall, S. J., 117, *130*
Buss, A. H., 45, *63*
Buss, D., 141, *150*
Bussell, D., 40, 42, 45, 62, *66*

C

Cacioppo, J. T., 197, *222*
Cain, V. S., 157, *171*
Camara, K. A., 84, *104*
Campbell, S. B., 137, *150*
Campos, J. J., 212, *222*
Cannon, W. B., 201, *222*
Cantwell, D. P., 191, *222*
Capaldi, D. M., 10, 11, 22, *37,* 55, *63,* 69, 76,
    78, 79, 93, 94, 99, 101, *103, 105*
Carella, E. T., 108, *129*
Carlsmith, J. M., 117, *130*
Carlson, C. I., 18, *36*
Carlson, E., 25, *35*
Carver, C. S., 44, *66,* 111, 128, *130, 132,* 176,
    188
Caspi, A., 6, 33, *34,* 47, *64,* 110, *130,* 136,
    151, 160, *171*
Cauce, A. M., 112, 115, *130*
Cerny, J. A., 114, *129*
Chamberlain, P., 76, 81, *105*
Chandler, M. J., 4, 20, *38*
Chapieski, M. L., 213, *224*
Chapman, M., 10, *37*
Chase-Lansdale, P. L., 67, 75, 76, 81, *103*
Cherlin, A. J., 67, 75, 76, 81, *103*
Cicchetti, D., 1, 3, 14, 20, 33, *34, 38,* 205,
    207, *222*
Cleary, S. D., 122, 126, *133*
Clifton, R. K., 197, *223*
Clingempeel, G., 7, 11, 16, 22, 23, 26, *36, 37,*
    43, 44, 47, *65*
Clingempeel, W. G., 47, 51, 54, 55, 61, *63,*
    65, 93, 94, *104,* 148, *152,* 190, *224*

Cohen, P., 40, 45, 46, *66*
Cohen, S., 108, 109, 127, *130*
Cohn, D. A., 12, 13, 15, *34, 35, 37*
Cohn, J. F., 210, *222*
Coie, J. D., 1, 32, *35*, 111, 113, 114, *130, 131*
Cole, R. E., *34*
Compas, B. E., 111, *130*
Conger, K. J., 43, 47, 48, 54, 55, 62, *64*, 110, 124, *130*, 176, *187*
Conger, R. D., 43, 47, 48, 54, 55, 62, *64, 66*, 80, 84, *103*, 110, 124, *130*, 176, *187*
Conor, R., 136, *151*
Corsaro, W., 214, *222*
Costello, E. J., 3, *35*
Cowan, C. P., 11, 12, 13, 15, 16, 17, 18, 23, 26, 30, 31, 32, 33, *34, 35, 36, 37*, 148, *152*
Cowan, P. A., 11, 12, 13, 15, 16, 17, 18, 23, 26, 29, 30, 31, *34, 35, 36, 37*, 148, *152*
Coward, R. T., 173, *187*
Cox, A., 190, *227*
Cox, M., 67, 84, 91, *104*, 108, *131*, 186, *187*
Cox, R., 67, 84, 91, *104*, 108, *131*, 186, *187*
Coyne, J. C., 69, *103*
Coysh, W. S., 26, 29, *35*
Crawford, D. W., 176, *187*
Crider, A., 195, *224*
Crnic, K. A., 22, *35*
Cronbach, L. J., 74, *103*
Cross, D., 140, *152*
Crouter, A. C., 176, *187*
Culver, C., 208, 209, *225*
Cummingham, D. A., 203, *224*
Cummings, E. M., 10, *37*
Curtis-Boles, H., 26, 29, *35*
Cutrona, C. E., 109, *130*

D

Daniels, D., 40, 45, 46, 51, *64, 66*
Darke, S., 193, *222*
Deal, J. E., 43, 44, 54, 55, 61, *65*, 141, *151*
DeBaryshe, B. D., 55, *65*, 115, 126, *132*
Deffenbacher, J. L., 193, 194, *222*
DeGangi, G. A., 200, 205, 207, *222*
DeLongis, A., 176, *187*
Delugach, J. D., 214, *223*
Derogatis, L. Q., 140, *151*
Derryberry, D., 189, 202, 206, *227*
Dickstein, S., 212, *222*

Dilworth-Anderson, P., 158, *171*
DiPietro, J. A., 198, 199, 200, 205, 207, *222, 223*
Dishion, T. J., 3, 4, *37*, 55, *65*, 68, 69, 74, 76, 77, 78, 81, 91, *103, 105*, 114, *130*, 137, *152*
Divitto, B., 209, *223*
Dixon, R., 157, 158, *171*
Dodge, K. A., 111, 112, 113, 114, *130, 131*, 148, *151*, 214, *222, 223*
Dodson, J. D., 194, *228*
Doherty, W. J., 117, *132*
Dolan, L. J., 189, 191, *224*
Dornbusch, S. M., 56, *63*, 110, 117, *130*
Downey, G., 69, *103*, 136, *151*
Doyle, A. C., 128, *130*
Duffy, E., 196, *223*
DuHamel, D., 114, *133*
Duncan, C. C., 191, *225*
Duncan, G. J., 84, 91, 92, *103*
Duncan, T. E., 81, *105*
Dunn, J., 40, 45, 46, 55, 56, *64*

E

Eagleston, J. R., 203, *224*
Easterbrook, J. A., 194, *223*
Edelbrock, C. S., 71, 73, 81, 94, 96, *102*, 137, *150*
Edelshn, G., 189, 191, *224*
Edwards, K., 111, *132*
Egeland, B., 25, *35, 38*
Eggebeen, D. J., 156, *171*
Eisenberg, N., 127, *130*, 213, *223*
Ekman, P., 218, *223, 225*
Elder, G. H., 43, 47, 48, 62, *64*, 157, 160, *171*
Elder, G. H., Jr., 6, 33, *34*, 47, 54, 55, *64*, 110, 124, *130*, 136, *151*, 157, *171*, 176, *187*
Elmen, J. D., 177, *188*
Emery, R. E., 82, *103*, 116, *130*, 177, *187*, 190, *223*
Engfer, A., 52, *64*
Ensminger, M. E., 3, 9, 10, *36*, 116, *131*
Epstein, D., 82, *104*
Epstein, S., 179, *187*
Ewart, C. K., 201, *223*
Eysenck, M. W., 192, 194, 195, *223*

F

Fabes, R. A., 127, *130*, 213, *223*
Falk, R. F,, 138, 145, *151*, 180, 181, *187*
Falk, R. R., 22, 23, *35*
Farley, R., 160, *171*
Farmer, A. E., 5, *36*
Fauber, R., 190, *225*
Feinleib, M., 202, 203, *223, 224*
Feldman, E., 214, *222*
Fendrich, M., 211, *223*
Fetrow, B., 91, *103*
Fetrow, R. A., 76, 94, 99, 100, *102*
Field, D., 18, *35*
Field, T., 201, 209, 210, *223, 228*
Filer, M., 128, *133*
Fincham, F. D., 3, *35*, 177, 178, *187*
Fish, M., 136, *150*
Fishman, H. C., 17, *37*
Fleeting, M., 51, *65*
Flewelling, R. L., 117, *130*
Folkman, S., 33, *37*, 108, 111, 128, *131*
Fondacaro, M. R., 110, *130*
Forehand, R., 46, *63*, 69, 93, *103*, 190, *225*
Forgatch, M. S., 47, 48, 55, *64*, 68, 69, 76, 80, 81, 84, 85, 86, 87, 88, 89, 90, 93, 94, 95, 99, 100, *102, 103, 104, 105*
Fornell, C., 180, *187*
Foster, E. M., 43, 47, *64*
Fox, N. A., 198, 199, 207, 208, 220, *223*
Frick, P. J., 136, *151*
Friedman, M., 203, *222*
Friesen, W. V., 218, *223, 225*
Frisch, R. O., 191, *221*
Furstenberg, F. F., 40, 45, 46, 47, *64*, 67, 75, 76, 81, *103*, 159, *171*

G

Gabriel, R., 173, *187*
Ganiban, J., 205, 207, *222*
Garmezy, N., 1, 9, 14, 15, 29, *34, 36, 37*, 39, 48, 51, *64, 65*, 108, 127, *130*, 136, *151*, 190, 191, *223*
Garrett, E., 26, 29, *35*
Ge, X., 80, 84, *103*
Gelles, R., 76, *105*
Gellhorn, E., 198, *223*
George, C., 12, *36*
Gerber, G., 177, *187*

Gershenson, H. P., 157, *171*
Gianino, A., 210, *223*
Gillespie, J., 20, *34*
Gjerde, P. F., 25, *34, 67, 103*
Glantz, M. D., 114, *131*
Glass, D. C., 201, 202, *223*
Goering, J., 137, *152*
Goldberg, K. E., 209, *222*
Goldberg, S., 209, *223*
Goldfarb, W., 139, *151*
Goldstein, M., 3, *36*
Goldstein, R. B., 129, *132*
Goldstein, S., 210, *223*
Goldwyn, R., 15, 33, *37*
Gordon, B. N., 48, *64*
Gottesman, I. I., 5, *36*
Gottman, J. M., 17, 22, *36*, 214, *227*
Graham, F. K., 197, *223*
Greenberg, E., 177, *187*
Greenberg, M. T., 22, *35*, 110, 115, *131*, 217, *223*
Greenspan, S. I., 21, 25, *38*, 51, *66*, 200, 205, 207, *222*
Gross, R. T., 117, *130*
Grotevant, H. D., 18, *36*
Gruenberg, E., 3, *36*
Grych, J. H., 3, *35*, 177, 178, *187*
Gunnar, M. R., 136, *151*
Gunnol, N. A., 191, *226*

H

Hagestad, G. O., 155, 157, 158, 160, *171*
Haggerty, R., 1, 29, 32, *37*
Halverson, C. F., 135, 136, 137, 138, 139, 140, 141, 147, *151, 152, 153*
Hamburg, B. A., 159, *172*
Handal, P. J., 126, *129*
Hanish, L., 213, *223*
Hansen, D. A., 18, *35*
Hanson, C. L., 114, *131*
Hareven, T. K., 157, *172*
Harper, L., 110, *131*
Harris, W. L., 201, *223*
Hartdagen, S. E., 136, *151*
Harter, S., 44, 56, 60, *64, 66*, 118, *131*
Hastorf, A. H., 117, *130*
Hastrup, J. L., 201, *223*
Hauser, S. T., 136, *152*
Hawkins, D., 1, 32, *35*

Haynes, S. G., 202, 203, *223, 224*
Healy, B., 210, *223*
Heckert, A., 93, *105*
Heft, L., 203, *224*
Heller, K., 110, *130*
Hellner, I., 114, *131*
Hembree, R., 193, *224*
Heming, G., 12, 23, 26, 29, 30, 32, *35*
Henderson, S. H., 40, 42, 45, 62, *66*
Hendricks Brown, C., 189, 191, *224*
Henggeler, S. W., 114, *131*
Henker, B., 203, 221, *228*
Heppner, P. P., 128, *131*
Herman, C. S., 191, *224*
Hess, R. D., 84, *104*
Hetherington, E. M., 7, 11, 16, 22, 23, 25, 26,
        36, 37, 40, 42, 43, 44, 45, 46, 47, 48,
        52, 54, 55, 61, 62, *63, 64, 65, 66*, 67,
        70, 84, 91, 93, 94, 95, *104*, 108, 112,
        116, 124, *131*, 136, 148, *151, 152*,
        186, *187*, 190, *224*
Hill, K. T., 194, *226*
Hill, R., 18, *36*
Hinchcliffe, M. K., 28, *36*
Hinde, R. A., 136, *151*
Hinshaw, S. P., 5, 33, *36*
Hirschi, T., 55, *65*
Hoelter, J., 110, *131*
Hoffman, S. D., 84, 91, 92, *103*
Hogan, D. P., 156, 159, *172*
Hollenbeck, B. E., 140, *152*
Hollier, E. A., 43, 44, 54, 55, 61, *65*, 116, *131*
Hooper, D., 28, *36*
House, J. S., 109, *131*
Houston, B. K., 201, *224*
Howard, J. H., 203, *224*
Howe, G., 40, 42, 45, 62, *66*
Howell, C. T., 122, *129*
Huck, S., 110, 124, *130*, 176, *187*
Humphrey, L. L., 179, 180, *187*
Humphreys, M. M., 199, 200, *226*
Huston, T. L., 176, *187*
Hynd, G. W., 136, *151*

I

Ianetti, R. J., 140, *152*
Ingraham, L. J., 6, *36*

J

Jacklin, C. N., 48, *65*
Jacobsen, B., 6, *36*
Jacobvitz, D. B., 33, *36*
Johnson, C. L., 158, *172*
Johnson, J. H., 91, *105*
Johnson, J. R., 190, *224*
Johnson, K. L., 215, *224*
Johnston, L. D., 116, *129*
Jones, O. H. M., 209, *224*
Jorgensen, R. S., 201, *224*
Jorgenson, S. R., 158, *172*
Jouriles, E. N., 190, *224*

K

Kahneman, D., 194, 195, 196, *224*
Kannel, W. B., 202, 203, *223, 224*
Kaplan, H. B., 114, *131*
Kaplan, N., 12, *36*
Karbon, M., 213, *223*
Kasser, T., *34*
Katz, L., 17, 22, *36*, 216, *228*
Kavanagh, K., 69, *103*
Kellam, S. G., 3, 9, 10, *36*, 116, *131*, 189,
        191, *224, 225*
Keller, M. B., 69, *103*
Kelley, S. L., 198, *228*
Kelly, J. B., 67, 84, 91, *105*
Kendall, P. C., 111, *131*
Kerig, P. K., 31, *36*
Kessler, R. C., 176, *187*
Kety, S. S., 6, *36*
Kiernan, K. E., 67, 75, 76, 81, *103*
Kilner, L. A., 136, *152*
Kirchner, G. L., 191, *224*
Kirmil-Gray, K., 203, *224*
Kiryluk, S., 117, *131*
Klein, D. M., 158, *172*
Kleinbaum, D. G., 3, *36*
Klerman, G. L., 69, *103*
Kliewer, W., 203, *224*
Kolligian, J., Jr., 112, *132*
Kolvin, I., 51, *65*
Kolvin, P. A., 51, *65*
Kopp, C., 205, 206, 213, 215, *224*
Korb, R. J., 200, *226*
Koslowski, B., 209, *222*
Kovacs, M., 44, *65*, 180, *187*

Krakow, J. B., 213, 215, *224*
Krantz, D. S., 203, *225*
Kretchmar, M. D., 33, *36*
Kreutzer, T., 25, *38*
Kropp, J. P., 47, *64*
Kuczynski, L., 10, *37*
Kuhn, C., 210, *223*
Kupersmidt, J. B., 111, 113, 114, *130, 131,*
    190, 220, *226*
Kupper, L., 3, *36*
Kurdek, L. A., 202, 203, *224*
Kusche, D. A., 217, *223*

L

Lacey, J. I., 196, 197, 199, *224*
Lahey, B. B., 47, *64,* 136, *151*
Lambert, N. M., 3, *36,* 136, *151*
Landis, K. R., 109, *131*
Landry, S. H., 213, *224*
Larkin, K., 136, *151*
Larsen, A., 136, 141, *151, 152*
Larson, R. W., 110, 121, *131*
Larson, S. K., 198, 199, *225*
Laub, J. H., 55, *65*
Laudolff, J., 189, 191, *224*
Lazarus, R. S., 33, *37,* 108, 111, 128, *131*
Lazelere, R. E., 55, *65,* 76, *104*
Leadbeater, B. J., 114, *131*
Lefebvre, R. C., 176, *188*
Lehr, U., 159, *172*
Leiderman, H., 117, *130*
Leitch, C. J., 110, 115, *131*
Levenson, R. W., 218, *223, 225*
Levine, S., 202, *224*
Leviton, A., 191, *226*
Levy, M. N., 197, 198, *222*
Lewinsohn, P. M., 111, *132*
Liddle, C., 19, *37*
Liem, J., 6, *37*
Light, K. C., 201, *223*
Liker, J. K., 136, *151*
Lillie, R., 202, 203, *224*
Lindner, M. S., 43, 44, 47, 54, 55, 60, 61, *65*
Linnemeyer, S. A., 199, *225*
Little, R. E., 191, *224*
Locke, H., 30, *37,* 43, *65*
Loeber, R., 55, *65*
Loehlin, J. C., 56, *63*
Lohmoeller, J. B., 138, *151,* 176, *187*

Long, B., 1, 32, *35*
Long, N., 190, *225*
Longfellow, C., 69, *104,* 176, *187*
Loofbourrow, G. N., 198, *223*
Lorenz, F. O., 47, 48, 54, 55, 62, *64, 66,* 110,
    124, *130,* 176, *187*
Lundberg, U., 202, *225*
Lytton, H., 136, 148, *151*

M

Maccoby, E. E., 48, 55, 61, *63, 65*
MacGregor Sandman, B., 191, *228*
Magovern, G. J., Sr., 176, *188*
Maher, C., 191, *226*
Main, M., 12, 15, 33, *36, 37,* 209, *222*
Malatesta, C. Z., 208, 209, *225*
Malatesta-Magai, C., 209, *225*
Mariani, J., 128, *133*
Markman, H. J., 1, 18, 32, *35, 37*
Martin, D. C., 191, *228*
Martin, J. A., 55, *65*
Martin, R. P., 140, *151*
Martin, S. S., 114, *131*
Martin, T. C., 92, 93, *103*
Masten, A. S., 1, 9, 14, 15, *36, 37, 38,* 39, 51,
    64, 65, 108, 127, *130, 131,* 136, *151*
Matthews, K. A., 176, *188,* 201, 202, 203,
    222, 225, 228
Matthews, S., 158, 160, *172*
Mayer, L. S., 189, 191, *224*
McArdle, J. J., 82, *104*
McBurnett, K., 136, *151*
McCabe, P. M., 198, *225, 228*
McCarty, J. A., 47, *64*
McClaskey, C. L., 111, 112, *130,* 214, *222*
McConaughy, S. H., 122, *129*
McCoy, J. K., 46, 49, *63*
McCranie, E. W., 203, *225*
McCubbin, H. I., 18, *37,* 141, *152*
McCubbin, M. A., 18, *37*
McEnroe, M. J., 108, *129*
McGillicuddy-DeLisi, A. V., 22, *37*
McGuffin, P., 5, *36*
McHale, S. M., 40, 46, *65*
McLaughlin, B., 137, *152*
McLoyd, V. C., 47, *65,* 176, 185, *187*
McNamara, G., 108, 113, 114, 115, 118, 119,
    121, 124, 126, *133*
Mednick, S. A., 3, *37*

Meehl, P. E., 74, *103*
Melby, J. N., 47, 54, 55, *64,* 110, 124, *130,*
    176, *187*
Meltzoff, A. N., 195, *225*
Meredith, W., 82, 86, 95, *104, 105*
Messer, D. J., 211, *226*
Miller, B., 158, *172*
Miller, F. J. W., 51, *65*
Miller, N. B., 11, 12, 16, 22, 23, 26, *35, 37,*
    47, 51, *65,* 138, 145, 148, *151, 152*
Miller, P., 109, *132*
Minuchin, P., 40, *65*
Minuchin, S., 17, *37*
Mirsky, A. F., 191, *225, 226*
Montague, R. B., 140, *152*
Moore, J. J., 141, *153*
Moore, M. K., 195, *225*
Moos, B. S., 141, *152*
Moos, R. H., 141, *152,* 176, *187*
Morgan, E., 33, *36*
Morgan, P. S., 156, *172*
Morgan, Y., 33, *36*
Morgenstern, H., 3, *36*
Morison, P., 108, *131*
Morrison, A., 177, *187*
Morrison, D. R., 67, 75, 76, 81, *103*
Mounts, N. S., 177, *188*
Mrazek, P. J., 1, 29, 32, *37*
Mueller, E., 213, *226*
Murphy, C. M., 211, *226*
Murphy, J. K., 201, *226*
Murray, D. M., 117, *132*
Murray, M., 117, *131*
Muxen, M., 141, *152*

N

Neale, J. M., 121, *132*
Needle, R. H., 117, *132*
Needleman, H. L., 191, *226*
Neubaum, E., 69, 93, *103*
Neugarten, B. L., 157, 158, *171, 172*
Newcomb, M. D., 117, 124, *132*
Nguyen, T. V., 110, *130*
Notarius, C. J., 18, *37*
Nottelman, E. D., 194, *226*
Nuechterlein, K. H., 1, *38*
Nunes, E. V., 129, *132*
Nydegger, C., 157, *172*

O

O'Boyle, C., 206, *227*
O'Connell, C., 117, *132*
O'Connor, T., 40, 42, 45, 62, *66*
O'Leary, K. D., 179, *188,* 190, *224*
O'Leary, S. G., 190, *224*
O'Malley, P. M., 116, *129*
Obrist, P. A., 201, *223*
Offord, D. R., 75, 78, 81, *104*
Olson, D., 141, *152*
Olweus, D., 79, *104*
Orthner, D., 173, 174, *187, 188*
Osborne, L. N., 3, *35*
Owens, J. F., 176, *188*

P

Parke, R. D., 17, *37,* 212, 222
Parker, J. G., 114, *132,* 212, *226*
Patterson, C. J., 190, 220, *226*
Patterson, G. R., 3, 4, 10, 11, 22, *37,* 47, 48,
    55, *64, 65,* 68, 69, 70, 74, 76, 77, 78,
    79, 80, 81, 84, 85, 89, 90, 91, 93, 94,
    99, 100, *102, 103, 104, 105,* 114, 115,
    126, *130, 132,* 136, 137, *152*
Patterson, J. M., 18, *37*
Pawletko, T. M., 40, 46, *65*
Pearlin, L. I., 157, *172*
Pearson, J., 12, 13, 15, *34, 35, 37*
Pederson, F. A., 139, *152*
Pellegrini, D., 108, *131,* 136, *151*
Peresie, H., 191, *226*
Perri, M. G., 128, *132*
Perry, C. L., 117, *132*
Perry, S., 210, *223*
Perry-Jenkins, M., 176, *187*
Peterson, A. C., 56, *63*
Peterson, D. R., 140, *152,* 180, *188*
Peterson, J. L., 67, *105*
Pettit, G. S., 111, 112, *130*
Pfiffner, L. J., 190, *224*
Phillips, E. L., 214, *226*
Piaget, J., 206, *226*
Pierce, G. R., 128, *132,* 193, *227*
Plath, D. W., 157, *172*
Platt, J. J., 111, *132*
Plomin, R., 40, 42, 45, 46, 49, 55, 56, 62, *63,*
    64, 66

Porges, S. W., 198, 199, 200, 205, 206, 207,
    208, 222, 225, 226, 227, 228
Porter, B., 179, 188
Porter, F. L., 207, 227
Posner, M. I., 192, 196, 206, 207, 208, 215,
    227
Poulin, R., 213, 223
Powell, G., 140, 153
Powers, S. I., 136, 152
Primac, D. W., 191, 226
Putallaz, M., 214, 227

Q

Quay, H. C., 140, 152, 180, 188
Quinn, R., 141, 152
Quinton, D., 19, 37, 51, 66, 190, 191, 227

R

Racine, Y. A., 75, 78, 81, 104
Radke-Yarrow, M., 3, 10, 37
Radloff, L. S., 15, 26, 30, 38, 43, 66, 86, 105,
    178, 188
Ragozin, A. S., 22, 35
Rakaczky, C. J., 201, 225
Ramey, S. L., 1, 32, 35
Ramsey, E., 55, 65, 115, 126, 132
Raskin, D. C., 199, 200, 226
Ray, J., 47, 48, 64, 68, 93, 94, 95, 104
Rebok, G. W., 189, 191, 224
Rechnitzer, P. A., 203, 224
Reed, R., 191, 226
Reid, J. B., 32, 38, 55, 68, 74, 76, 81, 105,
    114, 130
Reiss, D., 18, 38, 40, 42, 45, 62, 63, 66
Renouf, A. G., 56, 63
Repetti, R. L., 176, 188
Revitz, P., 214, 226
Riccobono, A., 126, 133
Richards, J. E., 200, 227
Richters, J., 3, 9, 13, 14, 38
Riley, M. W., 158, 172
Rindfuss, R. R., 156, 172
Ritter, P. L., 117, 130
Rivera, M., 198, 228
Robbins, C., 114, 131
Roberts, F. J., 28, 36
Robins, P. K., 67, 75, 76, 81, 103

Robinson, N. M., 22, 35
Robson, K. S., 209, 227
Rockwell, R., 157, 171
Rohde, P., 111, 132
Rolans, O., 190, 191, 227
Rolf, J., 1, 38
Rosenberg, M., 178, 188
Rosenman, R. H., 203, 222
Rosenthal, C., 158, 171
Rosenthal, D., 11, 38
Rossi, A., 157, 172
Rosvold, H. E., 191, 226
Rothbart, M. K., 189, 202, 206, 207, 208,
    215, 227
Rovine, M. J., 45, 62, 66, 136, 150
Rubin, B. R., 3, 9, 10, 36
Russell, D. W., 109, 130
Russell, G. A., 201, 223
Rutherford, R. B., 209, 222
Rutter, M., 1, 3, 9, 10, 13, 15, 19, 21, 25, 29,
    33, 36, 37, 38, 39, 40, 48, 51, 52, 55,
    66, 67, 105, 108, 127, 130, 132, 136,
    152, 190, 191, 220, 227
Ryff, C. D., 157, 171

S

Sachis, P. N., 198, 227
Sameroff, A. J., 3, 4, 9, 11, 21, 25, 34, 38,
    39, 51, 66, 136, 152
Sampson, R. J., 55, 65, 102, 105
Sandler, I. N., 109, 132
Sandman, C. A., 197, 222
Santa-Barbara, J., 18, 38
Sarason, B. R., 128, 132, 193, 227
Sarason, I. G., 91, 105, 128, 132, 193, 227
Saunders, E., 69, 104, 176, 187
Scaife, M., 211, 227
Schanberg, S., 210, 223
Scheier, M. F., 44, 66, 111, 128, 130, 132,
    176, 188
Schlundt, D. G., 214, 223
Schmid, L., 117, 132
Schneider, W., 192, 228
Schocken, I., 214, 223
Schulsinger, F., 3, 37
Schulz, M. S., 17, 23, 26, 35, 38
Scotch, N., 202, 224
Searight, H. R., 126, 129
Seeley, J. R., 111, 132

Seifer, R., 3, 11, 21, 25, *34, 38,* 39, 51, *66*
Seltzer, M., 157, *172*
Seracini, A. M., 129, *132*
Shapiro, D., 195, *224*
Sharpley, C., 140, *152*
Shenker, S., 214, *226*
Shepard, B., 208, 209, *225*
Shetterly, K., 139, *152*
Shiffman, S., 128, *132*
Shiffrin, R. M., 192, *228*
Short, J., 109, *132*
Shuck, E., 32, *35*
Shure, M. B., 1, 32, *35,* 111, *132*
Siegel, F. S., 191, *221*
Siegel, J. M., 91, *105,* 110, 115, 129, *131, 132,* 202, *228*
Sigel, I., 22, *38*
Silver, D. H., 13, *35*
Simmens, S., 40, 42, 45, 62, *66*
Simons, R. L., 47, 48, 54, 55, 62, *64, 66,* 110, 124, *130,* 176, *187*
Simpson, M. E., 203, *225*
Sison, C. E., 196, *228*
Skinner, H. A., 18, *38*
Skinner, M. L., 69, 80, 84, 85, 89, *104*
Skolnick, A., 18, *35*
Slater, E., 190, *225*
Smith, R. S., 13, 14, *38,* 108, 115, *133,* 190, 191, *228*
Smith, W. O., 173, *187*
Snow, M. E., 48, *65*
Snyder, C. R. R., 192, *227*
Snyder, J. J., 69, 85, 88, *105*
Sokolov, E. N., 196, *228*
Somes, G. W., 201, *226*
Spanier, G. B., 140, *152*
Spellman, M., 113, 121, *133*
Speltz, M., 217, *223*
Spivak, G. M., 111, *132*
Sprague, R. L., 200, *226*
Sprey, J., 158, 160, *172*
Sroufe, L. A., 25, *35, 38*
Staines, G., 141, *152*
Stanley Hagan, M., 43, 44, 54, 55, 61, *65,* 136, *151*
Stanley, B. J., 216, *228*
Steinberg, L., 110, *132,* 177, *188*
Steinglas, P., 4, *38*
Steinhauer, P. D., 18, *38*
Steinmetz, S., 76, *105*
Stern, R. M., 196, 206, 207, 208, 211, *228*
Sternberg, C. R., 212, *222*

Sternberg, R. J., 112, *132*
Stevens, J. A., 191, *226*
Stevenson-Hinde, J., 136, *151*
Stocker, C., 40, 55, *64*
Stone, A. A., 121, *132*
Stoneman, Z., 40, 46, 49, *63*
Stoney, C. M., 201, *225*
Stoolmiller, M. L., 69, 86, 87, 88, *104, 105*
Stouthamer-Loeber, M., 55, *65*
Straus, M. A., 43, *66,* 76, *105*
Streissguth, A. P., 191, *224, 228*
Su, S., 117, *132*
Sullivan, H. S., 5, *38*
Susman, E. J., 140, *152*
Swan, A., 117, *131*
Swanson, G. E., 18, *35*
Sweet, J. A., 92, 93, *103*
Swicegood, C. G., 156, *172*

T

Takeuchi, D. T., 110, 124, *132*
Tarter, R. E., 111, *132*
Taylor, S. E., 176, *188*
Teachman, J., 93, *105*
Teichman, M., 28, *38*
Teichman, Y., 28, *38*
Teitler, J. O., 67, 75, 76, 81, *103*
Tejerina-Allen, M., 40, 45, 46, *66*
Tellegen, A., 14, *36,* 108, 124, *131, 133,* 136, *151*
Teri, L., 43, *66*
Tesman, J., 208, 209, *225*
Thelen, E., 136, *151*
Thompson, W. D., 116, *129*
Thoresen, C. E., 203, *224*
Tilson, M., 111, *132*
Tinsley, B., 17, *37,* 108, *129*
Tisak, J., 82, 86, 95, *104, 105*
Tizard, J., 67, *105*
Toobert, D. J., 68, *104*
Toth, S. L., 20, 33, *34*
Treisman, A. M., 192, *228*
Trickett, P. K., 140, *152*
Troll, L., 160, *171*
Tronick, E. Z., 209, 210, 222, 223, *228*
Tryon, A., *66*
Tupling, C., 190, *227*
Turner, R. J., 116, *131*
Tursky, B., 195, *224*

U

Uhlenberg, P., 156, *171*
Umberson, D., 109, *131*

V

Vaccaro, D., 108, 113, 114, 115, 118, 119, 121, 126, *133*
Vaden, N. A., 190, 220, *226, 227*
Van Nyugen, T., 47, *64*
Vaughan, R., 108, 110, 121, *133*
Vaux, A., 109, *132*
Vega-Lahr, N., 201, *228*
Victor, J. B., 140, *152*
Viken, R., 91, *103*
Vogel, E. F., 177, *188*
Vygotsky, L., 108, *132,* 216, 217, *228*

W

Wagner, B. M., 40, 45, 46, *66*
Waldron, I., 203, *228*
Waldrop, M. F., 137, 139, *152*
Wallace, K., 30, *37,* 43, *65*
Wallerstein, J. S., 67, 84, 91, *105*
Walsh, F., 18, *38*
Walter, G. F., 200, *226*
Walters, L. H., 141, *153*
Wampler, K. S., 136, 140, 141, 147, *151, 152, 153*
Wampler, K. W., 135, 136, 137, 138, 142, *151, 152*
Waring, J., 158, *172*
Warner, V., 211, *223*
Wasserman, A., 214, *227*
Watson, C., 141, *153*
Watt, N. F., 1, 32, *35*
Weidner, G., 203, *224*
Weintraub, J. K., 111, *130,* 176, *188*
Weintraub, S., 1, 9, 13, 14, *38*
Weir, T., 109, 115, *130*
Weissman, M. M., 211, *223*
Wender, P. H., 6, *36*

Werner, E. E., 13, 14, *38,* 55, *66,* 108, 115, 119, 127, *132, 133,* 190, 191, *228*
West, S. G., 1, 32, *35*
Wethamer-Larson, L., 189, 191, *224*
Wethington, E., 176, *187*
Whalen, C. K., 203, 221, *228*
Whitbeck, L. B., 48, 62, *64,* 110, 124, *130,* 176, *187*
White, S. W., 91, *103*
Whitmore, K., 67, *105*
Wiedenfeld, S. A., 203, *224*
Wiley, E. S., 201, *226*
Willett, J. B., 45, *66*
Williams, C. L., 111, *131*
Williams, D. R., 110, 124, *132*
Wills, T. A., 108, 109, 110, 111, 113, 114, 115, 118, 119, 121, 122, 126, 127, 128, *129, 130, 133*
Wilson, B. J., 200, 214, 215, *228*
Wilson, H., 69, *105*
Wilson, M. N., 141, *152,* 176, *188*
Wirt, R. D., 191, *221*
Wolchik, S. A., 109, *132*
Woodall, K. L., 201, 203, *225, 228*
Wu, C., 54, *66*

Y

Yang, R. K., 47, *64*
Yerkes, R. M., 194, *228*
Yongue, B. G., 198, *225, 228*
Yule, W., 190, 191, *227*

Z

Zahn-Waxler, C., 3, *37,* 140, *152*
Zajonc, R. B., 218, *228*
Zax, M., 3, 11, 21, 25, *34, 38,* 51, *66*
Zeger, S., 201, *223*
Zelkowitz, P., 69, *104,* 176, *187*
Zerubavel, E., 157, *172*
Zevon, M. A., 124, *133*
Ziaie, H., 206, *227*
Zill, N., 44, *66,* 67, 81, *105*
Zimmerman, E. A., 210, *223*

Subject Index

A

Adaptation, 8
  depression, 26–28
ADHD, *see* Attention Deficit Hyperacticity
    Disorder
Adjustment
  boys, 67–102
  chronic problems, 74–76
    models, 76–80
  and competence, 114
  and coping, 114
  postseparation problems, 86–90, 102
    maternal antisocial qualities, 99–100
    repartnering, 90–98
  preseparation problems, 74–80
Adolescents
  competence, 117–129, 173–186
    academic, 118, 120–121
    measures, 119–120
    negative life events, 118–120
    peer, 120–121
  conduct disorder, 54–60
  coping, 117–129
  depression, 54–60
  differential treatment, 54–62
  and family structure, 116–117
  family support research program, 117–129

parental support, 55–60
positive self-concept, 44, 55–60
pregnancy, 158–159, 165–166
self-regulation, 177, 179, 183, 185–186
substance use, 118–126
temperament and differential parenting,
    48–52, 61–62
Adult attachment interview, 12, 15
African-Americans
  adolescent competence, 173–186
  family dynamics, 173
    cocaregiver support and conflict, 177,
      179, 183, 185–186
    marital interaction quality, 178–179
    parental depression, 176, 178, 185
    parental optimism, 176, 178, 185
    videotaping, 174–175
    youth self-regulation, 177, 179, 183, 185–186
  family structure, 155–170
    adolescent pregnancy, 158–159, 165
    intergenerational, 158–159, 164, 166
    life course perspective, 157–158
    parental timing, 157–159
    patterns, 169–170
    ripple effect, 155, 158
    role overload, 159, 166
    role responsibilities, 156–158, 162,
      165–166, 168

African-Americans *(Cont.)*
  family wages model, 175–177
    family wage per hour, 178, 185
    measures, 178–180
    path models, 183–184
    results, 181–184
    sample, 178
    structural modeling, 180–181
  urban study, 160–161
    great-grandmother, 165–166
    great-great-grandmother, 163–164
    mutual assistance patterns, 162–164
    off-time units, 160, 164–167
    on-time units, 160, 162–164
    primary care, 163–166
Alcoholism, 30
Attentional processes, 189–221
  ADHD, 191
  attention bottleneck, 192
  attention demanding, 192–193
  automatic, 192–193, 217–218
  cognitive psychology, 191–193, 217–218
  concentration, 191
  developmentally delayed children, 213,
    215–216
  emotional regulation, 190, 193–195, 218,
    220
    anxiety, 193–195
    arousal, 194–196
    attentional selectivity, 195
    attention narrowing hypothesis, 194
    performance, 194–195
  filtering model, 192
  infant–caregiver interaction, 208–209
    face-to-face, 209
    intersubjectivity, 212
    mutual regulation, 209–210
    sharing states, 211–212
    social referencing, 212
    still-face paradigm, 210
  infants, 205–208
  language, 216–217
  limited capacity model, 192–193
  peer relations, 212–216
    emotion regulation, 215
    frame of reference, 214
    play entry, 214–215
    rejection, 214
    stress inoculation, 220
  physiology, 189, 195–203
    autonomic, 197–198

    cardiovascular reactivity, 197–199, 201,
      218–219, 221
    defense response, 196–197
    directional fractionation, 196
    homeostasis, 204–205, 208, 219
    orienting response, 196–197
    parasympathetic nervous system,
      197–200, 204
    P300 wave, 196
    risk and, 191
    self-regulation, 206
    sympathetic nervous system, 197–198,
      204
    vagal tone, 197–200, 203, 218
    type A behavior, 201–203, 219
Attention Deficit Hyperactivity Disorder, 5,
    191
Attention narrowing hypothesis, 194
  type A behavior, 201–202

B

Becoming a Family Project, 12, 15
Behavior Events Inventory, 44
Behavior Problem Checklist, 140, 146
Behavior Problem Index, 44, 180
Black women, *see* African-Americans; Women
Block Childrearing Practices Report Q-Sort,
    139–140
Boys
  differential treatment, 31
  divorce and, 74–102
  Oregon Youth Study, 73–74
  postseparation adjustment problems, 81–84
    age factor, 82–85
    disrupted parenting, 84–85, 99
    harsh discipline, 86–88
    monitoring, 86–87, 99
    repartnering model, 90–99, 102
    socially disadvantaged/antisocial mother,
      99–101
    stress/depression models, 84–90
  preseparation adjustment problems, 74–80
    chronic problems, 75–80
    models, 76–80
Buffering, 7, 12–14
  parental support, 109–110, 121, 126–127
  peer support, 109–110
Buffering effect, 109–110, 121

C

Case-control studies, 5
Causal models, 4–6
Center for Epidemiological Studies in
    Depression Scale, 15, 30, 43, 178
Challenges, 108
    and coping, 111–112
Child adjustment problems measure, 89–90, 98
Childbearing, 155–170
    adolescent pregnancy, 158–159
    timing, 158–159
Child Behavior Checklist, 81, 94
Child Depression Inventory, 44
Child Monitoring and Control Scale, 44
Childrearing Issues Scale, 43
Children
    aggressive behavior
        marital conflict, 11
        permissive parenting, 79
    competence, 107–129
    coping skills, 107–129
    developmentally delayed, 213
        emotion regulation, 215–216
    deviancy, 102
        maternal stress, 80, 89–90
    externalizing behavior, 137, 139–140,
        142–143
        family effects, 145–150
        LVPLS model, 144–145
        minor physical anomalies, 142–150
    internalizing behavior, 137, 140, 142–143
        family factors, 148
        LVPLS model, 144–146
        minor physical anomalies, 142–150
    resilience, 14, 115, 135–150, 190–191
    risk, 135–150
    at risk, 10
        protective factors, 190, 220
    self talk, 216–217
    temperament
        and differential parenting, 48–52
        as protective factor, 190, 220
Children's Depression Inventory, 180
Children's Self-Control Scale, 179
Cognitive psychology and attentional
    processes, 191–193
Communication, 112–113
    affective challenges, 112
    and attentional processes, 212
    families, 107–108

information exchange, 113
    competence, 114–116
Competence
    academic, 118, 120–121
    and adjustment, 114
    definition, 113–114
    development process, 115–116
    and family support, 107–129
    information exchange, 114–116
    and substance use, 118–121
Concentration, 191
Conduct disorder, 54–60
Conduct Problems Prevention Research
    Group, 32
Conflict Tactics Scale, 43
Coping
    and adjustment, 114
    with challenges, 111–112
    definition, 110–111
    and family support, 107–129
    outcomes, 114
    resilience, 122
    transition to parenthood, 29–31

D

Depression
    adaptation, 26–28
    differential parenting, 54–60
    disrupted parenting model, 80
    gender-linked differences, 26–28
    mother, 27–28, 85–88, 181
    parental, 176, 178, 185
    parental trait model, 78
Developmental psychopathology and risk, 7–9
*Diagnostic and Statistical Manual of Mental
    Disorders,* 191
Directional fractionation, 196
Discipline, 68–70
    coercive, 57
    harsh, 86–88
    repartnering adjustment problems, 95–97
Disrupted parenting model, 77, 79–80
Divorce, 67–102
    adolescent behavior, 116–117
    Oregon Divorce Study, 70–74
    and separation adjustment, 74–102
Dyadic adjustment scale, 140
Dysfunction, 8

E

EAS temperament scale, 45
Energy Education Program, 174
Expanded Food and Nutrition Program, 174
Expression of Affection Scale, 43
Externalizing behavior
 age factor, 82–84
 boys, 81
 children, 137, 139–140, 142–143
 family effects, 145–150
 and marital conflict, 11
 minor physical anomalies, 142–150
 repartnering, 94–97

F

Facet-Free Job Satisfaction Questionnaire, 141
Families
 attachment relationships, 12–13
 blended family, 116, 123–124
 coercive cycles, 4
 communication, 107–108
 development cycle, 2
 economic stress, 47–48
 five-domain model, 26
 intact family, 124
 life course perspective, 157–158
 marital conflict, 11, 19–20, 26–28
 resilience, 1–34
 risk, 1–34
  coping strategies, 29
  multiple risks, 26–29
  path models, 22–23
  preventive intervention, 31–33
  research, 17–19
 at risk, 10
 single-parent, 116–117, 123–124
 structure
  and behavior, 116–117
  and substance use, 123–126
 timetables, 157, 162
 transition to parenthood, 29–31
Family Adaptability and Cohesion Evaluation
  Scales, 141
Family Adjustment and Adaptation Response
  Model, 18–19
Family Environment Scale, 141
Family relationships developmental model,
  107–108

Family stress theory, 18–19
Family support, 107–129
 buffering effect, 109–110, 121
 and coping, 121–122
 emotional, 109–110, 118–119, 121, 123
 research program, 117–129
 and resilience, 190–191
 and substance use, 118–126
Family systems theory, 40
Father
 depression, 27–28
 differential parenting, 48–54
 discipline, 57
 family stress effects, 50
 negativity, 57–60

G

Georgia Family Q-Sort, 141
Georgia Longitudinal Study, 135–150
 gender differences, 145
 measures, 139–142
 path models, 144–145
 results, 142–150
 sample, 138–139
Georgia Marriage Q-sort, 140
Girls
 differential treatment, 31
 in institutions, 19
 pregnancy, 158–159, 165–166
Global Severity Index, 140
Gospel Hill study, 161, 167, 169
 grandmothers, 167–169

H

Harter Self-Perception Profile for Adolescents,
  44

I

Illiteracy, 173
Infants
 attentional processes, 205–206
 high/low reactivity, 206–207
 infant–caregiver interactions, 208–209
  face-to-face, 209
  intersubjectivity, 212

sharing states, 211–212
social referencing, 212
still-face paradigm, 210
latency to peak arousal state, 207
primary circular reactions, 206
vagal tone, 207–208, 218
Internalizing behavior
children, 137, 140, 142–143
family factors, 145–148
minor physical anomalies, 142–150
Intersubjectivity, 212

L

Latent variable path analysis with partial least
squares, 138
Life Orientation Test, 44
Locke Wallace Short Marital Adjustment Test,
30
parenting differential treatment study, 43
LVPLS, *see* Latent variable path analysis with
partial least squares

M

Marital conflict
and externalizing behavior, 11
families, 19–20
parenting, 26–29
Mechanisms, 16–17
Megarisk index, 21–22
Models
additive, 19–20
causal models, 4–6
disrupted parenting model, 80
externalizing/internalizing behavior, 145–146
family adjustment and adaptation response
model, 18–19
family relationships developmental model,
107–108
family wages model, 175–177, 183–184
filtering model, 192
five-domain model, 26
limited capacity model, 192–193
parental trait model, 78
parenting between-family models, 53, 60
parenting mediational model, 67–70
path, 22–23
permissive parenting model, 77, 79

repartnering model, 90–99, 102
statistical, 21–22, 24
stress/depression models, 84–90
Mother
child deviancy and stress, 89–90
depression, 27–28, 85–88, 181
differential parenting, 48–54
discipline, 57
family stress effects, 49
and infant interactions, 208–212
negativity, 57–60
socially disadvantaged/antisocial, 99–101

N

National Academy of Science Institute of
Medicine, 32
National Institute of Mental Health National
Prevention Conference, 32

O

Ontario Child Health Study, 75
Optimism, 176, 178, 185
Oregon divorce study, 70–74
demographic characteristics, 72–73
sample, 70–71
Oregon Youth Study, 73–74
harsh discipline, 86–87
maternal depressed mood, 86–87
maternal stress, 89–90
monitoring, 86–87

P

Parental trait model, 76
depression, 78
marital transitions, 78–79
maternal antisocial behavior, 78
stress effects, 77–78
Parent–Child Relationship Scale, 43
Parenthood, 29–31
timing, 157–159
Parenting
differential treatment study, 40–63
adolescent psychopathology measures, 44
adolescent temperament assessment, 45
child temperament, 48–53, 61–62

Parenting *(Cont.)*
  differential treatment study *(Cont.)*
    economic stress, 47–48
    family stress effects, 48, 51–52, 56, 60–62
    family stress measures, 43
    negativity and coerciveness, 47–48, 55–61
    outcomes, 54–60
    overview, 40–41
    ownness effect, 50–54
    parenting assessment, 43–44
    predictors, 46
    procedure and measures, 42–45
    sample, 42
    scapegoat hypothesis, 53
    sibling depression, 54–60
    within-family differences, 45–46, 56–60
  discipline, 68–70
  disrupted, 77, 79–80
  family problem solving, 68–70, 92–93
  marital conflict, 26–29
  mediational model, 67–70
  monitoring behavior, 68–70
  parental involvement, 68
  permissive, 77, 79
  positive reinforcement, 68
  postseparation adjustment problems, 84–90
  and stress, 84–85
  style ratings, 26–28, 58–59
    fathers, 27, 50
    mothers, 27, 49, 57
Perceived Competence Inventory, 118
Permissive parenting model, 77, 79
Preschool Rating Scale, 140
Psychopathology, 2–9
  adolescent, 39–63
    measures, 44
    parental support, 55
  causal models, 4–6
  developmental, *see* Developmental
      psychopathology
  and trauma, 8
  within-family perspective, 40

Q

Quality of coparenting scales, 179

R

Relationship inventory, 140
Repartnering model, 90–99, 102

child adjustment problems, 90, 93–97
  age factor, 94–95
  discipline, 95–97
  externalizing behavior, 94–97
  problem solving, 95–97
  stepfathers, 94
  stress levels, 91–92, 98
Resilience
  children, 14, 135–150, 190–191
  coping, 122
  definition, 13–16
  in families, 1–34
  hypotheses, 15
  immunization versus acquisition, 15–16
Risk
  attentional processes and, 191
  children, 135–150
  concept of, 2–4, 9–10
  cumulative risk, 24–26
    developmental effects, 25–26
  definition of, 9–10
  developmental outcomes, 7–8, 24–25
  and developmental psychopathology, 7–9
  in families, 1–34
  magnitude of, 9
  megarisk index, 21–22
  models, 6–7
    development transactional models, 20
    dynamic statistical, 24
    multiple regression analyses, 22
    path models, 22–23
    structural equation, 22–23
  multiple risk, 21–29
  preventive intervention, 31–33
  research, 2–9
    family context, 17–19
    risk-process-outcome categories, 18
Rochester longitudinal study, 25

S

Scapegoat hypothesis, 53
Schizophrenia, 5–7
Self-Esteem Scale, 178
Social referencing, 212
Stepfathers, 94
Still-face paradigm, 210
Stress, 39–63
  inoculation, 220
  maintenance, 89–90

and parenting, 84–85
and resiliency, 190–191
Stress/depression models, 84–90

T

Teacher Strategy Q-sort, 141
Temperament Assessment Battery, 140
Turn-taking, 209
Type A behavior, 201–203, 219

V

Vulnerability, 7
concept of, 11
definition of, 10–12

functional relationships patterns, 11

W

Women, 155–170
great-grandmotherhood, 155–156
teenage mothers, 155–156, 158–159, 165
Women, Black, *see* Black women

Y

Yerkes–Dodson law, 194